"This is a highly stimulating work which makes a very helpful and useful contribution in its argument for utilizing the Trinitarian processions in a Frame/Poythress perspectival account of knowledge and apologetics. In terms of originality, I think the meat of the work lies there, and good meat it is too."
—**Mike Ovey,** Former Principal, Oak Hill College, London

"Triperspectivalism is a theological method based on the Bible's teaching about the One God in Three persons. Tim Miller's book presents an accurate formulation of this method and explores in depth the origin of the method in the doctrine of the Trinity. I recommend the book highly to those who aspire to be serious students of theological method and of the Trinity itself."
—**John M. Frame**, J. D. Trimble Professor of Systematic Theology and Philosophy, Reformed Theological Seminary, Orlando

The Triune God of Unity in Diversity

Reformed Academic Dissertations

A Series

Series Editor

John J. Hughes

The Triune God of Unity in Diversity

An Analysis of Perspectivalism, the Trinitarian Theological Method of John Frame and Vern Poythress

Timothy E. Miller

P U B L I S H I N G
P.O. BOX 817 • PHILLIPSBURG • NEW JERSEY 08865-0817

© 2017 by Timothy E. Miller

All rights reserved. No part of this book may be reproduced, stored in a retrieval system, or transmitted in any form or by any means—electronic, mechanical, photocopy, recording, or otherwise—except for brief quotations for the purpose of review or comment, without the prior permission of the publisher, P&R Publishing Company, P.O. Box 817, Phillipsburg, New Jersey 08865–0817.

Scripture quotations are from the ESV® Bible (The Holy Bible, English Standard Version®), copyright © 2001 by Crossway, a publishing ministry of Good News Publishers. Used by permission. All rights reserved. All quotations are from the 2007 text edition of the ESV.

Italics within Scripture quotations indicate emphasis added.

The Triune God of Unity in Diversity: An Analysis of Perspectivalism, the Trinitarian Theological Method of John Frame and Vern Poythress. Timothy E. Miller, Ph.D., M.Div., M.A. Submitted to Westminster Theological Seminary, Philadelphia, PA, 2015, for the Ph.D. degree. Supervisor: K. Scott Oliphint.

Printed in the United States of America

ISBN: 978-1-62995-310-6 (paper)
ISBN: 978-1-62995-311-3 (ePub)
ISBN: 978-1-62995-312-0 (Mobi)

For Hannah

INDEX

Public funding models (*cont.*)
   crowdloans, 738, 739
   DAICO, 739–743
   evaluations, 762
      fair launch model, 747
      investors, 747
      premine models, 747
   factors, 730
   ICO, 731–733
   IDO, 734, 735
   IEO, 733, 734
   IFO, 736
   steps, 760–762
   STO, 736, 737
   streamlined filtering, 751–760
   types of, 731
Python, 591

R

Realized capitalization, 412
   action steps, 416
   Bitcoin, 414
   evaluation, 417
   HODL Waves (*see* HODL Waves (realized cap))
   market cap *vs.* realized cap, 414, 415
   primary benefit, 413
   representation, 413
   unrealized profit/loss, 414
   UTXO networks, 413
Rewards
   beta testing, 670

   governance, 665
   incentive (*see* Incentive mechanisms)
   play-to-earn, 665, 666
   staking process
      advantages/disadvantages, 649
      conditions, 647
      Ethereum, 646
      investors, 641
      long-term investors, 645
      minted coins, 642
      minting *vs.* transaction fees, 642
      nominal staking rate, 645
      optimal ratio, 649–652
      ratio, 648
      real reward rate, 644–647
      slashing, 644
      Solana staking data, 647
      transaction fees, 643, 644
   strategies, 673
   unique strategies, 674
Roadmap project
   blockchain developer, 521
   categories, 530
   comparing competitors, 567–569
   conversations/communication.
   crypto project
      BNB Chain ter
      evaluation, F
      goals/obje

INDEX

relevant, 544
SMART objective
  analysis, 542
  steps, 545
  time-bound, 544
  TPS, 542
evaluation, 520
fundamentals, 520
investors, 530–533
  factors, 533
  sandbox, 531, 532
key elements, 523
  goals/objectives, 523
  milestone, 525–530
  motivation, 525
  SMART objectives, 523, 524
  vision/purpose, 524, 525
milestones (*see also* Milestones feasibility)
  budget control/delivery, 526
  clear direction, 526
  infrastructure requirements, 529
  performance, 529
  project planning, 526
  promising/deliverables, 528
  regulatory commissions, 527
  resource availability, 529
  resource management, 526
  risk management, 526
  stakeholders, 527
  team motivates, 526
  technical complexity, 528
  timeline, 526, 529

primary benefits
  clarity/direction, 522
  community engagement, 522
  investors, 522
  progress tracking, 522
  stakeholders, 522
  transparency and trust, 522
product development
  competitor analysis, 538
  Ethereum, 534–537
  factors contribute, 537
  features, 533
  goals/coordinate tasks, 534
  PoW, 534
strategic plan, 519
transparency/accountability
  evaluation, 564, 567
  real-time roadmap updates, 565
  responsibility, 565
  steps, 565
  transparency and accountability, 566
  update and communication, 564
vision/purpose
  alignment, 547, 548
  evaluation, 546, 554
  governance, 552
  internet, 549
  key deliverables, 549
  Matic network, 546
  POL tokenomics, 551
  Polygon network, 546

INDEX

Roadmap project (*cont.*)
    Polygon technology, 546, 547
    protocol architecture,
        550, 551
    review, 546
    steps, 553, 554
    value layer, 549–553
    vision alignment, 550, 551
    zkEVM validium, 549

S

SaaS, *see* Staking as a service (SaaS)
Scalability
    action steps, 243
    bandwidth, 218
    Bitcoin performance
        metrics, 242
    blockchain
        terminology, 218–221
    block time, 242
    consensus mechanics (*see*
        Consensus mechanics)
    definition, 215
    evaluation, 244
    first-and second-layer
        solutions, 230
    fundamental evaluation, 240
    latency, 217, 218
    lightning network, 218
    ongoing scaling solutions, 230
    polygon performance
        metrics, 243
    throughput, 229, 241
    throughput rate, 215, 217
    TPS/TPM, 216
Secondary incentive
        mechanisms, 666
    airdrops, 667, 668
    beta testing, 670
    loyalty incentives, 671
    platform incentives, 669
    referral programs, 670
    reward mechanisms, 667
Secure Hash Algorithm (SHA), 6
Security, 244–263
    cellular device, 259
    cold wallet, 260
    consensus mechanism,
        247–249
    custodial services, 259
    DDoS/BDoS attacks, 256
    digital assets, 250
    digital asset transactions, 261
    DoS attack, 256, 257
    double-spending, 249, 250
    evaluation, 263
    features, 244
    51% attack
        attackers, 245
        blocks, 245
        hash rate, 245
        likelihood of, 246
        proof-of-stake (PoS), 247
        slashing, 247
    forking, 250–255
    investor end-point, 257–261
    investors, 245

non-custodial software wallets, 259
phishing links, 260
protective measures, 257
steps, 261–263
Sybil attack
　fake identities, 255
　malicious nodes, 255
　Monero blockchain, 256
threat factors, 244
Security Token Offering (STO), 332, 333, 736, 737
Segregated Witness (SegWit), 234, 253
SegWit, *see* Segregated Witness (SegWit)
Semantic Web, 19
SEO, *see* Social Engine Optimization (SEO)
S2F, *see* Stock-to-flow (S2F) model
Shell programming language, 595
SLP, *see* SushiSwap Liquidity Provider (SLP)
Smart contracts
　anonymity and trustless, 576
　characteristics/benefits, 575
　definition, 574
　digital contracts, 574
　Ethereum, 576, 577
　self-executing, 575
　solidity, 575
　tamper-resistant/immutable, 575
　transparent, 576
Social Engine Optimization (SEO), 691
Social media network
　content engagement
　　comments/shares/likes/views, 694
　　engagement rate (ER), 695
　　ERR formula, 696
　　evaluation, 698
　　objective, 693
　　steps, 697, 698
　discord, 686
　evaluation, 688
　evaluation process, 684
　follower-count
　　competitor, 689
　　elements, 689
　　evaluation, 691
　　founding year, 689
　　social media platform, 689
　　steps, 690
　　subscribers, 689
　fundamentals, 679
　LinkedIn, 687
　Medium, 687
　platforms, 680
　post frequency
　　activity, 691
　　audience engagement, 692
　　competitor analysis, 693
　　concepts, 691
　　credibility, 691
　　evaluation, 693
　　post frequency, 692

INDEX

Social media network (*cont.*)
    reach/SEO, 692
    steps, 692
    primary media
        platforms, 685–688
    Reddit, 687
    sentiment analysis, 684
    steps, 688
    Telegram, 686
    X, 685
    YouTube, 686
Solidity programming
    language, 574
SQL, *see* Structured query
    language (SQL)
Staking as a service (SaaS), 637–639
    advantages, 639
    attributes, 638
    Blox Staking, 638
    bug bounty, 638
    consensus diversity, 638
    disadvantages, 639
    execution client, 638
    open-source, 638
    permissionless, 638
    self-custody, 638
Staking process
    advantages, 632
    block creators, 632
    centralized entities, 640
    digital asset, 631
    disadvantages, 633
    investors, 641–652
    liquid staking, 634–652
    primary sources, 641
    reward rate, 630
    slashing, 634
    validators, 632–634
    variations/processes, 632
STO, *see* Security Token
    Offering (STO)
Stock-to-flow (S2F) model, 489–492
    action steps, 491
    Bitcoin, 490, 491
    divergence tool, 490
    evaluation, 492
    financial concept, 489
    long-term investors, 489
    long-term price
        movements, 491
Streamlined filtering
    analytics platforms, 751
    annymous teams, 754
    fundamental checks, 751
    hard cap analysis, 755, 756
    imitation projects, 753
    investors, 751
    Neon labs, 755, 756
    Patex network, 752, 758
    poor grammar, 754
    price per coin, 757–760
    soft and hard caps, 754, 755
    Solana, 755
    summarization, 752–754
    token standard, 756, 757
    unclear timelines, 753
    unspecified fund allocation, 753
    vague detail, 753

whitepapers, 760
Structured query language (SQL), 593
Substack, 687
Supply metrics
    circulating supply, 365
    circulating *vs.* total supply, 366
    concepts, 362
    deflationary models, 363
    evaluation, 367
    maximum supply, 365, 367
    on-chain mechanisms, 362
    Polkadot networks, 363
    steps, 366
    total supply, 364
    whitepaper, 363, 366
SushiSwap Liquidity Provider (SLP), 655

T

TA, *see* Technical analysis (TA)
Tangible *vs.* intangible assets, 344
Team project
    aspects, 493
    background/experience
        activity, 504
        education history, 505
        evaluation, 508
        experience, 505
        followers/connections, 504
        fraudulent projects/scams, 502
        licenses and certifications, 506
        personal summary, 504
        profile picture, 504
        publications, 506
        recommendation, 506
        skills, 506
        steps, 507
        strategies, 502
    definition, 498
    developer team size
        crypto projects, 509
        evaluation, 511
        founding year, 509
        GitHub repository, 510
        objective, 508
        project—software, 508
        responsibilities, 508
        specialties, 508
        steps, 510, 511
    essential element, 493
    evaluation methods, 494, 501
    innovative, 493
    key professionals, 500–502
    project support
        accessible user education, 512
        assistance/clarification, 512
        community engagement, 513
        contributors, 511
        customer channels, 512
        evaluation, 514
        objective, 511

INDEX

Team project (*cont.*)
    resources, 512
    steps, 513
  public identity
    accountability, 495
    advantages, 495
    anonymous, 495
    challenges, 496
    community engagement, 495
    confidence, 496
    core product/service, 494
    evaluation, 498
    LinkedIn, 497
    online presence, 497
    partnerships, 496
    professionals, 496
    project website, 497
    steps, 497
    transparency, 496
    trust, 495
  specialists, 499
  steps, 501
  team interviews
    AMAs (Ask Me Anything), 514, 515
    credibility, 516
    evaluation results, 517
    investors/broader community, 514
    pre-/post official launch, 516
    responsiveness, 516
    social platforms, 515
    steps, 515
    testnet/builder phase, 517
    transparency, 516
    vision and strategy, 516
  team structures, 498
Technical analysis (TA)
  charting, 44
  EMAs technical indicators, 46
  stochastic oscillator, 46
  TradingView setup, 45
  traditional markets, 45
Technical documentation, 57, 60
Testnets
  advantages, 106, 107
  blockchain explorer, 108–110
  block explorer, 111–114
  continuous improvement, 112
  definition, 105
  Ethereum, 107, 108
  Goerli/Sepolia, 107
  MakerDAO, 108
  Moonbase Alpha block explorer, 114
  Polkadot block explorer, 113
  pseudo-anonymous, 111
  sandbox environment, 105
  TestNet, 114
  transaction hash, 110
TGE, *see* Token generation event (TGE)
Third-party wallet application, 259
Token design
  accrual processes, 350–357
  action steps, 349, 350
  Altcoins, 330
  asset tokenization, 344

built-in coins, 329
CAR tokens, 346
characteristics/rules, 327
cryptocurrency, 329
cryptographic tokens (*see* Cryptographic tokens)
evaluation, 350
fundamental evaluation, 346–348
fundamentals, 328
legitimacy, 346
protocol security, 345
real-world problem, 349
stakeholders, 345
standards
    cryptographic token, 343
    ERC-20, 340
    interaction, 339
    primary functions, 340
strategies, 327
traditional companies, 345
types of, 328
Token distribution model
    allocation categories, 379, 380
    benchmark, 382–384
    benchmark model, 385
    community/ecosystem development, 382
    competitor analysis, 385
    design phase, 379
    fundamental element, 386, 387
    investors funds, 383
    key elements/red flags, 378
    Moonbeam network, 387
    partnerships and advisors, 384
    public sales, 384
    stakeholders, 378
    steps, 384–386
    strategies, 378
    treasury, 383
    Uniswap, 381
Token generation event (TGE), 100, 390, 391, 515
Tokenomics (token + economics), 359
    design and implementation, 359
    distribution model, 378–387
    elements, 360
    fundamentals, 362
    investors, 361
    metrics, 362–367
    microtokenomics/macrotokenomics, 360, 361
    supplies, 368–378
    supply dynamics, 361
    supply dynamics data, 360
    vesting schedules, 387–398
Token supply models
    circulating *vs.* maximum supply, 375
    circulation, 372
    deflationary, 368–370
    evaluation, 377
    fixed supply model, 372–374
    inflationary, 376
    inflationary supply
        consensus mechanism, 370
        definition, 370

INDEX

Token supply models (*cont.*)
    KILT protocol, 371
    staking terms, 371
  steps, 374–377
  Web3/blockchain project, 368
Total transfer volume
  Bitcoin, 438
  different signals, 436
  evaluation results, 439
  objectives, 436
  on-chain/off-chain
    platforms, 436
  price action signals, 437
  steps, 438
Total value locked (TVL),
    49, 441–448
  chain, 442
  DeFi protocol, 441, 442
  evaluation, 448
  financial data, 444
  market capitalization, 445
  performance history, 445
  ratio, 443, 444
  reporting methodology, 446
  steps, 446–448
Total value staked (TVS)
  action steps, 440
  Ethereum, 440
  evaluation, 441
  Glassnode.com, 440
  representation, 439
TPS, *see* Transactions per
    second (TPS)

Traditional-to-traditional (T2T),
    766, 767
Transaction speed/gas cost
  accessibility/trading, 142
  affordability, 142
  Bitcoin average, 145
  business operations, 140
  competitiveness, 140
  consensus mechanism, 141
  encourage development, 142
  end-user experience, 139–150
  evaluation, 150
  fluctuations, 141
  gas-tracker tiers, 143–149
  GWei/USD Converter, 144
  historical oracle, 149
  investor analysis, 147, 148
  key metrics, 139
  lightning network, 145
  Polygon's transaction, 143
  proof-of-work (PoW), 140
  real-time transaction, 140
  steps, 148–150
  transaction gas cost, 141
  user experience, 140
  user retention, 140
Transactions per second (TPS), 216
Trilemma
  characteristics, 191
  decentralization, 190
  decentralized systems, 192–216
  elements, 190
  ongoing research, 190

2FA, *see* Two-Factor Authentication (2FA)
T2T, *see* Traditional-to-traditional (T2T)
TVL, *see* Total value locked (TVL)
TVS, *see* Total value staked (TVS)
Two-Factor Authentication (2FA), 257
TypeScript, 593

U

UFC, *see* Ultimate Fighting Club (UFC)
UGC, *see* User-Generated Content (UGC)
UI, *see* User interface (UI)
UI/UX product application
   aspects, 131
   blockchain, 132–134
   evaluation, 137
   interactive elements, 131
   investor analysis skills, 135
   Moonbeam networks, 133
   project websites, 134
   responsibility, 131
   steps, 135–137
Ultimate Fighting Club (UFC), 764
Uniform Resource Locator(URL), 16, 258
Uniswap (product/service)
   decentralized exchange interface, 90
   digital asset launch, 91
   digital asset trading, 90
   liquidity providers (LPs), 91
   service offering, 89
   value proposition
      definition, 91
      restrictions, 91
      revenue sharing proposal, 92
Unspent transaction output (UTXO), 412
URL, *see* Uniform Resource Locator (URL)
User experience (UX), 129, 131, *See also* End-user experience (UX); UI/UX product application
User-Generated Content (UGC), 17
User interface (UI), *see* UI/UX product application
UTXO, *see* Unspent transaction output (UTXO)
UX, *see* End-user experience (UX); User experience (UX)

V

Validators, 226
Vertical scaling solutions, 231, 232
   block compression, 235
   consensus mechanisms, 233
   SegWit, 234
Vesting schedules
   accredited investor allocations, 397
   action steps, 396–398

INDEX

Vesting schedules (*cont.*)
  benchmark structure, 394
  cliff parameters, 395–397
  cliff periods, 397
  cliffs, 388
  competitors, 398
  distribution Schedule, 397
  ecosystem development, 392, 397
  evaluation, 389–391, 398
  foundation reserve, 391
  fundamental analysis, 387
  IMX public sale, 393
  milestones, 389
  objectives, 387
  private sale tokens, 392, 393
  project development, 392
  project team, 393
  public sale tokens, 391
  terminology, 388, 389
  TGE summary details, 390
  token allocation, 390
Virtual Private Network (VPN), 260
VPN, *see* Virtual Private Network (VPN)

W

WBTC, *see* Wrapped Bitcoin (WBTC)
Web3 application
  centralized entities, 19
  concepts/features/limitations, 14
  decentralization, 20
  decentralized Internet, 19
  definition, 20
  digital ownership, 21–23
  evolution, 24–28
  fundamental concepts, 15
  fundamental elements, 18
  governance, 23
  HTTPS, 18
  interactions, 15
  interactive web/web2, 17–19
  permissionless, 23, 24
  principle, 14
  read-write-execute, 19
  semantic web, 19
  stateless, 16
  Web1/Static Web, 15–17
Whitepaper
  approaches, 74
  benefits, 64, 65
  Bitcoin, 60, 61
  commitment/progression, 74, 75
  content list, 63–65
  criteria, 76
  definition, 62
  editions, 70
  Ethereum, 62
  evaluation, 78

evaluation objective, 60
footnotes, 72–74
informative, 75
Moonbeam networks, 68
Polkadot network, 66, 67, 75
potential value, 76–78
product/service offering, 76
quality checks, 77
references, 71, 72
research/key points, 75
strategic process, 62
styles, 66–69
Wrapped Bitcoin (WBTC), 339

X, Y, Z

XCM, *see* Cross-Consensus Message Format (XCM)

GPSR Compliance

The European Union's (EU) General Product Safety Regulation (GPSR) is a set of rules that requires consumer products to be safe and our obligations to ensure this.

If you have any concerns about our products, you can contact us on

ProductSafety@springernature.com

In case Publisher is established outside the EU, the EU authorized representative is:

Springer Nature Customer Service Center GmbH
Europaplatz 3
69115 Heidelberg, Germany

Contents

Series Introduction   ix
Foreword by Vern S. Poythress   xi
Preface   xiii

1. Justification and Introduction to the Study   1
   Justification of the Study
   Summary of the Study

2. Method and Basis of General Perspectivalism   27
   Defining Perspectivalism
   The Method and Basis of General Perspectivalism

3. Implications of General Perspectivalism   77
   Perspectivalism and the Charge of Relativism
   Implications of General Perspectivalism
   Summary of the Basis of General Perspectivalism

4. Method and Basis of Triperspectivalism   105
   Introduction to Triperspectivalism
   The Trinity as the Ultimate Triad
   The Relationship of Simplicity and Perichoresis

5. Perichoretic-Simplicity   145
   Moderate Simplicity and Perichoresis
   Summary of the Perichoretic-Simplicity Model

6. Triperspectivalism and the Trinity   188
   Connection between God's Nature and Creation
   Perspectival Dynamics
   Types of Triads
   Summary of the Trinitarian Roots

7. Lordship, Trinity, and Perspectivalism   241
   The Centrality of Lordship
   Lordship as Control, Authority, and Presence
   Lordship and Perspectivalism
   The Lordship Attributes and Metaphysics
   The Lordship Attributes and Epistemology
   The Lordship Attributes and Axiology
   Summary of Lordship and Perspectivalism

8. Processional Triperspectivalism   264
   The Need for Processional Triperspectivalism
   The Concern over Persons and Priority
   Knowledge Triad: Processional Triperspectivalism
   Apologetics: Processional Triperspectivalism
   Summary of Processional Triperspectivalism

9. Conclusion   314

   Bibliography   319
   Index of Scripture   355
   Index of Subjects and Names   357

Series Introduction

P&R Publishing has a long and distinguished history of publishing carefully selected, high-value theological books in the Reformed tradition. Many theological books begin as dissertations, but many dissertations are worthy of publication in their own right. Realizing this, P&R has launched the Reformed Academic Dissertation (RAD) program to publish top-tier dissertations (Ph.D., Th.D., D.Min., and Th.M.) that advance biblical and theological scholarship by making distinctive contributions in the areas of theology, ethics, biblical studies, apologetics, and counseling.

Dissertations in the RAD series are *curated*, which means that they are carefully selected, on the basis of strong recommendations by the authors' supervisors and examiners and by our internal readers, to be part of our collection. Each selected dissertation will provide clear, fresh, and engaging insights about significant theological issues.

A number of theological institutions have partnered with us to recommend dissertations that they believe worthy of publication in the RAD series. Not only does this provide increased visibility for participating institutions, it also makes outstanding dissertations available to a broad range of readers, while helping to introduce promising authors to the publishing world.

We look forward to seeing the RAD program grow into a large collection of curated dissertations that will help to advance Reformed scholarship and learning.

John J. Hughes
Series Editor

Foreword

It is my pleasure to introduce Timothy Miller's book.

Miller's book has arisen from spending much time and energy in examining triperspectivalism, as developed especially by John Frame and me. Miller is a sympathetic analyst who has succeeded in understanding triperspectivalism from the inside, rather than from a distance, and so you will find in his book an accurate portrayal. The presentation is also clear and helpful for readers. At the same time, Miller has applied his own insights to explain triperspectivalism in his own way. He has rightly been willing to point out areas of weakness and areas that could use further development. He has offered some development himself, by proposing some terminological labels for clarification and by exploring whether there is an intrinsic "order" in some of the triples, an order mirroring the intrinsic order in the Trinity.

All this work makes his book a valuable resource on the subject. I am grateful that someone with Miller's ability has seen fit to offer the first published book-length study of triperspectivalism, and a good book at that. It has helped me to gain perspective (!) by hearing someone else's voice, and seeing details noticed that I had not attended to myself.

John Frame and I have hoped that the methods of triperspectivalism might be of service for the glory of God and for the edification of the people of God. May Miller's book also contribute to these goals, by helping the people of God to serve him with all love and faithfulness.

Vern S. Poythress
Professor of New Testament Interpretation
Westminster Theological Seminary
Philadelphia, Pennsylvania

Preface

The desire to write this book derived from reading John Frame's *Cornelius Van Til: An Analysis of His Thought*. The book was required reading for one of my first PhD classes at Westminster Theological Seminary. And while I did not embrace all of Frame's critiques of Van Til's thought (see the chapter on Processional Triperspectivalism), Frame's unique ability to write clearly provided substantial help in revealing Van Til's Trinitarian-based apologetic method. My final paper for that class concerned the relationship between Van Til and perspectivalism. That paper was my first attempt to understand the enigmatic world of triads, and it set me on a research trajectory that would ultimately end in a dissertation on the perspectival theological method. The present book is a modification of that dissertation.

This book is not a popularization of perspectivalism; rather, it is a detailed analysis of whether perspectivalism is—as Frame and Poythress argue—Trinitarian. My hope is that by defending the Trinitarian basis of perspectivalism, this book will prompt further exploration into the nature of the Triune God. Van Til believed the world was not properly understood unless viewed as a world produced by a Triune Creator. Perspectivalism seeks to do just that, and the final chapters of this book attempts to take perspectivalism one step further on that journey.

Thanks should be given to those who made this work possible. K. Scott Oliphint, William Edgar, and Lane Tipton, my instructors at Westminster, provided a robust Van Tillian framework, without which this work would not have been completed. These men pushed me to be a better researcher, student, and Christian. Special thanks should be given to Vern Poythress and John Frame who were willing to read my work, provide assistance, and correct my misunderstandings. Both men were exceptionally busy, but they thoroughly interacted with my questions over the space of three years. My editor, Marsha Love, made this work much better than it would have been otherwise. While I take all credit for any shortcomings in this text, I could not have written the work without those I have named in this paragraph.

The greatest expression of thanks must be directed toward the Triune God, who has faithfully provided for my family in inexpressible ways. He has sustained my wife, Hannah Miller, during the writing of this work, and added to our family three times over (Grace, Annie, and Danielle) while the work was in progress.

1

Justification and Introduction to the Study

During the late twentieth-century controversy over theonomy within American Reformed Orthodoxy, both Westminster Theological Seminary in Philadelphia and Westminster Seminary in California opposed the modern application of the Mosaic Law to the state.[1] But despite agreement that theonomy was exegetically and theologically problematic, individual critics of theonomy disagreed on both (1) what alternative should be offered and (2) how theonomy should be handled. Meredith Kline, one the one side, argued for an alternative, *intrusion ethic*, which closely resembled a two-kingdom approach.[2] His essay, *Comments on an Old-New Error*, indicates that theonomy is "a delusive and grotesque perversion of the teaching of Scripture."[3] John Frame and Vern Poythress, on the other hand, argued for a more nuanced position—embracing neither the

---

[1] Teachers from both schools contributed to the following book, critiquing theonomy from multiple vantage points: William Barker and W. Robert Godfrey, *Theonomy: A Reformed Critique* (Grand Rapids, MI: Zondervan, 1991).

[2] The substance of his view was originally published in the Westminster Theological Journal, but was later detailed more comprehensively: Meredith G. Kline, "The Intrusion and the Decalogue," *Westminster Theological Journal* 16, 1 (Fall 1953): 1–22; Meredith G. Kline, *The Structure of Biblical Authority* (Eugene, OR: Wipf and Stock, 1997), 154–71.

[3] Meredith G. Kline, "Comments on an Old-New Error," *Westminster Theological Journal* 41, 1 (Fall 1978): 172.

intrusion ethic nor a theonomy approach. Instead, they attempted to write sympathetically *and* critically, finding within theonomy both helpful and problematic elements.

During the controversy, Meredith Kline published a faculty paper at WSC arguing against Frame and Poythress's analysis.[4] The substance of his critique focused on the theological method of *perspectivalism* that Frame and Poythress embraced as they critiqued theonomy. Kline maintained that perspectivalism had impaired both theologians' abilities to critically assess theonomy. Further, Kline believed that perspectivalism could cause further problems in Reformed theology if not adequately addressed. In the faculty paper, written twenty-nine years ago (1986), Kline challenged his colleagues, "If we are to be responsible guardians of Reformed orthodoxy we must add to our agenda of study and discussion a scrutiny of multiperspectivalism. Is it an acceptable method of doing theology?"[5]

While theonomy and the intrusion ethic will not be the focus of the dissertation, that theological battle provided one of the earliest expressions of Reformed concern over perspectivalism. To date, no study of significant depth has been done on perspectivalism by anyone other than Frame and Poythress.[6] This dissertation will seek to partially fulfill Kline's request. More specifically, the dissertation will

---

[4] Meredith G. Kline, *A Paper Pursuant to the Faculty Forum* (Escondido, CA: Westminster Seminary in California, 1986).

[5] Ibid.

[6] The following two authors provide partial treatments of perspectivalism. Mark Karlberg wrote two articles on the method, but, due to the medium, could not engage deeply. Paul Elliott, the second critic, evaluated the method in only one chapter of his book. Mark W. Karlberg, "On the Theological Correlation of Divine and Human Language," *Journal of the Evangelical Theological Society* 32, 1 (March 1989): 99–105; Mark W. Karlberg, "John Frame and the Recasting of Van Tilian Apologetics: A Review Article," *Mid-America Journal of Theology* 9, 2 (Fall 1993): 279–96; Paul M. Elliott, "What Is Perspectivalism, and Why Is It Dangerous?," in *Christianity and Neo-Liberalism* (Unicoi, TN: The Trinity Foundation, 2005), accessed January 25, 2014, http://www.teachingtheword.org/apps/articles/?articleid=74632&columnid=5772.

seek to confirm, as John Frame and Vern Poythress have argued, that perspectivalism is a distinctively Trinitarian, creatively Reformed, and therefore eminently useful theological paradigm.[7] The remainder of this chapter will seek to further justify the study and lay out the method of the study.

Justification of the Study

We will mention four reasons an extended discussion of perspectivalism is needed. First, the influence of both Frame and Poythress in American Reformed Orthodoxy is vast and extensive. Because perspectivalism always follows in their wake, the broader their influence, the more important it is to evaluate their method. Second, perspectivalism has grown in influence, appearing in fields foreign to the expertise of Frame and Poythress. As perspectivalism multiplies in breadth of use, the importance of analyzing the method similarly multiplies. Third, the claims of perspectivalism—particularly that it is distinctively Trinitarian, principally Reformed, and eminently useful—are worthy of consideration. If they are true, perspectivalism deserves a wider hearing than it has heretofore obtained. Finally, Frame and Poythress have received very little thoughtful and critical engagement. This work seeks to provide some remedy for that lack.

The Influence of Frame and Poythress

John Frame is one of the most significant figures in twentieth-century conservative American Reformed Orthodoxy.[8] His influence

---

[7] This thesis is stated in a perspectival fashion. It will be our goal to prove that the method has normative (deriving from the Trinity), situational (grows out of the Reformed heritage), and existential (eminently useful as a theological construct) elements. This triad was not intentionally chosen for its adherence to perspectival form. Instead, the organization of the study naturally led in that direction, providing a way to demonstrate the usefulness of the method even while arguing for it.

[8] Feinberg sweepingly suggests, "it would be hard to imagine an evangelical theologian working broadly in the Reformed tradition during the latter part

can be discerned in the following ways: first, Frame has taught in the classroom for forty-five years at three of the most influential American Reformed schools (Westminster Theological Seminary, Westminster Seminary in California, and Reformed Theological Seminary, Orlando). Second, because of his prolific teaching career, Frame has influenced thousands of students. Of particular importance are the *influencers* he has influenced. *Influencers* are those who have a wide audience for their own teaching. Consider the following list of influential *influencers* Frame has taught:[9] Greg Bahnsen (previously Professor at Reformed Theological Seminary),[10] Richard Bedsoe (Professor at Rivendell College, Boulder), Mark Futato (Professor at Reformed Theological Seminary, Orlando), Wayne Grudem (Professor of at Phoenix Seminary),[11] Frank A. James (Professor at Gordon-Conwell Theological Seminary), James B. Jordan (Director of Biblical Horizons), Peter Leithart (Senior Fellow at New St. Andrews College), Vern Poythress (Professor at Westminster

---

of the twentieth century who didn't know of John Frame." John S. Feinberg, "Personal Words: John Feinberg," in *Speaking the Truth in Love: The Theology of John M. Frame*, ed. John J. Hughes (Phillipsburg, NJ: P&R Publishing, 2009), xliii. Derek Thomas adds, "John Frame is one of the most outstanding theologians of the twentieth century. Like most other geniuses, his greatness may not be fully uncovered until long after his passing." Derek Thomas, "Frame on the Attributes of God," in *Speaking the Truth in Love: The Theology of John M. Frame*, ed. John J. Hughes (Phillipsburg, NJ: P&R Publishing, 2009), 368.

[9] This is not to suggest that each of these individuals have embraced and reinforced the teaching of Frame. In fact, some will be the chief critics of perspectivalism.

[10] In an audio lecture critiquing Frame's apologetic method, Bahnsen indicated that after graduation from Westminster he told Frame, "As important as Dr. Van Til is to me, I really think the most influential of all my professors here at the seminary has been you." Greg Bahnsen, "Answer to Frame's Critique of Van Til," Covenant Media Foundation Transcript (Escondido, CA, April 1994), accessed January 25, 2014, http://www.cmfnow.com/answertoframescritiqueofvantil.aspx.

[11] Grudem dedicated his massively influential *Systematic Theology* to Frame (among others). Wayne Grudem, *Systematic Theology: An Introduction to Biblical Doctrine* (Grand Rapids, MI: Zondervan, 2000).

Theological Seminary), Richard Pratt (President of III Millennium Ministries and Adjunct at RTS, Orlando), John Sowell (President of The Reformed Theological Seminary, Atlanta), Lane Tipton (Professor at Westminster Theological Seminary), Kevin Vanhoozer (Professor at Wheaton College and Graduate School).[12] Added to these are those who have held professorships at Westminster in California: S. M. Baugh, R. Scott Clark, J. Van Ee, Bryan D. Estelle, Darryl G. Hart, Michael S. Horton, Dennis E. Johnson, Joel E. Kim, Julius J. Kim, James R. Lund, and David M. VanDrunen. While not everyone represented in the list above has embraced each (or any) of Frame's distinctive teachings, certainly his influence has been extended through this theological progeny.

Third, and perhaps the most important way Frame's influence has been evident, is through his writings. D. A. Carson states that Frame is among "a list of major contemporary figures whose works have helped shape me but whom I do not really know."[13] R. J. Gore, after noting the influence of Frame's writing on his own life, notes, "Like many others, I have never studied under John Frame, although I have been his student for two decades."[14] Frame's Lordship series has been his greatest and most influential work.[15] Beyond this series, Frame has written both extensively and widely,[16] delving into topics

---

[12] Vanhoozer also dedicated a book to Frame. Kevin Vanhoozer, *Remythologizing Theology: Divine Action, Passion, and Authorship* (Cambridge, UK: Cambridge University Press, 2010).

[13] D. A. Carson, "Personal Words: D. A. Carson," in *Speaking the Truth in Love: The Theology of John M. Frame*, ed. John J. Hughes (Phillipsburg, NJ: P&R Publishing, 2009), xxxix.

[14] R. J. Gore, "Personal Words: R. J. Gore," in *Speaking the Truth in Love: The Theology of John M. Frame*, ed. John J. Hughes (Phillipsburg, NJ: P&R Publishing, 2009), xlviii.

[15] As an indication of the importance of the series, the second volume, *The Doctrine of God*, won an ECPA gold medallion as Book of the Year in Theology and Doctrine. "ECPA Gold Medallion Book Award," *Library Thing*, last modified 2003, accessed February 14, 2014, http://www.librarything.com/book award/ECPA+Gold+Medallion+Book+Award.

[16] For the most recent bibliography of his works see, John M. Frame, "John

far beyond the range of most theologians.[17] While these works have not seen the popularity Frame's more systematic works have, nevertheless, they have broadened the reach of Frame's prolific, perspectival pen.[18]

A final element of Frame's influence comes through his online presence. His partnership with Vern Poythress on the Frame-Poythress website, where much of their published material is available for free, has given open access to Frame's (and Poythress's) perspectival method. Further, Reformed Theological Seminary's *iTunes University* audio ministry provides free access to two of Frame's classes,[19] giving Frame a wider hearing than the physical classroom alone.[20]

We have emphasized Frame's influence in order to show the extent to which perspectivalism has had a hearing within (and beyond) the American Reformed community. Wherever Frame has gone, his perspectival method has accompanied him. While the first major exposition of perspectivalism would not be written until the *Doctrine of the Knowledge of God* in 1987,[21] articles, reviews,

---

Frame's Bibliography," *The Works of John Frame and Vern Poythress*, last modified 2013, accessed February 14, 2014, http://www.frame-poythress.org/bibliographies/john-frame-bibliography/.

[17] Frame has written on culture, music, church union, and even wrote a series of film reviews.

[18] Frame's works are thoroughly saturated with perspectival triads. As one reviewer, A. T. B. McGowan, observed of Frame's writing, "There are more triads here than in Chinatown." A. T. B. McGowan, "The Doctrine of God," *Reformation & Revival* 12, 3 (2003): 178.

[19] One class is devoted to Apologetics, and the other to the History of Christian Philosophy. Both are saturated with perspectival methodology.

[20] James Grant and Justin Taylor note the influence RTS Mobile has had with their friend, Daniel Phillips: "Here is someone who had never met Frame, never taken a class from him in person, never even read a book by him—who in this digital age is being influenced by Frame's teaching and is suggesting it to others." James H. Grant, Jr. and Justin Taylor, "John Frame and Evangelicalism," in *Speaking the Truth in Love: The Theology of John M. Frame*, ed. John J. Hughes (Phillipsburg, NJ: P&R Publishing, 2009), 276.

[21] Frame calls this volume his "fundamental source for . . . triperspectivalism."

and personal testimony show that Frame had already developed the perspectival method early in his career.[22] These early essays indicate that while Frame's method would undergo some clarification in later years, even his earliest students and readers were introduced to his perspectival triads.[23] Indeed, William Edgar has argued, "John's triperspectival approach to knowledge . . . is essential for the entire structure of his worldview."[24] As such, there is relatively little within Frame's corpus of literature (either early or late) that has not been subject to perspectival exploration. In sum, it could be accurately said that all who have been exposed to John Frame have been exposed to perspectivalism.[25]

John M. Frame, "Recommended Resources," in *Speaking the Truth in Love: The Theology of John M. Frame*, ed. John J. Hughes (Phillipsburg, NJ: P&R Publishing, 2009), 1064.

[22] As early as 1973 Frame was developing his ethics along perspectival lines. A few years later, in 1976, Frame began using it as a method to critique other theologians' positions. John M. Frame, "The Institutes of Biblical Law: A Review Article," *Westminster Theological Journal* 38, 2 (Winter 1976): 215–17.

[23] Poythress shows how early perspectivalism entered Frame's teaching: "From an early point in his classroom teaching at Westminster Theological Seminary, John Frame deployed his key perspectival triads." He continues, "When I became at [sic] student at Westminster in 1971, Frame was already using as a major pedagogical tool both the triad for lordship (authority, control, and presence) and the triad for ethics (normative, situational, and existential)." Vern S. Poythress, "Multiperspectivalism and the Reformed Faith," in *Speaking the Truth in Love: The Theology of John M. Frame*, ed. John J. Hughes (Phillipsburg, NJ: P&R Publishing, 2009), 176.

[24] William Edgar, "Frame the Apologist," in *Speaking the Truth in Love: The Theology of John M. Frame*, ed. John J. Hughes (Phillipsburg, NJ: P&R Publishing, 2009), 404.

[25] Perspectivalism is the distinguishing mark of Frame's theology. J. I. Packer has suggested that "History will perhaps see this technique [of perspectivalism] as John Frame's major contribution to the conceptual toolkit with which systematic theology works." J. I. Packer, Foreword to *Speaking the Truth in Love: The Theology of John M. Frame*, ed. John J. Hughes (Phillipsburg, NJ: P&R Publishing, 2009), xxix.

Joyce Oldham Appleby, Introduction to *Common Sense and Other Writings*, by Thomas Paine (New York: Barnes & Noble Classics, 2005), xxxvii.

To the extent that Frame's widespread influence and ministry have been shown, we would argue an analysis of his perspectivalism is justified. But Vern Poythress, who describes himself as a student of Frame, has also embraced and developed perspectivalism.[26] Poythress's fields of study show only incidental connection to Frame's. That is, while Frame is a systematic theologian with a penchant for church unity, Poythress is a New Testament scholar with a penchant for the natural sciences. Where Frame's most distinctive work is his Lordship series in systematic theology, Poythress's most distinctive work is his series of *A God-Centered Approach*, which seeks to show how Biblical presuppositions influence various scientific and sociological fields.[27]

The distinction between Frame's and Poythress's areas of expertise indicates both that perspectivalism is flexible enough to be

---

[26] Having been asked about the influence Frame had on his perspectivalism, Poythress responded, "After the initial period that we had to interact, when I was a student in many of his classes, we did not actually talk or correspond with one another much at all. We just did our work, and it 'naturally' came out that our thinking corresponded. The influence of Frame on me, after a period of years, is pervasive. But for that very reason I generally don't in my informal moments single out some particular parts and try to say, 'Now this is Frame's, and this is mine.' Beyond some basic memories, I don't worry about sorting out which is which, because it is almost as if it were all Frame's and simultaneously all mine, in the sense that I have internalized it and I don't need to think, 'Now am I following Frame's thought accurately?'" Vern S. Poythress, e-mail message to the author, January 30, 2014.

[27] This series has focused on science, logic, math, language, sociology, and probability. Vern S. Poythress, *Chance and the Sovereignty of God: A God-Centered Approach to Probability and Random Events* (Phillipsburg, NJ: P&R Publishing, 2014); Vern S. Poythress, *Logic: A God-Centered Approach to the Foundation of Western Thought* (Wheaton, IL: Crossway, 2013); Vern S. Poythress, *Inerrancy and the Gospels: A God-Centered Approach to the Challenges of Harmonization* (Wheaton, IL: Crossway, 2012); Vern S. Poythress, *Redeeming Sociology: A God-Centered Approach* (Wheaton, IL: Crossway, 2011); Vern S. Poythress, *In the Beginning Was the Word: Language: A God-Centered Approach* (Wheaton, IL: Crossway, 2009); Vern S. Poythress, *Redeeming Science: A God-Centered Approach* (Wheaton, IL: Crossway, 2006).

applied to a wide range of topics and also that the influence of perspectivalism reaches beyond Frame's theological works. Vern Poythress's bibliography is just as impressive as Frame's in both breadth of material and theological acumen.[28] If we include the influence Poythress has had in the classroom as well,[29] we find that two of the most prolific and influential theologians in American Reformed Orthodoxy have embraced a theological method that has not been subject to any *considerable* external evaluation.

Uses of Perspectivalism Outside of Frame and Poythress

While Frame and Poythress have applied perspectivalism to a wide range of issues, including epistemology, theology proper, ethics, science, math, language, logic, and other disciplines, their followers have developed new applications of the method. The following are examples of perspectivalism in which the authors claim Frame as the origination of their organizational ideas.[30] The purpose of this section is not to develop others' views in detail. Rather, we will seek only to (1) show the general way each author uses perspectivalism and (2) make a notation of the author's reliance on Frame. Here it will be argued that the diversity of the ways perspectivalism has been applied provides ample justification for a study on the method.

In ethics, David Clowney, who previously held a professorship at WTS and presently teaches at Rowan University in New Jersey, has used perspectivalism as a method of developing environmental

---

[28] Vern S. Poythress, "Vern Poythress's Bibliography," *The Works of John Frame and Vern Poythress*, last modified 2014, accessed February 17, 2014, http://www.frame-poythress.org/bibliographies/vern-poythress-bibliography/.

[29] Poythress has been a Professor of New Testament Interpretation at Westminster Theological Seminary in Philadelphia from 1976–present.

[30] Because these authors cite Frame or Poythress as the origin of their perspectival view does not mean they properly understand perspectivalism. Further, because they put perspectivalism to use in various categories does not mean that Frame and Poythress would agree with their uses of the method. This section is merely a reflection of the influence and extent to which perspectivalism as a method has been used outside these two prolific authors.

ethics.³¹ While Clowney does not explicitly cite Frame as the origin point for his perspectival analysis, Frame has elsewhere argued that while Clowney was at Westminster the latter made "ample use of Van Til's work and of my multi-perspectival approach."³² Further, Clowney verified through personal correspondence that he continues to use perspectivalism.³³

As a second example, Esther Meek has built her epistemology on the foundation provided by John Frame and Michael Polanyi. From Frame she adopts the perspectival triad:

> Created reality everywhere evidences those aspects—the normative (or covenantally constitutive), the existential (or interpersoned intimacy), and the situational (the real, uncreated and created). I and many others have found that the Framean triadic motif proves most apt to develop and orchestrate the fundamental dimensions of most any subject.³⁴

Again, she notes, "John [Frame's] approach to a biblically shaped epistemology, in particular, his signature triad motif, has figured prominently both as a guide to my growing understanding and in my mature thought."³⁵ Frame's praised her book, *Longing to Know*, for its perspectival analysis, especially as it focused on knowing through the existential lens.³⁶ Her second epistemological work,

---

³¹ David Clowney, *Earthcare: An Anthology in Environmental Ethics*, ed. Patricia Mosto (Lanham, MA: Rowman & Littlefield, 2009), 8–11.

³² John M. Frame, "Systematic Theology and Apologetics at the Westminster Seminaries," in *The Pattern of Sound Doctrine*, ed. David Van Drunen (Phillipsburg, NJ: P&R Publishing, 2004), 96.

³³ David Clowney, e-mail message to the author, February 12, 2014.

³⁴ Esther Meek, "Servant Thinking: The Polyanyian Workings of the Framean Triad," in *Speaking the Truth in Love: The Theology of John M. Frame*, ed. John J. Hughes (Phillipsburg, NJ: P&R Publishing, 2009), 615.

³⁵ Ibid., 611; Esther Meek, *Longing to Know* (Grand Rapids, MI: Brazos Press, 2003).

³⁶ John M. Frame, "Review of Esther Meek's Longing to Know," *Presbyterion*

Loving to Know, further develops a covenantal epistemology built on Frame's unique insights.[37]

James Anderson also develops perspectivalism in epistemology. He has argued that while Frame's perspectivalism was "developed in an explicitly Christian context," it has application to mainstream epistemology.[38] Anderson seeks to prove this thesis by showing (1) how perspectivalism anticipates the threefold tradition in the history of philosophy (rationalism, empiricism, and subjectivism), (2) how perspectivalism correlates with the tripartite definition of knowledge, and (3) how Plantinga's understanding of warrant can be understood through the perspectival paradigm.[39] Anderson concludes by suggesting, "The fact that Frame's triad of normative, situational, and existential perspectives can be discerned here and elsewhere in 'mainstream' epistemological discussions suggests that Frame is on to something important."[40]

Perhaps the most popular way Frame's perspectivalism has been taught is in ecclesiology through the Prophet, Priest, and King distinction.[41] In addition to websites devoted to a perspectival

---

29, 2 (Fall 2003).

[37] Esther Meek, *Loving to Know: Introducing Covenant Epistemology* (Eugene, OR: Cascade Books, 2011).

[38] James N. Anderson, "Presuppositionalism and Frame's Epistemology," in *Speaking the Truth in Love: The Theology of John M. Frame*, ed. John J. Hughes (Phillipsburg, NJ: P&R Publishing, 2009), 441.

[39] Anderson notes, "Plantinga's sophisticated post-Gettier analysis of warrant also reflects Frame's triperspectival scheme. The normative perspective is found in the notion of proper function; a cognitive faculty can be said to function properly only if it proceeds according to certain design norms. The situational perspective is found in Plantinga's concept of a cognitive environment. Our cognitive faculties are designed to furnish us with true beliefs in specific environments. Finally, the existential perspective is found in Plantinga's suggestion that the degree to which a belief is warranted will depend (among other things) on the firmness or subjective confidence with which the belief is held. James N. Anderson, "Presuppositionalism and Frame's Epistemology," in *Speaking the Truth in Love: The Theology of John M. Frame* (Phillipsburg, NJ: P&R Publishing, 2009), 445–46.

[40] Ibid., 446.

[41] Dennis E. Johnson, "A Triperspectival Model of Ministry," in *Speaking the*

ecclesiology,[42] Tim Keller and Mark Driscoll have done much to popularize the perspectival triad. Mark Driscoll emphasized this triad in an address to the *Christian Counseling and Educational Foundation*, arguing that each church needs a balance of kingly, prophetic, and priestly pastors.[43] Keller, in harmony with Driscoll, sought to summarize the potential usefulness of this triad as it related to Keller's visit to Willow Creek Community Church:

> John Frame's 'tri-perspectivalism' helps me understand Willow [Creek]. The Willow Creek style churches have a 'kingly' emphasis on leadership, strategic thinking, and wise administration. . . . The Reformed churches have a 'prophetic' emphasis on preaching, teaching, and doctrine. . . . The emerging churches have a 'priestly' emphasis on community, liturgy and sacraments, service and justice.[44]

In a series of articles in the *Journal of Biblical Counseling*, Keller also developed the perspectival triad in the context of preaching.[45]

Truth in Love: The Theology of John M. Frame, ed. John J. Hughes (Phillipsburg, NJ: P&R Publishing, 2009), 631–58.

[42] The following blog provides links to others advocating this perspectival relationship. Drew Goodmanson, "Triperspectivalism," *Goodmanson: Leadership, Church Web & Tech, Mission Alignment (blog)*, last modified 2014, accessed February 17, 2014, http://www.goodmanson.com/category/church/triperspectivalism/.

[43] Driscoll recognizes Frame as the origin source for this triad in ecclesiological application. Mark Driscoll, "Fighting the Air War and Ground War," 2008, http://www.ccef.org/fighting-air-war-and-ground-war-1; Jamie Munson, "Prophet, Priest, King | The Resurgence," *The Resurgence*, last modified 2010, accessed February 17, 2014, http://theresurgence.com/2010/12/13/prophet-priest-king.

[44] Timothy Keller, "The 'Kingly' Willow Creek Conference," *Redeemer City to City (blog)*, September 13, 2009, accessed February 17, 2014, https://redeemercitytocity.com/blog/2009/the-kingly-willow-creek-conference/.

[45] Timothy Keller, "A Model for Preaching: Part One: Three Perspectives on Preaching & the Biblical Aspect," *Journal of Biblical Counseling* 12, 3 (1994): 36–42; Timothy Keller, "A Model for Preaching: Part Two: The Situational

In another field, Jeffrey Ventrella has applied perspectival insights to the Christ and Culture debate.[46] In his 28 page article, Ventrella attempts to show how one can "triangulate cultural restoration" through means of *thirty-five* triads.[47] Ventrella believes that the most helpful aspect of perspectivalism concerns the future: "Frame's triangles are certainly descriptive; yet they are also prescriptive, and therefore prospective. When employed prospectively, these triangles not only provide tactical insight, but identify strategic targets for cultural engagement and restoration: the robes of culture."[48]

A second way perspectivalism has been used in cultural studies is evident in the work of Nathaniel Claiborne.[49] In Claiborne's Th.M. thesis at *Dallas Theological Seminary*, he used perspectivalism as a method to develop a philosophy of film criticism. Within the thesis, he argued that one of his major goals was "to demonstrate the usefulness of Frame's triperspectivalism, being as it is 'generic Calvinism.' To offer a truly Calvinist philosophy of film, a triperspectival approach is the best framework available."[50] On his website,

---

Aspect," *Journal of Biblical Counseling* 13, 1 (1994): 39–48; Timothy Keller, "A Model for Preaching: Part Three: The Personal Aspect," *Journal of Biblical Counseling* 14, 1 (1995): 54–62.

[46] See also, John Barber, "John Frame's Theology in the Present Cultural Context," in *Speaking the Truth in Love: The Theology of John M. Frame*, ed. John J. Hughes (Phillipsburg, NJ: P&R Publishing, 2009), 884–907.

[47] Jeffrey J. Ventrella, "Passionately Demonstrating Truth: Triangulating Cultural Restoration," in *Speaking the Truth in Love: The Theology of John M. Frame*, ed. John J. Hughes (Phillipsburg, NJ: P&R Publishing, 2009), 856.

[48] Ibid., 882–83.

[49] Claiborne embraced perspectivalism through the ministry of Mark Driscoll. Nathaniel Claiborne, "Triperspectivalism: More Than Church Leadership Analysis," *Nate Claiborne (blog)*, last modified July 26, 2011, accessed February 19, 2014, http://nathanielclaiborne.com/triperspectivalism-more-than-church-leadership-analysis/.

[50] After his thesis was accepted, Claiborne presented it in absentia at the 2012 Evangelical Theological Society Conference. Nathaniel Claiborne, "Hollywood, Geneva, and Athens: A Reformed Philosophy of Film" (Th.M. thesis, Dallas Theological Seminary, 2011); Nathaniel Claiborne, "Hollywood, Geneva, and Athens: Towards a Reformed Philosophy of Film" (Oral

Claiborne has continued applying perspectivalism to further issues, noting that he found perspectivalism to have "numerous applications outside where Frame has made it and where I made it (film)."[51]

Harvie Conn, who was a missionary to Korea and later a professor of missions at *Westminster Theological Seminary*, also developed an application of perspectivalism to practical missionary ministry. In his *Eternal Word and Changing Worlds: Theology, Anthropology, and Missions in Trialogue*, Conn argues that theology with an eye to foreign contexts must take into account all three of Frame's perspectives. As a consequence, Western theology will be significantly affected.[52] But Conn believes that this should not be taken negatively:

> For the missionary this can be a liberating exercise. Theologizing becomes more of a dynamic process rather than one virtually completed in the West. More than simple indoctrination, it is transformed into a dynamic discovery engaged in by human beings in all human cultures. It is hemmed in and bombarded from three perspectives (to use the formulae of John Frame)—the normative perspective of the Bible, the situational perspective of cultural, social time and place, and the existential perspective of our humanity as images of God.[53]

By embracing such a system, Conn is convinced that theology can move forward in a way that embraces the perspectives of people from all nations.

Presentation presented at the Evangelical Theological Society, Milwaukee, WI, 2012), 41.

[51] Nathaniel Claiborne, "Perspectives on Triperspectivalism," *Nate Claiborne (blog)*, last modified September 25, 2011, accessed February 19, 2014, http://nathanielclaiborne.com/perspectives-on-triperspectivalis/.

[52] Harvie Conn, *Eternal Word and Changing Worlds: Theology, Anthropology, and Mission in Trialogue* (Phillipsburg, NJ: P&R Publishing, 1992), 338.

[53] Ibid.

Kevin Vanhoozer, one of the most broadly influential Christian theologians alive today, studied with Frame at Westminster for one year of intense study.[54] Though Frame left after Vanhoozer's first year, Vanhoozer secured Frame as the supervisor for his MDiv honors thesis.[55] The influence of perspectivalism can be seen in Vanhoozer's book, *The Drama of Doctrine*, where he proposes a theological method that seeks to triangulate doctrine in a way very similar to Frame's perspectivalism.[56] That Vanhoozer's *triangulation* is modeled after Frame's perspectivalism is implied both from the similarity in development and from the following dedication of a later book: "To John Frame: my first graduate-school theology professor, a master-pedagogue and triangulator extraordinaire, whose multiperspectival approach to the doctrine of God has been a source of continuing inspiration."[57]

It should not be surprising, considering that perspectivalism finds its "natural home in ethics,"[58] that counselors would find helpful themes in the method. David Powlison has described his own counseling as "Frame's ethics on wheels."[59] Later in the same

---

[54] Vanhoozer was one of the few students who successfully completed the program originally created for Vern Poythress. The advanced program allowed exceptional students to attend classes as desired while maintaining the rigor of required knowledge and competency through intense testing. In e-mail correspondence with James Grant and Justin Taylor, Vanhoozer revealed that he "took every class that Frame offered that year since Frame was leaving for California, and he obtained notes from other students for the courses he wasn't able to take with Frame." Grant, Jr. and Taylor, "John Frame and Evangelicalism," 281.

[55] Kevin Vanhoozer, "Personal Words: Kevin Vanhoozer," in *Speaking the Truth in Love: The Theology of John M. Frame*, ed. John J. Hughes (Phillipsburg, NJ: P&R Publishing, 2009), lxxix–lxxx.

[56] He brings together propositions/beliefs, experiences/feelings, and narratives/actions into one comprehensive act of developing theology. Kevin Vanhoozer, *The Drama of Doctrine: A Canonical-Linguistic Approach to Christian Theology* (Louisville, KY: Westminster John Knox Press, 2005).

[57] Vanhoozer, *Remythologizing Theology*, xix.

[58] John M. Frame, *The Doctrine of God* (Phillipsburg, NJ: P&R Publishing, 2002), 187.

[59] David Powlison, "Frame's Ethics: Working the Implications for Pastoral

article Powlison argues that "[Frame's] triperspectival outlook heads straight in the direction of counseling."⁶⁰ While the influences that have led to Powlison's prolific and significant career are more numerous than can be indicated here, Powlison reserves a significant place for Frame and his method of perspectivalism:

> Frame's influence was direct. I sat under his teaching in Doctrine of the Christian Life and Doctrine of the Word, two blockbuster courses at Westminster Theological Seminary in the late 1970s. The flexibility and adaptability of his triperspectivalism proved hugely provocative and helpful as I developed into a pastoral counselor.⁶¹

Finally, we will consider the perspectivally influenced works of Frame's students. Ezra Huyn Kim's DMin thesis under Frame is self-descriptive: *Biblical Preaching is Apologia: An Analysis of the Apologetic Nature of Preaching in Light of Perspectivalism*.⁶² Third Millennium Ministries has also published several articles from Frame's students, who have analyzed theological and cultural issues through a perspectival lens.⁶³

Care," in *Speaking the Truth in Love: The Theology of John M. Frame*, ed. John J. Hughes (Phillipsburg, NJ: P&R Publishing, 2009), 759.

⁶⁰ Ibid.

⁶¹ Ibid., 762.

⁶² Ezra Hyun Kim, "Biblical Preaching Is Apologia: An Analysis of the Apologetic Nature of Preaching in Light of Perspectivalism" (DMin, Westminster Theological Seminary, 2000).

⁶³ Robert Kemp, "Aesthetic Perspectivalism and the Nature of Art: Two Proposals," *IIIM Magazine Online* 5, 22 (June 2003), accessed October 18, 2014, http://www.thirdmill.org/files/english/practical_theology/6280~6_12 _2003_2-36-48_PM~PT.Kemp.epistemology.hall.frame.pdf; Michael Fourth, "Christian Reflections on the Phenomenological Epistemology of Maurice Merleau-Ponty," *IIIM Magazine Online* 5, 22 (June 2003), accessed October 18, 2014, http://thirdmill.org/files/reformedperspectives/hall_of_frame/HOF .Fourth.Merleau.Pointy.epistemology.pdf. While Third Millennium only published a few of these papers (those receiving the honor of Hall of Frame), it

As a consequence of their significant influence, Frame and Poythress's perspectivalism has been put to wide use within (and outside) Reformed theology. If perspectival methodology is flawed, it is essential that a critical analysis be formed, but if the method is essentially or even partially valid, a critical analysis should also be formed to emphasize the usefulness of the paradigm. Either way, an extended study is needed.

The Claims of Perspectivalism

A third justification for this study is the explicit claims of Frame and others in favor of perspectivalism. While many claims could be examined, perhaps the most important are the following three: (1) the claim that perspectivalism derives from the Trinity, (2) the claim that perspectivalism is a Reformed concept, and (3) the claim that perspectivalism is an eminently useful theological paradigm.

Perspectivalism as Trinitarian

Poythress unreservedly claims a Trinitarian focus for Frame's triads: "Frame's multiperspectivalism is grounded ultimately in the Trinity and is therefore possible only within the circle of Christian Trinitarian theology."[64] While Frame has historically vacillated over the Trinitarian origin of perspectivalism,[65] the overall trajectory of his thought leads the observant reader to conclude that Frame agrees with Poythress. For instance, in his inaugural book espousing the perspectival view, Frame asserted, "God's word tends to present relationships perspectively because it reflects the nature of God himself, I would surmise. God is one God in three persons; He is many attributes in one Godhead—the eternal one

---

would not be a stretch to believe that others have also written papers under Frame applying a perspectival grid to a variety of theological issues.

[64] Poythress, "Multiperspectivalism," 180n22.

[65] Frame's equivocation over the Trinitarian origins of perspectivalism will be examined later. For an example of his reservation, see, Frame, *The Doctrine of God*, 15n31.

and many."⁶⁶ More recently, in an interview written for his Festrichft, Frame confirmed, "[the perspectives] are ultimately based, I would say, in the Trinity: the Father, Son, and Spirit are all 'in' one another (*circumincessio*), so that to know one is always to know the others."⁶⁷

Because of the centrality of the doctrine of the Trinity in the Christian religion, Frame's claim that perspectivalism is Trinitarian takes on massive importance.⁶⁸ This is especially true for those engaged in apologetic dialogue with unbelievers who believe in a unitarian god. If it can be shown that all of creation reflects the Trinitarian nature of God, Van Til's transcendental methodology may be strengthened.

Van Til, following Herman Bavinck, believed that the world exhibited, as much as possible, the Trinitarian nature of God.⁶⁹ Frame is simply asserting that perspectivalism is one way God's reflection is shown in in creation. An evaluation of this claim from someone other than Frame or Poythress is overdue.

This dissertation will be chiefly concerned with this question,

---

⁶⁶ John M. Frame, *The Doctrine of the Knowledge of God* (Phillipsburg, NJ: Presbyterian and Reformed, 1987), 192.

⁶⁷ John M. Frame and P. Andrew Sandlin, "Reflections of a Lifetime Theologian: An Extended Interview with John M. Frame," in *Speaking the Truth in Love: The Theology of John M. Frame*, ed. John J. Hughes (Phillipsburg, NJ: P&R Publishing, 2009), 82.

⁶⁸ Frame does warn the reader about putting too much theological weight on the triads. Nevertheless, he suggests, "these triads are of some interest and that they may in some measure reflect, illumine, or provide evidence for the doctrine of the Trinity in some measure." Frame, *The Doctrine of God*, 743. Poythress seems to agree, arguing, "[perspectives] enjoy a mysterious coinherence testifying to God's Trinitarian character." Vern S. Poythress, "Reforming Ontology and Logic in the Light of the Trinity: An Application of Van Til's Idea of Analogy," *Westminster Theological Journal* 57, 1 (Spring 1995): 197.

⁶⁹ We will see this Reformed connection through Bavinck below. Cornelius Van Til, *An Introduction to Systematic Theology* (Nutley, NJ: Presbyterian and Reformed, 1974), 364–65.

for from it the other two claims are established.[70] If perspectivalism is Trinitarian, then it should be consonant with Reformed theology.[71] Further, if perspectivalism is a vestige of the Trinity, it will be the most practical of insights, showing how all things are reflective of and understood in light of the Trinitarian God.

Perspectivalism as a Reformed Concept

In *Doctrine of the Knowledge of God*, the first major exposition of perspectivalism, Frame recognized that many of his viewpoints were not consonant with other Reformed theologians.[72] Nevertheless, Frame believed, despite the lack of any direct argument for Reformed theology, his book would be an indirect argument for Reformed theology, showing the resources contained in Reformed orthodoxy that are unavailable to other theological persuasions.[73]

While perspectivalism is often noted as one of Frame's original developments, he says, "Strange as all of that may sound to Reformed people, I insist that this approach is nothing less than generic Calvinism." How is perspectivalism generic Calvinism? Namely, it stresses the interrelatedness of knowledge and creation as united under the sovereign, Trinitarian God. After expressing his continuity of thought from Calvin to Van Til, Frame suggests that only the Reformed could speak the way he does about the internal

---

[70] In the last chapter of the dissertation we will argue for a processional triperspectivalism in which the situational and existential flow from the normative. This pattern is evident here in the construction of the dissertation.

[71] What is the Reformed theology? We will follow Frame in indicating that it is both *reformed* (emphasizing the creeds and historical development) and *reforming* (emphasizing the continual refining of theology in light of Scripture). Further, we will argue that perspectivalism should be understood as Reformed in that it is grounded in the thought of Reformed theologians (*reformed*) and provides a step forward in theological understanding (*reforming*). John M Frame, "Introduction to the Reformed Faith," *Frame-Poythress*, last modified 1999, accessed April 1, 2011, http://www.frame-poythress.org/frame_articles/Trinitarian.htm.

[72] Frame, *The Doctrine of the Knowledge of God*, xv.

[73] Ibid., XV.

harmony of revelation. Perspectivalism, he insists, seeks "only to carry this [harmony] one step further."[74]

Not everyone agrees that perspectivalism is generic Calvinism. R. Scott Clark rhetorically asks, "Isn't the whole point of John's [perspectival] method to dispense with the [Reformed] tradition?"[75] Mark Karlberg contrasts Van Til as the defender of Reformed theology with Frame as the eclectic (i.e., broadly evangelical) perspectivalist.[76] William Dennison concurs, specifically arguing that while "Frame attempts to demonstrate that perspectivalism is in tune with historic Reformed theology . . . in the history of Reformed epistemology, the language is entirely new and foreign." Dennison concludes by suggesting that Frame has embraced "a principle which logical positivism would endorse."[77]

Clearly, Frame's claim that perspectivalism is congruent with Reformed theology is contested. Ironically, in light of the strong invective used against Frame and his approach, little serious work has been done to show the incompatibility between perspectivalism and the Reformed faith.[78] This dissertation will seek to do the

---

[74] Ibid., 90.

[75] Lane Keister, "John Frame's Newest Tome," *Green Baggins (blog)*, last modified August 20, 2008, accessed February 23, 2014, http://greenbaggins.wordpress.com/2008/08/20/john-frames-newest-tome/. In another post, Clark calls Frame's method a "cancer" in the Reformed community. R. Scott Clark, "Peace (with Evangelicalism) in Our Time," *The Heidelblog*, last modified October 7, 2009, accessed October 2, 2013, http://heidelblog.net/2009/10/subjectivism-and-peace-with-evangelicalism-tim-keller/.

[76] "Van Til is the uncompromising defender of the Reformed faith, Frame the genteel perspectivalist whose eclectic approach embraces diverse and contrary formulations." Karlberg, "John Frame and the Recasting of Van Tilian Apologetics," 281.

[77] William Dennison, "Analytic Philosophy and Van Til's Epistemology," *Westminster Theological Journal* 57, 1 (Spring 1995): 47.

[78] Some minor works have attempted to critique perspectivalism from a Reformed perspective. Notably, Mark Karlberg wrote two critical articles. His conclusion to the articles called for more interaction: "Hopefully, this critique of multiperspectivalism will stimulate constructive discussion among evangelical theologians who cherish the system of truth they find in Scripture in

opposite by showing that the foundation of perspectivalism is established in the Reformed heritage, particularly in the formative works of Herman Bavinck and Cornelius Van Til.

Perspectivalism as an Eminently Useful Theological Paradigm

Frame and Poythress have sought to confirm that perspectivalism is a useful method through the varied topics they have applied the method toward. More broadly, James Anderson has noted three ways that he finds perspectivalism useful: "(1) as a guard against imbalance and omission in our analyses, . . . (2) as a means of obtaining greater insight into any topic under examination, and (3) as a source of inspiration for new theories or methods."[79] Anderson's comments concern perspectivalism in epistemology, but he notes that it also applies "to ethics, theology, apologetics, psychology, and other fields."[80]

If, as Frame has argued, perspectivalism is a vestige of the Trinity present throughout creation, then it is of utmost importance that a study be done to ascertain its proper function. In this way, it can be used to describe, analyze, and predict the elements of the world that God has called man to subdue. While the dissertation will not seek to directly address this question, the usefulness of the method will be constantly expressed as we defend its Trinitarian basis and apply the method to various theological and philosophical issues.

Need for Critical Analysis

That Frame has desired critical engagement with his work is the final reason this dissertation is needed. In his recent festrichft, Frame lamented, "one blessing I've largely missed has been that of

---

the face of modern-day theological eclecticism." Karlberg, "Theological Correlation of Language," 105; Karlberg, "John Frame and the Recasting of Van Tilian Apologetics." We will interact with Karlberg and other critics throughout the dissertation.

[79] Anderson, "Presuppositionalism and Frame's Epistemology," 446.
[80] Ibid., 446n39.

sympathetic, critical analysis. . . . I have wished for someone to come along and give my work a professional going-over, a careful analysis and evaluation."[81] Notice that Frame desires a *sympathetic* and *critical* analysis. He has had his share of non-critical and non-sympathetic critics.[82] The fountains of Frame's thought are deep in both theological and philosophical sophistication, and most of his critics have failed to dig as deeply as necessary to see the intricate connections flowing within.

In honor of Professor Frame and of his service to the church, his call for a sympathetic-critical analysis needs to be heeded. As he approaches full retirement, the time for his enjoyment of such an analysis is drawing shorter. It is the goal of this dissertation to provide a partial answer to Frame's request.

Summary of the Study

The first chapter has sought to develop the significance of perspectivalism by analyzing the importance of the two major theological figures representing the method. Further, the chapter has served to show that an analysis of perspectivalism has been called for in light of (1) its wide use within and outside Reformed theology, and (2) its central claims to be Trinitarian, Reformed, and eminently useful. If successful, this first chapter has shown the necessity of the following chapters.

In chapter two we will examine the two types of perspectivalism

---

[81] John M. Frame, "Preface," in *Speaking the Truth in Love: The Theology of John M. Frame*, ed. John J. Hughes (Phillipsburg, NJ: P&R Publishing, 2009), xx–xxi.

[82] Garcia notes, "Frame has experienced what far too many working in our day also experience: the near absence of criticism that reflects a careful, extensive reading of one's work as the necessary prelude to assessment, or, alternatively, the absence of reasonable charity in the handling of it." He continues, "In addition, the standards of analysis frequently fall far short of what we as Christians should expect of one another, and Frame has had more than his fair share of incompetent critics." Mark A. Garcia, "The Word Made Applicable,"

(general perspectivalism and triperspectivalism) and clarify the language used in reference to the system. Having made the necessary clarifications, we will develop the metaphysical basis of general perspectivalism by an examination of both man's knowledge and God's knowledge. More specifically, we will show that the dual effects of sin and finitude necessitate creaturely perspectival knowledge. Further, we will show that neither sin nor finitude is the *ultimate* basis for the perspectives; rather, the innate perspectival knowledge of the triune persons provides the model by which the perspectives exist, are distinct from one another, and yet are able to cohere. Because knowledge has historically been considered an attribute of the essence and not the individual persons of the Trinity, it will be necessary to examine the Trinitarian theology of Cornelius Van Til, who argues for the equal ultimacy of the one and many. There we will develop what Van Til meant by God being a "tri-conscious being." Armed with the equal ultimacy of the one and many, we will have the resources to show that the foundation of man's diversity of perspectives is ectypally reflective of the archetypal intra-Trinitarian knowledge.

Considerations provided in chapter two necessitate a discussion of both the major implications and the major critiques of general perspectivalism in chapter three. We will begin by answering the common criticism concerning the relationship between perspectivalism and relativity. In order to show that perspectivalism is not inherently relativistic, we will show that a belief in a divergence of perspectives does not necessarily lead to relativism. Further, we will contrast Frame and Poythress's perspectivalism with the relativistic systems of Friedrich Nietzsche, Charles Sanders Peirce, and Werner Kriegelstein. While these men have developed relativistic systems that are similar in name to perspectivalism, they differ substantially in content. Having answered the charge of relativism, we will turn to a discussion of the major implications of general perspectivalism.

---

in *Speaking the Truth in Love: The Theology of John M. Frame*, ed. John J. Hughes (Phillipsburg, NJ: P&R Publishing, 2009), 247.

These implications will help the reader recognize the utility of perspectivalism.

Chapter four will introduce the second form of perspectivalism, triperspectivalism. The chapter will begin with a brief overview of the method of triperspectivalism. This overview is designed merely to introduce the system in order that the Trinitarian basis may be examined. A further exploration of the depths of triperspectivalism will await chapter six. After the brief introduction to the method, we will propose the Trinity as the foundational triad. In order to do so, we will need to first address two potential criticisms: first, whether Frame really believes perspectivalism is Trinitarian; and second, whether referring to the Trinity as perspectival entails Sabellianism. Having answered these criticisms, we will explore both perichoresis and simplicity as the models of unity in diversity whereby Frame grounds his perspectival groupings. But in order to ground perspectivalism in both simplicity and perichoresis, we will have to fashion a model by which we can relate perichoresis and simplicity together. We will introduce the need for such a perichoretic-simplicity model by examining the weakness of the simplicity model of Thomas Aquinas. By examining the Trinitarian shortfalls of his simplicity account, we will set the foundation for the next chapter in which we will develop a perichoretic-simplicity model.

Chapter five will show the benefit of adopting the perichoretic-simplicity model by comparing it to Aquinas's understanding of the nature and persons of the Godhead. We will maintain that perichoretic-simplicity is beneficial for the following reasons: first, it is born out of Trinitarian revelation; second, it is capable of maintaining proper predication (contra Aquinas's model); third, it provides a foundation for unity; fourth, it shows the similarity of function in the unity and diversity of the *persons* and *attributes* of the Godhead; fifth, it maintains the aseity of God; sixth, it is the product of absolute personality; seventh, it is not entirely a-historical in that Duns Scotus offered some of the fundamentals necessary for such a system. After arguing for the model, we will summarize the implications of perichoretic-simplicity, showing that the product of the model is consonant with how Frame and Poythress describe perspectival relationships. As such, this chapter is critical in showing that perspectivalism is ectypally reflective of the archetype of God's attributes (simplicity) and persons (perichoresis).

Chapter six will continue showing the Trinitarian basis for triperspectivalism by making explicit the three reasons Frame and Poythress believe creation necessarily reflects the Trinitarian Creator. First, God's nature as *absolute* implies ectypal manifestation of his archetypal nature. Second, God's work of imaging in man and creation provides extensive reasons to seek analogies of his nature in creation. Third, God's creation as the product of his speech implies Trinitarian reflection into creation. That Frame and Poythress seek vestiges of the Trinity in creation is ultimately sourced out of the pioneering work of Herman Bavinck on *vestigia trinitatis*. Therefore, we will develop Bavinck's views, showing how Frame and Poythress follow his lead in developing the Trinitarian analogies. Having established the foundations for *vestigia*, we will turn to the ectypal manifestation of the Trinity in perspectival dynamics. These dynamics are the core attributes of perspectival groups, and they will show the foundational relationship of the perichoretic-simplicity model to perspectivalism. To finish the chapter, we will seek to show the way Frame and Poythress derive their triads. In doing so, we will see that the derivation is not random or unreflective, but is intentionally Trinitarian, aligning the various triads according to the nature, persons, and acts of the triune God. Here we will see that not every triad in Frame is perspectival. Further, not ever triad is built upon lordship. Instead, there are at least three ways of deriving perspectival triads, for which the ultimate commonality is the unity in diversity of the triune Godhead.

Chapter seven focuses on Frame's most prolific triad, the lordship triad. Because many of Frame's triads are a reflection of his analysis of God's lordship in triperspectival fashion, we will develop and defend that model. We will seek first to show that authority, control, and presence are accurate reflections of the theme of lordship. We will observe this theme in God's covenants, his acts, and biblical descriptions of his character. That each of the lordship characteristics is associated predominantly with one of the members of the Trinity is critical to perspectivalism, and it shows the connection between perspectivalism and God's Trinitarian nature. While each characteristic is not exclusive to one member of the Trinity, the Father is predominantly identified as the authority, the Son as the controller, and the Spirit as the presence of God. It is this foundation that provides the key to understanding the majority of Frame's triads. As such, this chapter argues that Frame is seeking to understand creation through the lens (i.e., perspective) of God's lordship, which is necessarily Trinitarian.

Chapter eight will seek to show that while perspectivalism is Trinitarian it is not yet sufficiently Trinitarian. More specifically, we will argue that perspectivalism is not Trinitarian enough in that the method eliminates all order and priority, yet order and priority are fundamental to the Trinitarian persons. On this basis we will develop a model of processional perspectivalism, which images the order and priority of persons. We will apply processional perspectivalism to two issues in order to show the benefit of the system. First, we will apply it to the knowledge triad in order to show why God's norms maintain a priority over all of life. Second, we will apply it to Frame's apologetics, seeking to show that Frame's position on presuppositional apologetics and the transcendental argument are sourced out of a perspectivalism that dismisses priority and order. If priority and order are reintroduced through processional perspectivalism, Frame's criticisms of Van Til's presuppositional approach are considerably reduced. Overall, this chapter seeks to refine perspectival methodology in an even more robust Trinitarian direction.

Because of the limitations necessary for this dissertation, it is not possible to cover all of the important aspects of perspectivalism here. Much work needs yet to be done, so the final chapter will conclude the dissertation by focusing on research questions yet to be adequately answered.

2

Method and Basis of General Perspectivalism

R. Scott Clark has argued that perspectivalism is analogous to a rigged game: "The best way I know to describe such a view is to describe it as a kind of wheel of fortune. Someone has to start the wheel and someone has to stop it and someone has to say what it means and, in my experience, only authorized persons (Frame, Poythress or another one approved by [Frame]) get to play."[1] Clark also offers another analogy:

When we try to play we're told "You don't know the rules, go away" or "your throw doesn't count because you broke the rules."
"What are the rules?"
"Well, there's first base, second base, and third base."
"Great, that makes sense."
"Wait, there's more. After the game begins, first base modifies second base, and second base modifies third base."
"Uh, okay. I guess I can imagine how that might be."
"There's more. When the game really heats up, first base, second base, and third base become identical."

---

[1] R. Scott Clark, comment, October 24, 2009, on "Frame's Negative Review of Horton's Christless Christianity," Kim Riddlebarger, *The RiddleBlog*, October 22, 2009, accessed March 7, 2014, http://kimriddlebarger.square space.com/the-latest-post/2009/10/22/frames-negative-review-of-hortons -christless-christianity.html#comments.

"Uh, who says when that happens?"
"The ump."
"Who wrote the rules?"
"The ump"
"Who says who gets to play?"
"The ump"
"Who says what the score is?"
"The ump"

You can see that this not exactly a field of dreams or perhaps it is.[2]

Clark is arguing that perspectivalism is a method without definitive rules, and, more importantly, that it is a method relative to those who employ it. If true, this would be a devastating critique to the perspectival method as well as the theological corpus of Frame and Poythress. They would be found to embrace a method that systematically allowed them to construct theology according to their own whims. It will be argued in this chapter that Clark is substantially wrong in his assessment.

But Clark's misunderstanding of perspectivalism may result from what is perceived to be a lack of clarity on perspectival methodology. Brant Bosserman claims that "very little has been done . . . to incorporate the mass of perspectivalist insights into a tight-knit system."[3] He suggests that the character of perspectivalism as a methodology that shifts from specificity to generality might be the source of the problem. That is, Bosserman suggests that perspectivalism is inherently against systemization. We will argue that this position is partially mistaken.[4] Everything necessary to provide the

---

[2] Ibid.
[3] Brant Bosserman, "The Trinity and the Vindication of Christian Paradox: An Interpretation and Refinement of the Theological Apologetic of Cornelius Van Til" (PhD Diss., University of Bangor, 2011), §156.
[4] Because the ultimate basis of perspectivalism is Trinitarian, a full systemization is impossible. Thus, Bosserman is partially correct. Nevertheless, God

system is available, yet the method is not systematically presented in any of Frame's or Poythress's writings.[5] In these next chapters, we will explore the writings of these men in order to explain this system as systematically as possible.

Further, and more importantly, we will seek to show that perspectivalism in both its general and more specific form is grounded in the doctrine of the Trinity. While Frame and Poythress have built perspectivalism on the revelation of the Trinity, they have not thoroughly developed the Trinitarian connection.[6] Bosserman notes the problem, suggesting that "without a more thorough and precise explanation of the mutual implication of a Trinitarian theology and a perspectivalist epistemology, it is not at all clear that the latter is even the exclusive property of the former."[7] In light of this critique, we will seek to develop the connection between the Trinity and perspectivalism by showing how an understanding of God's Trinitarian knowledge, his perichoretic relations, and his simple nature all point to a unity in diversity reflected in creation. This reflection is what Frame and Poythress have called perspectivalism.

So what is perspectivalism, how does it function, and how is it related to the Trinity? These questions will be the focus of the

---

has given the resources to provide a basic understanding of how such a system should be organized, and this dissertation will seek to develop that basic understanding as presented in the writings of Frame and Poythress.

[5] Both Frame and Poythress have written books emphasizing perspectivalism. However, both books had a central focus outside of perspectivalism itself. Frame's *Doctrine of the Knowledge of God* focused on epistemology, and Poythress's *Symphonic Theology* focused on interpretation. While these were two helpful avenues through which to express perspectival methodology, they did not seek to systematize the method. Frame's article-length introduction to perspectivalism, *A Primer on Perspectivalism*, is helpful as well. However, its brevity limits its usefulness.

[6] Poythress has made greater strides than Frame in this field. But while he has dedicated small sections of books and articles to the connection, and while he has connected many of the triads to the workings of the Trinity, there is no place in his corpus where the idea is as developed at length as it will be here.

[7] Bosserman, "The Trinity and Christian Paradox," §153.

dissertation. In this chapter, we will distinguish the two major kinds of perspectivalism, define what is meant by *perspective*, describe the method of general perspectivalism, and finally relate general perspectivalism to Trinitarian epistemology.

Defining Perspectivalism

As noted above, the two major proponents of perspectival methodology are John Frame and Vern Poythress. Poythress learned perspectivalism under the teaching of Frame,[8] and he argues that, in terms of perspectivalism, "I am in complete agreement with Frame."[9] Frame, for his part, also argues for continuity of thought between the two.[10] While there are some methodological differences between them (some of which will be discussed later in the dissertation), on the whole both men agree that they argue for the same perspectival methodology. As such, we will freely quote from Poythress as well as Frame in defining perspectivalism.

Types of Perspectivalism

One of the potentially confusing aspects of perspectivalism is the multiplicity of names given to the method. Among the

---

[8] Poythress confirms, "In 1971 I became a student at Westminster Theological Seminary in Philadelphia, where John Frame was teaching. I was attracted to his teaching, including its triperspectival dimensions, and adopted it as my own." Vern S. Poythress, "Multiperspectivalism and the Reformed Faith," in *Speaking the Truth in Love: The Theology of John M. Frame*, ed. John J. Hughes (Phillipsburg, NJ: P&R Publishing, 2009), 182.

[9] Vern S. Poythress, "God's Lordship in Interpretation," *Westminster Theological Journal* 50, 1 (Spring 1988): 29n4.

[10] "I wrote *Doctrine of the Knowledge of God*, introducing my triperspectival approach. It was published in 1987. Lo and behold, that same year Vern published his *Symphonic Theology*, which told the same story more concisely and arguably more cogently." John M. Frame and P. Andrew Sandlin, "Reflections of a Lifetime Theologian: An Extended Interview with John M. Frame," in *Speaking the Truth in Love: The Theology of John M. Frame*, ed. John J. Hughes (Phillipsburg, NJ: P&R Publishing, 2009), 78.

multisyllabic words used are *perspectivalism, general perspectivalism, triperspectivalism, multiperspectivalism, broad perspectivalism, narrow perspectivalism, special perspectivalism*, and *Symphonic Theology*. To the unacquainted, these may be viewed as distinct types or as mere synonyms. In order to proceed, we must define our terms.

We will argue for two major types of perspectivalism, which we will call *general perspectivalism* and *triperspectivalism*.[11] The word perspectivalism can refer to either form, and is, therefore, limited in specificity. Nevertheless, it is rich in intensiveness, allowing us to speak of the implications of both general perspectivalism and triperspectivalism at once. Careful attention should be paid to the use of *perspectival* or *perspectivalism* (without a prefix), for it can refer to the entirety of the method or to one of the more specific forms (figure 2.1). Frame makes the same major distinction we are making here by noting that *general perspectivalism* is a general concept, while *triperspectivalism* is a specific method.[12]

A second potential confusion can be derived from the multiplicity of names in perspectival methodology. Sometimes, when referencing the more specific form of triperspectivalism, Frame and Poythress use the term multiperspectivalism.[13] These terms are sometimes used as synonyms,[14] but there is a slight difference

---

[11] Other names have also been suggested for these two forms, including *Narrow and Broad and General and Special*. Trumper uses the Narrow/Broad categories. Tim J. R Trumper, "John Frame's Methodology: A Case Study in Constructive Calvinism," in *Speaking the Truth in Love: The Theology of John M. Frame*, ed. John J. Hughes (Phillipsburg, NJ: P&R Publishing, 2009), 160. Frame uses the General and Special perspectivalism in John M. Frame, "Directory of Frame's Major Ideas," in *Speaking the Truth in Love: The Theology of John M. Frame*, ed. John J. Hughes (Phillipsburg, NJ: P&R Publishing, 2009), 978.

[12] John M. Frame, "A Primer on Perspectivalism," in *John Frame's Selected Shorter Writings* (Phillipsburg, NJ: P&R Publishing, 2014), 3.

[13] Poythress prefers *multiperspectivalism*, but Frame uses it infrequently. On the other hand, Frame uses *triperspectivalism* frequently, but its use is relatively rare in Poythress's work.

[14] See Torres, who uses *multiperspectivalism, triperspectivalism,* and

between them—namely, Frame and Poythress use triperspectivalism for triads, whereas they use multiperspectivalism for both triads and those items exhibiting perspectival relations no matter the size (e.g., the Ten Commandments). For this reason, we will seek to eliminate confusion by speaking of the more specific triune method as triperspectivalism and refrain from using multiperspectivalism (except where it is used in the source documents).

Thus, in order to clarify the use of terms in this dissertation, *general perspectivalism* will be used to designate the general concept, which is explained in this chapter. In summary, general perspectivalism describes the implications of the epistemological fact that humans come to knowledge by means of various points of view. *Triperspectivalism* will be used to refer to the specific method and will be explained in the following chapters. In summary, triperspectivalism is a method whereby certain groups of *three* serve as comprehensive points of view. Finally, *Perspectivalism* will be used to speak of the entire system (figure 2.1).

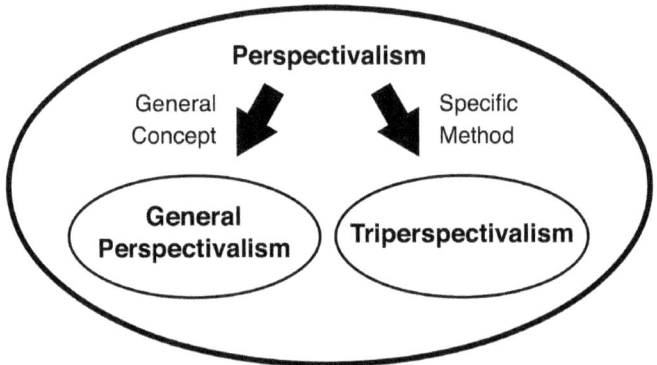

Fig. 2.1. Forms of Perspectivalism

---

perspectivalism interchangeably. Joseph Emmanuel Torres, "Perspectives on Perspectivalism," in *Speaking the Truth in Love: The Theology of John M. Frame*, ed. John J. Hughes (Phillipsburg, NJ: P&R Publishing, 2009), 112n2.

Defining a Perspective

Before explaining the fundamentals of general perspectivalism, we must answer a foundational question: What is a perspective? Nowhere in the literature on perspectivalism do Frame or Poythress seek to give an explicit definition.[15] Nevertheless, it appears that Frame and Poythress use the term *perspective* in two different but related ways: it can speak of (a) *a person's viewpoint on a matter* or (b) *a lens through which a subject is understood*. We will discuss, distinguish, and illustrate both.

The first sense of perspective (a) we will call a *personal perspective*. Personal perspectives can be defined broadly as *a person's viewpoint on a matter*. This refers not to a physical place, but an epistemological position. For example, imagine a person, Todd, who is asked about his understanding of money, sex, politics, and sports. His answers would indicate Todd's personal perspective on each of those categories; namely, Todd's personal perspective on money, Todd's personal perspective on sex, etc. More specifically, his personal perspective on, e.g., money would be the total sum of Todd's propositional beliefs concerning that specific topic as well as the foundational beliefs (presuppositions) that led him to such beliefs.[16]

It is important to note that personal perspectives can express truth, error, or a mixture of truth and error.[17] For instance, the

---

[15] This is, in part, due to their focus on their definition of meaning as use. Poythress suggests that the best way of understanding perspectivalism is through examples (i.e., its use). It does not seem that they would be opposed to a definition, but they have not found it necessary in light of their manifold examples. We will seek both to give a definition and show by example how that definition is appropriate.

[16] We follow Oliphint in defining a presupposition as "any religious, foundational proposition, principle or state of affairs assumed to be necessary for another given proposition, principle or state of affairs." K. Scott Oliphint, "Presuppositionalism," *Simple Apologetics (blog)*, 2014, n7, accessed August 28, 2014, http://simpleapologetics.com/presuppositionalism.html.

[17] By true, we mean that a personal perspective is in accord with the way things really are; that is, the way God has constituted, revealed, and known them. Of course, man does not personally know as God does, for man's

Apostle John gives his personal perspective on the life of Christ in his gospel. His personal perspective *as given in the gospel*, because inspired, is true.[18] On the other hand, Rudolph Bultmann also has a personal perspective on the life of Christ as evidenced in his article, *New Testament and Mythology*.[19] Because this personal perspective contradicts John's inspired viewpoint,[20] we can say that Bultmann's perspective contains many false propositional beliefs (though he may grasp some valid truth-claims).[21] Thus, personal perspectives entail truth-claims (figure 2.2).

The second type of perspective (b), we will call a *focal perspective*. These differ from personal perspectives in that they do not entail truth-values. In other words, the focus of focal perspectives is only on the *way* something is examined.[22] For example, we might ask about the Apostle John's focal perspectives on the life of Christ?

---

knowledge is a finite replica of God's. By truth, then, we are suggesting that someone's personal perspective is analogically imaging God's knowledge. Cornelius Van Til, *The Defense of the Faith*, ed. K. Scott Oliphint, 4th ed. (Phillipsburg, NJ: P&R Publishing, 2008), 62–69.

[18] John M. Frame, *The Doctrine of the Word of God* (Phillipsburg, NJ: P&R Publishing, 2010), 40–45.

[19] Rudolf Bultmann, "New Testament & Mythology," in *New Testament & Mythology* (Minneapolis, MN: Fortress Press, 1984), 1–44.

[20] For a Reformed critique, see Cornelius Van Til, *The New Hermeneutic* (Nutley, NJ: Presbyterian and Reformed, 1974).

[21] By grasping truth-claims, we mean that unregenerate men display epistemological diversity. Dispositionally they are fundamentally contrary to biblical truth, yet they are creatures living in God's world and exposed to God's common grace. As such, they sometimes grasp truth-claims, yet because of the context of that knowledge, it cannot properly be called true. Van Til, *The Defense of the Faith*, 194–99.

[22] Someone may object here, arguing that there are wrong and right ways to view things. Consequently, it would seem, there are right and wrong focal perspectives. For example, it is never right to think autonomously. While this is true, Van Til argued for thinking like an unbeliever *for the sake of argument*. While engaging in his two-step apologetic, the critique of the unbeliever's thought does not occur outside of submission to Christ. In the same way, one can view the gospels from Bultmann's focal perspective of demythologizing while maintaining epistemological submission to God. Ibid., 122–23.

Method and Basis of General Perspectivalism

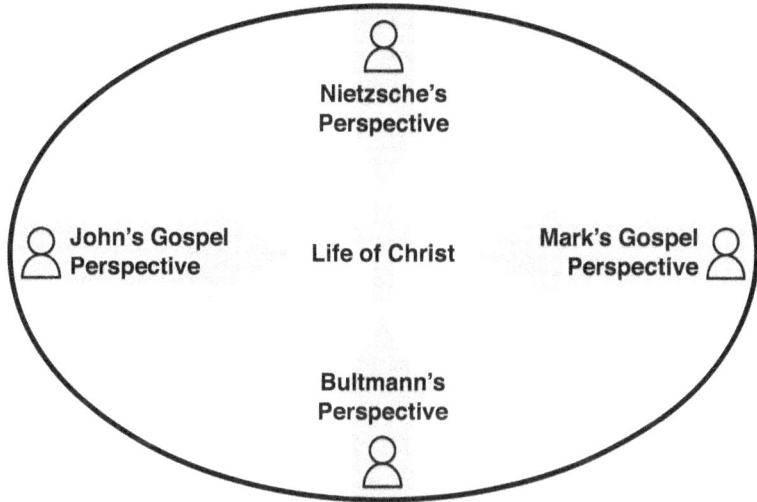

Fig. 2.2. Personal Perspectives

Here we would be asking, what are the lenses by which John seeks to understand and explain the life of Christ? One of John's points of view through which the life of Christ is explained is the divine focal perspective.[23] But if we asked about Matthew's focal perspectives, we would get a different answer. For example, Matthew uses the kingship of Christ as a focal perspective to examine the life of Christ.[24] This does not suggest that the object (i.e., the Life of Christ) being described by the two focal perspectives is contradictory;[25] rather, it indicates the richness of the life of Christ, which cannot be exhausted from only one point of view. While someone

---

[23] John makes more explicit references to the divinity of Christ than any of the other gospel writers (1:1–18; 2:19; 5:17–23; 8:58; 10:30–33; 16:15).

[24] Matthew's gospel begins by noting that Jesus is a son of David (1:1), bringing to focus the kingship of Christ. It ends with a focus on Jesus' kingship with a promise of his kingly presence and future return for full kingship (26:64; 27:11; 27:29; 28:18). Further, the gospel mentions the kingdom of God forty times.

[25] In the case of the inspired gospel accounts there are no contradictions. Frame, *The Doctrine of the Word of God*, 40–45.

could abstract either of these focal perspectives from its context and incorrectly use it to reach heretical conclusions,[26] if the person using the focal perspective is *faithful to the revelation of God*, he or she will derive rich, varied, and yet compatible (i.e., not contradictory) implications (figure 2.3).

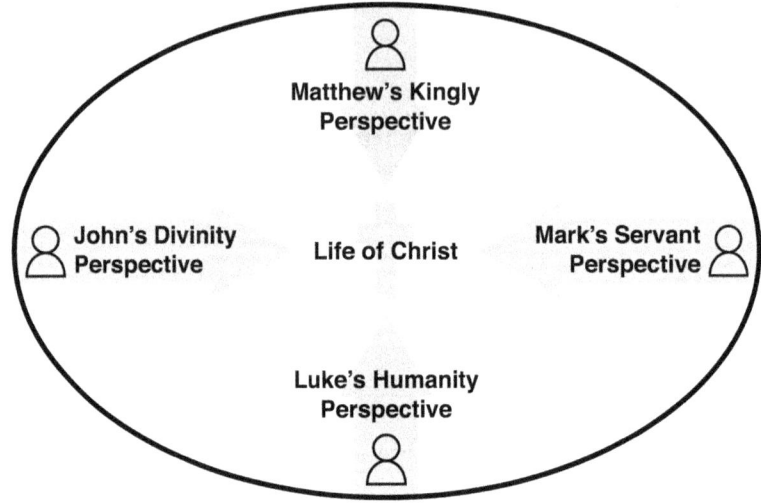

Fig. 2.3. Focal Perspective

So while Christians should challenge the *personal perspective* of Bultmann on the life of Christ (as far as it claims to be true), one of his the *focal perspectives* could be helpful. Further, by recognizing the traces of positive truth-claims that Bultmann has grasped, we can show the inconsistency of his own system in light of those truth-claims.[27] We can do this because there is a unity of truth according

---

[26] For example, someone could argue that the focal perspective in the book of John leads to a gnostic or Sabellian view of Christ.

[27] As Oliphint notes, "There is value . . . in using the language of the philosophers, poets, and others to show them just how the truth of Christianity fulfills the aspirations expressed in that language." K. Scott Oliphint, *Reasons for Faith: Philosophy in the Service of Theology* (Phillipsburg, NJ: P&R Publishing,

to the self-consistency of God. Any accurate truth-claim can be maintained only within God's ultimate system of truth.[28]

Prescription glasses provide an example of how focal perspectives work—when one looks through a pair of glasses, he or she views reality in a different way. The objects in existence remain the same, but the viewer can now see them in a new light. In the same way, a focal perspective allows the viewer to see the object of epistemological reflection in a new way. Frame and Poythress even suggest focal perspectives that can enlighten the way we view *all of reality* (fig 2.4). For example, Frame encourages his readers to view theology through the focal lenses of God's control, authority, and presence. This *lordship triad* is central to perspectivalism and will have a more thorough treatment below. We introduce it here to indicate the richness of the focal perspective.

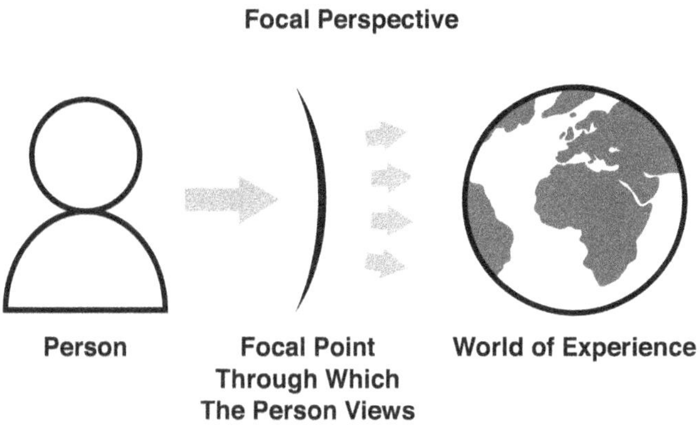

Focal Perspective

| Person | Focal Point Through Which The Person Views | World of Experience |

Fig. 2.4. Focal Perspectives as Lenses

2006), 31.

[28] An illustration might help: Bultmann argues for the humanity of Scripture, which he believes implies that Scripture needs to be demythologized. Indeed, viewing the Scripture through an anthropological focus is important (e.g., by expressing covenantal condescension, etc.). Van Til, however, shows that the humanity of Scripture can only be maintained in the light of the absolutely personal God of Scripture. So if Bultmann wishes to maintain

The two types of perspectives (personal and focal) are related to one another. First, listening to another person's personal perspective can introduce one to new focal perspectives. For example, when Meredith Kline elucidated the covenant scheme of the Ancient Near East, he provided a fresh focal perspective through which the covenants of Scripture could be understood.[29] Second, *personal perspectives can be focal perspectives*. For instance, Bill might want to think about an event from the personal perspective of Todd. In this way, Bill would be seeking to understand the event from the unique life-situation of Todd.

While Frame and Poythress use the first sense of perspective (personal), the majority of their uses align with the second variety (focal). For this reason, any use of *perspective* without a modifier in the dissertation will refer to focal perspectives.

The Method and Basis of General Perspectivalism

In this section we will explain the method of general perspectivalism and show how it is ultimately based on the Trinitarian God and his reflection in his image bearers. To do so we will begin by showing that man is fashioned to think according to perspectives. Second, we will show that God also knows according to perspectives, not because of finitude or sin, but because of his nature as triune and his plan as one and many. Finally, we will show how God's Trinitarian nature serves as a foundation for man's perspectival knowledge.[30]

---

the humanity of Scripture, then he must give up his autonomous theological system. Bultmann, "New Testament & Mythology"; Cornelius Van Til, *A Christian Theory of Knowledge* (Nutley, NJ: Presbyterian and Reformed, 1969), 341–84.

[29] Meredith G. Kline, *Treaty of the Great King: The Covenant Structure of Deuteronomy: Studies and Commentary* (Eugene, OR: Wipf and Stock, 2012).

[30] The phrase *perspectival knowledge* will be used throughout this dissertation to refer to knowledge that is characterized as being known through a personal perspective by means of various focal perspectives.

Man's Knowledge and General Perspectivalism

General perspectivalism is built upon obvious facts about human beings. Because "we are finite, sinful, and therefore fallible, we need to guard against error by looking at the truth from many angles or perspectives."[31] From this statement, two key aspects emerge necessitating general perspectivalism. First, man is finite; consequently, infinity in knowledge is outside of man's grasp.[32] This recognition should lead one to the conclusion that he or she is liable to error; humans are limited by previous knowledge, experiences, and other sociological factors. In sum, Poythress concludes, "admitting you are a creature leads naturally to [general perspectivalism]."[33]

If each individual's knowledge is limited by the factors noted above, then seeking other perspectives can broaden one's own knowledge.[34] How can one benefit from other perspectives? James Anderson gives some examples: "by shifting our point of view, either physically or conceptually; by reordering or reorganizing our data; by considering different emphasis or 'entry points;' and by consulting with others and allowing their insights to complement our own."[35] Emphasis should be placed on the value of other people's personal perspectives, because each person has different proficiencies, backgrounds, and cultural experiences, which inevitably affect his or her understanding.

An example might help illuminate this concept. Imagine a couple buying their first car. When shopping, they ought to view

---

[31] John M. Frame, *The Doctrine of God* (Phillipsburg, NJ: P&R Publishing, 2002), 767.

[32] It is not merely finitude that prevents omniscience. The fundamental distinction is the Creator-creature distinction. More will be said about this distinction below.

[33] Poythress, "Multiperspectivalism," 195.

[34] Nevertheless, one is still viewing from his or her personal perspective when seeking to view from another perspective.

[35] James N Anderson, "Presuppositionalism and Frame's Epistemology," in *Speaking the Truth in Love: The Theology of John M. Frame* (Phillipsburg, NJ: P&R Publishing, 2009), 437.

the car from various perspectives. The most obvious would be spatial perspectives. That is, one should view the car from the front, side, back, and even underneath if possible. But, of course, other perspectives are important as well. For instance, the personal perspective of a well-trained mechanic would give a helpful assessment on the condition of the vehicle. Other focal perspectives could also be sought (miles per gallon, safety, etc.). In the end, the more focal perspectives used, the more knowledgeable the purchase will be. Human finitude, then, compels humans to seek many perspectives.[36]

The second basis for general perspectivalism is human sinfulness. It is important to note that sin did not create either the need for thinking according to perspectives or the benefit of seeking others' personal perspectives. Even in the Garden of Eden, God created mankind with different skills and abilities. There were things that Adam, as the representative head, would have noticed that Eve, as the helpmeet, would not (and vice versa). Thus, even in the Garden of Eden man was designed to think and relate according to perspectives. Sin does affect perspectives, however. When Adam sinned, humanity fell with him. The effect was not only spiritual; it affected every aspect of man—including his mental faculties. The fall into sin provided a sinful, selfish inclination to each person's personal perspective, ultimately enhancing the need for others' personal perspectives.[37] But, since every human personal

---

[36] Such finitude is a significant aspect of Harvie Conn's missional strategy. He argues that American theology is limited to the extent that it does not listen to the voices of those with different life experiences in foreign contexts. His position, as seen above, is influenced by perspectivalism. See, Harvie Conn, *Eternal Word and Changing Worlds: Theology, Anthropology, and Mission in Trialogue* (Phillipsburg, NJ: P&R Publishing, 1992).

[37] How might others help? One way might be shown in that not everyone will express his or her depravity in the same way. Consequently, what fallen Adam twisted, fallen Eve may not have twisted in the same way. Poythress says, "The introduction of sin did not create diversity but rather made it contentious." Vern S. Poythress, *Symphonic Theology* (Grand Rapids, MI: Zondervan, 1987).

perspective is liable to error, the greatest need is God's personal perspective.[38]

God's Knowledge and General Perspectivalism

God's knowledge is unique in that it is infinite, including every *possible* personal and focal perspective. God knows the personal perspective of every human that ever lived, and he even knows the perspective of the fly on the wall—even if a fly is not on the wall.[39] By calling God's knowledge a personal perspective, we do not intend to indicate that he is subject to sin or finitude. Indeed, it would be a mistake to univocally compare God's personal perspective to man's personal perspective, since God's personal perspective is both infinite and metaphysically distinct from man's personal perspective.[40] A key metaphysical distinction here is that God knows all personal perspectives by knowing himself. God knows the perspective of the fly on the wall because God's exhaustive plan included the perspective of the fly on the wall.[41] But if man's perspectival thought is, in part, a result of his finitude, then how could God's thought be described as in any way perspectival?

---

[38] Frame notes, "My limited perspective gives me no excuse to doubt that I have five fingers, or that 2+2=4, or that God exists. Our finitude does not imply that our knowledge is erroneous, or that certainty is impossible. But we do, in most cases, need to guard against mistakes." Frame, "A Primer on Perspectivalism," 4.

[39] "God knows, not only everything about my typing, but also how that typing appears to the fly on the wall. Indeed, because God knows hypothetical situations as well as actualities, God knows exhaustively what a fly in that position would experience—if such a fly were present—even if it is not." Ibid.

[40] In his first major work on perspectivalism, Frame shows how man's knowledge and God's knowledge are metaphysically distinct yet epistemologically relatable. We will develop these differences later. See, John M. Frame, *The Doctrine of the Knowledge of God* (Phillipsburg, NJ: Presbyterian and Reformed, 1987), 21–40.

[41] And God knows the perspective of the potential fly on the wall by knowing himself as well, since he knows everything he *could have* created.

Method and Basis of General Perspectivalism

The Problems with Claiming God's Knowledge Is Perspectival

The most significant problem with claiming God's knowledge is perspectival is that it appears to contradict God's simplicity.[42] Simplicity of God's being implies simplicity of knowledge, but if God's knowledge is diverse, then there must be *parts* of God's knowledge. A potential way to resolve this difficulty is to argue that the appearance of diversity in God's knowledge is a condescension to man's finitude. Thus, God's knowledge is actually a unity without diversity, but in order to reveal truth to finite man God must communicate according to knowledge distinctions. So, for example, God's view of the life of Christ is a unity without diversity, but in order to communicate to man, who unlike God cannot know all facts as one, God must communicate in parts.

We will argue against such a position on three fronts. First, we will argue that intra-Trinitarian considerations necessitate understanding God's knowledge as both ultimately one and many. Second, we will argue that Scripture indicates both the unity *and* diversity of God's knowledge. Finally, we will argue that simplicity does not demand God's knowledge to be a unity without diversity.

Trinitarian Considerations and God's Perspectival Knowledge

The Trinitarian persons necessitate understanding God's knowledge as a unity with diversity. Here we will argue that the Father, Son, and Spirit each have a distinct personal perspective. This means that the Father's knowledge is not *in all ways* like the Son's knowledge, nor is the Son's knowledge *in all ways* like the Father's knowledge. This is a difficult claim and will have to be defended.

---

[42] Simplicity will play a large part in later chapters, so we will merely introduce it here. In summary to argue for simplicity, "is to say that there is no composition in [God's] being. Specifically, there is no composition of physical parts, form and matter, actual and potential, genus and differentia, substance and accident, God and his essence, essence and attributes, attributes and one another, essence and *esse*. God is not, then, in any sense made up of parts." Frame, *The Doctrine of God*, 225.

An obstacle to arguing for such a thesis is that God's knowledge has often been recognized as an *essential* attribute and not as a *personal* attribute. That is, God's knowledge has been understood as a function of the unity of the Godhead (i.e., essence) rather than the diversity (i.e., persons) of the Godhead. Charles Hodge appears to argue in this way: "As the essence of the Godhead is common to the several persons, they have a common intelligence, will and power. There are not in God three intelligences, three wills, three efficiencies. The three are one God, and, therefore, have one mind and will."[43] Van Til cites Hodge on this point approvingly, which initially suggests that both Hodge and Van Til would argue against a personal perspective view of the knowledge of the three persons.[44]

Van Til's Trinitarian Theology

Despite his approving citation of Hodge, Van Til was not against the personal perspective knowledge of the three persons.[45] In order to understand why, it is necessary to appreciate the distinctive Trinitarian theology of Van Til. The context of Van Til's unique contribution to Trinitarian theology must be understood lest we accuse him of heresy or anti-creedalism.[46] While his Trinitarian theology is certainly distinctive, he did not believe it contradicted any of the creeds. Indeed, he suggested that "If the true doctrine [of the

---

[43] Charles Hodge, *Systematic Theology*, vol. 1 (New York, NY: Scribner, 1873), 461.

[44] Cornelius Van Til, *An Introduction to Systematic Theology* (Nutley, NJ: Presbyterian and Reformed, 1974), 357.

[45] We will not seek to address whether this is a proper understanding of Hodge. We will only focus on Van Til, since he is central to the argument below.

[46] Horton holds Van Til's Trinitarian theology as anti-confessional in its assertion of one person and three persons. Gordon Clark calls it a heresy. Michael S. Horton, *The Christian Faith: A Systematic Theology for Pilgrims on the Way* (Grand Rapids, MI: Zondervan, 2011), 285,n40; Gordon Clark, "The Defense of the Truth: John Frame and Cornelius Van Til" (MP3, presented at the Gordon-Conwell Lecture on Apologetics, Hamilton, MA, 1980), accessed June 26, 2014, http://thegordonhclarkfoundation.com/defending-the-faith/.

Trinity] was to be maintained it had to be continually restated and refined."[47] Van Til may be following Murray, who argued that stagnancy in doctrine leads to corruption of that same doctrine.[48] Nevertheless, what is clear is that Van Til believed that he was asserting the historic doctrine of the Trinity, yet he was casting it in a modern light, that is, in light of modern difficulties.

What were those difficulties? Ralph Smith describes the problem Van Til was addressing: "Our modern (postmodern) world presents it [sic] own unique challenges. . . . The Enlightenment challenged the authority of the Bible and denied that faith in the Biblical God was the true starting point and ultimate standard for human knowledge. Van Til had to address the modern West and its pretended intellectual autonomy."[49] He more specifically notes, "The challenge to the Gospel in our day is the attempt to claim an ultimate impersonalism, to find the unity of the world in an impersonal principle or formula (or to deny unity altogether)."[50]

Van Til believed God was one person and three persons. How does the denial of the ultimate authority of God relate to impersonalism? For Van Til, creation was the product of the absolutely personal God of Scripture. By *absolute*, Van Til referred to the aseity of God, whereby God was independent of the world and self-contained. By *personal*, Van Til includes God's thinking, acting, desiring, and relating to himself and his creation.[51] Unbelief

---

[47] Van Til, *An Introduction to Systematic Theology*, 357.

[48] "As it is true that ecclesia *reformata reformanda est* so also is it true that *theologia reformata reformanda est.* When any generation is content to rely upon its theological heritage and refuses to explore for itself the riches of divine revelation, then declension is already under way and heterodoxy will be the lot of the succeeding generation." John Murray, "Systematic Theology (Part One)," *Westminster Theological Journal* 25, 2 (May 1963): 141–42.

[49] Ralph Smith, "Van Til's Insights on the Trinity," *Global Missiology English* 2, 2 (2005): 3.

[50] Ibid.

[51] Oliphint, in a footnote to Van Til's notation of the absolute personality of God, includes "mind, consciousness, and will" in the concept of personality.

denies one or both of these principles, but only by maintaining both could knowledge be possible.⁵² Therefore, Van Til was seeking to emphasize the absolute personality of God as the answer to modern epistemological difficulties.

Theologians generally agree that the persons of the Godhead are personal. Indeed, the classical treatment of God as one essence and three persons lends itself to such an understanding. Van Til, however, believed that there was *no trace* of impersonality anywhere in the Godhead. If personality was only attributable to the diversity of God, the unity of God must be impersonal. If so, God could not be described as an absolute person, for there would be some abstract quality of which the three persons consist. This would leave the door open for brute fact,⁵³ which would destroy the entire epistemological enterprise. Because of these considerations (along with others), Van Til argued that God was both one person and three persons.⁵⁴ In

---

Clearly, Van Til's concept also addresses a *personal presence* of favor or potential disfavor as much as he correlates divine personalism with man's personalism through the representational principle, which establishes the covenantal relation amidst the Trinity and consequently in creation. Van Til, *The Defense of the Faith*, 33n17; Cornelius Van Til, *A Survey of Christian Epistemology*, Logos Digital Collection. (Nutley, NJ: Presbyterian and Reformed, 1977), 78–79.

⁵² Van Til, *The Defense of the Faith*, 33–34.

⁵³ For Van Til, brute fact was a mute fact without interpretation and meaning. Because God is an absolute person, he is both responsible for the creation of all facts and is personally present to every fact giving each their interpretation and meaning. But if God is not absolutely personal, then there are some brute facts, and if they are uninterpreted by God, then he is not omniscient. But if God is not omniscient then nothing can be known, for knowledge is of one cloth. That is, because knowledge is ultimately interrelated, if God does not know and give the meaning to every fact, then a *new* fact God learns could change everything God knows. In the end, Van Til shows that impersonalism leads to brute fact, leading to the impossibility of epistemology. Ibid., 161.

⁵⁴ Van Til states his most controversial Trinitarian claim in the following passage: "It is sometimes asserted that we can prove to men that we are not asserting anything that they ought to consider irrational, inasmuch as we say that God is one in essence and three in person. We therefore claim that we have not asserted unity and trinity of exactly the same thing. Yet this is not the

saying this, Van Til was not going against the creeds, but rather, he sought to move the doctrine forward, bringing its truth to clearer light.[55]

Van Til believed there was an equal ultimacy between the one and the many. In order to see the applicability of Van Til's Trinitarian theology to the personal perspectives of the Father, Son, and Spirit, we must understand another aspect of his theology. Van Til believed there was an *equal ultimacy* between the unity and diversity of God.[56] He applied this equal ultimacy to both the attributes and persons, and he argued that the Trinitarian equal ultimacy was the archetypal pattern from which God created the unity and diversity of all creation.[57] More will be said about these aspects of Van Til's theology and their relation to perspectivalism in the next chapters. Here, we simply want to note that Van Til would not allow impersonalism at the level of God's ultimate unity, because that would imply impersonalism throughout. Just as the diversity of persons was personal, so the unity of the Godhead was personal as well.[58]

So the personhood of God's essence can be seen as a fruit of Van Til's emphasis on the equal ultimacy of the one and many. If we are not careful, we can do the opposite; that is, we can personalize the essence of God and depersonalize the persons![59] We noted above

---

whole truth of the matter. We do assert that God, that is, the whole Godhead, is one person." Van Til, *An Introduction to Systematic Theology*, 363.

[55] For a more prolific defense of Van Til's claim of one person and three persons, see, Lane G. Tipton, "The Triune Personal God: Trinitarian Theology in the Thought of Cornelius Van Til" (PhD Diss., Westminster Theological Seminary, 2004); John M. Frame, *Cornelius Van Til: An Analysis of His Thought* (Phillipsburg, NJ: P&R Publishing, 1995), 65–71.

[56] Van Til, *An Introduction to Systematic Theology*, 353.

[57] Ibid., 363–64.

[58] While Bavinck is not the only influence towards equal ultimacy, Bavinck's Trinitarian theology certainly led in this direction. Bavinck says, "In God both are present: absolute unity as well as absolute diversity." Herman Bavinck, *Reformed Dogmatics*, ed. John Bolt, trans. John Vriend (Grand Rapids, MI: Baker, 2003), 2.332.

[59] Ralph Smith warns, "The threeness of God is equally ultimate with

that Oliphint defined *personal* as involving mind, consciousness, and will.[60] Van Til includes in *personal* self-conscious, intellectual, and moral elements.[61] Therefore, while Van Til certainly maintains the unity of knowledge in God (as the quote from Hodge suggests), on the basis of his ultimate equality of the one and many, each of the persons *as persons* have personal knowledge as well.[62] Indeed, Van Til says, "Unity and plurality are equally ultimate in the Godhead. The persons of the Godhead are mutually exhaustive of one another, and therefore of the essence of the Godhead. *God is a one-conscious being, and yet he is also a tri-conscious being.*"[63] Van Til also says that it is not a valid objection

> To say that you cannot speak of a covenant [i.e., personalistic] relation within the Trinity because there is only one will in God. The same argument would also *destroy genuine personality*. There is, to be sure, one will only in the Godhead but here exactly lies the *mystery* of the relation of the divine persons to the divine substance. So also there is only one will of God with relation to the creature, and yet also *there is a threefold relation*.[64]

---

the oneness of God. Any compromise of the ultimacy of God's threeness would be utterly destructive of Van Til's whole project." Ralph Smith, *Paradox and Truth: Rethinking Van Til on the Trinity* (Moscow, ID: Canon Press, 2003), 42.

[60] Van Til, *The Defense of the Faith*, 33n17.

[61] Ibid., 33.

[62] Van Til notes, "We are always in danger, [Bavinck] says, of turning in the direction of Sabellianism by allowing the absolute unity of the being of God to do despite to the genuine personal distinctions in the Godhead, or of turning to Arianism by allowing the distinctions of the persons in the Godhead to do despite to the absolute unity of the being of God." Van Til, *An Introduction to Systematic Theology*, 362–63.

[63] Ibid., chap. 17. Emphasis added.

[64] Cornelius Van Til, "The Will in Its Theological Relations," in *Unpublished Manuscripts of Cornelius Van Til*, ed. Eric H. Sigward, Logos Digital Collection. (New York, NY: Labels Army Company, 1997). Emphasis added.

So Van Til is willing both to argue that there is one will in God, but in order to maintain the personality of the persons, Van Til is not willing to eliminate the unique will of each of the persons. Ultimately, Van Til calls this the "mystery of the relation of the divine persons to the divine substance."

Van Til believed the one and many were aligned through perichoresis. While the quote by Hodge does not necessarily indicate a lack of diversity in God's knowledge, it can help us understand the relationship of unity and diversity. Directly after noting that "There are not in God three intelligences, three wills, three efficiencies. The three are one God, and, therefore, have one mind and will," Hodge immediately adds, "This intimate union was expressed in the Greek Church by the word perichoresis, which the Latin words 'inexistentia,' 'inhabitatio,' and 'intercommunio,' were used to explain."[65] The unity of God's knowledge is a function of perichoresis; whereby, the three persons of the Godhead infinitely and exhaustively interpenetrate. We will examine the function of perichoresis in perspectivalism in later chapters. Here we desire to note that the unity and diversity of the Godhead is coordinated through perichoresis, and as such, it is not improper to note that God has one will, mind, and intelligence. Truly, through perichoresis, God has one mind, will, and intelligence.[66] Again Van Til shows this connection when, after noting that the "three persons, though together the one divine being, are in so far distinct that they assume objective relations to one another," he seeks to explain the unity of that personal relationship by means of perichoresis.[67]

But if we allow the identity in the essence to overshadow their

---

[65] Hodge, *Systematic Theology*, 1:461.

[66] Anderson and Welty note the connection between the individual persons's thoughts and perichoresis: "Taking a cue from the patristic doctrine of perichoresis, a Christian theist could hold that the three persons of the Trinity *literally share one another's thoughts*." Greg Welty and James N. Anderson, "The Lord of Noncontradiction," *Philosophia Christi* 13, 2 (2011): 20n33.

[67] Van Til, "The Will in Its Theological Relations."

distinction in the persons, we have done so only by ignoring the ultimate unity and diversity. Indeed, we do so at the cost of the absolute personality of the Godhead. Ralph Smith makes the same argument as he reflects on Van Til's work. Notice how he speaks of God's united knowledge as a perichoretically-shared knowledge that does not eliminate God's personality:

> Father, Son, and Spirit have different perspectives on the things they share. The Father, Son, and Spirit all know the cross and they all know it in multiple ways. Their mutual indwelling means that the Father's knowledge of the cross includes sharing the Son's knowledge, but the full and complete sharing of all things through mutual indwelling must not be thought to rule out the reality of their distinct perspectives, for that would *eliminate the meaning of their personhood.*[68]

In summary of our argument to this point, we may say that Van Til's distinctive Trinitarian theology emphasized the absolute personal nature of both God's unity and diversity. To attribute knowledge merely to the unity of God (i.e., essence) without equal attribution to the persons would do damage to the equal ultimacy. On this basis, we can indeed argue for one mind, will, and intelligence in God, but we must also balance this with the distinctive knowledge of each of the triune Persons. If the preceding argumentation is sound, we can describe God's knowledge as personally perspectival; that is, we can describe it as a unity in diversity, since such knowledge is the knowledge of a Trinitarian being.

Van Til's Covenant Structure and Triune Knowledge

Perhaps another insight from Van Til will help establish our point. We would argue that the *representational principle* offers us

---

[68] Smith, "Van Til's Insights on the Trinity," 11. Emphasis added.

another vantage point from which to view the necessity of ascribing diversity to God's knowledge. Within the covenant structure, as built upon the representational principle, Van Til suggests personal knowledge distinctions in the Godhead. In order to understand how, we will need to quote Van Til at length:

> It were quite legitimate and true to say that the foundation of all personal activity among men must be based upon the personality of one ultimate person, namely, the person of God, if only it be understood that this ultimate personality of God is a triune personality. In the Trinity there is completely personal relationship without residue. And for that reason it may be said that man's actions are all personal too. Man's surroundings are shot through with personality because all things are related to the infinitely personal God. But when we have said that the surroundings of man are really completely personalized, we have also established the fact of the representational principle. All of man's acts must be representational of the acts of God. Even the persons of the Trinity are mutually representational. They are exhaustively representational of one another. Because he is a creature, man must, in his *thinking, his feeling and his willing*, be representative of God. There is no other way open for him. He could, in the nature of the case, *think nothing at all unless he thought God's thoughts after him, and this is representational thinking*. Thus man's thought is representative of God's thought, but not exhaustively representative.[69]

There is much here that we can't fully develop, but for our present purposes, we should note that Van Til argues for the basis of covenant on the representation principle: "The covenant idea is

[69] Van Til, *A Survey of Christian Epistemology*, 78–79. Emphasis added.

nothing but the expression of the representational principle consistently applied to all reality."[70] So what Van Til appears to be suggesting is that because the intra-Trinitarian relations are absolutely personal (what he calls covenantal), God's relation to creation is ectypally personal (i.e., covenantal).[71] This absolute personalism in the Trinity, then, is the foundation of the covenant God makes in creation.[72]

Now note how Van Til suggests that the personalism exhaustively expressed in the Godhead is analogically[73] related to the

---

[70] Ibid., 96.

[71] Van Til develops this point in the following way: "All the decrees, having reference to creation or recreation, i.e, to all finite existence, are accordingly of the nature of an agreement between the persons of the Divine Essence; i.e., the relation between the Divine persons is a covenant relation. In this eternal covenant, the covenant of the decrees, God deals with man. In one sense these decrees are opera ad intra, because they still effect nothing historical, yet in another sense they are opera ad extra, because they have reference to that which will historically occur. But in each case they are a covenant activity within the Godhead by which the relations of man to God are established." Van Til, "The Will in Its Theological Relations."

[72] Van Til probably derives this view from Bavinck who notes, "The dogma of the trinity . . . tells us that God can reveal himself in an absolute sense to the Son and the Spirit, and hence, in a relative sense also to the world. For, as Augustine teaches us, the self-communication that takes place within the divine being is archetypal for God's work in creation." We will develop Bavinck's Trinitarian theology later in the dissertation, but for now it is enough to recognize with Brian Mattson that "An assumption latent within Bavinck's argument is that a divine-world relationship requires an antecedent 'relationality' or 'reciprocity' in God's being or essence; or, at the very least, there must be an innate capacity for relationship." Bavinck, *Reformed Dogmatics*, 2.333; Brian G. Mattson, *Restored to Our Destiny: Eschatology and the Image of God in Herman Bavinck's Reformed Dogmatics* (Boston, MA: Brill, 2011), 38–39.

[73] Van Til's understanding of analogy is important to understand. he defines analogical in the following way: "By [analogy] is meant that God is the original and that man is the derivative. God has absolute self-contained system within himself. What comes to pass in history happens in accord with that system or plan by which he orders the universe. But man, as God's creature, cannot have a replica of that system of God. He cannot have a reproduction

personalism expressed in reality. His example of the personalism in reality is in man's thinking, feeling, and willing. These elements need to be brought into conformity with God's thinking, feeling, and willing. Now if we take the analogy back to its source, we find that the triune persons are thinking, feeling, and willing, yet they do so in harmony through perichoresis. The disanalogy should be obvious. We are not in a perichoretic relationship with God, nor can we as creatures know qualitatively like God. However, the analogical relation between God and man allows us to affirm an analogy between God's thinking and our own. We, as individuals under covenant, ought to conform our knowledge to the God who is always present (ectype), just as the persons of the Trinity, in eternal relation with one another, have their personal knowledge in perichoretic union with one another (archetype).[74] Again, as Van Til says,

> The reality and vitality of the personal and therefore covenant relation within the Trinity, however unharmonizable it is for our logic, with the Oneness of the divine essence also forms the basis for a real freedom of the finite person. God can thus also enter into historical covenant relation with man, and have this relation be real and vital, giving to man a genuine free finite covenant personality. The covenant relation is therefore the only relation in which the finite stands to the infinite, because the eternal persons of the divine Trinity stand to one another in covenant relation.[75]

---

of that system. He must, to be sure, think God's thoughts after him; but this means that he must, in seeking to form his own system, constantly be subject to the authority of God's system to the extent that this is revealed to him." Van Til, *A Christian Theory of Knowledge*, 16.

[74] This is not to suggest that the persons of the Trinity are learning about one another, or having to conform their knowledge to one another. Their knowledge is eternally conformed and complete because of identity through perichoresis.

[75] Van Til, "The Will in Its Theological Relations."

Personal Triune Knowledge and Aseity

Van Til's theology offers a third reason to maintain the diversity of personal perspectives in the persons of the Trinity—to safeguard the aseity of God. One of the apologetic thrusts of Trinitarian theology is in its ability to show how God can be self-existent and not correlative to the world. This was one of Van Til's most significant reasons for his unique Trinitarian theology: "The one main concern of the Church has been to keep God and man in the proper relation to one another without confusing them. God exists as triune. He is therefore self-complete. Yet he created the world."[76] By this Van Til means that the Trinity needs nothing from the world in order to exist. For example, if God were unitarian (rather than Trinitarian), the essential attribute of love would require correlativity to the world. God would be love, but he would need an object for that love.[77] If the object is the world or anyone it in, then for God to be who he is, he would need the world. Alternatively, as Trinitarian, the persons of the Trinity are both the subject and object of love. On this account, there is no correlativity to the world. While God may subsequently love the world, this is merely a reflection of the archetypal love the Trinity has eternally expressed in relation to one another.[78] In a similar way, in order for God to have knowledge (which requires both a subject and object)[79] without being correlative to the world,

---

[76] Van Til, *An Introduction to Systematic Theology*, 359.

[77] Bavinck references this argument approvingly while noting that "in love there is always a subject, an object, and a bond between the two." Bavinck, *Reformed Dogmatics*, 2:327.

[78] For a fuller expression of this argument from a patristic father, see Richard of St. Victor. His developed argument suggests that love is an essential characteristic of God from eternity. Each member of the Trinity loves the others and each knows that they are loved by the others. Richard argues that true charity-love requires one both to love an equal and to be loved by an equal. His language indicates a personal perspective of love for each of the divine members in order for love to be perfected love. Richard of Saint Victor, *On the Trinity*, trans. Ruben Angelici (Cambridge, UK: James Clarke & Co, 2012), 113–37.

[79] Poythress notes a similar connection between love and knowledge as

he has to be Trinitarian. In this way, the personal perspective knowledge of the persons is essential to the aseity of God.[80]

So we have made three arguments from the Trinity in order to indicate that God's knowledge is both united (i.e., one through perichoresis) and diverse (i.e., three through the distinction of persons). First, we noted that the equal ultimacy of the one and many indicates the personal knowledge of both the unity and diversity of the Godhead. Second, we noted that the covenant structure, as built upon the representational principle, provides the analogy whereby man is covenantally required to think God's thoughts after him. The analogy invokes the personal, perichoretic knowledge of the Trinitarian persons, indicating diversity in the knowledge of God. Finally, we indicated that the aseity of God required that the Trinitarian persons know one another in eternity. Having argued for our position on the basis of the Trinitarian persons, we will now turn to an argument from Scripture that confirms much of what we have argued in this section.

Scripture Indicates Personal Triune Knowledge

God's revelation indicates that the persons *as persons* have personal knowledge.[81] Poythress gathers from Scripture that "There are

---

inherently personal: "The word knowledge involves a relationship, namely between the knower and the known. So does the language of speaking and hearing . . . and the language of loving." Vern S. Poythress, e-mail message to the author, July 5, 2014.

[80] Van Til makes a similar point when he notes, "These three persons, though together the one divine being, are in so far distinct that they assume objective relations to one another, they address and love one another." And lest one imagine that Van Til is speaking only in reference to the economical Trinity, Van Til says a few lines later, "Now as God is, so he works. This ontological Trinity forms the basis of the economical Trinity." In other words, Van Til's comments concern the ontological, which is reflected in the economical. Van Til, "The Will in Its Theological Relations."

[81] We will argue for the truthfulness of God's revelation later in the dissertation. For now, we will assume what will later be argued; namely, that when God reveals himself, that revelation is necessarily true and properly predicated

three ultimate perspectives on truth—the [personal] perspectives of the Father, the Son, and the Holy Spirit—and these three are *not* identical with one another in every respect."[82] Why are these different personal perspectives? Because (1) Scripture describes the persons of the Godhead as distinctively related to one another, and (2) Scripture describes the activities of the divine persons as distinct, and (3) Scripture describes the distinct knowledge of individual members of the Trinity.

Starting with (1), we would say that Scripture presents the persons of the Trinity in particular roles. Thus, the Father knows the Son as *the one who is begotten of the Father* from the personal perspective of the begetter. The Son knows this same relationship from the personal perspective of one begotten. Now, the Father knows the personal perspective of the Son as a focal perspective, in which he exhaustively knows what the Son knows. The same could be said of all the persons in relation to the processions.[83] Thus, the processional distinctions necessitate personal knowledge distinctions. To suggest otherwise would, according to Van Til, "destroy genuine personality."[84]

---

of him (though certainly not exhaustive).

[82] The main difference is not the nature of truth, but rather that the Son sees the Father as Father, and the Father sees the Son as Son. These are different perspectives. Poythress, *Symphonic Theology*, 51.

[83] Augustine notes this distinction in triune knowledge: "Therefore God the Father knows all things in himself, knows all things in the Son; but in himself as though himself, in the Son as though his own Word which Word is spoken concerning all those things that are in himself. Similarly the Son knows all things, viz. in himself, as things which are born of those which the Father knows in himself, and in the Father, as those of which they are born, which the Son himself knows in himself. The Father then, and the Son know mutually; but the one by begetting, the other by being born." Augustine, On the Trinity, 15.14.23

[84] In other words, if we cannot maintain a distinction in the knowledge of the triune persons in eternity, then we cannot legitimately call God tri-personal. And if we cannot, then the ectype of personality in man has no ultimate archetype in God. But for Van Til this would denigrate the entire personalistic, covenant structure of creation. Van Til, "The Will in Its Theological Relations."

Our second point (2) shows that the differing activities of the Godhead in relation to creation necessitate a distinction in knowledge. In light of the cross, "Only the Son actually experienced death for sin. Only the Father actually experienced the self-sacrificial pain of giving the Son. Only the Spirit suffered with the Son by indwelling the Son and enabling the Son to suffer."[85] These distinctions are not arbitrary, for orthodox theology has refrained from suggesting that the Father was on the cross.[86] Now, the Father knows the pains of the cross as much as the Son, but he knows it through the perichoretic relationship with the Son. This does not denigrate the Father's knowledge (as though it is inferior to the Son's knowledge), for in perichoresis there is absolute interpenetration. However, this also does not entirely eliminate the distinctiveness of the Son's personal knowledge of actually experiencing the cross.[87]

So we have argued that (1) the processional distinctions of the Trinity and (2) the diverse descriptions of the actions of the individual members of the Trinity lead us to believe the knowledge of God pertains both to the persons and essence of God. But are there (3) direct statements of Scripture in support of such a notion? It appears so. Consider Matthew 11:27 (English Standard Version): "No one knows the Son except the Father, and no one knows the Father except the Son." Someone may suggest that such language is reflective of only the Son as incarnate, but 1 Corinthians 2:10–11 refers to the distinct knowledge of the Spirit: "The Spirit searches everything, even the depths of God. For who knows a person's thoughts except the spirit of that person, which is in him? So also

---

[85] Smith, "Van Til's Insights on the Trinity," 11.

[86] See, Rob Lister, *God Is Impassible and Impassioned: Toward a Theology of Divine Emotion* (Wheaton, IL: Crossway, 2012), 100.

[87] Frame's comments here are enlightening. He argues that we must not do damage to either the unity or diversity of God by saying either that the Father was not affected or that the Father had the same experience as the Son. Frame leaves the issue in mystery though he does note the presence of perichoresis as a model by which the issue can be framed. Frame, *The Doctrine of God*, 611–16.

no one comprehends the thoughts of God except the Spirit of God." Poythress points out the import of these verses in light of perichoresis by arguing that the Father knows all things in knowing the Son and Spirit, even while the Spirit knows all things by knowing the Father and Son, etc. On this interpretation, the knowledge of the Godhead is shot through with personality.[88] There is no knowledge abstracted from personhood, for the knowledge is both known *by a person and through a person*.[89] Poythress's conclusions appear to complement Van Til's representational personalism, whereby the reason man seeks to align his thoughts after God is because the persons of the Trinity, in perichoresis, have eternally had their knowledge in alignment. All knowledge comes through a person.[90]

One potential criticism should be handled here. Could it be that these references to the distinction of the knowledge of the persons pertain merely to the economic Trinity? In other words, what if the knowledge distinctions are a product of God's free will to create, and are therefore not reflective of the ontological Trinity? But in answer, we must recognize that our knowledge of the ontological

---

[88] "The content of the truth is both one and many. It is not merely analytically precise and isolated bits, plus analytically cold relations between these bits and relations between the relations. The Father knows the Son, and the Son is one person. Yet this one person includes all treasures of wisdom and understanding (Col. 2:3)." Poythress, *Symphonic Theology*, 51.

[89] "The Father knows God in knowing the Son and the Holy Spirit. The knowledge of all three persons agrees, since all three know God, and know all the thoughts of God. There is perfect harmony among the three persons, but also a distinction of persons. Therefore, there is also a distinction of personal perspectives on knowledge." Vern S. Poythress, *Redeeming Philosophy: A God-Centered Approach to the Big Questions* (Wheaton, IL: Crossway, 2014), 58.

[90] Such personalism shows Van Til's apologetic to be both biblical and refreshing. It is biblical in that it makes sense of Romans 1:18–20, whereby the personal knowledge of God comes through creation. It is refreshing in that it makes the knower aware of the covenantal presence of God in all of life. Indeed, Poythress argues that *all* knowledge comes through a person. All of our knowledge comes through the Spirit as he reveals in Christ the plan of the Father. Poythress, "Multiperspectivalism," 190–91.

comes by means of the economical. Poythress notes, "We cannot make strictly or exhaustively functional (economic) or ontological statements about the Trinity. For a creature to do so would be a repudiation of creaturehood."[91] In other words, because our only medium of knowing God is through his functional revelation, we cannot neatly divide the economic from the ontological. However, we have confidence that God can communicate who he is to man, and thus we should recognize the ontological in the economical expressions. As Frame says, "God reveals himself as he really and truly is. His economic dealings with us, particularly his revelation in Scripture, do not distort his true nature."[92] The lordship of God guarantees that he can communicate who he ontologically is through functional manifestations. Frame and Poythress ultimately derive this principle from Van Til:

> It is this self-contained, mysterious being who has deigned to reveal himself to man. He has revealed himself as necessarily existing as he exists. Therefore we may say that God exists necessarily as a trinitarian God. When Scripture ascribes certain works specifically to the Father, others specifically to the Son, and still others specifically to the Holy Spirit, we are compelled to presuppose a genuine distinction within the Godhead back of that ascription. On the other hand, the work ascribed to any of the persons is the work of one absolute person.[93]

Conclusion to Trinitarian Knowledge Distinctions

Where does this leave us? We have argued for the ultimacy of the distinction of knowledge in the persons as well as the ultimacy

---

[91] Vern S. Poythress, *God-Centered Biblical Interpretation* (Phillipsburg, NJ: P&R Publishing, 1999), 43.

[92] John M. Frame, *Systematic Theology: An Introduction to Christian Belief* (Phillipsburg, NJ: P&R Publishing, 2013), 490.

[93] Van Til, *An Introduction to Systematic Theology*, 362.

of the unity of that knowledge through perichoresis in the persons. Ralph Smith asks the logical question and provides the only available answer:

> How is it that by virtue of their mutual indwelling the three Persons share all things without limit, without defect, without mystery, while at the same time they also have something that might be called an individual perspective? We are simply confronting the mystery of the Trinity, the incomprehensibility of the one and the many, in another realm. We are back to the place that we can only confess and adore.[94]

Because the entire structure of thought just presented is built upon Van Til's distinctive Trinitarian theology, this answer should not be surprising. Van Til argued that all knowledge, because it is based on the personal unity and diversity of the Godhead, is mysterious. Here we are looking directly into the magnificent light of God's unity in diversity; consequently, we should expect nothing less than mystery.[95]

Scripture Necessitates God's Knowledge as United and Diverse

We have been developing how God's Trinitarian nature provides evidence for the one and many relationship of God's knowledge, but we could argue it from a different vantage point as well.

---

[94] Smith, "Van Til's Insights on the Trinity," 11.

[95] The following words are given shortly following the notation that God is one person and three persons: "As Christians we say that this is a mystery that is beyond our comprehension. It surely is. God himself in the totality of his existence, is above our comprehension. . . . the facts of the world are created facts, facts brought into existence as the result of a fully self-conscious act on the part of God. So then, though we cannot tell why the Godhead should exist tri-personally, we can understand something of the fact, after we are told that God exists as a triune being, that the unity and the plurality of this world has back of it a God in whom unity and the plurality are equally ultimate." Van Til, *An Introduction to Systematic Theology*, 364–65.

Method and Basis of General Perspectivalism

That is, another support for a general perspectival view of God's knowledge comes from the multiplicity of divine revelation itself. Frame and Poythress contend that each gospel account is one of God's many focal perspectives.[96] Of course, this means there could have been an incalculable number of gospels, since God's knowledge includes innumerable focal perspectives. For example, God could have recorded a gospel from the *personal perspective* of James, Martha, or even Pilate. God could have also have used different *focal perspectives* to reveal the life of Christ. Earlier we noted that the gospels have different focal perspectives. Luke appears to focus on the humanity of Christ, paying attention to the downcast, poor, and socially ostracized, but God could have given us a gospel focused on the successful, rich, and socially prosperous. Nevertheless, God in his infinite wisdom determined that man needed only these four distinct and harmonizable gospels.

God's revelation also reveals other forms of general perspectivalism: the two historical records of Israel's monarchy in Scripture (e.g., Samuel, Kings, and Chronicles); poetic descriptions of previously recorded historic events (e.g., prose description in Exodus 12–14 and poetic description in Exodus 15); and the repetition of theological truths (e.g., different analogies to show eternal security in Christ in John 10:27–29, Romans 8:34, and 2 Corinthians 1:22). All of these express different focal perspectives from which we can view God's knowledge.

Now one could say that the gospels are four accommodated epistemological reflections of the non-diverse knowledge of God. If so, the gospels are merely condescension to human finite limitations. On this reading, God's knowledge is not like the limited, accommodated perspectives He offers man. Instead, his knowledge is the united, non-diverse knowledge of this life-event.

---

[96] Frame says, "God's revelation to us of *his own perspective is itself multi-perspectival in structure*. He has, for example, given us four gospels, rather than one." Frame, "A Primer on Perspectivalism," 7.

But did God in eternity *not know* Matthew's personal perspective on the life of Christ as distinct from John's perspective? Yes, he knew both in knowing himself. Such knowledge does not eliminate the diversity of John's and Matthew's personal perspectives on the life of Christ; rather, it is the foundation for the distinction. In other words, in the eternal act of knowing himself, God knows his plan in both its full unity and diversity. Thus, as he knows the life of Christ, he knows it exhaustively (the one) from the perspective of John, Matthew, Mark, Mary, Thomas, etc. (the many). This is not because he is dependent on their perspectives, but because he is the sovereign Creator of their perspectives.

It appears that such an understanding is the only way to avoid brute fact, for if God did not sovereignly create Matthew's perspective, then that perspective was not a product of God's interpretation of his thoughts, and thus was not filled with meaning by him. But Poythress, following Van Til, argues that there is no such thing as brute fact: "there are no self-existent or autonomous states of affairs independent of divine prior knowledge of them. Each one stands in relation to God, who ordains them."[97] Poythress continues, arguing that once these brute facts are rejected, "we are driven back to ask what *God's* view is of the historical events recorded in the Gospels. The surprising answer is simply that God's view is the Gospels themselves, in their unity *and* diversity."[98] By starting with God's knowledge as constitutional of the facts, Poythress argues that the planned diversity in the life of Christ must, in the nature of the case, imply the diversity of God's knowledge.

Simplicity Does Not Demand a Lack of Diversity in God's Knowledge

At this point we should take up the most significant argument against ascribing diversity to the knowledge of God. We have hinted at this argument above, but we will express it in its fullness here. The

---

[97] Poythress, *Symphonic Theology*, 49.
[98] Ibid.

argument can be found in Augustine, who says that the Father and Son see

> simultaneously all things that are in their knowledge, in their wisdom, in their essence: *not by parts* or singly, as though by alternately looking from this side to that, and from that side to this, and again from this or that object to this or that object, so as not to be able to see some things without at the same time not seeing others; but, as I said, sees all things simultaneously, whereof there is not one that he does not always see.[99]

Thomas Aquinas agrees, noting that the main problem with ascribing diverse knowledge to God is that this diverse knowledge has to be accounted for.[100] Aquinas believes that coming to such knowledge would indicate a lack in God, showing either that God would be subject to succession, or that God would be limited in having to learn one thing after another. To Aquinas, neither option is allowed, for both challenge God's aseity.

Aquinas provides the following argumentation for why diversity cannot be attributed to God's knowledge:

> Now just as [God] knows material things immaterially, and composite things simply, He knows enunciable things not after the manner of enunciable things, as if in his intellect there were composition or division of enunciations. For he knows each thing by simple intelligence, by understanding the essence of each thing; as if we by the very fact that we understand what man is, were to understand all that can

---

[99] Augustine, "On the Trinity," trans. Arthur West Haddan, *New Advent*, 15.14.23, last modified December 1, 2009, accessed December 1, 2009, http://www.newadvent.org/fathers/1301.htm. Emphasis added.

[100] Thomas Aquinas, *Summa Theologica* (New York, NY: Cosimo, 2013), 1.14.7.

be predicated of man. This, however, does not happen in our intellect, which discourses from one thing to another, forasmuch as the intelligible species represents one thing in such a way as not to represent another. Hence when we understand what man is, we do not forthwith understand other things which belong to him, but we understand them one by one, according to a certain succession. On this account the things we understand as separated, we must reduce to one by way of composition or division, by forming an enunciation. Now the species of the divine intellect, which is God's essence, suffices to represent all things. Hence by understanding his essence, God knows the essences of all things, and also whatever can be accidental to them.[101]

To summarize, Thomas argues that God has simple intelligence (or simple knowledge), meaning that his knowledge is not properly predicated as diverse for the following reasons: (1) God knows all things in knowing his own essence; (2) By knowing his own essence, God knows the essence of all other things, including all their accidents; (3) diverse knowledge is creaturely, for man, unlike God, knows through composition, division, and succession.

K. Scott Oliphint further confirms that God's necessary knowledge "is identical with who he is . . . like God, it is not composed of parts."[102] He clarifies his position by following Bénédict Pictet, who says,

> Concerning the manner (modus) in which God knows all things, we must speak cautiously and not attribute anything unbecoming or unworthy to the ultimate majesty. . . . Now

---

[101] Ibid., 1.14.14.
[102] K. Scott Oliphint, *God with Us: Divine Condescension and the Attributes of God* (Wheaton, IL: Crossway, 2011), 96.

we must not at all imagine that God knows things in the same manner as men, who understand one thing in one way, and another thing in another way, and the same thing sometimes obscurely and at other times more clearly, and who, from things known proceed to things unknown. The divine knowledge is of such a mode, as not to admit of any discursive imperfection, or investigative labor, or recollective obscurity, or difficulty of application. God comprehends all things by one single act, observes them as by a single consideration, and sees them distinctly, certainly, and therefore perfectly.[103]

Pictet and Oliphint are arguing that a true diversity of knowledge appears to entail (1) knowing as man knows, (2) knowing imperfectly, (3) and knowing by means of discursive accumulation.

Before responding to some of these arguments, we will also examine Alston's argument for God's non-diverse knowledge.[104] He suggests that while Aquinas's argument against God's diverse knowledge is dependent on simplicity (a doctrine he calls "a lot to swallow"), the argument can be fashioned without the doctrine.[105] His reasoning is attractive, because he begins with the distinction between God as a knowing subject and man as a knowing subject (i.e., by positing a Creator-creature distinction). Alston argues that man's knowledge has limitations, and two are of utmost importance

---

[103] Bénédict Pictet, *Christian Theology*, trans. Frederick Reyroux (London: R. B. Seeley and W. Burnside, 1834), 80.

[104] To be clear, Alston is arguing against God having propositional thoughts. Because such a discussion would take us too far off-track, we are limiting the discussion to the question of whether God has a diversity of knowledge. In this way, we are ascertaining whether (1) God has a diversity of thoughts, or (2) whether his knowledge is a unity of which human categories of description do not pertain.

[105] William P. Alston, "Does God Have Beliefs," *Religious Studies* 22, 3/4 (October 1986): 291.

for the present argument. First, man "cannot grasp any concrete whole in its full concreteness."[106] Instead, he has to break knowledge into digestible units. Of course, this does not apply to God. Second, as creatures, we must separate truths in order to relate them logically.[107] Again, this does not apply to God, since he knows all as a cohesive unit. In recognizing these two differences between men and God, Alston believes one can establish the non-diverse knowledge of God without recourse to simplicity.

The following list summarizes the arguments given above:

1. Diversity of knowledge indicates that God's knowledge is complex, which is incompatible with his simplicity (and simple knowledge).
2. Diversity of knowledge is incompatible with the fact that God knows by knowing himself.
3. Diversity of knowledge entails the following creaturely habits: knowing discursively, successively, and inferentially.

The Case for God's Diverse Knowledge

The case for the diversity of God's knowledge is important to general perspectivalism. We are seeking to show that man's knowing through perspectives is derived from the Trinitarian God. We have already shown that general perspectivalism is Trinitarian in the personal perspectives of the Son, Father, and Spirit. Here we are seeking to show that God, while knowing the world as an absolute unity, also knows the world through a variety of focal perspectives. But if so, God's knowledge must be describable as diverse. This is not to suggest that God *comes to knowledge* (mode of knowledge) by way of the focal perspectives; rather, we are arguing that God's knowledge contains all the focal perspectives (content of knowledge). It is this latter fact that makes it possible for

---

[106] Ibid.
[107] Ibid.

man to think God's thoughts after him. Thus, in seeking to know through focal perspectives, we are seeking to think God's thoughts after him.

A few questions arise in consideration of the question of the diversity of God's knowledge. First, why suppose God has thoughts? Second, even if God has thoughts, why suppose that they are constituted like our thoughts?

In answer to the first question, we would argue that Scripture presents God as having thoughts. Psalm 139:17 says, "How precious to me are your thoughts, O God! How vast is the sum of them!"[108] Micah 4:12 says that those who are unbelieving "do not know the thoughts of the LORD; they do not understand his plan." Psalm 92:5 adds, "How great are your works, O LORD! Your thoughts are very deep!"

This leads us to the second question. Could it be that while God is presented as having thoughts, these verses are actually not to be taken as speaking of God's essential knowledge? In other words, could it be that God is condescending to speak to man in terms of *thoughts* while in his essence there is no such reality? On the surface, this appears to be a fruit of the doctrine of divine simplicity. James Anderson offers a reply,

> If the objection here is that talk of 'God's thoughts' is problematic because it implies diversity within God, then I have two comments in response. First, the Bible speaks directly about God's 'thoughts' (e.g., Isa. 55:8–9) but it doesn't speak directly about divine simplicity (even if [simplicity] turns out to be a reasonable inference from other biblical teachings). So anyone who claims to accept the Bible but denies that God has thoughts has some explaining to do.[109]

---

[108] Unless otherwise indicated, all Scripture quotations are from The Holy Bible, English Standard Version, copyright © 2001 by Crossway Bibles, a division of Good News Publishers. Used by permission. All rights reserved.

[109] James N. Anderson, "God and Propositions: The Saga Continues,"

Anderson does not reject simplicity; instead, "Those of us committed to the *doctrine of the Trinity* have to affirm *some real ontological diversity within God*."[110] In other words, a proper understanding of the Trinity leads Anderson to allow a measure of diversity in the Godhead. We are here reminded of Van Til, who argued on the basis of the one and many in the Trinitarian persons an equal ultimacy of the one and many in the attributes of God.[111] Anderson is expanding this insight to suggest a real diversity in God's knowledge.

Anderson continues, "Any resources that the defender of DDS [doctrine of divine simplicity] might deploy to explain how DDS can be reconciled with the (indispensable) notion of divine attributes could be redeployed to explain how DDS can be reconciled with the (equally indispensable, in my view) notion of divine thoughts."[112] Anderson's comparison here is rich in that it shows that whatever problems simplicity has with the attributes can be aligned with the problems it will have with God's knowledge. In both cases, we are dealing with a unity that is truly diverse. If we take the ontological Trinity as our interpretive concept everywhere,[113] we should understand this as an ultimate unity in diversity. The distinctions of the persons of the Godhead are as real as the unity. The distinctions of the attributes are as real as their unity in the person of the Godhead. The distinctions of God's knowledge are as real as their unity in the

---

Analogical Truths (blog), July 31, 2012, accessed July 11, 2014, http://www.proginosko.com/2012/07/god-and-propositions-the-saga-continues/.

[110] Ibid. Emphasis added.

[111] Such agreement between Van Til and Anderson is not surprising, since Anderson is the administrator of the VanTil.info website. Van Til, *An Introduction to Systematic Theology*, 364–65.

[112] Anderson, "God and Propositions: The Saga Continues."

[113] Van Til states that the "Ontological Trinity must be our interpretive concept everywhere." In context, he is speaking of the problem of knowledge being solved by the correlativity of fact and universal—or the one and many. It is solved because we can know there is a unity in diversity of knowledge because there is back of it a unity in diversity in the ontological Trinity. Cornelius Van Til, *Common Grace and the Gospel* (Nutley, NJ: Presbyterian and Reformed, 1972), 64.

person of the Godhead.[114] Thus, by beginning with the clear revelation of the Trinitarian persons, we have the resources to provide for genuine diversity of God's knowledge.

According to Thomas, if God knows all things through knowledge of his essence, then such knowledge indicates a lack of divisions or complexity in that knowledge.[115] But if we begin with the ontological Trinity, who is both one and many, we can maintain that in knowing his own essence, God knows a unity in diversity. Truly, the essence is one, yet he is equally three persons. In knowing his own essence, God knows the unity and multiplicity of persons and their personal knowledge distinctions. Further, in knowing his essence, *he knows both the unity and diversity of his plan*. While it is not wrong to speak of the unity of God's knowledge, it would be wrong to exclude the diversity on account of it. In Van Til's terms, this is not properly grasping that there is an *equal ultimacy* of the one and many. Further, knowing through his own essence does not appear to give any reason to deny diverse content on that basis. If God's plan is diverse, then God knows the plan in all its diversity, and, therefore, his thoughts can accurately be described as diverse.

But even if what we have said above is accurate, there remain two problems. First, we have not shown clearly why a Thomistic account of knowledge is lacking. Second, the argument that division

---

[114] We will develop the shared one in many relationship between the persons and attributes to a greater extent in chapters four and five. What is stated here is more fully argued there.

[115] The opposite of *simple* is the separability of parts not complexity. So Frame says that Thomas's arguments for simplicity, "do not rule out all complexity within the divine nature. Imagine a distinguishable aspect of God's nature (such as an attribute or a person of the Trinity) that is no less noble than himself, that cannot be removed from him, that necessarily belongs to him apart from any causal process, that is not the result of a movement from potentiality to actuality. It would not be inconsistent with the above doctrine of simplicity for God to have many such aspects." Frame, *The Doctrine of God*, 227.

in God's knowledge entails creaturely attributes (discursive, successive, and inferential knowledge) has not been answered. We will handle these in order.

First, Aquinas's doctrine of simple knowledge indicates that God's knowledge is a veiled mystery for which we have no access. Alston summarizes, noting that for Aquinas,

> We cannot even make a start at seeing how [God's knowledge] is brought off. We do not have real understanding of how so simple a state of affairs as that this rose is red could be known by a subject without that subject's cognitive state somehow reflecting the complexity of that fact. Hence when we have occasion to speak of God's knowledge we are forced to represent it on the model of human knowledge, and weak of God as knowing, e.g., that the Israelites were being held in slavery in Egypt, even if we hold that this is not how God's knowledge is in itself. . . . [Aquinas] would be quick to acknowledge, indeed to insist, that *we have no real understanding of what God is like*.[116]

The last statement of Alston's quote is critical and points to the weakness of Aquinas's simplicity account. Thomas's construction of analogy presents a God who is entirely unknowable. While Scripture reveals certain attributes of God, and while we can, by analogical reasoning, say these are true of him, we have no way possible to know who he really is.[117] Similarly, when applied to knowledge, we have no clue what God really knows. This is absolutely damning to an epistemological program designed to *think God's thoughts after him*.

---

[116] Alston, "Does God Have Beliefs," 289. Emphasis added.

[117] We cannot develop the weaknesses of Thomas's account in full here, but we will do so in chapter four. For now, it is enough to say with Paul Maxwell that Aquinas's analogy is merely an attempt to say "not univocal and

Anderson provides a way forward, showing how simplicity has been understood as it pertains to the attributes, and how that can apply to God's knowledge:

> 'It's acceptable to speak about God's attributes,' the defender of DDS will say, 'so long as we understand that ultimately each of God's attributes is identical to God.' In that case, why can't we say that it's also acceptable to speak about God's thoughts, so long as we understand that ultimately each of God's thoughts is identical to God? If the champion of DDS can accommodate a meaningful distinction between God's omniscience and God's omnipotence, there's no reason to think he can't also accommodate a meaningful distinction between God's thought *that he is omniscient* and God's thought *that he is omnipotent*.[118]

So just as we do not have to fully understand what it means for God's attributes to be distinct yet identical to God's essence, so we can say the same with his knowledge. This does not denigrate the knowledge we have; rather, it indicates that the knowledge we have is true yet incomplete.[119] In this way, we can say that the diversity of God's knowledge is not opposed to a simplicity account of that knowledge.

Having argued for the compatibility of diversity of knowledge

---

not equivocal." However, Thomas gives us no way to bridge such a gap. Put succinctly, Maxwell says the doctrine of analogy in Thomas "is merely the duct taping together of univocism and equivocism, with an inexplicable leap betwixt." Paul Maxwell, "The Formulation of Thomistic Simplicity: Mapping Aquinas's Method for Configuring God's Essence," *Journal of the Evangelical Theological Society* 57, 2 (June 2014): 397.

[118] Anderson, "God and Propositions: The Saga Continues."

[119] This knowledge is quantitatively and qualitatively distinct from God's knowledge. The qualitative arises because God knows by knowing himself. This does not falsify the content of the knowledge we have, but it does protect the Creator-creature distinction.

within a simple knowledge paradigm, the major opposition to God having diverse knowledge is averted. That is, a primary reason God's diverse knowledge is challenged is because it is seen to be a challenge to simplicity. If, however, simplicity is understood in Trinitarian terms (i.e., as one and many), there is no problem with the diversity of God's knowledge if that diversity is understood to have an ultimate unity in the person of the Godhead.[120]

Now we can turn to the final matter of concern. How does an account of God's knowledge as diverse deal with the accusation that it *humanizes* God? In other words, how can we maintain the model in light of the accusations that it entails God's knowledge as derived *discursively, successively*, and *inferentially*. This objection is rather significant, but it is not clear how it follows from the claims above. If God knows all things in knowing himself, then he knows the entirety of his plan in both its unity and diversity.[121] That is, he knows his plan exhaustively, immediately, intuitively, non-inferentially, and simply. The method of *coming to knowledge* is certainly distinct in man. We cannot know exhaustively, immediately, intuitively, non-inferentially,

---

[120] It should be noted that there is disagreement within Thomistic scholarship concerning how to understand Aquinas's view of the diversity of God's knowledge. James Dolezal notes two major positions. One position holds that the appearance of diversity in God's knowledge is merely accommodation. God has no real diversity of knowledge. The second position, and the one Dolezal holds, argues that there are genuine distinctions in the content of God's knowledge, yet the source of such knowledge is always simple in that it derives from God's essence. This latter group suggests that there is a deep disparity between God's knowledge and attributes such that there can be genuine distinctions in knowledge, but there can be no similar distinction in the attributes. The position of this dissertation, as will be seen below, is that there is a genuine distinction both in the attributes and knowledge of God. James E. Dolezal, "God Without Parts: Simplicity and the Metaphysics of Divine Absoluteness" (PhD Diss., Westminster Theological Seminary, 2011), 217n22.

[121] William Hasker uses the image of a "mental map" to describe God's thought. He suggests that in order for God to know that at T^1 Bill is under wrath and at T^2 Bill is transferred to the realm of grace, then God must have the thought content inherent in those two ideas. William Hasker, "Yes, God Has Beliefs!," *Religious Studies* 24, 3 (September 1988): 388–91.

and simply. Thus, there is a vast difference between God's knowledge and our own.

It is at this point we should emphasize the difference between one's mode of knowing and the content one knows. As Oliphint says, "There are actually two aspects of God's knowledge that are traditionally emphasized—the *mode* and the *object*."[122] That distinction is important to our point here. The mode of God's knowing is through an immediate awareness of his own plan. The object of his knowledge is his own plan in both its unity and diversity. Thus, while we can say that God does not discursively, successively, or inferentially obtain knowledge, this does not necessarily entail that he does not have diverse knowledge.

Creaturely knowledge is necessarily discursive because man is limited in noetic function, but God knows all through one single act of vision (i.e., in knowing himself), so he knows the unity and diversity immediately. The same can be said of succession. God does not need to add to his knowledge piece by piece; rather, he knows all immediately. Finally, while God knows inferential truths, he does not depend on them for his knowledge. Thus, we would agree with Alston: "God does not mentally distinguish subject and predicate and then unite them by a copula. he does not analyze reality into various separate facts, each of which is itself internally complex, and then organize them into some kind of system."[123] Nevertheless, we would question whether having a diversity of knowledge entails such development of thought. If God's knowledge is an ultimate unity and diversity, the diversity does not precede the unity, just as the unity does not precede the diversity. Both are known eternally in God's self-knowledge.

Conclusion to the Argument for God's Diverse Knowledge

We noted that the arguments against God having diversity of knowledge could be summarized in the following three propositions:

---

[122] Oliphint, *God with Us*, 95n14.
[123] Alston, "Does God Have Beliefs," 288.

1. Diversity of knowledge indicates that God's knowledge is complex, which is incompatible with his simplicity (and simple knowledge).
2. Diversity of knowledge is incompatible with the fact that God knows by knowing himself.
3. Diversity of knowledge entails the following creaturely habits: knowing discursively, successively, and inferentially.

Having argued for a model of God's diverse knowledge, we can now answer these three more directly. As for (1), there is nothing inherent to the diversity of knowledge that entails a denial of a biblically defined simplicity. If God's knowledge of himself (and thereby his eternal plan) is exhaustive, immediate, intuitive, and non-inferential, this can be a simple kind of knowledge. This is predicated on the idea that simplicity does not eliminate complexity (e.g., triunity or abundance of attributes), rather simplicity argues for an identity of the multiplicity in an absolute unity.

Argument (2), when properly understood, actually appears to confirm the diversity of knowledge. When God knows himself, he knows his plan. But clearly his plan is a unity in diversity. If so, he knows it as a unity in diversity. Thus, he knows it all simply and in accordance with its truth function as he has designed it. Further, since God's thought is constitutional of the facts, he must know creation in every way. This highlights the fact that while some indicate that ascribing diversity to God's knowledge brings God down to the level of the creature, the opposite is the case. If God did not know all diversity, he would have *to come to know it*.

The third argument against our position is again answered by a proper understanding of God's knowledge. Once we understand his knowledge as absolute, exhaustive, immediate, intuitive, simple, and non-inferential, we understand that there is nothing creaturely about his mode of knowledge. So, while God could explain a syllogism, he is not dependent on that process of reasoning to know the conclusion, for God's creative thought produced both the premises and conclusion.

Conclusion to the Defense of God's Perspectival Knowledge

We have argued for God's knowledge being a unity in diversity from three major vantage points. First, we developed the implications of God's Trinitarian nature, showing that each of the three persons has a distinct personal knowledge perspective. Second, we indicated that Scripture itself led to the conclusion that God's knowledge was best understood in both its unity and diversity. Finally, we argued that simplicity does not necessarily eliminate the diversity of God's knowledge.

Before pointing out the import of these considerations on general perspectivalism, we should note that the Trinity is central in all the conceptions we have made here. The reason Scripture posits a genuine diversity of knowledge in God is because, as triune, he has genuine knowledge distinctions. Indeed, the reason that God has the essential capability of knowing the created world is because he has known himself as triune eternally. The Father has always known the truth, *the second member of the Trinity loves the first member of the Trinity* as distinct from the truth, *the first member of the Trinity loves the second member of the Trinity*. Thus, God's knowledge of the world is reflective of his knowledge of his own being.[124]

God's Perspectival Knowledge and Man's Perspectival Knowledge

We have noted that man's knowledge is gained through personal perspectives because of finitude and sin. Further, we have noted that God's knowledge can be described as perspectival because of his Trinitarian nature. But is there a connection between the two? Poythress argues affirmatively, contending that God's knowledge

---

[124] This is important to maintain, for if God's knowledge is dependent on the world, then God is dependent on the world to be who he is. Just as the love of the Father for the Son in eternity provides the basis for God's love of humanity, so God's knowledge of himself provides the basis for God's knowledge of the world. Consequently, a unitarian God could not provide the necessary resources for knowledge.

has implications for derivative knowledge—the knowledge by creatures. As creatures we have knowledge that is an ectype, a derivative knowledge, rather than the archetype, the original infinite knowledge of God. Ectypal knowledge must inevitably show the stamp of its Trinitarian archetype, because all knowledge, insofar as it is true knowledge at all, is knowledge of truth, and archetypal truth is God's truth, truth in his mind.[125]

Because God's knowledge is the standard of truth, any true knowledge will be reflective of his knowledge. This is a key idea in Van Til's theology, wherein he argued that the key to epistemology was the unity in diversity of the Godhead, who in himself knows all truth exhaustively.[126]

We have seen that God's knowledge is a unity in diversity, whereby we may consider the diversity of his knowledge as various focal perspectives on the whole. Consequently, if man seeks to have knowledge, he must model his knowledge after God's epistemological unity in diversity. God has provided the way to do so through the perspectives. Of course, this does not imply that we will ever know in the way that God knows, nor does it imply that we can unite our knowledge to the exhaustive unity of his knowledge. Nevertheless, it is the creaturely way of thinking God's thoughts after him. Seen in this light, man's knowing through perspectives (both focal and personal) is not primarily a function of his finitude or sin but is ultimately reflective of his creation in the image of God.[127]

In sum, Poythress and Frame believe that man's knowledge through perspectives is founded on the God's knowledge of perspectives. Because God's knowledge is a unity in diversity, those who

---

[125] Poythress, "Multiperspectivalism," 191.
[126] Van Til, *A Christian Theory of Knowledge*, 16.
[127] If Adam had not fallen into sin, there still would have been personal and focal perspectives, and while it is essential to man's nature to be finite, it is not because of finitude alone that we know through personal perspectives.

think his thoughts after him must, if they want true knowledge, seek to know the way God does, and in the diversity of his knowledge, God knows according to perspectives.[128]

---

[128] Of course this does not imply that God desires us to know absolutely, exhaustively, immediately, intuitively, and non-inferentially. In making us in his image, he does not make exact *divine* replicas. In the realm of knowledge, this means that while our thoughts have to be fashioned after his, they must be fashioned in a creaturely way. The relation between our knowledge and his is grasped through the diversity of his plan but will never exhaustively embrace either the fullness of the diversity or the full unity of that plan. The more we understand the diversity of God's plan, the closer we come to a replicated unity. Nevertheless, this replica is just that—a replica.

3

Implications of General Perspectivalism

Having sought to show the foundations of general perspectivalism, we are now in a position to develop some of its epistemological implications. We will do so first by showing that general perspectivalism does not lead to relativism as many critics have asserted. Second, we will work through some of the positive implications before summarizing the main features of general perspectivalism. This will put us in a position in the next chapter to develop the further Trinitarian foundations of the more specific form of perspectivalism—triperspectivalism.

Perspectivalism and the Charge of Relativism

Having worked through a description of perspectivalism as it pertains to both man and God, we should now turn to the most critical objection to Frame and Poythress's method. Is perspectivalism relativistic? If the analysis in the previous chapter is correct, then we should be confident that such an account of knowledge does not lead to relativism. Nevertheless, in order to answer this important concern, we will express and answer the reasons people fear perspectivalism leads to relativism.

There are three reasons critics think perspectivalism is relativistic: first, because proponents of the method find value in listening to many diverse perspectives; second, because of the name *perspectivalism*; third, because perspectivalism assumes the lack of non-subjective certainty; and fourth, because multiple perspectives may lead to incommensurability.

Listening to all Perspectives Does Not Necessarily Lead to Relativism

Frame and Poythress argue for the potential benefit of listening to many diverse perspectives. William White, recognizing this tendency in both Frame and Poythress, complained that the two professors were indicating "that we as mature believers can sit down . . . and *learn* from those who reject the sovereignty of God and his only-begotten Son, that is, from liberation theologians, Marxists, feminists, and all manner of unbelievers."[1] D. G. Hart similarly argued that, unlike Frame, Reformed Christians should believe there is nothing of substance to be learned from non-Reformed Christians.[2]

William White is correct in his assessment that Frame and Poythress argue for potentially helpful perspectives being offered by people of many theological persuasions. In this, they are following Van Til, who was willing to recontextualize truth-claims that were gleaned by unbelievers through common grace.[3] Nevertheless, they do not suggest that *all* personal perspectives are equally helpful in seeking truth. Rather, by emphasizing both God's common grace and the limitation of context on perspective, Frame and Poythress are suggesting that, at times, unbelievers will have a helpful vantage point (i.e., focal perspective) that may be missed by the believer.

---

[1] William White, "Bill White Contra John Frame," *Journey*, June 1988, 13.

[2] John M. Frame and D. G. Hart, "The Regulative Principle: Scripture, Tradition, and Culture," *The Works of John Frame and Vern Poythress*, last modified 1998, accessed September 4, 2013, http://www.frame-poythress.org/the-regulative-principle-scripture-tradition-and-culture/.

[3] Arguably Van Til's greatest contributions to theology are reflective of his understanding of Christianity through the biblically modified focal lenses of Kantian and Idealist traditions. See also, Cornelius Van Til, *A Christian Theory of Knowledge* (Nutley, NJ: Presbyterian and Reformed, 1969), 43–44.

Implications of General Perspectivalism

Listening to the unbeliever (i.e., seeking to see from his focal lens) will allow one to see the compatibility of one aspect of his or her truth-claims with God's revelation.[1] As such, each truth-claim is evaluated on the basis of its compliance with revelation. This is not a relativistic acceptance of any belief; rather, it is a robust awareness of God's working in his creation whereby, through common grace, even unbelievers recognize helpful ways of viewing the world.

A similar criticism comes from Meredith Kline, who argued that perspectivalists "are prone, as I perceive it, in spite of their protestations to the contrary, to view antithetical positions as merely differing but compatible emphases."[2] The context of this quote concerns the debate within American Reformed theology over theonomy.[3] Kline believed that Frame and Poythress were saying that both sides were correct, and that the other side needed to embrace the other's emphases. Poythress, in response, says, "I may have not been as clear as I should have been between a *method* of using perspectives and the *conclusions* that one draws." He further recognizes, "It is always a danger that the use of multiple perspectives could serve to

---

[1] This is not to suggest that the unbeliever's viewpoint is *true*. As Van Til argued, truth is a united whole, and the unbeliever's false starting point spoils all claims to true knowledge. Thus, we speak of *truth-claims* here, suggesting that some of the claims being made are compatible with truth if recontextualized. Cornelius Van Til, *The Defense of the Faith*, ed. K. Scott Oliphint, 4th ed. (Phillipsburg, NJ: P&R Publishing, 2008), 199.

[2] Meredith G. Kline, *A Paper Pursuant to the Faculty Forum* (Escondido, CA: Westminster Seminary in California, 1986).

[3] Greg Bahnsen, a graduate of Westminster, ignited much of the debate with his publication of *Theonomy in Christian Ethics*. He argued that theonomy, the application of Old Testament legislation in the modern day, was the product of a true Reformed theology. Kline, on the other side, argued for an intrusion ethic, whereby eschatological consummation provided the structure under which both Old Testament and New Testament ethics should be understood. As such, Old Testament legislation did not have a *direct* bearing in the New Testament. Greg Bahnsen, *Theonomy in Christian Ethics*, 3rd ed. (Nacogdoches, TX: Covenant Media, 2002); Meredith G. Kline, "The Intrusion and the Decalogue," *Westminster Theological Journal* 16, 1 (Fall 1953): 1–22.

blur distinctions about conclusions."[4] Here Poythress has made a distinction between using various focal perspectives and the theological conclusions drawn from those perspectives. Reading the source texts in context shows that neither Frame nor Poythress were indicating a relativistic form of acceptance of both positions.[5] Nor were they suggesting that at bottom both positions were the same. Instead, they were suggesting that *when understood as related to the question of the role of the law in the New Testament economy* Kline's position and Bahnsen's position were on a spectrum. Kline argued for the discontinuity of the law; while Bahnsen argued for continuity.

The following example may help. Imagine infralapsarianism and supralapsarianism on a spectrum detailing the order of priority election holds in God's eternal plan relative to creation. On the one side, supralapsarianism emphasizes election as having first priority in the mind of God. On the other hand, infralapsarianism, while holding strongly to the importance of election, prioritizes God's will to create.[6] While such a spectrum on the role of election may be helpful in showing each side where and why they disagree, it is not capable of providing a full answer the question of the order of God's will. In the same way, Poythress and Frame were not seeking to definitively answer the question of theonomy by the spectrum they offered; rather, they were seeking to clarify the differences. By looking from the perspective of the applicability of God's law to the New Testament situation, both men were able to clarify some of the major differences that needed to be addressed in order for the larger controversy to be settled.

---

[4] Vern S. Poythress, e-mail message to the author, January 30, 2014.

[5] The following are their major works on theonomy: John M. Frame, "Review of Bahnsen's Theonomy in Christian Ethics," *The Presbyterian Journal* 36 (August 1977): 18; John M. Frame, "Penultimate Thoughts on Theonomy," *Reformed Perspectives Magazine*, August 2001; Vern S. Poythress, *The Shadow of Christ in the Law of Moses* (Phillipsburg, NJ: P&R Publishing, 1995).

[6] Clearly more than election is evident in the debate, but by focusing on the one perspective of election, we can help clarify the larger debate.

So while Frame and Poythress do suggest that we ought to be willing to listen to many diverse perspectives, this does not necessarily lead to relativism for the following reasons: first, because God's truth is revealed not only to the elect, but also to the non-elect;[7] second, because even in sharp disagreements (e.g., Kline and Bahnsen) there are differences based on focal perspective that can be used to aid in understanding the larger disagreement; and third, because all conclusions gleaned by use of any focal perspective are accepted only on their positive relation to the revelation of God.

The Name of Perspectivalism Does Not Necessarily Lead to Relativism

The name *perspectivalism* can mislead people into believing the method is relativistic.[8] Frame recognizes the weakness of this name: "It is somewhat unfortunate that the name perspectivalism has been attached to the view I am advocating. I'm not sure who is responsible for the name; maybe I am."[9] The problems with the name derive from its use by three philosophers. First, Friedrich Nietzsche developed *perspectivism*, a relativistic system of epistemology.[10] Frame

---

[7] We cannot develop the difficult issue of common grace here. We take for granted what we suggested earlier about Van Til's conception of common grace. Frame and Poythress are following Van Til's thought. Van Til, *The Defense of the Faith*, 194–99.

[8] For a clear example, see Elliott's unsubstantiated claim that perspectivalism is rooted in Nietzsche's philosophy. Paul M. Elliott, "What Is Perspectivalism, and Why Is It Dangerous?," in *Christianity and Neo-Liberalism* (Unicoi, TN: The Trinity Foundation, 2005), chap. 8, accessed January 25, 2014, http://www.teachingtheword.org/apps/articles/?articleid=74632&columnid=5772.

[9] John M. Frame, "A Primer on Perspectivalism," in *John Frame's Selected Shorter Writings* (Phillipsburg, NJ: P&R Publishing, 2014), 5n6. Since Frame's introductory work on the topic contains the term *triperspectivalism*, Frame appears responsible for the terminology. John M. Frame, *The Doctrine of the Knowledge of God* (Phillipsburg, NJ: Presbyterian and Reformed, 1987), 265.

[10] For more on Nietzsche's position, see Michael Lacewig, "Nietzsche's Perspectivism," in *Philosophy for A2: Philosophical Problems* (New York, NY: Routledge, 2014), 200–201.

says, "Note, [Nietzsche's] perspectivism, not perspectivalism. I have preferred the latter term, to distinguish my view from Nietzsche's relativism."[11] So, while the name is not exactly the same, they are close enough to cause confusion.

Second, Charles Sanders Peirce proposed *perspectivalism* (including the suffix) as a method of collaborative learning. John Howie provides a succinct and cogent explanation of Peirce's perspectivalism:

> Charles Sanders Peirce insisted that human knowledge is unavoidably perspectival. In light of a doctrine he called 'fallibilism,' Peirce argued for collaborative inquiry, based on scientific method, in order to maximize our potential for understanding reality. However, he did not use the terms *truth* or *knowledge* to signify the result of his pragmatic, maximizing method; rather, he called the result 'belief,' defining this as a plan or habit of action. Peirce thus distinguished between truth as the ultimate goal of inquiry and the conclusions that human beings reach in their ongoing search for knowledge. What is known and knowable through experience in this unfinished world is inevitably partial but not relative. Although we cannot achieve omniscience, we can minimize our errors or mistakes through collaboration.[12]

There are some striking similarities between Frame's perspectivalism and Peirce's system. But while Peirce's method is not *explicitly* relativistic, it is found within a system that does not embrace absolute truth.[13] In other words, Frame's perspectivalism is only possible

---

[11] John M. Frame, *A History of Western Philosophy and Theology* (Phillipsburg, NJ: P&R Publishing, 2015), chap. 9.

[12] John Howie, *Ethical Issues for a New Millennium* (Carbondale, IL: SIU Press, 2002), 83–84.

[13] Peirce's position eliminates the possibility of absolute truth because he does not seek to establish truth in the ontological Trinity. While he wants to avoid

within the Christian theistic worldview, because it is based on the triune God. Without such a foundation, Peirce's system cannot ultimately escape relativism.

The third philosophical use of the term perspectivalism is found in the writings of Werner Krieglstein. his transcendental perspectivism aligns with Nietzsche's perspectivism, but it seeks to go beyond it by more consistently situating the perspectives in an explicitly naturalistic environment. On his website, *perspectivism.com*, Krieglstein notes the following as the foundational points of his perspectivism:

1. Transcendental Perspectivism recognizes truth as experiential and personal, but *not as objective and universal.* Therefore all religious beliefs including agnosticism and atheism are respected equally, as long as these do not impose their values on others.
2. Transcendental Perspectivism *prefers diversity,* difference over singularity. These are assumed to be more natural and beneficial in evolutionary terms.
3. Transcendental Perspectivism aims for *cooperation and connectiveness* over competition and survival of the fittest. This, too, is seen to be more natural and adaptive.[14]

Clearly, from the very first point we see the relativism of Krieglstein's method. Further, his system, as shown in points two and three, assumes the truth of metaphysical naturalism. Thus, this perspectivism is only analogous to Frame's general perspectivalism in linguistic commonality.

These three uses of perspectivism/perspectivalism may cause confusion for some readers. However, if these same readers would look past the terminology to the concepts underlying Frame and

---

relativism, he has no ground for the consistency of or the ultimate origin of truth.

[14] Werner Krieglstein, "Perspectivist Manifesto," *Perspectivism,* last modified

Poythress's language, they would find that relativism is far distant from general perspectivalism.[15] While there is an appreciation for multiple perspectives, this appreciation derives from the unity of those perspectives under the sovereignty of God. Indeed, Frame contends that general perspectivalism "presupposes absolutism" because its metaphysical grounding is in the Trinitarian God who has revealed several aspects of his personal perspective to man.[16] Because of God's absoluteness, truth is fully dependent on him. As such, God grounds both the multiplicity of vantage points on truth (perspectives) and the ultimate unity of that truth.

While these three advocates of perspectivism/perspectivalism used similar language, their metaphysical assumptions naturally lead them to relativity rather than diversity in unity. General perspectivalism, because of the inherent nature of the Trinity, embraces the latter rather than the former.[17] In summary, Frame acknowledges, "My perspective would be relativistic if it were not for my presupposition, derived from scripture, that each perspective brings us into contact with God's truth. And that truth is infallible, absolute, and ultimate."[18]

2010, accessed March 8, 2014, http://perspectivism.com/perspectivist-mephesto/. Emphasis added.

[15] Frame laments that theological battles often concern the language used rather than the concepts behind that language. John M. Frame, *Systematic Theology: An Introduction to Christian Belief* (Phillipsburg, NJ: P&R Publishing, 2013), 484.

[16] Frame, "A Primer on Perspectivalism," 5.

[17] Poythress called perspectivalism Symphonic Theology, but he recognized that "the term multiperspectivalism is more precisely descriptive, and so it has remained the more conventional label." No other name has been proposed, and after forty years, the outlook for a new name does not look promising. Vern S. Poythress, "Multiperspectivalism and the Reformed Faith," in *Speaking the Truth in Love: The Theology of John M. Frame*, ed. John J. Hughes (Phillipsburg, NJ: P&R Publishing, 2009), 184.

[18] John M. Frame, "Epistemological Perspectives and Evangelical Apologetics" (presented at the Evangelical Theological Society, Biola University, CA, 1982), accessed September 3, 2013, http://www.frame-poythress

The Lack of Non-Subjective Certainty Does Not Necessarily Lead to Relativism

The third way critics of perspectivalism have argued for its relativism is by emphasizing its lack of *non-subjective certainty*. In any discussion of certainty, a distinction between epistemic and psychological certainty must be maintained.[19] Epistemic certainty is absolute in that such certainty cannot be wrong. This form of certainty is objective of any human person holding the belief. Psychological certainty, however, is fundamentally concerned with human persons. It is the state of a subject whereby he or she is convinced, e.g., of the truth or falsity of a matter. Consequently, we could say that the existence of a triune God is epistemically certain.[20] However, a subject exposed to arguments for God's triunity may not have psychological certainty of such a fact.

When we speak of objective *certainty*, we are speaking of psychological certainty, the certainty of the believing subject. *Objective* here is used in its most natural sense to refer to a lack of personal bias or subjective influence. Once fully defined, it should be clear that we are not suggesting that for Frame and Poythress there is no psychological certainty; rather, we are affirming that man can only have a subjective (i.e., highly personalistic) form of psychological certainty. Before describing what this subjective certainty looks like, we will give an example.

Frame is clear that our understanding of Scripture can never be objectively certain:

> We just have to accept the fact that our interpretation of Scripture will be fallible, subject to correction, and then do

---

.org/epistemological-perspectives-and-evangelical-apologetics/.

[19] Baron Reed, "Certainty," ed. Edward N. Zalta, *The Stanford Encyclopedia of Philosophy*, 2011, accessed July 15, 2014, http://plato.stanford.edu/archives/win2011/entries/certainty/.

[20] See Van Til's argument that there is an "absolutely certain proof for the truth of Christianity." Van Til, *The Defense of the Faith*, 381.

the best we can. That fact need not inject any fear or thanklessness into the process! Hesitation at times, yes. But at the same time thankfulness and boldness because God is using this process to lead his people into more and more truth.

Critics may attribute this statement to two elements of perspectivalism. First, since man is bound to his personal perspective, this may lead to skepticism and relativism. The argument proceeds in the following fashion: If I can never transcend my own personal perspective, then I am trapped, obliterating the possibility of objective certainty. Second, if man's personal perspective is finite and marred by sin, and if men can only understand Scripture through their own personal perspective, doesn't such knowledge necessarily lead to skepticism and relativism?

The charge of skepticism fails on the first charge because man *is designed by God* to appropriate the personal perspectives of others. God's creative purposes in designing man included a diversity of gifts and functions that harmonize in order to fulfill the creation/cultural mandate (Gen. 1:28). These differing gifts and functions require communal sharing of knowledge (personal perspectives) in order to carry out God's command. But even more importantly, God created man to know him (Rom. 1:18–20), and this implies that man can, as much as God intends, embrace God's revealed knowledge. We are not trapped in epistemological solipsism. God has made meaningful connections between men and between himself and man.

Perhaps we could say that the diversity of perspectives is the only way to escape skepticism. Man confirms his own experiences by comparing them to the personal perspectives of others, viewing them from a multitude of focal perspectives provided by others. Through such a process, he reforms his concepts in light of the truth-claims brought by other personal perspectives. The personal perspective most needed is God's, and he has provided that through revelation. In this way, the God-ordained situational position of the creature as one who is to come to know God through a creaturely perspective guarantees that his or her knowledge does not lead to skepticism. Seen in this light, the multiplicity of perspectives becomes a partial solution to the threat of epistemological skepticism.[21]

But this leaves the second concern over skepticism remaining. How is it possible that man's finite personal perspective, influenced as it is by sin, can appropriate God's knowledge? Put theologically, if all of man's epistemological faculties are affected by depravity, how can he interpret revelation (even scriptural revelation) correctly? Tom Chantry brings accusation against perspectivalism on this front, suggesting that the method "makes the Word something other than perspicuous. It may only be guessed at, never truly apprehended. That is the essential character of relativism." He continues by noting that Frame's perspectivalism "is a toxic dose of individualism" which he believes fails to have "a rich dependence on the Spirit."[22]

Chantry's main concern is that perspectivalism maintains the necessity of a *personal* perspective, yet this *personal* perspective is not objective. It is always influenced by subjective considerations (feelings, emotions, desires, etc.), and because man is sinful, Chantry believes that the personal subjective factors will always override truth. Accordingly, Chantry summarizes Frame by saying, "The objective word of God ought to affect the way in which I view the opinions formed from my own personality and my context, but *at the same time and in the same way* my personality and context ought to inform my understanding of the word of God." He then concludes, "That, my friends is relativistic hermeneutic—plain and simple."[23]

---

[21] Stated differently, because God has chosen to reveal himself through multiple perspectives, and because man's knowledge is necessarily composed of and gained by means of various perspectives, there is no alternative to learning through perspectives. Thus, if we are to have knowledge, it must be through perspectives.

[22] Tom Chantry, "Confessional Redefinition and the Virtue of Honesty," *Chantry Notes* (blog), February 20, 2014, accessed July 15, 2014, http://chantrynotes.wordpress.com/2014/02/20/confessional-redefinition-and-the-virtue-of-honesty/.

[23] Tom Chantry, "Re-Framing Reformed Baptist Doctrine," *Chantry Notes* (blog), February 17, 2014, accessed June 16, 2014, http://chantrynotes

Multiple answers can be provided to Chantry's critique. First, as we will show in a following chapter, Frame believes Scripture is the covenant document by which all other thought must be in subjection. Thus, he clearly denies Chantry's claim that in perspectivalism personality and context apply *the same way* to Scripture as Scripture applies to them.

Second, God's sovereign plan included the fall and the epistemological situation after the fall. If it can be shown that man knows by means of subjective factors (e.g., personality and context), then Frame and Poythress's position is not a denigration of epistemology; rather, it is the full exposition of a biblically informed epistemology. Further, God through grace and the work of the Spirit transforms people noetically, limiting the effects of the fall and allowing successful communication to his elect (1 Cor. 2:6–16).

Third, Chantry's major problem is his desire for an objective form of knowledge, that is, a form of knowledge freed from the constraints of any personal subjectivity. Notice how Chantry not only argues against the personalistic nature of perspectivalism, but also is embarrassed by any hint of personalism: "The Reformed thinker, then, may acknowledge that his personality and his context play a role in his reading of Scripture, but he views this as a shameful fact, a result of his fallen nature and continuing sin—something to be fought against with all the power of the Spirit."[24] We should read Chantry most charitably by suggesting that he is embarrassed by his *fallen* personality and his *fallen* context. Nevertheless, the overall point he is stressing is that we need to *get past* personality and context to the truth—a truth standing outside personal subjectivity and contextual factors.

Poythress and Frame, however, do not believe any such truth exists. They deny that there is any non-subjective truth waiting to be

---

.wordpress.com/2014/02/17/re-framing-reformed-baptist-doctrine/. Emphasis added.

[24] Ibid.

known behind personal and contextual factors. The primary reason to deny such *truth* is because God's knowledge is not objective (i.e., non-subjective). God is an absolute person, and, as such, his knowledge is exhaustively *personal*.[25] This is reflective of Frame's understanding of Van Til's adherence to God's absolute personality. In the context of arguing for man having both a proximate as well as an ultimate starting point for knowledge, Van Til says,

> Man is and can be a subject of knowledge in a derived sense because God is the subject of knowledge in the absolute sense. Theologically expressed, we say that man's knowledge is true because man has been created in the image of God. And *for this reason too there can be no dispute about the relative priority of the intellect and the feeling of man. Since the personality of God is a complete unity, so also the personality of man is a unity.*[26]

Here Van Til is noting the similarity of man's knowledge with God's knowledge. Because man is the image of God, man can obtain knowledge. The latter section is of massive importance. Van Til suggests that man's emotions are just as important as his intellect in the acquisition of knowledge. There is no priority, for man is made in the image of God, and God is an absolute person. Thus, what God knows, he knows emotionally as well as intellectually, and he knows these inseparably.

That God's knowledge is fundamentally an emotional knowledge may appear to contrast with the Westminster Confession of Faith, which posits that God is without passions.[27] However, Hodge

---

[25] We could also argue that God knows contextually in that his knowledge is known within the context of the three divine persons.

[26] Cornelius Van Til, *A Survey of Christian Epistemology*, Logos Digital Collection. (Nutley, NJ: Presbyterian and Reformed, 1977), 133. Emphasis added.

[27] "There is but one only, living, and true God, who is infinite in being and perfection, a most pure spirit, invisible, without body, parts, or passions."

did not read the confession this way. Note how he speaks of the necessity of God's emotion in love:

> The schoolmen, and often the philosophical theologians, tell us that there is no feeling in God. This, they say, would imply passivity, or susceptibility of impression from without, which it is assumed is incompatible with the nature of God. . . . [if so] the word [love] has for us no definite meaning; it reveals to us nothing concerning the real nature of God. Here again we have to choose between a mere philosophical speculation and the clear testimony of the Bible, and of our own moral and religious nature. Love of necessity involves feeling, and if there be no feeling in God, there can be no love. . . . unless the children of God are the objects of his complacency and delight, they are not the objects of his love. He may be cold, insensible, indifferent, or even unconscious; he ceases to be God in the sense of the Bible, and in the sense in which we need a God, unless he can love as well as know and act. *The philosophical objection against ascribing feeling to God, bears, as we have seen, within equal force against the ascription to him of knowledge or will.* If that objection be valid, he becomes to us simply an unknown cause, what men of science call force; that to which all phenomena are to be referred, but of which we know nothing. We must adhere to the truth in its Scriptural form, or we lose it altogether. We must believe that God is love in the sense in which that word comes home to every human heart. The Scriptures do not mock us . . . God is love; and love in him is, in all that is essential to its nature, what love is in us. Herein we do rejoice, yea, and will rejoice.[28]

"Westminster Confession of Faith," 1646, 2.1, accessed December 9, 2009, http://reformed.org/documents/wcf_with_proofs/.

[28] Charles Hodge, *Systematic Theology*, vol. 1 (New York, NY: Scribner, 1873), 428–29. Emphasis added.

B. B. Warfield speaks in similar language when describing God's love:

> Herein is a wonderful thing. Men tell us that God is, by the very necessity of his nature, incapable of passion, incapable of being moved by inducements from without; that he dwells in holy calm and unchangeable blessedness, untouched by human sufferings or human sorrows for ever . . . *Let us bless our God that it is not true. God can feel*; God does love. We have Scriptural warrant for believing, as it has been perhaps somewhat inadequately but not misleadingly phrased, that moral heroism has a place within the sphere of the divine nature. . . . But is not this gross anthropomorphism? We are careless of names: it is the truth of God. And we decline to yield up the God of the Bible and the God of our hearts to any philosophical abstraction. We have and we must have an ethical God; a God whom we can love, and in whom we can trust.[29]

The commonality between the quotes of these Reformed theologians is in their adherence to Scriptural description of God. If a philosophical speculation argued otherwise, then the philosophical speculation should be cast aside or modified.

But how could these men who subscribed to the Westminster Confession of Faith appear to reject its statement about God's impassibility? Indeed, how could Hodge, who stated, "I have had but one object in my professional career and as a writer, and that is to state and to vindicate the doctrines of the Reformed Church. I have never advanced a new idea, and have never aimed to improve

---

[29] This quote is given in the context of a message concerning the incarnation. However, Warfield's language shifts from Christ to God in order to show that emotion is properly attributed to the Godhead. Benjamin Breckinridge Warfield, "The Example of the Incarnation" (Sermon, Princeton Theological Seminary, January 8, 1893), accessed July 16, 2014, The gospelcoalition.org/blogs/justintaylor/files/2010/09/Warfield-Imitating-the-Incarnation2.pdf.

on the doctrines of our fathers,"[30] put forward such a position? Oliphint helps here by noting that in scholastic terminology a passion is that which brings an internal change to an agent from an external source.[31] Thus, "when the Confession denotes God to be 'without passions,' what it is saying is that, however and whatever God 'feels,' he does so according to his own sovereign plan and not because he is dependent or because something independent of him caused him to *re*-act to something outside himself."[32]

Therefore, the Westminster Confession can be maintained if we understand God's emotional knowledge to be reflective of his eternal plan.[33] God did not *come to love* the elect (as though through process) but has from all eternity in his free will determined love towards them. In like manner, God's knowledge of all reality is a personal knowledge, including emotional, volitional, and intellectual elements.[34] Properly understood, these are not separate parts of

---

[30] Archibald Alexander Hodge, *The Life of Charles Hodge* (New York, NY: Scribner, 1880), 430.

[31] K. Scott Oliphint, *God with Us: Divine Condescension and the Attributes of God* (Wheaton, IL: Crossway, 2011), 87.

[32] Ibid.

[33] Compare with Frame: "Doctrines like God's eternal decree, his immutability and his aseity sometimes lead us to think that God can never 'respond' to what happens in the world. Responding seems to assume passivity and change in God. Now, emotions are usually responses to events. They are, indeed, sometimes called passions, a term that suggests passivity. This consideration is one reason why theologians have resisted ascribing emotions to God. But although God's eternal decree does not change, it ordains change. It ordains a historical series of events, each of which receives God's evaluation. God evaluates different events in different ways. Those evaluations themselves are fixed in God's eternal plan. But they are genuine evaluations of the events. It is not wrong to describe them as responses to these events." John M. Frame, *The Doctrine of God* (Phillipsburg, NJ: P&R Publishing, 2002), 610.

[34] Frame adds that there are some truths that cannot be spoken without an attending emotion (e.g., Rom. 11:33–36), and if they are communicated without that emotion, they are falsified. From this Frame makes an argument for God's knowledge necessarily containing emotional aspects: "we see a kind of coalescence between emotion and intellect, and an argument in favor of asserting

God's knowledge; rather, they are an integrated whole as the person of God knows his eternal plan.

Coming back to our point then, we see that man's knowledge, as a consequence of being fashioned after God's knowledge, should not be objective (non-subjective) either. Man, as the image of God, does not seek to rid himself of personal subjectivity when coming to knowledge; rather, he comes to knowledge by means of personal subjectivity. His feelings, emotions, and will are not expendable when considering truth. Thus, the search for non-subjective truth is doomed from the start. Even in eternity, man will know in light of personality and context, for that is part of what it means to be made in the image of God.

Poythress, however, shows that the problem is greater than merely desiring non-subjective knowledge:

> People who are addicted to human rationalism will never find themselves satisfied with an approach [like perspectivalism]. We are tempted to want to reduce everything to mechanical technique, to pin everything down. We fear that the only alternative to nailing down every aspect of interpretation is a boundless, irrational subjectivity. To those who are addicted in this way, I must point out that the only remedy is spiritual, and that it cannot be fathomed or reduced to technique. . . . Autonomous rationalists want perfect control and transparency that is reducible to technique. But only God controls transcendently. God's word controls us, our every thought, and our every move in interpretation. God calls us to humble ourselves and admit that we are but weak, emotion-laden creatures.[35]

---

divine emotions: without emotions, God would lack intellectual capacity, and he would be unable to speak the full truth about himself and the world." Ibid., 611.

[35] Vern S. Poythress, *God-Centered Biblical Interpretation* (Phillipsburg, NJ: P&R Publishing, 1999), 220.

According to Poythress and Frame, the answer to the threat of skepticism is *trust in the sovereignty of God*. Interpretation is inevitably affected by sin and finitude, because individual persons are sinful and finite. Man can never escape finitude, and in the present creation, he cannot escape sin. The answer is not to capitulate to skepticism; rather, it is to trust in the God who truly reveals himself. It is within this trust that we can find *subjective* certainty.[36]

By *subjective certainty*, we are referring to a psychological certainty gained through a *personal* knowledge of God. Thus, while personal perspectives are limited and subject to sin, God can and does break through such limitations and reveal himself. Thus, while we can never have purely objective assurance of our interpretation of Scripture (e.g., by looking past/behind our own perspective), we can have subjective, personal assurance, knowing that God is sovereign over our every interpretation.[37] Frame calls such certainty *cognitive rest*.[38]

Perspectivalism Does Not Lead to Incommensurability

A final concern relating to perspectivalism and relativism concerns whether perspectivalism leads to incommensurability. Does the multiplicity of perspectives lead to a lack of a final standard for truth? As has been noted above, perspectivalism argues that truth is thinking God's thoughts after him. As such, he is the ultimate standard of truth. His perspective, which he has given to us in Scripture, is ultimate. All personal perspectives that deny his revealed perspective are false and should not be considered alongside truth.

---

[36] Frame, *The Doctrine of the Knowledge of God*, 134–35.
[37] Of course, this does not eliminate the necessity of diligent study; rather, it presupposes diligent study, for God will grant to those who seek after him, knowledge of himself. Further, this does not suggest that we will have indubitable or exhaustive knowledge. In finitude, we might embrace claims that are not true, but in the midst of such a belief, we have confidence that God is sovereign over our interpretation of the Word.
[38] Frame, *The Doctrine of the Knowledge of God*, 152–53.

Being false, however, does not mean that they are not perspectives. Neither does it mean that such a perspective is not useful. For example, God has revealed the perspective of Satan in the Garden of Eden. Is Satan's perspective on God's actions as voiced to Eve *true* (e.g., that God wanted to withhold good from Adam and Eve)? No. Nevertheless, such a perspective can be useful to know. When a Christian begins to doubt God's goodness, the Christian can remember that he is thinking according to Satan's perspective, a perspective laden with false claims.

A critic might respond that while perspectivalism may recognize Scripture as the ultimate standard of truth, the multiplicity of interpretations of Scripture lead directly back to incommensurability. A few things can be said in response. First, every Christian epistemology has the same problem. If one believes the Scripture to be the ultimate authority, the problem of interpretation is bound to arise. Second, perspectivalism has a better answer than many other epistemological positions. Because perspectivalism recognizes the limitations of one's own experience and the influence of sin even over the interpretation of Scripture, proponents of perspectivalism seek out the perspectives of others who are likewise committed to Scripture. While this does not solve the hermeneutical issues, it provides a way for Christians to be exposed to viewpoints of brothers and sisters in the faith whose reading of Scripture is informed by experiences that may enlighten the text in a way unanticipated by others. In other words, by recognizing their own limitations, perspectivalists are able to learn from others, allowing their perspectives to challenge their own. The ultimate standard does not change, but one can add new focal perspectives, allowing them to better understand the revelation God has given to man.

Implications of General Perspectivalism

Having answered the major accusation against general perspectivalism, we can now show the epistemological implications of embracing the method. These implications will further clarify the method and show that it is epistemologically fruitful.

Recognition of the Value of other Personal Perspectives

General perspectivalism naturally leads to a more mature recognition of the potential benefit of other perspectives. The recognition that we are created to *think God's thoughts after him in community* leads to a willingness to listen to other people's vantage points.

Perspectivalism takes seriously both the limitations and uniqueness of each individual. As for limitations, one individual cannot experience or investigate everything. We are dependent on one another for most of our knowledge. Seeking the personal perspectives of others follows naturally from such limitation. As for uniqueness, even if we were to have the same experiences as another person, our unique skills, temperaments, and interests would lead to different aspects of knowledge (i.e., our different focal perspectives would allow us to discover aspects of the truth). Thus, in order to grasp the fullness of any experience, we need the perspectives of others.

The benefit of listening to others also applies to unbelievers as well. While the perspective of an unbeliever will necessarily be impacted by his twisted worldview, nevertheless, he is a creature who lives in God's world and is made in God's image. Further, he is a creature who is perpetually face-to-face with the truth (Rom. 1:18–20). No concepts he ever contemplates are completely foreign to the world God has made him to live in.[39] Therefore, even unbelievers grasp truth-claims (though falsified by their larger context of

---

[39] Barber makes this connection: "Art, music, and every other form of human creativity, once they are accomplished, are nothing more than an image of something that exists in God's universe. The painter cannot paint anything more than what his eye can see, or his imagination can take from nature and elaborate on." John Barber, "John Frame's Theology in the Present Cultural Context," in *Speaking the Truth in Love: The Theology of John M. Frame*, ed. John J. Hughes (Phillipsburg, NJ: P&R Publishing, 2009), 894.

knowledge—Acts 17:28).[40] By recognizing God to be whom he has revealed himself to be, the general perspectivalist is open to learning something from even the most ardent unbeliever.

Poythress has connected listening to others' perspectives to God's knowledge in the intra-Trinitarian fellowship. Because of eternal love within the ontological Trinity, the persons in the Godhead understand one another, exhaustively knowing each other's perspective. Poythress analogically applies this love to our love for neighbors: "If we love them, we listen to them and begin to appreciate their perspectives. The diversity of people leads naturally to acknowledging a diversity of perspectives. In addition, we begin to incorporate a second or a third perspective into our mind."[41]

Recognition of the Possibility to Preempt the Opponent's Strong Points

General perspectivalism offers the opportunity to embrace whatever aspect of truth one's opponent admits and to use that truth to show the opponent the failure of the non-biblical position. Even when someone embraces a wrong position, there are still aspects of his personal or focal perspective that can be helpful. Poythress has emphasized this implication in his book, *Understanding*

---

[40] For example, Paul, when citing unbelieving poets when at Athens (Acts 17), never indicated that the unbelievers spoke truth; rather, they had had grasped a claim that in the *right context* was true. See, K. Scott Oliphint, *The Battle Belongs to the Lord: The Power of Scripture for Defending Our Faith* (Phillipsburg, NJ: P&R Publishing, 2003), 143–73; Greg Bahnsen, "The Encounter of Jerusalem With Athens," *Ashland Theological Bulletin* 13 (Spring 1980): 4–40. Reprinted in Greg Bahnsen, *Always Ready: Directions for Defending the Faith*, ed. Robert Booth (Texarkana, AR: Covenant Media, 1996), 235–76.

[41] To be clear, the analogy is not that the divine persons *come to know* one another's perspectives. Instead, the analogy is that the persons eternally *know* one another's personal perspectives. But because we are limited, we must *come to know* (through process) other personal perspectives. Vern S. Poythress, *Logic: A God-Centered Approach to the Foundation of Western Thought* (Wheaton, IL: Crossway, 2013), 298–99.

Dispensationalists.[42] While Poythress holds firmly to Covenant Theology and holds Dispensationalism to be a *contradictory* system to Covenant Theology, he nevertheless uses the truth-claims dispensationalists accept to attempt to show them that their system is wrong. Poythress calls his method *preempting the opponent's strong points* and describes it in the following way:

> Sometimes we are dealing with outright error, not just a harmonizable difference of viewpoint. In such cases, it is often worthwhile trying to figure out what other people fear and what are the strongest points in their arguments. We should try to find some grain of truth in their fears, in their strong points, and in the things that they care for most intensely. Even if there is only a distant similarity between what they assert and what is actually true, we can find the primary points of similarity. Starting with the actual truth closest to their viewpoint, we can develop a perspective from which to expand to the truth that we want them to learn. We can, in other words, 'steal their thunder,' or preempt their strong points.[43]

Poythress's method depends on the unity of truth undergirding reality. Because God maintains the consistency of truth, Poythress can begin with any truth and show how it can only be true in light of other truth. In this way, any positive truth-claim an opponent may embrace can be used as a focal perspective to lead that opponent to a fuller understanding of truth.[44]

---

[42] Vern S. Poythress, *Understanding Dispensationalists*, 2nd ed. (Phillipsburg, NJ: P&R Publishing, 1994).

[43] Vern S. Poythress, *Symphonic Theology* (Grand Rapids, MI: Zondervan, 1987), 90.

[44] An example of Poythress's method is shown in his analysis of the term *literal* in dispensational material. Poythress confirms that the intention behind such language is good, yet he suggests that if dispensationalists desire a *literal*

Implications of General Perspectivalism

Recognition of the Need for Humility in Epistemological Conclusions

A third practical result of embracing perspectivalism is epistemological humility. Because man is limited, finite, and sinful, it is always possible that he has failed to see from a potentially foundation-changing focal perspective. Humility does not eliminate subjective psychological certainty, however. While often these two are pitted against one another, they are not opposites. Further, humility does not prevent theological and philosophical conviction. That is, once the general perspectivalist has embraced a truth he believes is from God, only God could make him doubt that truth.[45] On matters concerning which Scripture does not clearly speak, general perspectivalists remain open to ideological emendation. Because only God knows all truth exhaustively, he alone has the right to be believed without exception.

Recognition that Some Disagreements are Based on Perspective

Frame's most notorious article, *Machen's Warrior Children*, illustrates a fourth practical ramification of general perspectivalism; namely, the belief that many disagreements occur because of differences in focal perspective.[46] Because people understand reality from different vantage points, they sometimes fail to see that their opponent is looking at the same truth from a complementary but distinct focal perspective. On the surface, their conclusions may not appear

---

interpretation, then they are seeking a grammatical-historical interpretation. From there, Poythress can argue for covenant theology as a more *literal* (i.e., consistent grammatical-historical) interpretation. Poythress, *Understanding Dispensationalists*, 78–96.

[45] Frame argues, "When God speaks to us in Scripture . . . the human knowledge we obtain is warranted by his own exhaustive perspective . . . Scripture tells me that God created the heavens and the earth. That knowledge can never be invalidated by any other perspective. It is true from any possible perspective." Frame, "A Primer on Perspectivalism," 5–6.

[46] John M. Frame, "Machen's Warrior Children," in *Alister E. McGrath and Evangelical Theology*, ed. Sung Wook Chung (Grand Rapids, MI: Baker, 2003), 113–46.

harmonious, but the complexity of truth often masks the inner congruence. Here we must keep in mind that general perspectivalism does not embrace relativism; there are such things as contradictory beliefs.[47] Either Christianity's Yahweh or Islam's Allah is Lord. The difference here is not merely focal perspective. General perspectivalists, however, maintain that too often people assume they entirely disagree when, instead, they are viewing the same reality from a complementary focal perspective.

Frame provides an example in what is often called the Van Til-Gordon Clark debate.[48] The debate centrally concerned the incomprehensibility of God as it pertained to the relationship between God's knowledge and man's knowledge. Both men argued for incomprehensibility, but Van Til believed Clark denied it in practice. Van Til was chiefly concerned to maintain the Creator-creature distinction. Clark was chiefly concerned to maintain the revelatory power of God's communication. We can view these two concerns as a focal perspective through which each man viewed the question of knowledge. From the focal perspective of the Creator-creature distinction, Van Til believed Clark violated the distinction by suggesting that propositions were the *exact same* for both man and God.[49] Clark, by focusing on the focal perspective of the clarity of revelation, believed Van Til maintained a two-level theory of truth whereby what was revealed was not what God knows and, therefore, has no connection with truth.[50]

---

[47] Ibid., 142.

[48] In using this example, I am not seeking to defend Frame's position on the debate. That would take us too far off field. It is used here because it is one of Frame's chief examples of a difference based on perspective.

[49] In the Complaint, the signers, of whom Van Til was one, stated, "We dare not maintain that [God's] knowledge and our knowledge coincide at any single point." John Betzold et al., "The Text of a Complaint: Against Actions of the Presbytery of Philadelphia in the Matter of the Licensure and Ordination of Dr. Gordon H. Clark," 1944, 5, accessed July 23, 2014, http://godshammer.wordpress.com/2010/07/the-complaint.pdf.

[50] Clark says, "The proposition Christ died for our sins, has a single, definite

John Frame, in his analysis of the debate, suggests that both men were viewing the relationship between God's knowledge and man's knowledge from helpful focal perspectives. However, their failure to see from the other's personal (and focal) perspective convinced them that they were in near total opposition. But in the end, Frame contends that "Van Til . . . did not deny what was most important to Clark, namely that God and man can believe the same proposition and thus can agree as to what is objectively true." And on the other side, "Clark expressed, in his discussion of the 'mode' of God's knowledge, what was important to Van Til, namely the radical difference between the nature and workings of the divine mind and the human."[51]

While Frame does not indicate that all of the differences between Van Til and Clark were based upon a failure to view from the other's personal perspective,[52] he does suggest that the major arguments expressed in *The Complaint* and in *The Answer* did not treat the opponent's view adequately.[53] In sum, if each man would have sought to view the issue from the personal perspective of the other, they would have found more agreement than was expressed in *The Complaint* and *The Answer*.

---

plain meaning. To say that God places some other, undiscoverable meaning upon these words is to empty the Bible of truth and to deny that it really reveals God's mind." Alan Tichenor et al., "The Answer to a Complaint Against Several Actions and Decisions of the Presbytery of Philadelphia Take in a Special Meeting Held on July 7, 1944," 1944, 17, accessed July 23, 2014, godshammer.files.wordpress.com/2010/07/the-answer.pdf.

[51] Frame, "Machen's Warrior Children," 121.

[52] Many of these differences can be seen in the later development of both Clark and Van Til's epistemology. In hindsight, it appears that Van Til was aware of some problems in Clark's epistemology, but *The Complaint* did not clearly get to the bottom of those differences. This may have been because Van Til was only one of many people constructing *The Complaint*.

[53] For the most extensive analysis see, John M. Frame, *Cornelius Van Til: An Analysis of His Thought* (Phillipsburg, NJ: P&R Publishing, 1995), 97–114.

Summary of the Basis of General Perspectivalism

Having finished our treatment of general perspectivalism through an analysis of its metaphysical basis, of its chief critique, and of its major positions, we can now summarize the method before turning to triperspectivalism.

The major themes of general perspectivalism can be understood under the following three statements. First, *God's knowledge is ultimately independent from all human perspectives.* He, being the Creator, remains distinct from his creation. Two conclusions follow from this. First, while his infinite knowledge includes the exhaustive knowledge of all the perspectives of his finite creatures, these perspectives are a result of God's free desire to create and are, therefore, not ontologically necessary to him.[54] Second, his knowledge is constitutive of the things he knows, but man's knowledge is merely non-original replications of God's knowledge.

Maintaining that God's knowledge is independent from all human knowledge does not eliminate perspectives, however. This is the case for three reasons. First, as a triune being, God has multiple personal perspectives on all reality—the perspective of the Father, Son, and Spirit. Further, these perspectives can be seen as focal perspectives.[55] Second, God exhaustively knows the personal perspectives of all his creatures because he knows his own eternal plan, which is constructive of the personal perspectives of his creatures. Third, God knows creation through the focal perspectives he creates in reality. Like the personal perspectives, he does not know the focal perspectives as a result of their creation; he creates them as a result

---

[54] This is a difficult metaphysical claim. It would take us too far off field to examine it in depth here. For a helpful summary of one way to handle the issue see, K. Scott Oliphint, *Reasons for Faith: Philosophy in the Service of Theology* (Phillipsburg, NJ: P&R Publishing, 2006), 232–55.

[55] For instance, the Father knows the focal perspective of the Son. This implies that the Son knows the focal perspective of the Father as the Father knows the focal perspective of the Son, *et cetera*.

of his knowledge of them. Thus, he does not grow in knowledge by knowing all the focal perspectives; rather, the immensity of focal perspectives shows the exhaustiveness of God's creative thought.

Second, *man's knowledge is dependent on God's* knowledge. As noted above, man's knowledge, if it is to be accurate knowledge, must think God's thoughts after him. Therefore, it must analogically replicate God's original knowledge. The dependence of man's perspectives on God's knowledge allows perspectivalism to avoid relativity. Other systems of epistemology that embrace a quasi-perspectival view ultimately fall into abject relativism, because they do not have a stable foundation on which multiple perspectives can ultimately coalesce. Because God knows all truth, and because man is seeking to replicate, on a creaturely scale, God's knowledge, multiple personal and focal perspectives do not present an epistemological problem. Further, because God has revealed himself in Scripture, the world, and man's own constitution, one should have confidence that God's knowledge can be embraced (to the extent he has made this knowledge available).

That *man's knowledge is interdependent on other humans' perspectives* is the third summarizing feature of general perspectivalism. Because we are finite, we cannot know as God knows (innately, exhaustively, etc.). One implication of this fact is that we cannot *fully* know creation until we know it from everyone's perspective. For even seeking others' personal perspectives *is* seeking after God's perspective, since his knowledge is foundational to the creation of all perspectives.[56] Further, because God's knowledge is productive of all reality, we can seek out all perspectives, knowing that each focal perspective, when fully explored, may shed new light on every other perspective.[57]

---

[56] God's knowledge includes (and is determinative of) even unbelieving personal perspectives. If not, man is unilaterally creative and his thought is antecedent to God's knowledge. Of course, this implies that God knows many false truth-claims, but he knows them as false.

[57] We will discuss this to a greater extent later. For now, it is enough to say

Implications of General Perspectivalism

In light of these three summarizing features, perhaps the shortest summary of general perspectivalism available would be the following: God's knowledge is *independent* of man's personal perspectives, man's knowledge is *dependent* on God's ultimate personal perspective, and man's knowledge is *interdependent* on other men's personal perspectives.[58] Once these statements have been understood within a biblical metaphysic, general perspectivalism naturally follows.

Before turning to triperspectivalism, the Trinitarian basis for general perspectivalism should be reemphasized. God's knowledge is inherently perspectival, because he is irreducibly Trinitarian and because his plan is a unity in diversity. God created man according to his own constitution (in his image), and, therefore, man's knowledge is personally perspectival (imaging the distinction of persons) and focally perspectival (imaging the unity in diversity of God's plan). Consequently, man can seek after God's ultimate personal perspective in two ways: first, by coming to know the unity of God's creative plan through the diversity of revelatory focal perspectives he has provided; second, by knowing in community, replicating on a creaturely scale the intra-Trinitarian relations of the Trinity. Therefore, general perspectivalism is a reflection of the Trinitarian nature of God in epistemology.

---

that because God's knowledge is constructive of reality and his knowledge is a unity in diversity of perspectives, then the perspectives will ultimately harmonize and reflect one another.

[58] This summary of general perspectivalism conforms to triperspectivalism, which will be examined below. God's knowledge is the *normative*, man's interdependence within the created world is *situational*, and man's appropriation of God's knowledge is *existential*.

4

Method and Basis of Triperspectivalism

Frame's perspectival method is best known for its triads—group of three items that coinhere. We will begin this chapter with a short example of triperspectivalism. This will allow us to have a familiarity with perspectival triads before developing their Trinitarian base. Second, we will address some preliminary issues, including whether Frame really believes triperspectivalism is Trinitarian and whether the Trinity can be legitimately called perspectival. Third, we will seek to show the Trinitarian foundations for triperspectivalism. More explicitly, we will show how Frame's triperspectivalism is built upon the relationship of unity and diversity of God's persons and attributes. Stated differently, we will show how perichoresis and simplicity are reflected into creation. Finally, having argued for the similarity of perichoresis and simplicity, we will attempt to build a case for the development of a perichoretic-simplicity model that is necessary for the future of perspectival methodology.

Introduction to Triperspectivalism

Two major directions for the presentation of triperspectivalism are possible. First, we could develop triperspectivalism at length and later show the Trinitarian origins of the method. Alternatively, we could begin with the Trinitarian reflections and later show how they are foundational for the structure of perspectivalism. We have chosen this second direction in order to emphasize more fully the Trinitarian nature of the program. This means that a full analysis of triperspectivalism will have to wait until we have developed perichoresis and simplicity as functions of God's unity and diversity. For this reason, we will simply introduce triperspectivalism here without deep analysis of the method. Deeper analysis will be provided in later chapters.

Triperspectivalism can be described as a method where distinct elements cohere in perfect harmony. We will provide one of Frame's chief epistemological examples, showing how it builds on the insights provided by general perspectivalism. Triperspectivalism is more specific than general perspectivalism in that it argues for *three* distinct focal points from which knowledge can be viewed. For example, one can view his or her knowledge from the *normative* perspective, focusing on the standards by which knowledge is apprehended. One can view knowledge from the *situational* perspective, focusing on the facts that can be correlated with the law. Finally, one can view knowledge from the *existential* perspective, focusing on the role personality plays in knowledge acquisition. Frame argues that, while these can be distinguished from one another, in the act of knowing, they are identical,[1] or, in other words, they cohere.[2] A fact (situation) cannot be known without the law (normative) and the person (existential). But of course, the law (normative) can only be known by means of facts (situational) through a person (existential). This interrelation could be extensively expounded, showing how each element is absolutely necessary for and constitutive of any act of knowing. In Frame's terminology, the normative, situational, and existential are perspectival, cohering with one another.

---

[1] We will develop what Frame means by *identical* in chapter six.
[2] For a more explicit statement of this triad, see, John M. Frame, *The Doctrine of the Knowledge of God* (Phillipsburg, NJ: Presbyterian and Reformed, 1987), 65–73.

Another influential triperspectival triad derives from ethics.[3] We will develop this triad using the same terminology above.[4] For every ethical decision there is a law (normative) that should be applied to a situation (situational) by a person (existential). The entirety of an ethical decision depends on all three. Thus, they are distinct in regards to their identification, yet they are all essential to one another in the act of ethical decision-making. For example, an ethical decision cannot be made if there is no law (normative) by which the situation (situational) is to be understood by the person (existential). Further, without any situation (situational), the laws (normative) remain impotent and uninterpretable to the person (existential). Finally, without a person (existential) there is no one to bring the laws (normative) in connection to the situation (situational). All three are absolutely essential for the ethical task, interrelating with one another. Frame, therefore, calls them perspectival.

Admittedly, using only two examples is insufficient for understanding triperspectivalism. However, this section is merely introducing the topic, which will be further elucidated in the following chapters.

---

[3] Frame embraced the triad from Van Til, who spoke of the right motive (existential), standard (normative), and goal of ethics (situational). Van Til, for his part, was merely working out the implications presented by the Westminster Confession of Faith: "Works done by unregenerate men, although for the matter of them they may be things which God commands; and of good use both to themselves and others: yet, because they proceed not from an heart purified by faith; nor are done in a right manner, according to the Word; nor to a right end, the glory of God, they are therefore sinful and cannot please God, or make a man meet to receive grace from God: and yet, their neglect of them is more sinful and displeasing unto God." "Westminster Confession of Faith," 1646, 16.7, accessed December 9, 2009, http://reformed.org/documents/wcf_with_proofs/. The ethical triad is most clearly developed in John M. Frame, *The Doctrine of the Christian Life* (Phillipsburg, NJ: P&R Publishing, 2008), 33–36.

[4] Frame argues, following Van Til, that epistemology is a subdivision of ethics. As such, it is not surprising that the same triad is useful in both fields. Frame, *The Doctrine of the Knowledge of God*, 62–64.

The Trinity as the Ultimate Triad

Frame and Poythress have developed perspectivalism out of Trinitarian concerns. We have already observed how general perspectivalism flows out of a proper understanding of God's Trinitarian knowledge. In this section, we will describe how perichoresis and simplicity provide the foundation for the *perspectival dynamics* evident within all triperspectival groups. Before developing perichoresis and simplicity, however, we will need to deal with two preliminary concerns.

Preliminary Considerations

Before developing the Trinitarian triad, two issues must be addressed. The first concerns whether the Trinity is really the source of the triads and the other concerns a potential Trinitarian critique.

Does Frame Believe Perspectivalism Is Trinitarian?

First, does Frame really believe the Trinity is the ultimate source of the perspectival triads? Frame appears to express an uncertain answer to this question. Since this question is central to our thesis, we will spend some time discerning Frame's viewpoint.

Poythress leaves the reader without doubt as to his belief that the Trinitarian nature is the ultimate ground of triperspectivalism.[5] Scarcely a triad is mentioned in Poythress work without some reference to the divine archetype.[6] For instance, notice how Poythress establishes his triad of imaging in the following terms:

---

[5] "Perspectivalism of a Trinitarian kind has its ultimate roots in the Trinitarian character of God." Vern S. Poythress, "Multiperspectivalism and the Reformed Faith," in *Speaking the Truth in Love: The Theology of John M. Frame*, ed. John J. Hughes (Phillipsburg, NJ: P&R Publishing, 2009), 190.

[6] For instance, in his book, *God's Lordship in Interpretation*, Poythress argues for the following triads in explicitly Trinitarian categories by aligning the Trinitarian persons with the distinct perspectives: Triad of meaning, purpose, imaging, partition, love, understanding, communication, and transmission. Vern S.

> We can reexpress [the idea of imaging] using the triad of terms that we already introduced: originary, manifestational, and concurrent aspects or perspectives. Start with the Son imaging the Father. The Father is Originary; the Son is Manifestational; the Spirit who represents the relation between them is Concurrent. When God made man, God was originary, man was manifestational, and the permanent relation of imaging, brought about through inbreathing (Gen. 2:7), was concurrent.[7]

More will be said about the relationships present within this and other triads below. Here, we desire to show the following two points: first, Poythress frequently indicates a Trinitarian ground for his triads, and second, he also often associates the various poles of a triad with individual members of the Trinity.

Frame is not always as clear as Poythress. While he sometimes aligns the poles of his triads with the Trinity,[8] he does not do so as consistently or prolifically as Poythress. Further, while Poythress has never publicly cast doubt on the Trinitarian nature of triperspectivalism, Frame has done so on multiple occasions: "*Perhaps* the ultimate source of these triads is the doctrine of the Trinity."[9] In more explicit terms he has stated,

> Readers should make up their own minds as to how seriously they should take all these triads. I vacillate in my own thinking about them. Sometimes I think I have uncovered a deep layer of Trinitarian meaning in the Scriptures; at other times I think I have merely hit upon a useful pedagogical device.

Poythress, "God's Lordship in Interpretation," *Westminster Theological Journal* 50, 1 (Spring 1988): 27–64.

[7] Ibid.

[8] Notably he does so in the lordship triad, which we will discuss below.

[9] John M. Frame, *Salvation Belongs to the Lord: An Introduction to Systematic Theology* (Phillipsburg, NJ: P&R Publishing, 2006), 331. Emphasis added.

And there are times when I think even less of the scheme—as a kind of mental crutch, or at worst a procrustean bed for theological mutations. Certainly I am trying to avoid the worst kind of schematic thinking, in which the main motive is to make the scheme work, even at the expense of exegetical cogency.[10]

Finally, in a remark to his listeners at Trinity Evangelical Seminary Frame said,

You may be thinking by now that these threefold distinctions are getting to be a little too schematic, too neat; I think so too, but I find them hard to avoid. Sometimes I think that I'm hooked into some mysterious Trinitarian deep structure of Scripture; other times I think it's just a useful pedagogical device. Perhaps it all comes from sleeping through too many three point sermons as a child.[11]

These statements seem to conflict with other statements made by Frame that suggest the Trinitarian basis for triperspectivalism is more secure. For instance Frame writes, "All of God's activities in the world, therefore, are Trinitarian. . . . And all the covenantal triads I have employed in the Theology of lordship books arise out of the unity and complexity of God's Trinitarian being."[12] Likewise, in a recent interview, Frame told Sandlin that the perspectives "are ultimately based, I would say, in the Trinity: the Father, Son, and Spirit are all 'in' one another (circumincessio), so that to know one is always to know the others."[13] Most recently, in January of 2014,

---

[10] John M. Frame, *The Doctrine of God* (Phillipsburg, NJ: P&R Publishing, 2002), 15n31.

[11] John M. Frame, *Perspectives on the Word of God: An Introduction to Ethics* (Phillipsburg, NJ: Presbyterian and Reformed, 1990), 20.

[12] Frame, *The Doctrine of God*, 728.

[13] John M. Frame and P. Andrew Sandlin, "Reflections of a Lifetime

Frame confirmed in correspondence with the author, "I do believe that the Triperspectival nature of God (the Trinity) is ontological. That would include all the interrelations of triads and all the sub-triads. Then when God contemplates and creates a world outside himself, the world is an image of his triadic nature."[14]

What causes the apparent inconsistency of language from Frame? One could resolve the tension by arguing that Frame really is ambivalent. The times when he is more certain, he makes the latter statements, but the times he is less certain, he adds the caveats above. However, as we will argue below, Frame's system depends on triperspectivalism deriving from the Trinity. The epistemological system cannot stand without an ontological basis. Frame, as much as Van Til, demands an ontological reason for all epistemological positions.[15]

An alternative proposal for reconciling Frame's apparently contradictory statements is to appeal to Frame's ecumenical tendencies and humility. First, Frame is one of the foremost advocates within Christian orthodoxy for church union. Non-essential teachings that bring division in the church are antithetical to Frame's ideal.[16] With great sadness, Frame recognizes the controversy produced by perspectivalism. For instance, in his list of twenty-one divisions within Machen's Reformed heritage, Frame lamented that his own triperspectivalism, while designed to bring

---

Theologian: An Extended Interview with John M. Frame," in *Speaking the Truth in Love: The Theology of John M. Frame*, ed. John J. Hughes (Phillipsburg, NJ: P&R Publishing, 2009), 82.

[14] John M. Frame, e-mail message to the author, January 28, 2014.

[15] Poythress confirms, saying, "There can be no other ultimate foundation for perspectives than in God himself. God alone is absolute. Thus absoluteness, a key concept in Reformed theology of God, serves naturally as a key incentive for moving toward multiperspectival thinking in human practice, a multiperspectivalism that imitates the coinherence of the persons in the Trinity." Poythress, "Multiperspectivalism," 199.

[16] John M. Frame, *Evangelical Reunion: Denominations and the One Body of Christ* (Grand Rapids, MI: Baker, 1991).

Reformed brethren together, "has become a focus of controversy in Reformed circles."[17] Perhaps, as a result, when his perspectivalism causes potential disunity, Frame is unwilling to dogmatically claim a Trinitarian reality to perspectivalism.

In his *Penultimate Thoughts on Theonomy*, Frame explicitly notes how he consciously sought to establish the truth of perspectivalism in a different way than he theonomy had been introduced:

> After some reflection, I have come to the conclusion that theonomy (like Dooyeweerdianism in the 1960s) is a good case study of how theological ideas *should not be introduced*. Forgive the personal reference, but consider this: In my *Doctrine of the Knowledge of God* I introduce a 'multi-perspectival' approach to theology. Now imagine how I might have written the book in a very different way: I might have said that multi-perspectivalism was the clear teaching of Scripture and the Reformers, but that since the Reformation down to the present the church has been dominated by wicked mono-perspectivalists who have impoverished and disempowered the church by their stupid and wilful heresy. With the right rhetoric, I might have sent my students forth to start all sorts of battles in churches, denominations, Christian schools and other organizations between 'monoperspectivalists' and 'multiperspectivalists.' Eventually I might have become the founder of a denomination called the 'Multiperspectivalist Presbyterian Church' (MPC, of course). And perhaps in time I might have been interviewed by Bill Moyers.
>
> I could have made a case for such a polemical and partisan approach. In fact, I believe that Scripture is multi-perspectival and that most good theology (like that of the

---

[17] John M. Frame, "Machen's Warrior Children," in *Alister E. McGrath and Evangelical Theology*, ed. Sung Wook Chung (Grand Rapids, MI: Baker, 2003), 142.

Reformers) is also multi-perspectival. I also believe that the church has been impoverished by certain narrower approaches which absolutize certain 'emphases,' 'orders,' over against others and which overgeneralize and misapply Scriptural principles by ignoring perspectives other than their own. Such theology creates rifts in the church. That is denominationalism, in essence; see my *Evangelical Reunion.*

But I did not present my case that way; for *I hate ecclesiastical factionalism* (1 Cor. 1–3) as much as I love multi-perspectivalism. And I believe that the best way to communicate multi-perspectivalism is gently, leading Christians to see that this is what they already believe in their heart of hearts, rather than creating adversary relationships with my readers before they even understand what I am saying.[18]

These words suggest that Frame is hesitant to divide his Reformed brethren on a point that is not central to the gospel. While he may believe perspectivalism Trinitarian, he wants to allow variance of opinion that would otherwise be limited by an unwavering claim for the Trinitarian origins of perspectivalism.

A second reason Frame may avoid being fully expressive of the Trinitarian basis of perspectivalism resides in his humility. Frame is quite concerned that he will fall into the trap other theologians have fallen into, namely, "When we develop a system or strategy that is useful in communicating the truth, we often get puffed up with pride and think that system is really the reflection of some deep, hitherto undiscovered truth about something hidden in the divine nature."[19] Frame applies this concern to his own system: "I have to keep reminding myself of that problem when I meditate on my Triperspectivalism, which, sometimes, seems to me to reflect

---

[18] John M. Frame, "Penultimate Thoughts on Theonomy," *Reformed Perspectives Magazine*, August 2001. Emphasis added.

[19] Frame, *The Doctrine of the Knowledge of God*, 265.

something very deep in God's trinitarian nature."[20] Thus, the combination of a rare humility and a deep desire for church unity may be responsible for Frame's unwillingness to definitively claim a Trinitarian origin of perspectivalism.

To be clear, we do not believe Frame has deceived his readers. He is not simply acting as though he is unsure of the Trinitarian basis for perspectivalism for the sake of church unity and the persona of humility. Instead, we are arguing that Frame's personal disposition towards belief of the Trinitarian foundation for triperspectivalism is affected by genuine humility and a fervent desire for church unity. Nevertheless, if the Trinitarian basis were firmly established, then a more overt method of teaching *should* be expressed—a method more in line with Poythress's presentation. However, even as we maintain ambivalence in Frame's *thought* concerning triperspectivalism, his *method* demands a Trinitarian basis. To this we will turn after dealing with one more preliminary matter.

Is the Trinity Merely Perspectival?

The second preliminary matter to discuss before addressing the Trinitarian triad is a potential critique: calling the Trinity a perspectival triad may appear to some as Sabellianism.[21] If the distinction between the Trinitarian persons is *merely* one of man's epistemological focal perspectives, then the critique stands. Frame attempts to curtail this critique in his perspectival primer: "'Perspective' does not exhaust the ways in which the three persons are distinct. . . . But if the three persons are not mere perspectives on the Godhead, they nevertheless are perspectives."[22] While one can describe the difference among the Trinitarian persons as a difference in perspective

---

[20] Ibid.

[21] Determined to be a heresy in multiple early church councils, Sabellianism is the view that the distinctions within the Godhead are *merely* manifestations of *one person* in three different ways.

[22] John M. Frame, "A Primer on Perspectivalism," in *John Frame's Selected Shorter Writings* (Phillipsburg, NJ: P&R Publishing, 2014), 9–10.

(for we do know the one true God through the Father, Son, and Spirit), to maintain *only* this distinction would be heretical. Of course, this same critique applies to other theological statements as well. For instance, if the distinctions amongst the Trinitarian persons were *merely* a description of acts within redemption (Father plans, Son accomplishes, and the Spirit applies), the distinction would be Sabellian as well.

Perichoresis and Simplicity

Having dealt with the two preliminary matters, we can turn to an examination of the Trinity as the basis for perspectival triads. Since, as Poythress maintains, "Perspectivalism of a Trinitarian kind has its ultimate roots in the Trinitarian character of God," the Trinity is a perfect place to begin.[23] In examining the Trinity, we will look at two core characteristics of the Trinity that lead Poythress and Frame to perspectivalism.

Perichoresis

The first core characteristic of the Trinity concerns the unity and diversity of the *persons*. *Perichoresis* (Greek) or *circumincessio* (Latin) is the doctrine formulated by the church out of the necessity to describe the scripturally attributed relations among the triune persons (John 10:28, 30; 14:10, 11; 17:21).[24] It comes from relating the Greek words *chora* (χώρα), meaning *location* or *place*, and *choreo* (χωρέω), meaning *to move* or *to go forward*.[25] Van Til summarized the doctrine as follows:

---

[23] Poythress, "Multiperspectivalism," 190.

[24] While the doctrine was originally formulated to describe the relationship of the two natures in Christ, John of Damascus modified the concept to align with the Trinitarian persons. For a history of the term and why it is more appropriately used of the Trinitarian persons, see, Danut Manastireanu, "Perichoresis and the Early Christian Doctrine of God," *Archaevs* 11/12 (October 2008): 61–93.

[25] Paul Molnar warns that some have confused χωρέω with χωρεύω. The latter refers to dance and can too easily lead away from the idea of identity to

The persons of the Godhead exist mutually in one another (Jn 17:21). There is a sort of inward circulation of the Godhead, an eternal movement within the being of God. The persons are distinct from the Divine Essence not *modaliter*—Sabellianism, nor *essentialiter*—Tritheism, nor *formaliter* or *ratione*, but *realiter*, which can have meaning for us only by negation of the others because admittedly we here peer into mystery.[26]

Van Til sought to maintain the mysterious relationship by explaining the perichoretic relationship in negative terms, indicating that while there is a true distinction between the persons and essence, the exact relation is not entirely expressible. Nevertheless, he also indicated that the ultimate unity of this diversity could be partially understood through mutual indwelling. By describing it as an "eternal movement" he suggests that it is a never-ending, ever-penetrating, and exhaustively-circular relationship. Each member is exhaustively represented in one another, yet none lose their distinctiveness.

Thomas Torrance gives another useful and concise summary of the doctrine: "In the Holy Trinity all subsistent relations are in eternal movement mutually containing and interpenetrating one another in such a way that in and through their distinctive properties they constitute a perfectly homogenous communion in one Being as Three in One and One in Three."[27] Torrance, like Van Til, maintains the distinctiveness and unity of the Trinity in somewhat mysterious terms. If *eternal* is beyond our mental abilities to comprehend, then an *eternal movement* is as well. The mystery, however,

---

a relation of mere harmony. Paul Molnar, *Thomas F. Torrance: Theologian of the Trinity* (Burlington, VT: Ashgate, 2013), 62.

[26] Cornelius Van Til, *Unpublished Manuscripts of Cornelius Van Til*, ed. Eric H. Sigward, Logos Digital Collection. (New York, NY: Labels Army Company, 1997).

[27] Thomas Forsyth Torrance, *Trinitarian Perspectives: Toward Doctrinal Agreement* (T&T Clark, 1994), 33.

does not bring into disrepute the truth. The members of the Trinity, while maintaining their unique distinctions, harmoniously and endlessly interpenetrate, producing a unity in diversity which cannot legitimately be separated nor conflated.

Because we will discuss the connection between perichoresis and the Trinitarian relations below, it is helpful here to examine the writings of Hilary of Poitiers on this point.[28] Hilary argues that the johannine stress on perichoresis, that is, the Father being in the Son and the Son being in the Father, is ultimately reflective of the Trinitarian relations: "The Father is in the Son because the Son is from him; the Son in the Father because he is not a Son from anywhere else; the only-begotten is in the unbegotten because the only-begotten is from the unbegotten."[29] In other words, Hilary argues that the perichoretic relations are necessarily reflective of the biblical description of begetting (and "breathing" of the Spirit). Hilary does warn, however, that the perichoretic relations are not fully comprehended by God's creatures.[30] Humans, because created, have limitations imposed by their created finitude, and when a creature seeks to go beyond his finitude, he "glorifies that which is erroneously given the name of wisdom."[31] In this case, human reason assumes perichoretic

---

[28] It is also helpful to hear Hilary on the perichoretic relation in light of our previous discussion about God's knowledge. Hilary notes that "[The Father and Son] are one, that is to say, he who is has nothing that will not also be found in him from whom he is. Whenever you hear the Son declare: 'I and the Father are one,' apply this statement to the persons, and allow to the begetter and the begotten the truth that has been revealed concerning them." In other words, Hilary argues that there can be nothing in the one that is not found in the other. The knowledge the one has, the other possesses in totality. Saint Hilary of Poitiers, *The Trinity*, trans. Stephen McKenna, vol. 25, The Fathers of the Church (Washington, DC: Catholic University of America Press, 1954), 68.

[29] Ibid., 25:67.

[30] "That which is imperfect cannot form an idea of that which is perfect, nor can that which derives its existence from something else have a perfect understanding either of its author or of itself." Ibid., 25:86.

[31] Ibid.

unity through the Trinitarian processions is impossible, yet "what man cannot conceive is possible with God."[32]

How does Trinitarian perichoresis influence perspectivalism? Both Frame and Poythress argue that perichoresis is the foundation for perspectivalism.[33] That is, the relationship existing among the perspectives within Frame and Poythress's method derive their core characteristics from God's inherent perichoretic relations. Poythress makes the connection by citing the principle of the absoluteness of God:

> We can never exhaustively understand the Trinity, but the Trinity is at the root of our epistemology. Together, these thoughts naturally lead to seeing the roots of multiple perspectives in the knowledge relations among the persons of the Trinity. These knowledge relations touch on the coinherence of the persons. The coinherence of the persons guarantees the coherence of perspectives at the deepest ontological level. There can be no other ultimate foundation for perspectives than God himself. God alone is absolute. Therefore, absoluteness, a key concept in Reformed theology of God, serves naturally as a key incentive for moving toward multiperspectival thinking in human practice, a multiperspectivalism that imitates the coinherence of the persons in the Trinity.[34]

In other words, because there can be no other ultimate foundation for reality than the Trinity, and because God, in his being and

---

[32] Ibid., 25:65.

[33] Poythress favors perichoresis, and Frame favors simplicity as the basis for perspectivalism. Nevertheless, both are willing to describe the relation in line with the other person's language. For instance, in personal correspondence, Frame was willing to call perspectivalism a *covenantal form of perichoresis*. John M. Frame, e-mail message to the author, March 25, 2014. Poythress also uses both concepts in Vern S. Poythress, *God-Centered Biblical Interpretation* (Phillipsburg, NJ: P&R Publishing, 1999), 36–47.

[34] Poythress, "Multiperspectivalism," 199.

knowledge, exhibits perichoretic relations, when perichoretic-like relations are found to exist in creation (in man and the world), perspectivalists seek to make explicit the connection between the perichoretic-like relations in creation and the perichoretic relations originally exhibited by God. This reflection of perichoresis in creation is called perspectivalism.

Simplicity

Just as the first core characteristic of the Trinity concerned the relationship of unity and diversity of the *persons*, so the second core characteristic concerns the relationship of unity and diversity of the *attributes*. Theologians call the relationship God's attributes maintain with the essence and one another *simple*.[35] The doctrine of simplicity does not refer to *ease of understanding* or *lack of complex ideas*, as the word often suggests. Instead, it is used in a less obvious sense of the word, referring to *a lack of parts*. This doctrine is not explicitly mentioned in Scripture, but it is defended as a natural consequence of biblical metaphysics.[36] James Dolezal summarizes the doctrine in the following way: "There is nothing in God that is not God. If there were . . . something other than God himself would be needed to account for his existence, essence, and attributes. But nothing that is not God can sufficiently account for God. He exists in all his perfection entirely in and through himself."[37]

Gerrit Immink notes three essential notions in the formulation

---

[35] For the latest discussion of the doctrine along with a robust defense of Thomistic account see, James E. Dolezal, "God Without Parts: Simplicity and the Metaphysics of Divine Absoluteness" (PhD Diss., Westminster Theological Seminary, 2011). Also published as James E. Dolezal, *God Without Parts: Divine Simplicity and the Metaphysics of God's Absoluteness* (Eugene, OR: Pickwick Publications, 2011).

[36] "The doctrine [of simplicity] is not revealed by Scripture but is used to secure God's aseity and otherness, and this aseity and otherness is certainly taught by Scripture." Frederik Gerrit Immink, *Divine Simplicity* (Kampen, Netherlands: J. H. Kok, 1987), 35.

[37] Dolezal, "God without Parts," iv.

of simplicity in scholastic theology: "first the notion that God displays aseity; second that God is transcendent and 'wholly other' than his creation, and third the notion that God displays a unique degree of unity."[38] Immink is arguing that these are the three motivations for the doctrine of simplicity. We will seek to explain each one.

First, if God truly is *a se*, there is nothing outside of him that could provide a reason for his existence. If we were to embrace *love* as a standard outside God, then we must ask where this standard of love derives. Thus, biblical metaphysics refuses to accept anything as eternally existent alongside God, for it refuses to accept the dependence that this eternal companion would place upon God. Therefore, the doctrine of simplicity implies that all of the attributes of God are *one* with him or, put differently, *they are him*.

Second, the doctrine of simplicity is motivated by the transcendence of the unique triune God. While the characteristics of man are separable from him (e.g., goodness, holiness, etc.), God is not so composed. In Aquinas's system, this form of transcendence results in major problems of predication, because the statement *God is wise* indicates both a subject and predicate. However, there is no such distinction in reference to God. We will discuss Aquinas's solution to such a problem below. For now it is enough to indicate that Aquinas maintains that such problems of predication are the inevitable result of God's simple being. God is so transcendent that he is beyond proper human predication.

Third, simplicity safeguards the unity of God. Immink suggests that while unity is not the *primary* motive for simplicity, it is a clear result.[39] There are two forms of unity important in theology proper: *unitas singularitatis* and *unitas simplicitatis*. The former reflects that we serve one God (rather than three). The latter unity, which is what we are concerned with here, is most often defended by suggesting that God is *identical* with his attributes. In this way, proponents of

---

[38] Immink, *Divine Simplicity*, 27.
[39] Ibid., 163.

simplicity indicate that there is no inconsistency in God's being for his will, attributes, knowledge, etc. are One.

Frame argues that perspectivalism derives from the relationships inherent in simplicity:

> 'God is Spirit' (John 4:24), 'God is light' (1 John 1:5), 'God is love' (1 John 4:8, 16). These expressions state what God really and truly is. In other words, they describe his essence, not merely what he happens to be on some occasions. But note that there are three of these attributions, not just one. So God's essence can be described in three different ways. I am inclined to say that these expressions describe the whole divine essence from *three different perspectives*.[40]

In other words, the attributes are focal perspectives (though not only focal perspectives) through which the unity and diversity of God's being may be viewed. Therefore, while we stated earlier that perichoresis (as the unity and diversity of persons) is the Trinitarian basis for perspectivalism, here we find that simplicity (as the unity and diversity of God's nature) is as well.

The Relationship of Simplicity and Perichoresis

If both perichoresis and simplicity provide the foundation for perspectivalism, the natural question arises—what relationship do simplicity and perichoresis have to one another? Or what is the relation between the *unity in diversity of the persons and the essence* and the *unity and diversity of the attributes and the divine nature*. Are perichoresis and simplicity synonyms, complementary conceptions, or is one derivative of the other? These questions are central to the task of confirming a Trinitarian basis for perspectivalism. In that light, it is unfortunate that proponents of perspectivalism have not been

---

[40] Frame, *The Doctrine of God*, 228. Emphasis added.

as explicit as necessary in the development of both perichoresis and simplicity in relationship to perspectivalism.[41] The lack of explicitness in aligning the two has caused some confusion.[42] It has also been the source of at least one misguided critique.[43]

Having noted that the literature is not as explicit as we would wish, we should also note that Frame and Poythress are not silent on the matter. For instance, when referencing the perspectival relationships within Scripture, Frame mentions both simplicity and perichoresis as reflective of the nature of God:

> God's Word tends to present relationships perspectivally because it reflects the nature of God himself, I surmise. God is one God in three persons; he is many attributes in one Godhead—the eternal one-and-many. None of the persons is 'prior to' the others; all are equally eternal, ultimate,

---

[41] To be fair, Frame does deal with both in his *Doctrine of God*. Nevertheless, the central questions we are posing here are not explicitly answered. Poythress is less to be blamed in that he has not published on the doctrine of God.

[42] R. Scott Clark struggles to connect Frame's view of simplicity with the Trinitarian nature: "So, we began with an *apparently* clear, boldfaced affirmation of divine simplicity but as we continue we find that, via a dialectical method, God is *also* complex. How is he complex? It is not clear. At points in the discussion it seems as if he is suggesting that the Trinity itself implies complexity in God. At other points it seems as if the existence of attributes might be the reason. I'm not sure but he does say that God is complex." R. Scott Clark, "Should I Buy It? (1)," *The Heidelblog*, 355, last modified December 2013, accessed January 22, 2014, http://heidelblog.net/2013/12/should-i-buy-it-1/. See also Thomas's comments: Derek Thomas, "Frame on the Attributes of God," in *Speaking the Truth in Love: The Theology of John M. Frame*, ed. John J. Hughes (Phillipsburg, NJ: P&R Publishing, 2009), 355.

[43] See Scrivener's critique, which argues that Frame should construct perspectivalism on perichoresis instead of simplicity. As we will show, Frame would agree with Scrivener's critique. Nevertheless, Scrivener's critique is helpful in a different way, which will be expressed below. Glen Scrivener, "How Frame's Doctrine of the Knowledge of God Might Shape and Inform the Christian Study of Ethics" (Bth Paper, Oak Hill Theological College, 2006), http://www.christthetruth.org.uk/Frame.htm.

absolute, glorious. None of the attributes is 'prior to' any of the others; each is equally divine, inalienable, and necessary to God's deity.[44]

As shown in this quote, Frame clearly aligns perichoresis and simplicity as analogous reflections of the unity and diversity of God.

If perichoresis and simplicity are related, what unites them? Is one derivative of the other? One could argue that the relations expressed in the perichoretic unity in diversity of the personal triune Godhead finds its expression in the unity in diversity of the attributes of God. But the opposite might be said as well: the unity and diversity of the attributes in God finds its expression in the perichoretic relations among the persons of the Trinity.[45] In other words, neither the attributes nor the persons are primary to one another. Both are essential expressions of the triune God. Thus, we cannot say that one is foundational to the other. So what is the foundational relation?

It appears that Frame perceives the connection between simplicity and perichoresis through the lens of his mentor, Van Til. One of the most substantial concerns for Van Til was the correlation between the one and the many, or unity and diversity. Within the Scriptures and the Reformed faith, Van Til believed he had found the answer to this perplexing epistemological and ontological quandary. What was the answer? In one place Van Til boldly asserted, "The so-called problem of the one and the many receives a definite answer from the doctrine of the *simplicity* of God."[46] However, in another place he seems to argue that the explanation is in the triune

---

[44] Frame, *The Doctrine of the Knowledge of God*, 192.

[45] So Frame says, "I do not believe that we can make such a neat separation between nature and persons. Certainly the persons are essential to God's being, just as essential as any attribute. It is not evident to me why 'triunity' should not be considered an attribute of God along with the others." Frame, *The Doctrine of God*, 228.

[46] Cornelius Van Til, *The Defense of the Faith*, ed. K. Scott Oliphint, 4th ed. (Phillipsburg, NJ: P&R Publishing, 2008), 31. Emphasis added.

nature: "the unity and the plurality of this world has back of it a God in whom unity and the plurality are equally ultimate. Thus we may say that this world . . . shows analogy to the *Trinity*. This world . . . may be thought of as revealing God as he exists. And God exists as a *triune being*."[47] So which is it? Is the ultimate source of unity and diversity the triune persons (as related in perichoresis) or in the relation of the divine attributes (as related in simplicity)?[48]

In order to answer this question, we must step further back. What is the similarity between the divine nature and the divine persons? In Van Til's theology, an essential similarity is their expressiveness of God's absolute personality. In this light we can see that both perichoresis and simplicity come together in Van Til's theology. Notice how Van Til fluidly works from absolute personality to both perichoresis and simplicity:

> In God as an absolute personality, who exists as the triune God, we have the solution of the one and many problem. The persons of the Trinity are mutually exhaustive. This means that there is no remnant of unconsciousness of potentiality in the being of God. Thus there cannot be anything unknown to God that springs from his own nature. Then too there was nothing existing beyond this God before the creation of the universe.[49]

---

[47] Cornelius Van Til, *An Introduction to Systematic Theology* (Nutley, NJ: Presbyterian and Reformed, 1974), 365. Emphasis added.

[48] Bosserman notes that "On occasion Van Til himself speaks as if the one-many problem is solved by the diversity and simplicity of the divine attributes, and not specifically the oneness and threeness of persons." In his opinion, "Van Til's statement in this context is out of place, and potentially misleading." In our opinion, Van Til was not mistaken; rather, he was indicating that the same one and many relationship evident in the persons was evident in the attributes as well. Brant Bosserman, "The Trinity and the Vindication of Christian Paradox: An Interpretation and Refinement of the Theological Apologetic of Cornelius Van Til" (PhD Diss., University of Bangor, 2011), §155.

[49] Cornelius Van Til, *Psychology of Religion*, Logos Digital Collection.

So the solution to the one and many problem is *God's absolute personality*, which implies both that God is *a se* and that he is exhaustively present in both his unity and diversity. Such absolute personality is expressed and reflected in perichoresis and simplicity, with the result that every distinction in God is expressive of him absolutely. In fact, this is exactly how Frame has understood the relationship between the two in Van Til's works: "[According to Van Til,] God's plan is a *personal* one and many, because his nature is one and many. The 'manifoldness' of God is seen in the diversity of his attributes, his thoughts, and his plans. But it is seen pre-eminently in the three persons of the Trinity."[50] So for Van Til, the problem of the one and many is resolved in the absolutely personal God who is manifested as a unity in diversity in both his persons and attributes.

Taking these ideas from Van Til and going a step beyond, Frame can describe simplicity as *perichoresis applied to the attributes*.[51] Of course, because of their equal expression within the nature of God, perichoresis could be described as *simplicity applied to persons* of the Godhead as well. Yet, this way of describing simplicity appears to be at odds with the Thomistic account of simplicity. Aquinas does not correlate simplicity and perichoresis, and he would not formulate, as Frame does, simplicity along perichoretic lines.

There is considerable controversy over the doctrine of simplicity in modern thought. We will follow Cooper in suggesting that there are presently two major models of simplicity being defended today. The *strong version of simplicity* "affirms that the divine nature in itself is absolutely without distinctions. In God, everything is logically identical. All theological distinctions are limited human concepts that do not truly apply to God."[52] The *moderate version* of

---

(Nutley, NJ: Presbyterian and Reformed, 1971), chap. 4.

[50] John M. Frame, *Cornelius Van Til: An Analysis of His Thought* (Phillipsburg, NJ: P&R Publishing, 1995), 75. Emphasis added.

[51] In personal correspondence, Frame mentioned that this was a "good way of putting it." John M. Frame, e-mail message to the author, May 13, 2014.

[52] John Cooper, *Panentheism: The Other God of the Philosophers-From Plato to*

simplicity defines "simplicity not from absolute identity but from God's self-sufficiency. Because God is not created or dependent on anything outside of himself, he is not composed of principles, properties, or constituents more basic than himself. Thus he is ontologically (not logically) simple."[53] The benefit of the latter, according to Cooper, is that the moderate version "rules out composition but not complexity in God—genuine distinctions among the persons of the Trinity, God's attributes, his essence and existence, and his nature and freedom."[54]

Which position does Aquinas take? According to Cooper, "Aquinas is ambiguous . . . between these two senses of simplicity, sometimes seeming to assert absolute identity."[55] Frederik Immink likewise says that it is possible that when Aquinas was speaking of the attributes he "didn't really mean to affirm *identity* . . . but only some substantial equivalence."[56] We will not seek to argue this point here; rather, we will take the historically accepted position that Aquinas did intend the stronger version.[57] In the following section, we will show the need for perichoretic-simplicity by showing the weakness of the strong simplicity account.

The Need for a Model of Perichoretic-Simplicity

Discussions of God's simplicity have often taken place alongside discussions of Trinitarian theology in Reformed doctrine.[58]

---

the Present (Grand Rapids, MI: Baker, 2006), 326.

[53] Ibid., 327.

[54] Ibid.

[55] Ibid., 137n8.

[56] Later in the work, Immink does attribute the strong version to Aquinas. Immink, *Divine Simplicity*, 176.

[57] We will follow James Dolezal's interpretation of Aquinas's doctrine of simplicity. Dolezal, "God without Parts."

[58] For example, Oliphint observes, "Calvin's affirmations of the simplicity of God take place, for the most part in the *Institutes*, in the context of his discussion of the Trinity." K. Scott Oliphint, *God with Us: Divine Condescension and the Attributes of God* (Wheaton, IL: Crossway, 2011), 65n33.

Nevertheless, discussion of simplicity as a perichoretic-like relation has not been prominent. While there are the resources for such within Van Til's writing, he did not *explicitly* develop it at length. Further, while Frame's perspectivalism relies on such an analogous relation, he has only to a limited extent shown how they relate to one another in the perspectival method. How would such a relation proceed?

In order to set the ground for a perichoretic-simplicity model, we will begin by showing the central weakness of the strong simplicity position. In the next chapter, we will show how a moderate simplicity position can appropriate the main tenets of perichoresis, providing a harmony of relation within the unity and diversity of God's persons and attributes.

Strong Simplicity and Moderate Simplicity

In the strong version of simplicity, stress is placed upon unity, while diversity is attributed to creaturely accommodation. Notice how Thomas speaks of God's being:

> God, however, as considered in himself, is *altogether one* and simple, yet our intellect knows him by different conceptions *because it cannot see him as he is in himself.* Nevertheless, although it understands him under different conceptions, it knows that one and the same simple object corresponds to its conceptions.[59]

In classic statements of the Trinity in perichoresis, on the other hand, both unity and diversity are upheld as equally ultimate. One could not say for example:

> God, however, as considered in himself, is altogether one *person*, yet our intellect knows him *as three persons* because it

---

[59] Thomas Aquinas, *Summa Theologica* (New York, NY: Cosimo, 2013), 71. Emphasis added.

cannot see him as he is in himself. Nevertheless, although it understands him under different conceptions—i.e., *as three persons*, it knows that one and the same *person* corresponds to its conceptions.

This conflict in the nature of the unity in diversity of the persons and attributes is disconcerting in light of Van Til's statements above. If the problem of the one and many is solved by both unity and diversity of the attributes and persons, one should expect more similarity between them. In the following section, we will examine the way Aquinas understood the distinction between persons and attributes before proposing an alternative.

The Perceived Weakness of a Strong Simplicity Account

Many philosophers and theologians believe Aquinas failed to bring Trinitarianism and simplicity together in his system. Christopher Hughes, after attempting to reconcile Aquinas's view of simplicity with biblical Trinitarianism, concluded that the only options for Aquinas were Sabellianism (and thus giving up Trinitarianism) or a reworking of the strong version of simplicity. In sum, Hughes says, "the full-strength account of divine simplicity (the one Aquinas presupposes and deploys in his metaphysics of the Trinity) describes a God who *could not possibly be triune*."[60] Jay Richards agrees, suggesting that those who employ a strong account of simplicity "lack any consideration of the problems the doctrine of the Trinity raises for the notion."[61] He further argues, "Given the centrality of the trinitarian claim to the Christian doctrine of God, if there is such a conflict between it and strong simplicity, then surely the latter

---

[60] Christopher Hughes, *On a Complex Theory of a Simple God: An Investigation in Aquinas' Philosophical Theology* (Ithaca, NY: Cornell University Press, 1989), 239–40. Emphasis added.

[61] Jay W. Richards, *The Untamed God: A Philosophical Exploration of Divine Perfection, Simplicity and Immutability* (Downers Grove, IL: InterVarsity Press, 2009), 229.

should give way."[62] John Cooper adds a third voice, suggesting that Aquinas's position on simplicity "implicitly denies the genuine distinctions among the persons of the Trinity."[63]

Brian Leftow appears to believe that Aquinas's concept of simplicity *cannot* be reconciled with the Trinitarian distinctions. Instead, Leftow insinuates that Thomas divides his philosophy from his theology at this point. In other words, while his philosophy (i.e., simplicity) would lead to a denial of his theology (i.e., Trinitarianism), Aquinas chose to accept theological Trinitarianism despite his philosophical concept of simplicity.[64]

But according to Frame, Aquinas did seek to reconcile his theology and philosophy. However, instead of understanding simplicity in light of Trinity, Aquinas understood Trinity in light of strong simplicity, resulting in a subversion of the real Trinitarian distinctions to merely notional or apparent distinction.[65] Cornelius Plantinga agrees:

> Thomas simplifies things so aggressively that even that difference is eventually washed out. For each person is identical with his relevant relation: the Father just is paternity; the son just is filiation; the Spirit just is procession. Further, these relations themselves, Thomas explicitly says, are all really the same thing as the divine essence. They differ from it only in intelligibility, only in perception, only notionally, not ontologically.[66]

---

[62] Ibid., 230.

[63] Cooper, *Panentheism*, 326.

[64] "On Aquinas's view, God is simple relative to the distinctions metaphysics is equipped to make, and yet Trinitarian theology affirms that God is complex relative to further distinctions theology alone is equipped to draw." Brian Leftow, *Time and Eternity* (Ithaca, NY: Cornell University Press, 2009), 68.

[65] John M. Frame, *Systematic Theology: An Introduction to Christian Belief* (Phillipsburg, NJ: P&R Publishing, 2013), 430, 486.

[66] Cornelius Plantinga, "The Threeness/Oneness Problem of the Trinity," *Calvin Theological Journal* 23, 1 (April 1988): 47.

Such a position, Frame and Plantinga argue, suggests something close to modalism, and as Frame argues, betrays a view whereby "unity must always be prior to multiplicity, so that God, who is prior to everything, must have no multiplicity."[67]

Dolezal's Defense of Aquinas's Strong Simplicity and Trinitarianism

James Dolezal correctly notes that the present debate is not only about simplicity and Trinitarianism, but it is also foundationally about how to "conceive the relationship between the divine persons and divine nature and among the three persons themselves."[68] Dolezal presents the most complete modern defense of Thomas's relation between simplicity and Trinity, and, therefore, we will seek to express his view here. He suggests that Thomas's chief concern is to avoid God having parts. Specifically, Thomas seeks to explain how God is without *accidents*, which determine the subject to a reality above that which the subject has in substance alone. Any such accident would indicate that God is composed of something for which is not his divine substance. As Dolezal says, such an accident would mean that God "would not be sufficient to account for the full range of his actuality—he would depend upon something non-divine (i.e., the accident) for some aspect of his being."[69]

On the most obvious reading, it would appear that the divine persons would make God a subject with accidents (personal relations). The easiest way out of such a conundrum is to suggest that these relations are like the attributes; they are only nominal and not real. However, Dolezal recognizes that such a position is modalistic and contradicts the nature of relation, which "requires genuine otherness."[70] Thus, he follows Aquinas, who indicates that the relations are real. Such a position leads to a potential problem, because real

---

[67] Frame, *Systematic Theology*, 430.
[68] James E. Dolezal, "Trinity, Simplicity and the Status of God's Personal Relations," *International Journal of Systematic Theology* 16, 1 (January 2014): 81.
[69] Ibid.
[70] Ibid., 82.

relations appear to negate simplicity. To avoid this problem Thomas argued that the notion of relation as pertaining to God is equivocal from the creaturely understanding of relation.[71] In man, relations between persons are sometimes notional, but in God, because the relations exist within the self-same Being, the relations are real.[72] Now, because we know it is not necessarily of the character of relation to be accidental (i.e., because relations can be notional in creation), they are not accidental in God even though they are real.

Further proof for the non-accidental nature of relations in God is gained by distinguishing the relations from real accidents. Accidents refer to the subject in which the accident inheres. Relations, however, refer to something external to the subject. So Aquinas says, "the true idea of relation is not taken from its respect to that in which it is, but from its respect to something outside."[73] But in God, this something outside is not really *outside* for it references the divine subsistence. In light of these facts, a relation is not an accident, and, therefore, we can say that God has personal relations without inferring both a subject and accident.

A final reason to deny the accidental character of relations in God is stated by Thomas:

> Now whatever has an accidental existence in creatures, when considered as transferred to God, has a substantial existence; for there is no accident in God; since all in him is his

---

[71] Dolezal says of the concept of relation in terms of God, "Clearly, this is a *sui generis* notion of relation that Thomas proposes." Ibid., 83.

[72] Aquinas explains, "Relations exist in God really; in proof whereof we may consider that in relations alone is found something which is only in the apprehension and not in reality. . . . But when something proceeds from a principle of the same nature, then both the one proceeding and the source of procession, agree in the same order; and then they have real relations to each other. Therefore as the divine processions are in the identity of the same nature, as above explained (27.2, 4), these relations, according to the divine processions, are necessarily real relations." Aquinas, *Summa Theologica*, 28.1.

[73] Ibid., 28.2.

essence. So, in so far as relation has an accidental existence in creatures, relation really existing in God has the existence of the divine essence in no way distinct therefrom. But in so far as relation implies respect to something else, no respect to the essence is signified, but rather to its opposite term.[74]

In other words, because God is simple, we know that relations *cannot be* accidental. In another context Aquinas says this more clearly:

> Given that there are relations in God we are bound to say that they are the divine essence: else we would have to say that there is composition in God and that the divine relations are accidents, since whatever adheres to a thing besides its substance is an accident. It would also follow that something that is not the divine substance is eternal; and all these things are heretical.[75]

In light of this point, Dolezal remarks, "If one were not committed to the axiom of simplicity that there are no accidents in God it is rather doubtful that one would arrive at such a strong identity between the essence and personal relations of God. At least there would be no apparent ontological reason to do so."[76]

But what does Thomas mean by opposition in the above quote? In sum, opposition refers to distinction. And while these relations require distinction, they do not imply composition. Further, Thomas indicates that this distinction applies only to the diversity of God's persons and not the unity of the essence: "The very nature of relative opposition includes distinction. Hence, there must be real distinction in God, not, indeed, according to that which is absolute—namely,

---

[74] Ibid.

[75] Thomas Aquinas, *On The Power of God*, trans. by the English Dominican Fathers (Westminster, MD: Newman Press, 1952), 8.2, accessed July 29, 2014, http://dhspriory.org/thomas/QDdePotentia.htm.

[76] Dolezal, "Trinity, Simplicity and God's Personal Relations," 84–85.

essence, wherein there is supreme unity and simplicity—but according to that which is relative."[77] Dolezal suggests that this provides another reason to deny the accidental nature of the divine relations. Namely, by proposing that the oppositions (distinctions) of the relations are not to be attributed to the essence (relation to essence), but only between the relations (relation to relation) accidentality could not apply to the essence.[78]

For Aquinas, this form of distinction (or opposition) is different from any creaturely form. As necessary relations in the substance of the triune God, relatives cannot exist without one another. This implies that there was no lack in God from all eternity in which something external to him supplied what was lacking. Rather, from all eternity God is his relations. As Dolezal says, "In God real relation adds nothing to the subject. It simply denotes that there are within him relatives which refer to one another."[79]

Having argued that the relations are not properly understood as accidents, Dolezal turns to a related problem. How can God be three persons with distinct personal relations and not in some sense be composite? Dolezal offers such an argument before answering it: "The relations that distinguish each of the divine persons indicate that the three divine subjects are composed of personal essence and differentia, such as the personal properties of paternity, filiation and spiration. Therefore, the persons *as persons* are not simple."[80]

Aquinas's answer is to deny creaturely *personhood* in God. God's persons are not univocal with persons in creation:

> There cannot be a distinction of suppositum in creatures by means of relations, but only by essential principles; because in creatures relations are not subsistent. But in God relations

---

[77] Aquinas, *Summa Theologica*, 28.3.
[78] Dolezal, "Trinity, Simplicity and God's Personal Relations," 85–86.
[79] Ibid., 87.
[80] Ibid.

are subsistent, and so by reason of the opposition between them they distinguish the supposita; and yet the essence is not distinguished, because the relations themselves are not distinguished from each other so far as they are identified with the essence.[81]

So while *person* in creatures refers to distinct substances, in God, because the relations are subsistent (meaning, at minimum, eternal and essential) to God's essence, they should not be understood as reflecting a multiplicity, but a unity within the essence. Thus, *person* applied to God literally means relation: "But since relation, considered as really existing in God, is the divine essence Itself, and the essence is the same as person, as appears from what was said above (39.1), relation must necessarily be the same as person."[82] Later, Aquinas shows that this implies "Personal properties are the same as the persons . . . *paternity is the Father himself, and filiation is the Son, and procession is the Holy Ghost.*"[83]

But what should be said about the distinction between the divine nature and persons? Dolezal says, "the Father is wholly divine yet divinity is not wholly the Father, and so forth for the Son and Spirit."[84] This distinction would seem to argue against *identity* in the strong simplicity account. Dolezal argues otherwise by noting that the distinctions between the persons and the essence are "not in fact *real*."[85] So Aquinas says, "relation as referred to the essence does not differ therefrom really, but only in our way of thinking."[86] The distinctions are modal distinctions, which must be understood in opposition to creaturely modal distinctions. In the latter, modes add some quality to the thing in which it inheres. In God, modes subsist,

---

[81] Aquinas, *Summa Theologica*, 39.1.
[82] Ibid., 40.1.
[83] Ibid. Emphasis added.
[84] Dolezal, "Trinity, Simplicity and God's Personal Relations," 95.
[85] Ibid.
[86] Aquinas, *Summa Theologica*, 39.1.

and so are deprived of any addition. These modal distinctions are not *real* because they are *conceptual distinctions*. However, such conceptual distinction is not *primarily* in the creaturely knower; rather, it is in God's essence itself.[87]

The key to understanding Aquinas's position then is to recognize that the idea of person is *qualitatively different* in God than in man. Under the creaturely understanding of *person*, three persons must indicate three individual substances. For God, however, *person* simply indicates a divine-logical distinction of one simple being. The distinction between the persons is real, but the distinction between each person and the divine essence is not real. Dolezal indicates that we maintain the distinction of the persons and essence in our theology because it is fitting for a creaturely mode of predication, but also because "if we were to predicate of the relations by way of divine substance we would not be able to express the real distinctions between them."[88] In conclusion Dolezal says,

> Given that we are composite creatures who can only think and speak compositely, it is no argument against divine simplicity that we are compelled to predicate of the simple Father, Son and Holy Spirit according to the double way of relation and essence. Whatever distinction we make in that regard is merely conceptual and not real.[89]

---

[87] Richard Muller says that there is "no real distinction between the three persons and the divine essence, as if the essence were one thing (*res*) and the three persons another thing, for God is a simple and noncomposite being. Rather the persons are rationally or conceptually (*ratione*) distinct, not merely in the mind of the finite knower but in *ipsa re*, that is, in the Godhead or divine essence itself." Richard A. Muller, *Post-Reformation Reformed Dogmatics: The Rise and Development of Reformed Orthodoxy, Ca. 1520 to Ca. 1725 (Divine Essence and Attributes)*, 2nd ed., vol. 4 (Grand Rapids, MI: Baker, 2003), 191.

[88] Dolezal, "Trinity, Simplicity and God's Personal Relations," 97.

[89] Ibid., 98.

Critique of Strong Simplicity and Trinitarianism

Dolezal has benefitted modern theology greatly by his clear expression of Aquinas's concept of strong simplicity in light of Trinitarian concerns. However, we find that his account is lacking. One major problem is that such a proposal brings the Trinitarian persons into the same problems of predication that a strong simplicity account of the attributes has. On Aquinas's notion of simplicity, predications of God are non-proper (non-literal).[90] That is, to say, e.g., that God is good is to declare both a predicate and a subject. According to the Thomistic simplicity, however, in consideration of God's being, the predicate cannot be properly distinguished from the subject. Goodness, when stated as a predicate toward a subject, is distinguishable from God and, therefore, would be a *part* of God. Unfortunately, this way of speaking is necessary to creatures, argues Thomas. So how can we resolve the problem inhering between the way God is and the way we speak of/know God? It is here that Aquinas introduced his *rei significandi* and *modus significandi* distinction. The former referred to the concept being discussed (e.g., goodness), which is properly attributed to God, and the latter is the way in which that concept is spoken, which is non-proper or non-literal. These provided the path by which analogical predication might be made under his system.[91]

There are serious problems with such a construal however. First, it is not clear how we know the *rei significandi*. For instance, Aquinas says, "with reference to the mode of signification there is in every name that we use [of God] an imperfection, which does not befit God, even though the thing signified in *some eminent way* does befit God."[92] It is not clear what this eminent way is, and Aquinas

---

[90] Again, Aquinas says, "God, however, as considered in himself, is altogether one and simple, yet our intellect knows him by different conceptions because it cannot see him as he is in himself." Aquinas, *Summa Theologica*, 13.12.

[91] Ibid., 13.3.

[92] Thomas Aquinas, *Summa Contra Gentiles*, ed. Joseph Kenny, trans. Anton

never explains it.⁹³ Second, our knowledge of God comes through Thomas's philosophy of analogy, but, as Maxwell explains, Thomas's analogy, "is merely the duct taping together of univocism and equivocism, with an inexplicable leap betwixt."⁹⁴ On the one hand, Aquinas will not allow univocism, for this would indicate that God is really like our construal of him. On the other hand, Aquinas desires to avoid equivocism because he realizes that mysticism or skepticism is the end of such a line of thought. Despite his desire to avoid these two positions, Aquinas never develops resources to bridge the gap between the Creator and creature.⁹⁵ Further, since in Aquinas's method "even revelation gives us analogical knowledge,"⁹⁶ Aquinas's

---

Pegis et al. (New York, NY: Hanover House, 1957), 1.30, accessed July 30, 2014, http://dhspriory.org/thomas/ContraGentiles1.htm.

[93] See also, Paul Maxwell, "The Formulation of Thomistic Simplicity: Mapping Aquinas's Method for Configuring God's Essence," *Journal of the Evangelical Theological Society* 57, 2 (June 2014): 397–98n65.

[94] It would seem that this inexplicable leap is actually the distinction between *rei significandi* and *modus significandi*. Ibid., 397.

[95] The key text in Aquinas says, "*Univocal predication is impossible between God and creatures.* The reason of this is that every effect which is not an adequate result of the power of the efficient cause, receives the similitude of the agent not in its full degree, but in a measure that falls short, so that what is divided and multiplied in the effects resides in the agent simply, and in the same manner . . . this term 'wise' applied to man in some degree circumscribes and comprehends the thing signified; whereas this is not the case when it is applied to God; but it leaves the thing signified as incomprehended, and as exceeding the signification of the name. Hence it is evident that this term 'wise' is not applied in the same way to God and to man. The same rule applies to other terms. Hence no name is predicated univocally of God and of creatures. *Neither, on the other hand, are names applied to God and creatures in a purely equivocal sense,* as some have said. Because if that were so, it follows that from creatures nothing could be known or demonstrated about God at all . . . Therefore *it must be said that these names are said of God and creatures in an analogous sense, i.e., according to proportion.*" Aquinas, *Summa Theologica*, 13.5. Maxwell shows that the analogy of proportion is never able to span the Creator-creature divide. Maxwell, "The Formulation of Thomistic Simplicity," 388–400.

[96] Maxwell, "The Formulation of Thomistic Simplicity," 395n56.

system does not have the resources to speak *meaningfully* and *intelligibly* about the Trinity.

This is an aspect of Aquinas's larger problem, which is shown clearly in Dolezal's work. Namely, the most significant critique of Aquinas's strong simplicity account of the Trinity is that biblical references are essentially non-existent in either Dolezal's major account of simplicity or his more specific account of the relation of simplicity and Trinitarianism.[97] While we do not seek simple text-proofs, it is central when speaking of God to reference what he has said concerning himself.[98] Because theology proper is not the primary fruit of natural theology, Scripture is essential. Dolezal's problem is reflective of the method of Aquinas. In a recent study on Aquinas's doctrine of simplicity, Maxwell argued that Thomas subscribed to *Compositional Constructionism*, which means "The use of Scripture and reason to formulate one's doctrine of God and/or one of his attributes, giving a methodological priority to reason."[99]

More specifically Maxwell claims that in Aquinas's system "Aristotelian substance metaphysics forges the conceptual tank that is *only later* filled with the content of divine revelation."[100] Maxwell explains this in three points, which align with figure 4.1: "Thomas (1) builds a philosophical construct for created reality out of the principles of Nature A (AFR), (2) builds a philosophical construct for divine reality through the principles of Natural Reason B (APR),

---

[97] Only Exodus 3:14 is referenced in the dissertation, but as we will show later, this passage defends aseity not strong simplicity. In his review of Dolezal's major work on simplicity, James Anderson noted, "In the book's index, 'Trinity' is conspicuous by its absence—likewise 'Bible' and 'Scripture.' Dolezal, *God without Parts*; James N. Anderson, "Review of God Without Parts by James Dolezal," *Themelios* 37, 2 (July 2012): 366.

[98] John Feinberg says, "In consulting various systematic theologies, one is hard pressed to find one that offers biblical support for the notion [of simplicity]." John S. Feinberg, *No One Like Him: The Doctrine of God* (Wheaton, IL: Crossway, 2006), 327.

[99] Maxwell, "The Formulation of Thomistic Simplicity," 372.

[100] Ibid., 380.

and (3) fills the second construct with theological data from Scripture (REV)."[101]

Scientific Tool	Nature A (AFR) (Affirmative Reason)	Nature B (APR) (Apophatic Reason)	Grace (REV) (Revelation)
Scientific Object	Creation	Creator A	Creator B
Scientific Method	*Separate essence* (Humanity [passive potential]) *from existence* (Aristotle's existence as a human [active embodiment of human substance])	*Conflate essence* (divinity) *with existence* (God [pure actuality]) to form DDS.	*Add* revealed truth (grace [e.g., the personal distinctions, freedom, love, covenantal qualities, etc.) *onto* reasoned truth (nature [e.g., simplicity, efficient causality, etc.])

Fig. 4.1. Aquinas's Epistemology[102]

Notice how Maxwell indicates that such a process produces conflicts in Aquinas's theology whereby natural reason through apophatic (reasoning by negation) process leads to one understanding of God (Creator A), while revelation leads to a second understanding of God (Creator B).[103] Most important to our purposes, Maxwell includes the personal distinctions as revealed and in potential conflict with Aquinas's apophatic reasoning.

[101] Ibid., 379–80.
[102] Reproduced by permission from Paul Maxwell, "The Formulation of Thomistic Simplicity," Table 1. © 2014 by Paul Maxwell.
[103] Maxwell further notes, "Thomas's use of use of REV creates a schism in his own doctrine of God, thereby creating the option to either (1) subsume the content of God's own self-revelation into the already extant, non-revelatory construct of divine essence (according to Aristotelian categories); or (2) simultaneously affirm irreconcilable doctrines of God (Creator A and Creator B), each defined according to their respective methods of construction." Ibid., 401.

We can see this pattern in Aquinas's treatment above. First, he begins with the construct of relations in creation. Second, he abstracts from that concept whatever is unbefitting of an Aristotelian conception of God. Third, he adds divine revelation of the persons, subsuming any theological analysis to the preconceived philosophical conclusions. He must do this because, in Aquinas's method, "in terms of man's ability to make metaphysical-theological formulations, man reaches God through reason before God reaches man through revelation."[104]

But the result of such a process makes it difficult to reconcile Scriptural descriptions of God's persons with Aquinas's account of personhood. For instance, what does it mean to say that a divine-notional relation came to earth and prayed to another divine-notional relation of opposition? Consider that the person of the Son "lifted up his eyes to heaven, and said, 'Father, the hour has come; glorify your Son that the Son may glorify you, since you have given him authority over all flesh, to give eternal life to all whom you have given him'" (John 17:1–2). While we would be wrong to claim a lack of unity between the Father and Son when considering these verses (John 10:30; 17:21), it is apparent that denying any *real* (i.e., non-notional) diversity of the persons is problematic as well.

Further, limiting the persons to mere relations is problematic. We agree with Robert Letham who argues,

> That the three persons of the Trinity are *not simply subsistent relations* is demonstrated by the Incarnation. In becoming flesh, the Son took a human nature into personal union, and that for eternity. This the Father and the Holy Spirit did not do. The Son is forever united to humanity, which is not the case with the Father and the Spirit. This points to the fact that the three are different from each other, irreducibly different, in ways we cannot understand. The Son is eternally

---

[104] Ibid., 377.

different from the Father and the Holy Spirit. Likewise, we can rightly conclude, the Holy Spirit is different from the Father and Son.[105]

Further, relations do not exist unless they relate something, and in this case, they relate *persons*. It does not appear one can reduce persons to relations, for relations presuppose persons. Frame makes a similar point:

> Relations do not subsist on their own, apart from the things they relate. Paternity doesn't exist by itself, apart from the persons (Father, Son) related to one another by paternity. And to suggest that relation is somehow a better term than person to designate the members of the Trinity is, I think, wrong. The persons are not 'really' relations, rather than true persons. They are persons standing in relation.[106]

Certainly Aquinas wants to maintain a diversity of persons.[107] Indeed, Dolezal critiques Frame for his assertion that "we should reject Aquinas's view that the three persons are distinct only notionally, only in our minds."[108] But as much as Aquinas's position makes the *persons distinct from the essence* only notionally in the divine mind, it is hard to indicate he has done any better. Further, while Dolezal sought to escape modalism by suggesting that the modes are in a non-creaturely sense, it is hard to see how that saves the position from modalism. If the difference in the persons from the essence is merely notional (whether in man or God), then there is no *real*

---

[105] Robert Letham, *The Holy Trinity: In Scripture, History, Theology, and Worship* (Phillipsburg, NJ: P&R Publishing, 2004), 382. Emphasis added.

[106] Frame, *Systematic Theology*, 486.

[107] He says, "those who follow the teaching of the catholic faith must hold that the relations in God are real." Aquinas, *On The Power of God*, 8.1.

[108] Dolezal, "Trinity, Simplicity and God's Personal Relations," 83n14; Frame, *The Doctrine of God*, 702.

diversity of the persons. Letham, while he does recognize Aquinas's distinction between real-notional and merely notional relations, concludes that Aquinas's "model does entail a strong bias in a modalist direction. Above all, his powerful doctrine of simplicity of God drastically inhibits his Trinitarianism." Further, "It becomes very difficult for him to conceive of three different persons while maintaining such a powerful idea of simplicity, for three persons imply complexity and counteract absolute simplicity." Letham concludes that such a problem is the result of the "conflict between an Aristotelian doctrine of God and a biblical one."[109]

It is clear why Aquinas holds such a position on the relation of the persons and the essence. Throughout the argument above, we noted that Aquinas assumes the Trinity must be of a particular sort because of the doctrine of simplicity.[110] And while simplicity itself is never mentioned in Scripture, we did argue that it *could be* understood as the result of biblical metaphysics. In other words, it is sometimes understood as the good and necessary consequence of biblical descriptions of God (Ex. 3:14). The central question, however, is whether Aquinas's strong simplicity account is what is required by biblical descriptions of God.

The chief text Aquinas uses to defend simplicity is Exodus 3:14, where God identifies himself to Moses. Aquinas says of simplicity and Exodus 3,

> This sublime truth Moses was taught by our Lord. When Moses asked our Lord: 'If the children of Israel say to me: what is his name? What shall I say to them?' The Lord replied: 'I AM WHO AM.... You shall say to the children of Israel: HE WHO IS has sent me to you' (Exod. 3:13, 14). By this our Lord showed that his own proper name is HE WHO IS. Now, names have been devised to signify

---

[109] Letham, *The Holy Trinity*, 236.
[110] Aquinas, *Summa Theologica*, 28.2; Aquinas, *On The Power of God*, 8.2.

the natures or essences of things. It remains, then, that the divine being is God's essence or nature.[111]

While such an analysis of Exodus 3:14 does justice to the character of the text as a metaphysic proclamation, the way that Thomas uses the text is without exegetical warrant. Maxwell notes, "This is philosophical eisegesis.... Thomas's use of Scripture in this instance is as an adjunct to his philosophy, not an authority."[112] John Wippel agrees, noting the unique character of Aquinas's proposal:

> As for Aquinas's view that esse or the act of being is the act of all acts and the perfection of all perfections, I am aware of no explicit prior philosophical (or theological) source for this. It has been suggested by Gilson (and others) that Thomas took this notion from Scripture at Exodus 3:14 where, according to the Latin Vulgate, God refers to himself as *Ego sum qui sum*. I would rather argue that it is precisely because Aquinas had already worked out philosophically his understanding of esse or the *actus essendi* as intrinsic causality that he could then claim to recognize it in the text of Exodus. For instance, in SCG I, c. 22, which Gilson cites, Thomas first offers a series of philosophical arguments to prove that in God essence and esse are identical. Only at the end of the chapter does he refer to the text from Exodus for additional confirmation. And this is in accord with his usual practice in the first three books of SCG in which, as he writes at Bk I, c. 9, he intends to pursue by following the way of reason those things that faith professes and human reason can investigate about God.[113]

---

[111] Aquinas, *Summa Contra Gentiles*, 1.22; Aquinas, *Summa Theologica*, 1.13.11.

[112] Maxwell, "The Formulation of Thomistic Simplicity," 383.

[113] John Wippel, *Metaphysical Themes in Thomas Aquinas II* (Washington, DC: Catholic University of America Press, 2007), 281.

What does Exodus 3:14 teach? While we cannot develop it at length here, the central teaching is that God is *a se*. Oliphint offers an insightful analysis of the text and concludes with this summary: "This revelation in Exodus tells us . . . Yahweh is *a se*. He is the 'I am.' He depends on nothing to be who he is. Not only so, but his name attaches to his character in such a way that there is no possible way that he could be anyone else, or that he could give up who and what he is."[114] Using the categories developed earlier, Maxwell suggests that "the DDS is pure APR, conceived on the basis of Aristotelian metaphysics (AFR), but the doctrine of aseity is a positive statement about God's being that he gives about himself (REV). Whereas the DDS is a list of metaphysical redactions (APR), the doctrine of aseity is God's metaphysical self-attestation (REV)."[115]

Thus, what Exodus indicates is *aseity* not *simplicity* as such. Of course, *aseity* may imply simplicity, but that must be established and not merely assumed. Here we will argue that aseity does not require the strong account of simplicity, but it does seem to require a moderate simplicity account. To such an account we will turn in the next chapter.

---

[114] Oliphint, *God with Us*, 61–62.
[115] Maxwell, "The Formulation of Thomistic Simplicity," 385.

5

Perichoretic-Simplicity

Moderate Simplicity and Perichoresis

Having argued that the strong account of simplicity is not compatible with Scriptural expressions of Trinitarian doctrine, we can now begin to show how a perichoretic form of simplicity can provide all the resources desired by the strong simplicity account without subverting theology to philosophy. In this way, we are seeking to embrace Compositional Receptionism, which Maxwell defines as "The use of Scripture and [scripturally informed] reason to formulate one's doctrine of God and/or one of his attributes, giving a methodological priority to Scripture."[1]

Perichoretic-Simplicity Maintains Trinitarian Revelation

The key advantage to this model is that it allows us to begin with the revelation of God.[2] While Aquinas, as a believer in

---

[1] We add *scripturally informed* to emphasize that reason must be understood in light of what Scripture says concerning it. Paul Maxwell, "The Formulation of Thomistic Simplicity: Mapping Aquinas's Method for Configuring God's Essence," *Journal of the Evangelical Theological Society* 57, 2 (June 2014): 372.

[2] On this basis, Frame begins his treatment by saying, "I believe that the truth in these classic treatments like that of Aquinas may more easily be ascertained, stated, and argued from a biblical standpoint than from the standpoint of scholasticism's own natural theology." John M. Frame, *Systematic Theology:*

Christ, was incredibly perceptive, he often allowed philosophical constructs to guide his theology.³ Oliphint, amidst a critique of Thomistic theology, confirms that "the *fundamental* interpretive context with respect to the knowledge of God is (the content of God's) revelation rather than abstract being or the combination of being and essence."⁴ By developing his theology in light of his philosophy, Aquinas presented simplicity in light of Aristotelian and neo-Platonic concerns.⁵

The present proposal, in contrast, seeks to look first at the revelation of God and afterward to compare the results with potential philosophical constructions. This allows Scripture to stand as the authority, while also providing the avenue for God to express himself in ways beyond our ability to reason (though not ultimately unreasonable). If we were to begin with philosophical constructs, then Christian paradox (which is necessarily present due to the Creator/creature distinction) would potentially be eliminated in favor of the creature's autonomous paradigm.⁶

How does the present model start with Scripture? Namely, by

An Introduction to Christian Belief (Phillipsburg, NJ: P&R Publishing, 2013), 428–29.

³ See Van Til's analysis of Thomas's philosophical method: Cornelius Van Til, "Nature and Scripture," in *The Articles of Cornelius Van Til*, ed. Eric H. Sigward, Logos Digital Collection. (New York, NY: Labels Army Company, 1997), 2.3; Cornelius Van Til, "Confessing Jesus Christ," in *Scripture and Confession*, ed. John H. Skilton (Nutley, NJ: Presbyterian and Reformed, 1973), 217–46.

⁴ K. Scott Oliphint, *Reasons for Faith: Philosophy in the Service of Theology* (Phillipsburg, NJ: P&R Publishing, 2006), 114.

⁵ Two additional resources help show the influence of Aristotelian and Platonic philosophy on Aquinas's simplicity model. Barry D. Smith, *The Oneness and Simplicity of God* (Eugene, OR: Wipf and Stock, 2013), 23–56; Frederik Gerrit Immink, *Divine Simplicity* (Kampen, Netherlands: J. H. Kok, 1987), 36–73.

⁶ Not every element of simplicity is foreign to Scripture. Some of the constructions are necessary on the basis of biblical revelation. Here we are simply arguing for scriptural primacy.

beginning with the revelation of God as a Trinity of persons in perichoretic relation. The perichoretic relationship is clearly an implication of John's language in his gospel (John 10:30, 38; 14:9–11, 18, 20; 17:21) and is an inference from the mutuality of God's actions (Gen. 1; John 1:3; Col. 1:16; Ps. 104:30).[7] If the exegetical basis for perichoresis is correct, then we have a model by which both the unity and diversity of God's persons can be maintained.

Letham, in his recent exposition of the doctrine of the Trinity, noted five essential elements that must be maintained in light of biblical exegesis: the three persons

1. Are equally ultimate with the being of God;
2. Are identical in being;
3. Mutually indwell one another in perichoresis;
4. Are irreducibly different from one another;
5. Are irreversibly ordered according to their appropriate dispositions.[8]

Aquinas, by uneven emphasis on the second element, did not do justice to the fourth, but if we embrace the fullness of the third point, the others follow. Perichoresis maintains (1) by showing that there the three cannot be understood without the one, nor the one without the three. They are equally ultimate. In this sense, Gregory Nanzianzen, the first to develop the doctrine of perichoresis for the Trinitarian persons, could say,

> No sooner do I conceive of the one than I am illuminated by the splendor of the three; no sooner do I distinguish them than I am carrried back to the one. When I think of any one of the three I think of him as the whole, and my eyes are

---

[7] For a further development of the biblical case for perichoresis, see, John M. Frame, *The Doctrine of God* (Phillipsburg, NJ: P&R Publishing, 2002), 693–96.

[8] Robert Letham, *The Holy Trinity: In Scripture, History, Theology, and Worship* (Phillipsburg, NJ: P&R Publishing, 2004), 381–83.

filled, and the greater part of what I am thinking escapes me. I cannot grasp the greatness of that one so as to attribute a greater greatness to the rest. When I contemplate the three together, I see but one torch, and cannot divide or measure out the undivided light.⁹

Because perichoresis is consonant with the equal ultimacy of both the unity and diversity of God's persons and essence, (2) and (4) are maintained. Of course, these appear antithetical to one another. How can the persons be described as identical in being and yet irreducibly different as well? Van Til helps: "The persons are distinct from the Divine Essence not *modaliter*—Sabellianism, nor *essentialiter*—Tritheism, nor *formaliter* or *ratione*, but *realiter*, which can have meaning for us only by negation of the others because admittedly *we here peer into mystery*."¹⁰ In other words, it is precisely at this point that we should keep the united essence and the distinct persons as limiting concepts on one another.¹¹ We must not allow the united essence to overshadow the distinct persons, but we also cannot allow the distinct persons to overshadow the united essence.¹² Though

---

⁹ Gregory Nanzianzen, "Orations," in *Nicene and Post Nicene Fathers*, ed. Kevin Knight, Philip Schaff, and Henry Wace, trans. Charles Gordon Brown and James Edward Swallow, vol. 7 (Buffalo, NY: Christian Literature Publishing, 1894), 40.41, http://www.newadvent.org/fathers/3102.htm.

¹⁰ Cornelius Van Til, "The Will in Its Theological Relations," in *Unpublished Manuscripts of Cornelius Van Til*, ed. Eric H. Sigward, Logos Digital Collection. (New York, NY: Labels Army Company, 1997).

¹¹ While Van Til takes the phrase, *limiting concept*, from Kant, he recontextualizes the phrase to speak of concepts that balance other concepts. For instance, while one may inaccurately infer from God's love that he will save all people, a balanced approach will show that God's love is a love that is in harmony with *justice*. For an exposition of Van Til's use of limiting concepts see, John M. Frame, *Cornelius Van Til: An Analysis of His Thought* (Phillipsburg, NJ: P&R Publishing, 1995), 165–69.

¹² We have not shown the relationship between perichoresis and (5) above. We will do so below, but for now it is enough to say that perichoresis must be understood in light of (5), and that, because of the nature of the relations as

ultimately mysterious, Van Til's key to maintaining "both identity and distinction," that is, both unity in the diversity and the diversity in the unity, is perichoresis.[13]

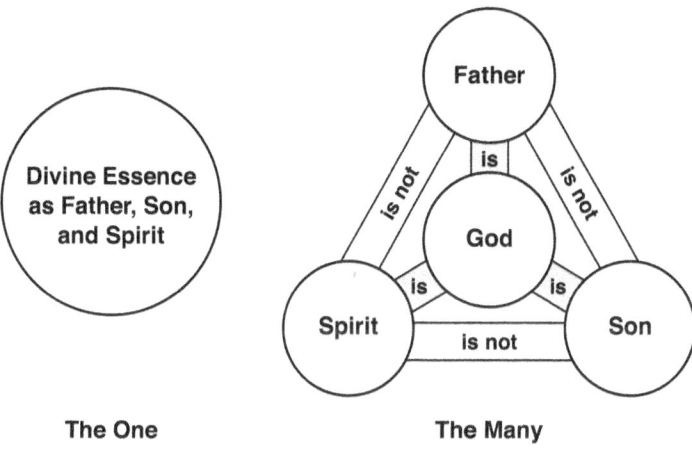

Fig. 5.1. Equal Ultimacy of the One and Many

If the unity and diversity of the *persons* and *essence* is partially understood through perichoresis, is it a stretch to understand the unity and diversity of God's *attributes* and *essence* in a similar fashion? Oliphint appears to be congenial to such a claim: "Arguing from the greater to the lesser, since orthodox theology has consistently maintained that the one, simple God is distinctly (i.e., differently) Father, Son, and Holy Spirit, it is no theological stretch to maintain as well that the real distinctions present in God's character and attributes are, themselves, the one and simple God as well."[14] What does he mean by *arguing from the greater to the lesser*? Perhaps he means to

---

eternal, the relations do not do damage to the unity and diversity of the essence and persons.

[13] Cornelius Van Til, *The Great Debate Today* (Nutley, NJ: P&R Publishing, 1970), chap. 5,E,1,b.

[14] K. Scott Oliphint, *God with Us: Divine Condescension and the Attributes of God* (Wheaton, IL: Crossway, 2011), 249n53.

say from the more definitively revealed to the less revealed or from the clearly stated to the implied. If so, he is expressing what we are seeking to say here. Revelation should be the primary method of predication concerning God's nature.

Thus, the strength of this model is that it is more explicitly biblical in that it seeks to model the unity and diversity of the attributes on the analogous relation of unity and diversity in the persons. This is appropriate because we are given no other model of relating unity and diversity *in Scripture*.

Perichoretic-Simplicity allows for Proper Predication

Another way the model is helpful is that it resolves a second problem present in Aquinas's model; namely, the present model allows for proper predication of God. On Aquinas's notion of simplicity, predications of God are properly false (non-literal).[15] Aquinas maintains this position for the following reasons. First, to say that God is good is to declare both a predicate and a subject, but according to Thomistic simplicity, one cannot distinguish a predicate and subject in reference to God. Goodness, when stated as a predicate toward a subject, is distinguishable from God and, therefore, would be a *part* of God.[16] Second, Aquinas desired to preserve God's independence. If a predicate could be properly stated concerning God, that predicate could be distinguished from him, raising the question concerning the derivation of the property/attribute. Finally, Aquinas was particularly careful not to ascribe

---

[15] Again, Aquinas says, "God, however, as considered in himself, is altogether one and simple, yet our intellect knows him by different conceptions because it cannot see him as he is in himself." Thomas Aquinas, *Summa Theologica* (New York, NY: Cosimo, 2013), 13.12.

[16] It is here that Aquinas introduced his *rei significandi* and *modus significandi* distinction. The former referred to the concept being discussed (e.g., goodness), which is properly attributed to God, and the latter is the way in which that concept is communicated, which is properly false or non-literal. These provided the path by which analogical predication might be made under his system. Ibid., 13.3.

creaturely properties to God,[17] and univocal predication appeared to do precisely that.

The perichoretic-simplicity model allows proper predication. Scripture never struggles to speak of the multiplicity of persons of the Godhead. For example, it is not improper (or non-literal) to speak of the Father, for through the Father that we know the Godhead. The same can be said of the Spirit and Son. As argued earlier, our knowledge of God is knowledge of the Father through the Son by the Spirit. Thus, it is through the multiplicity of persons that we know the fullness of the Godhead.

In the same way, it is not illegitimate to speak of God's power, love, grace, etc., for it is through these that God reveals himself. The equal ultimacy of the one and many indicates that the many (attributes/persons) can be spoken of properly despite the fact that they are reflective of one (God). Just as the one (God) can be spoken of properly despite the fact the he is many (attributes/persons). Further, since Scripture does speak of God's goodness, righteousness, wrath, mercy, and other attributes, then these are properly predicated of him. Revelation trumps philosophical constructs.

In a similar fashion, Charles Hodge argued for true predication of God and warned against the dangers of the strong account of simplicity. While Hodge did not provide the resources to fashion a complete alternate conception, he recognized that the classical account of simplicity had the potential to destroy man's knowledge of God.[18] He further believed there were two options before him. Should he follow a metaphysical construct or revelation? He chose the latter:

---

[17] Though he did not maintain the Creator/creature distinction as fervently as the doctrine requires. Oliphint, *Reasons for Faith*, 96.

[18] "To say, as the schoolmen, and so many even of Protestant theologians, ancient and modern, were accustomed to say, that the divine attributes differ only in name, or in our conceptions, or in their effects, is to destroy all true knowledge of God." Charles Hodge, *Systematic Theology*, vol. 1 (New York, NY: Scribner, 1873), 371.

> We are not to give up the conviction that God is really in himself what he reveals himself to be, to satisfy any *metaphysical speculations* as to the difference between essence and attribute in an infinite Being. The attributes of God, therefore, are not merely different conceptions in our minds, but different modes in which *God reveals himself to his creatures* (or to himself).[19]

While Hodge did recognize the motive for Thomas's account of analogous speaking according to simplicity,[20] he believed that in strong simplicity speculation had usurped revelation. Frame follows Hodge in this assessment, arguing that when Scripture presents God as having different attributes, they are real distinctions, which truly describe God. This is why Frame maintains that while God is simple, he is also complex. Complexity, Frame maintains, is not the opposite of simplicity. Rather, it is a recognition that within God's simple being there are true distinctions, which align with the way that he has revealed himself to creatures.[21] These distinctions are analogous to the distinctions found within the persons of the Trinity.

Ultimately, the reason Frame believes in the real distinction of attributes is because God reveals himself that way, and Frame believes that God as Lord is not impeded by human language in revealing himself:[22] "If God is transcendent as the Lord, involved

---

[19] Ibid., 1:374. Emphasis added.

[20] "There is indeed danger in either extreme; danger of degrading God in our thoughts, by reducing him to the standard of our nature, and danger of denying him as he is revealed. In our day, and among educated men, and especially among students of philosophy, the latter danger is by far the greater of the two." Ibid.

[21] Frame, *The Doctrine of God*, 227.

[22] Frame is following Hodge, who argues that a strong account of simplicity implies a failure of special, general, and existential revelation: "If in God eternity is identical with knowledge, knowledge with power, power with ubiquity, and ubiquity with holiness, we are using words without meaning when we attribute any perfection to God. We must, therefore, either give up the attempt

in our history and revealing himself in his Word, then we can make the distinctions he himself has revealed to us."[23] The following quote indicates Frame's reticence to accept Thomistic analogy and also his reason for rejecting it:

> [Aquinas] assumes that human language is fit in itself only to deal with the natural world. 'Univocally,' literally, it refers only to this world. To make it apply to God, we must adjust it, twist it, use it in extraordinary ways ('analogously'). On a biblical basis, however, we need to affirm that although God is very different from us, we can speak of him in very ordinary language. God made language so that we could speak, not only of the world and to each other, but also of God and to him. And he has given us his word in Scripture, which guides us in the use of our language in all these areas. When Scripture says 'God is love' (1 John 4:8) it describes a love that is greater than we can imagine. But I don't believe it uses the term 'love' in a non-literal sense. In other cases, too, biblical language about God is clearly univocal. When Scripture says that God is 'not a liar (as Titus 1:2)' it distinguishes God from literal liars, not analogous or figurative ones.[24]

A major point should be made in connection with Frame's quote above. Taken alone, this quote could indicate a rejection of analogy and a complete acceptance of univocity of predication by Frame. Such an understanding would be mistaken. Frame upholds *complete*

---

to determine the divine attributes from our speculative idea of an infinite essence, or renounce all knowledge of God, and all faith in the revelation of himself, which he has made in the constitution of our nature, in the external world, and in his Word. Knowledge is no more identical with power in God than it is in us." Hodge, *Systematic Theology*, 1:372.

[23] Frame, *Systematic Theology*, 476.

[24] John M. Frame, *A History of Western Philosophy and Theology* (Phillipsburg, NJ: P&R Publishing, 2015), chap. 4.

analogy and literal (what he calls univocal) predication.[25] The key to understanding how he can maintain both is by understanding the distinction between Aquinas's analogy and Van Til's analogy.

Frame argues that Aquinas's epistemological concept of analogy is built upon the metaphysical structure of the analogy of being. As such, language used by beings on the same level of being can be said to be literal (i.e., univocal),[26] but when referencing one on a higher level, the language must be analogous.[27] This analogous language is properly false, though it does communicate something of the truth (non-literal truth). Van Til's concept of analogy is quite distinct, however. For Van Til, analogy maintains the absoluteness of the Creator/creature distinction. There is no analogy of being in which God is simply a greater manifestation than creatures. Instead, man is the ectype of the divine archetype. The analogy exists, not through a univocal concept of being, but through the *imaging* relationship between God and creation. Gilbert Weaver is correct, then, to say that for Van Til, "analogy applies not to terms, but to the overall process of human thought: man is God's created analogue in both his being and his knowledge."[28]

---

[25] Analogy is necessary for Frame because, "Our knowledge is the knowledge of creatures, which receives the reality and interpretation of its objects from God. There is no continuum between God's knowledge and ours. There is no midpoint, no ladder to heaven for us to ascend to gain a knowledge that is increasingly divine." Frame, *The Doctrine of God*, 218.

[26] Frame says of Aquinas that in "His short early work, *On Being and Essence* . . . there is no hint of any doctrine of analogy, no suggestion that terms like essence and *esse* apply to God in any way other than univocally. So in Aquinas's treatment of essence, we lose the sense of divine transcendence that permeates his doctrine of analogy." Ibid., 224.

[27] Frame says, "In Aquinas's view of language, 'univocal' is more or less equivalent to 'literal,' and 'equivocal' to 'merely metaphorical.' 'Analogical' language is figurative language, but somehow closer to the literal than equivocal language is." He then states in a footnote, "I am making vague distinctions. I don't believe that his own account can be made more precise than this." Frame, *Cornelius Van Til*, 91.

[28] Gilbert Weaver, "Man: Analogue of God," in *Jerusalem and Athens: Critical*

Frame, following Weaver, suggests that the distinction between Aquinas and Van Til's concepts of analogy is so significant that Van Til may have been clearer by not using the term *analogy*. What is most significant about the distinction, however, is that Aquinas's position requires non-literal predication while Frame argues that Van Til's system of analogy does not require it. Further, Frame argues that Van Til's understanding of the anthropomorphic nature of God's revelation lends more credibility to some measure of univocity in predication than for no measure of univocity.[29]

By maintaining analogy in a Van Tillian sense, Frame is not required to call language Scripture uses entirely non-literal. Because of his adherence to analogy through the archetype/ectype distinction, Frame does not believe that literal statements about God disrepute his transcendence. Consequently, "God's essence is not some dark, unrevealed entity behind God's revealed character. Rather, God's revelation tells us his essence. It tells us what he really and truly is."[30] And as much as Scripture speaks of God as having various attributes, these are *true* statements, indicating the reality of the distinctions.

Before turning to another advantage of the perichoretic-simplicity model, we should note that such a position not only allows for proper predication, but it also indicates the way in which progressive knowledge of God in eternity may be gained. In other words, the perichoretic-simplicity model integrates the infinity of God in such a way that, while maintaining his simplicity, it allows the human mind to be open to further understanding of God. In the end, the

---

Discussions on the Theology and Apologetics of Cornelius Van Til, ed. E. R. Geehan (Nutley, NJ: Presbyterian and Reformed, 1971), 327.

[29] Frame said that he asked Van Til about whether human language concerning God was literal, "and his reply was that he had never thought much about it and had not formulated a position on the question. Evidently it was not an issue he considered important to his epistemology...I suspect that Van Til held...that there are degrees (and perhaps kinds) of literality and no such thing as purely literal language." Frame, *Cornelius Van Til*, 94.

[30] Frame, *Systematic Theology*, 431.

strong account of simplicity ends in ignorance and stifles the progressive knowledge of God.[31] On that model one can say that God is love, but he or she does not *really* know what that love is. On the perichoretic-simplicity model, we know what that love is (granted that we do not know it exhaustively or as God knows it).[32] Bosserman draws our attention to the practical import of this insight:

> Because God is infinite, believers know that the future will yield new and surprising expressions of the divine nature. And yet, because God is infinite in the sense that every attribute characterizes the others, believers may rest assured that future disclosures will only enhance, rather than contradict their present knowledge of God's power, goodness, truth, etc. as revealed directly in the written Scriptures.[33]

Rather than shutting the door on future learning by arguing that our language does not speak *properly* of God, this account provides the

---

[31] Frame says, "Van Til is not calling us, as did Aquinas's doctrine of analogy, to *greater agnosticism*, but to greater confidence. He is not trying to say that apparently literal expressions are really figurative, but that apparently figurative expressions contain some element of literal truth." Frame, *Cornelius Van Til*, 93–94. Emphasis added.

[32] The difference between God's love and man's love is not only of degree. God's love is infinite and essential to him. This understanding parallels Frame's conception of God's knowledge. The difference between man's knowledge and God's knowledge is not merely the amount of knowledge (though that is certainly present); rather, it is the way in which God knows. God knows by knowing himself. Thus, man and God can have the same object of thought, yet there remains a distinction: God knows the fact (e.g., rose) by knowing himself (as well as by knowing it infinitely), while man knows it through revelation by creaturely senses and reason. In a similar fashion, man has an attribute similar to God's essential attributes (e.g., love) by means of creation, while God has that attribute in himself eternally. John M. Frame, *The Doctrine of the Knowledge of God* (Phillipsburg, NJ: Presbyterian and Reformed, 1987), 20–40.

[33] Brant Bosserman, "The Trinity and the Vindication of Christian Paradox: An Interpretation and Refinement of the Theological Apologetic of Cornelius Van Til" (PhD Diss., University of Bangor, 2011), §186.

avenue by which the knowledge of God can ever-increase without exhausting the character of God. Further, it provides the boundaries by which we can be assured that our knowledge today is true, while incomplete. Once we understand that each of God's attributes is infinitely interrelated (analogous to the infinite relation of the persons), we have an infinite field of exploration which eternity cannot exhaust.

Perichoretic-Simplicity Provides the Basis for Unity

Perichoresis assumes a genuine otherness, a genuine complexity in God. Immediately this challenges the strong account of simplicity, for if everything in God's essence is identical, then there is no true multiplicity. Indeed, there cannot be such multiplicity. However, we will argue that even Dolezal, in his defense of God's Trinitarian simplicity, could not help but posit *some form* of non-identity or true complexity in God:

> While each person can be said to be divine he cannot be said to be the other persons.... Since the divinity is communicable to all three and the unique personal relations are not, the notion of the divine nature is not adequately comprehended in the consideration of any single divine person. Another way of expressing this is to say that the Father is wholly divine yet divinity is not wholly the Father, and so forth for the Son and Spirit.[34]

The implication is clear—the Father is *not identical* with the Son because each has *unique personal relations*. Further, the Father is not *entirely* identical with the essence, for identity indicates an equal relationship from both sides (A=B *and* B=A). How does Dolezal

---

[34] James E. Dolezal, "Trinity, Simplicity and the Status of God's Personal Relations," *International Journal of Systematic Theology* 16, 1 (January 2014): 95. Emphasis added.

seek to relieve this tension? This is where he posits the non-creaturely modal distinction. By means of such a modal analysis, he suggests that the distinction between the personal relations and the essence is not real but is in our way of speaking/knowing.[35] Thus, "We cannot comprehend a substance so perfectly in act that it is really identical with its mode(s) of subsistence, much less speak adequately of such a being."[36] Here, we are face to face with the dual problems of (1) non-proper predication in Aquinas's system and (2) the elevation of a philosophical construct above revelation.

While it would be wrong to claim that the differences between the persons in Aquinas's system are merely notional (in light of his own claims), a stronger claim is actually being made about the essence. Namely, we can't know anything properly about the persons and their relation to the essence *other than that the distinctions cannot be real*. But clearly, as we saw in Van Til's statement above, we must posit a real distinction even if we can't fully express how those real distinctions exist. Indeed, we must posit the real distinctions, for revelation makes it clear that they exist. Further, we must posit some distinctions if we are to take seriously Dolezal's own comment that "the Father is wholly divine yet divinity is not wholly the Father." Put differently, *A is wholly B, yet B is not wholly A*.

Perichoresis provides an alternative rationale for *identity through unity*. In other words, one might ask how to provide for the unity of the persons if strong simplicity is denied. Perichoresis provides the way. The persons are truly one essence in three persons, coalescing through infinite mutual interpenetration. They are not identical *in every way*; rather, they are truly distinct yet truly one. There is an equal ultimacy of both the one (essence) and the many (persons).

---

[35] "God's persons and his nature may appear to undermine the strong classical account of simplicity, it has traditionally been argued by simplicitists that it does not since it is *not in fact real*." Here it must be remembered that Dolezal is arguing that the relations are real, but he is denying that the relations are really distinct from the essence. Ibid. Emphasis added.

[36] Ibid., 96.

What does it mean to say that they are not identical in every way? It would seem that something that is identical with something else is identical in every way, but the type of identity expressed through perichoresis is a *sui generis* form of identity unique to the Godhead. Through mutual interpenetration, the persons coalesce having in the essence everything of the Godhead. In this sense, they are identical in the person of the Godhead (the one). Nevertheless, as much as they are distinct in their persons, they each have unique attributes not expressed in relation to the other persons. Thus, we can say that the Father is God, the Son is God, and the Spirit is God, but the Spirit is not the Son, the Son is not the Spirit, and so forth (the many).[37] Again, this is excellently displayed in the classic image of the Trinity (figure 5.1).

In holding to the equal ultimacy of the one and many, Frame believes that Aquinas both went too far and did not go far enough. He went too far by allowing the persons to be swallowed into the essence, arguing that the distinctions were merely modal. In this way, Aquinas did not give justice to the equal ultimacy of the many.

But Aquinas did not go far enough either, and so brought the equal ultimacy of the one into question. Because the three persons are one God, each attribute of the persons applies to the entirety of the Godhead. So Frame could not say with Aquinas that "the notion of the divine nature is not adequately comprehended in the consideration of any single divine person."[38] Frame believes that perichoresis demands that any attribute of the individual persons is an attribute of the united essence. Frame realizes that personal properties are often spoken of as distinct from attributes in the history of Trinitarian discussions, yet Frame says, "properties are attributes

---

[37] As Calvin says, "I wish, indeed, that . . . all would concur in the belief that the Father, Son, and Spirit, are one God, and yet that the Son is not the Father, nor the Spirit the Son, but that each has his peculiar subsistence." John Calvin, *Institutes of the Christian Religion: 1536 Edition*, trans. Ford Battles (Grand Rapids, MI: Eerdmans, 1995), 1.13.5.

[38] Dolezal, "Trinity, Simplicity and God's Personal Relations," 95.

grammatically and metaphysically. Certainly Father, Son, and Spirit are *beings*, subjects of predication, just as is the Godhead as a whole. . . . And the personal properties are predicates of those substantival subjects, attributes of the persons."[39] By maintaining the equal ultimacy of the one and many, Frame believes it is necessary to argue that one can predicate truly of the unity or diversity of the Godhead. And through perichoresis, what is truly predicated of the persons applies to the divine nature. So Frame can say, with Scripture, "God is a Father (Mal. 1:6; John 5:18; 1 John 3:1), a Son (John 1:1, 14, 18), and a Spirit (John 4:24)."[40]

Such a position does cause some difficulty. For instance, did the Father share in the suffering on the cross? Frame addresses this issue asking, "Are these experiences only of the Son, and not of the Father? The persons of the Trinity are not divided; rather, the Son is in the Father and the Father in the Son (John 10:38; 14:10–11, 20; 17:21). Theologians have called this mutual indwelling *circumcessio* or *circumincessio*."[41] But Frame continues, noting the necessary distinctions: "The Son was crucified; the Father was not. Indeed during the crucifixion, the Father forsook the Son as he bore the sins of his people (Matt. 27:46)." Frame later asks, "Was the Father, nevertheless, still 'in' the Son at that moment of separation? . . . I have not heard any scripturally persuasive [answer]. But we must do justice to both the continuity and the discontinuity between the persons of the Trinity."[42] We might suggest that, in *consideration of their unity* through interpenetration, there is nothing unique to any of the persons, yet in *consideration of their diversity*, each has distinctions not shared by the others. While such a statement appears contradictory, we should embrace with all gusto the apparent paradox in order to maintain revealed truth. In other words, the two limiting concepts that must be kept

---

[39] Frame, *Systematic Theology*, 488.
[40] Ibid.
[41] Frame, *The Doctrine of God*, 613.
[42] Ibid.

in balance here are that Father shares in everything of the Son (John 10:38; 14:10–11, 20; 17:21), yet the Father did not die on the cross (Matt 27:46).

Frame asks more generally, "How can the three persons be distinct from each other when each is coterminous with the whole divine being?" He answers by reference to simplicity: "I believe that my account of divine simplicity, in which the identity of everything divine with the divine being indicates (rather than negates) the complexity of this being, is of some help."[43] In other words, Frame uses the concept of simplicity to describe the relation of unity and diversity of the persons just as he uses the unity and diversity of the persons to describe the concept of simplicity. But how does his concept of simplicity help? Namely, by suggesting that God is irreducibly united-in-diversity: "That God is a Father, a Son, and a Spirit indicates real complexity in God's nature, a nature that encompasses real distinctions. . . . Each says something different, something distinct, about God. . . . But we do not know the precise nature of that complexity-in-unity."[44] Speaking of such a mystery, Frame argues that it is not irrational even if we cannot fully comprehend it. God has only given a glimpse of his inner life; a glimpse that, while ultimately mysterious, must not be denied. In the end, Frame argues that theologians should "acknowledge our ignorance of the precise distinction between substance and person in God and of the precise interactions between these."[45]

In this light, we might describe the difference between Frame's and Aquinas's conceptions of God's nature as a difference in the place of mystery. Both men recognize the necessity of mystery in the doctrine of God, yet they place the mystery in different places. For Aquinas, who starts with reason before revelation, the mystery is

---

[43] Frame, *Systematic Theology*, 488–89.
[44] Ibid., 489.
[45] Ibid.

that a being, who is totally and irreducibly one, could be triune. This results in damage being done to both the diversity and unity of God. For Frame, who starts with the revelation of God, the mystery is that a being who is irreducibly described as *both* one and many, could in fact be *both* one and many. Frame's position leads to problems of paradox on both sides. On the one hand, Frame must maintain the distinctions even in consideration of the essence,[46] and on the other

---

[46] Perhaps the most controversial way Frame has done this is by suggesting that triunity is an attribute of God. Frame's claim is given in opposition to Aquinas' view that simplicity applies only to the divine nature and not the persons. However, Frame argues that the persons and essence cannot be separated so neatly, ultimately arguing, "the persons are essential to God's being, just as essential as any attribute. It is not evident to me why 'triunity' should not be considered an attribute of God along with the others. Certainly it is true to say that God's being is triune." Ibid., 431. Bruce McCormack suggests that Frame's attribution of triunity is problematic, because it does not seem to apply to the persons individually. Thus, it is an abstraction that is inapplicable to the personal God of Scripture. Bruce McCormack, *Engaging the Doctrine of God: Contemporary Protestant Perspectives* (Grand Rapids, MI: Baker, 2008), 178n22. Frame's response should be clear from what has been said previously. All of the attributes of the persons apply to the essence and vice versa. The Father is triune in that through the Father one recognizes the fullness of the divine being. Thus, the Father perichoretically exemplifies the Father, Son, and Spirit, and, therefore, can be called triune. Such an ascription is not abstract. Michael Horton argues against Frame's position by suggesting that a hard distinction between the essence and persons was what settled the controversy between the Cappadocians and the Arians. By positing a distinction in the persons *and not in the essence*, one could maintain the deity of the Son. Michael S. Horton, *The Christian Faith: A Systematic Theology for Pilgrims on the Way* (Grand Rapids, MI: Zondervan, 2011), 285n40. However, it is not clear that such a hard distinction is necessary. If, as Frame argues, God is irreducibly one and many, then the Son is truly distinct from the Father yet is wholly one with him. The problem Horton provides is only a problem if one does not maintain God's nature as equally ultimate in unity and diversity.

One potentially problematic interpretation of Frame's attribution of triunity to the Godhead would be to say that the persons become attributes, but Frame is clear that the persons are distinct from the attributes. The personal comes before the impersonal, and only persons can have attributes. Viewing

hand, he must maintain the unity even when considering the persons. In this light, Frame could argue that a true Trinitarian position might sometimes be confused with both modalism (because of the insistence on the ultimacy of the one) and tritheism (because of the insistence on the ultimacy of the many).

By positing such a unique form of identity, we can maintain the Scriptural ascription of both *one God* that is truly *three persons*. Further, because of the analogy present between the unity and diversity of the persons and the unity and diversity of the attributes, the same could apply to the attributes. Each attribute is exhaustively representative of God such that there is a full expression of divinity in the attribute. Nevertheless, as considered in its diversity, these attributes are distinct from one another. Thus, one could say that God is love, God is omnipotent, God is wisdom, and yet still reject the fact that love is in all ways identical with omnipotence, etc. (figure 5.2).[47] In this way, we can maintain the equal ultimacy of the one and many of the attributes, following Van Til who spoke of the "God of the historic Christian creeds who is ultimately simple and whose simplicity is *fully and eternally exhausted by his diversity*."[48]

---

triunity this way has the effect that all of God's attributes are exhaustively and personally triune (because all of the attributes are descriptive of the others). Thus, God's wisdom is triune, his omnipotence is triune, etc. Frame's emphasis on triunity as an attribute may derive from Bavinck, who said, "It belongs to God's very essence to be triune." Perhaps it should not be surprising that Bavinck also argues for "absolute unity as well as absolute diversity" in God. Herman Bavinck, *Reformed Dogmatics*, ed. John Bolt, trans. John Vriend (Grand Rapids, MI: Baker, 2003), 2.303, 332.

[47] But even while considering the real distinctions, we are drawn back to considering their real unity *in the person of God*: "Does God's simplicity, then, mean that his eternity is the same as his love, or that his knowledge and justice are identical? The attributes do differ in perspective and emphasis, but they ultimately coalesce. Yes, God's eternity is the same as his love: for his eternity is the eternal existence of a loving person, and his love is the love of that eternal person." Frame, *The Doctrine of God*, 288.

[48] Cornelius Van Til, "A Sacramental Universe," *Westminster Theological Journal* 2, 2 (Spring 1940): 183.

Perichoretic-Simplicity

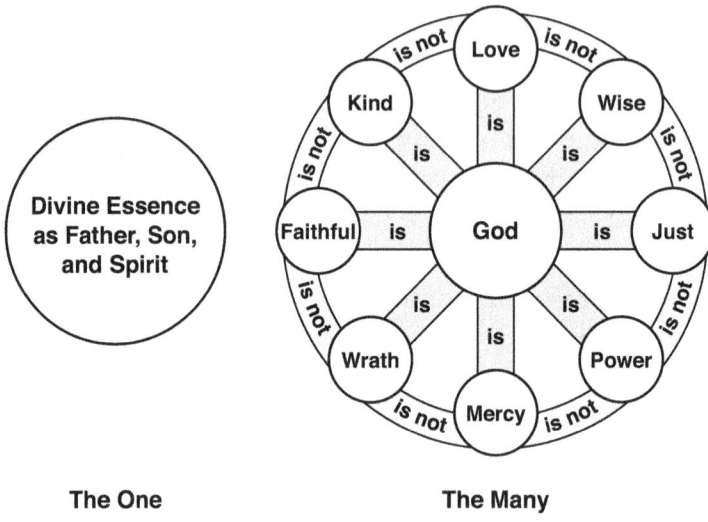

Fig. 5.2. Equal Ultimacy of the Attributes as One and Many

While Dolezal categorizes Frame with those who deny identity among the attributes,[49] this is not entirely accurate. Frame believes that the persons and the attributes can be described as identical to the entire fullness of the Godhead:

> God is not simple in the sense of lacking all complexity, but in the sense that each of his necessary attributes exhausts his being. We saw that each necessary attribute is a way of looking at God's complete nature. Each attribute, indeed, includes all the others. . . . So we can now take a similar approach to the persons of the Trinity. Each exhausts the divine being; each bears all the divine attributes, and, indeed, each is in the other two (*circumincessio*).[50]

---

[49] James E. Dolezal, "God Without Parts: Simplicity and the Metaphysics of Divine Absoluteness" (PhD Diss., Westminster Theological Seminary, 2011), 158n3.

[50] Frame, *Systematic Theology*, 486.

Perichoretic-Simplicity

This identity is had through perichoresis, and it provides the avenue both for unity (identity) and the diversity (complexity).[51]

But even if the one and many are equally ultimate, how should we understand their relationship to one another? That is, why can't we say that there are two Gods—the one and the many? Frame says, "the Trinity shows us, at least in very general terms, how ultimate unity and diversity can be reconciled. They can be reconciled, if they are seen not as abstract qualities, but as qualities of a *person*."[52] The last statement of his quote is paramount. Our analysis does not seek to understand love *qua* love; rather, it understands love as an expression of the absolutely personal triune God. Thus, when divine love is compared with divine wrath, we do not simply correlate abstract love and abstract wrath. Instead, we correlate *God's* love and *God's* wrath. The former abstract concepts, as separated from a person, are void and may potentially conflict.[53] The latter concepts, as attributes of the infinite triune God, are absolutely harmonious and, in connection with his person, are absolutely embracive of one another. And, as Frame argues, "God relates to us as a whole person, not as a collection of attributes."[54] Frame's construction of unity and diversity in light of

---

[51] R. Scott Clark argues that Frame holds to dialectical theology whereby he can maintain "p and ~p at the same time and about the same thing." He further argues that Frame's dialectical theology is "shown chiefly in the simplicity question, where Frame affirms simplicity and complexity in God." We will agree that Frame does affirm both simplicity and complexity; however, it is hard to see how this is dialectical theology. If understood in Trinitarian terms as representative of the absolute equality of the one and many, Frame's comments are quite distant from dialectical theology. R. Scott Clark, "Should I Buy It? (1)," *The Heidelblog*, last modified December 2013, accessed January 22, 2014, http://heidelblog.net/2013/12/should-i-buy-it-1/.

[52] Frame, *Cornelius Van Til*, 76.

[53] Frame connects this view to God's lordship, arguing that "covenant lordship means personalism. The personal is prior to the impersonal. God's personal goodness defines any legitimate abstract concept of goodness." Frame, *Systematic Theology*, 432.

[54] Ibid.

Perichoretic-Simplicity

the persons of the Trinity is unarguably a reflection of Van Til's influence.

A final issue that should be addressed is how one might speak of and know the diversity of the persons. Within Trinitarian theology, the diversity of the persons is often stated as a function of the processions: the Father is unbegotten, the Son is begotten (of the Father), and the Spirit is spirated (from the Father and Son). Frame suggests that "the economic roles played by the three persons must be roles appropriate to their natures." Further, "That the Son, rather than the Father or the Spirit, became incarnate, was a free decision among the persons of the Trinity, but not an arbitrary one."[55] Thus, Frame is indicating an eternal diversity within the unity of the Godhead. Each of the three persons has unique qualities that distinguish him from the others.

Is there a similar relation distinguishing the divine attributes? There does not appear to be any processions of attributes. However, if the processions are viewed as *definitional*, there may be an analogy. That is, the processions are definitional statements of the distinctions between the persons (e.g., the Son is *he whom is begotten*, etc.). While Thomism regards processions as merely relations and *not* properties or attributes, if the processions are understood in their natural sense as properties/attributes of the persons, then they are definitional.[56] This is not to suggest that the only distinctions are definitional; rather, it is to suggest that we know the diversity of God by means of the definitional distinctions he reveals.

In the same way, the attributes are definitional in that they are experienced, understood, and defined as distinct from other attributes.[57] Such a construction would allow attributes to maintain

---

[55] Frame also argues that God's economic dealings with creation are truly reflective of his nature. Ibid., 490.

[56] Frame, *The Doctrine of God*, 705.

[57] Duns Scotus also makes a distinction between the attributes in terms of their definitional distinctions. Cross summarizes, showing that for Scotus "There are formal distinctions between the various divine perfections. The

their distinctiveness by means of their definitional character.[58] So, just as the Son could be defined as *he who is begotten of the Father*, so love, for example, could be defined as *that aspect of God's eternal nature whereby he decided (if he would create, etc.) to send his Son to die for the sins of mankind*.[59] Again, this is not to suggest that the persons are attributes; rather, it is to argue that the unity and diversity of the persons and attributes can be understood in congruent fashion.

Perichoretic-Simplicity Correlates Unity and Diversity of Persons and Attributes

Another advantage of the model is that it allows us to correlate the unity and diversity of God's persons and attributes. In other words, unlike simplicity this model does not run into the conflict between God's nature and persons. Indeed, Frame finds the union of the two in the similarity of their relation as unity in diversity: "the triunity of God does not conflict with his simplicity, understood as I have described it. Each of the three persons is 'in' the other two (*circumincessio*), and therefore each exhausts the divine nature, just as every attribute includes the whole divine nature."[60] Stated differently, when simplicity is understood as an analogous relation of ultimate unity and diversity of perichoresis, the tension is permanently

---

reason is that this intensional commonality includes the basic definition of each perfection, and the basic definitions of the various perfections are simply and irreducibly distinct." Richard Cross, *Duns Scotus on God* (Burlington, VT: Ashgate, 2005), 109.

[58] A key element in both Frame and Poythress's thought concerns the vagueness or imprecision of language. Definitions are never absolute, yet they do reflect what is truly experienced. Frame, *The Doctrine of the Knowledge of God*, 216–21; Vern S. Poythress, *Symphonic Theology* (Grand Rapids, MI: Zondervan, 1987), 55–68.

[59] We are not suggesting that this is the only or even the best definition of love (though there is biblical warrant for it in 1 John 3:16). The model we are proposing here does not depend on precise, exact, and inflexible definitions. The attributes of God can be expressed in diverse ways.

[60] Frame, *The Doctrine of God*, 230.

relieved. Put in the simplest terms, "The relationship between unity and multiplicity is the same in regard to persons as it is in regard to attributes."[61]

Brant Bosserman, in his dissertation detailing the implications of Van Til's Trinitarian theology, suggests another way to relate the unity and diversity of the persons and attributes. Just as the Father infinitely interrelates with the Son in seamless interpenetration, so God's attributes infinitely interrelate in seamless interpenetration with each other. Bosserman sees this as a function of God's personality,[62] for the attributes are not unrelated, abstract concepts. Instead, they are *attributes of persons*, and each of the triune persons has all of the attributes. Thus, Bosserman argues that the infinite interrelatedness, as expressed in the perichoretic relation of the triune persons, implies an infinite expression and interrelatedness of God's attributes.[63]

The connection between persons and attributes leads Bosserman to conclude, "the Triune God must possess an infinitude of attributes (Ps. 16:11, Rom. 11:33), because there can be no limit to the circuminsession of a deity who is self-contained in a tri-personal fashion."[64]

---

[61] Frame, *Systematic Theology*, 433.
[62] Bosserman, "The Trinity and Christian Paradox," §199.
[63] Ibid., §185.
[64] Bosserman argues for a position on simplicity similar to Frame. Bosserman says that a proper understanding of the attributes indicates that "God's nature cannot be simple unless it is infinitely diverse, or vice versa." He argues that the conclusion follows "on its own (Trinitarian) terms, and is further established by the impossibility of the contrary positions, which render God, ultimate reality, and thus, all things wholly unknowable." By contrary position, Bosserman is referring to the Thomistic position, which he argues fails in the following ways. First, it fails by assuming an analogy of being whereby attributes abstracted by the human subject are univocal with the attributes God has. Second, he argues that if every distinction were incompatible with God, then we could not even predicate God as simple. Finally, such an understanding of simplicity is incompatible with the triune persons. Ibid., §186.

Perichoretic-Simplicity

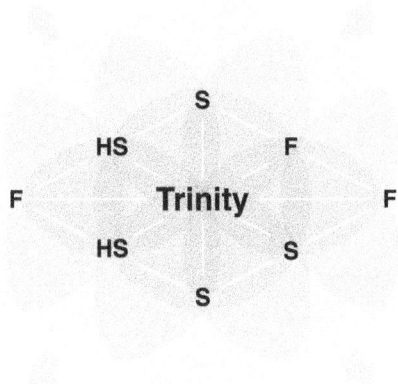

Fig. 5.3. Interpenetration of the Persons through Perichoresis, Leading to Infinite Attributes[65]

Perichoretic-Simplicity Maintains Aseity

A fifth way perichoresis helps us understand simplicity is by providing the resources to maintain the aseity of God, without recourse to a strong account of simplicity.[66] Indeed, God's aseity does not require the strong account of simplicity.[67] Frame argues that a moderate simplicity account that safeguards aseity could be forged in light of Aquinas's four main reasons to embrace strong simplicity.[68]

1. Nothing in God is less noble than himself.

---

[65] Reproduced by permission from Brant Bosserman, "The Trinity and Christian Paradox," fig. 37. © 2011 by Brant Bosserman.

[66] For a thoroughly biblical defense of aseity without recourse to strong simplicity see, Frame, *The Doctrine of God*, 600–608.

[67] Feinberg says, "there is no need to hold simplicity in order to protect aseity and sovereignty." See, John S. Feinberg, *No One Like Him: The Doctrine of God* (Wheaton, IL: Crossway, 2006), 337.

[68] Frame summarizes these four qualities of simplicity from Thomas Aquinas, *Summa Contra Gentiles*, ed. Joseph Kenny, trans. Anton Pegis et al. (New York, NY: Hanover House, 1957), 1.18, accessed July 30, 2014, http://dhspriory.org/thomas/ContraGentiles1.htm.

Perichoretic-Simplicity

2. Nothing in God can be removed, for nothing in him can not be.
3. God's many attributes are not caused, for he is the first cause.
4. God is pure act, without passive potentiality.[69]

After arguing for real (not notional) distinctions among the attributes, Frame shows how these real distinctions are consonant with the concerns of aseity:

> Imagine a distinguishable aspect of God's nature (such as an attribute or a person of the Trinity) that is no less noble than himself, that cannot be removed from him, that necessarily belongs to him apart from any causal process, that is not the result of a movement from potentiality to actuality. It would not be inconsistent . . . for God to have many such aspects.[70]

A perichoretic-simplicity account satisfies these concerns.

Dolezal disagrees, suggesting that Frame has embraced a "harmony account" of simplicity.[71] Dolezal's two criticisms of Frame's position are as follows. First, his proposal, opposite the original intention of the doctrine of simplicity, is more concerned about defending God's unity than defending God's existence "as the absolute self-sufficient first cause of being."[72] Second, Frame's proposal emphasizes the *necessity* of the attributes, but the original intention of the doctrine of simplicity was to establish God as the sufficient reason for his attributes.[73]

Dolezal's first critique does not follow from Frame's position.

---

[69] Frame, *Systematic Theology*, 429.
[70] Ibid., 430.
[71] Categorically, Frame should not be considered in line with the harmony account, since he does maintain identity. Ibid., 487. Nevertheless, we will answer Dolezal's critiques in order to show that Frame's account does not fall to his critiques.
[72] Dolezal, "God without Parts," 179.
[73] Ibid.

That is, while Frame does maintain a harmony among all the attributes (as any biblical theologian should), he is *equally concerned* to defend God's existence as the absolute self-sufficient first cause of being. Dolezal believes that maintaining a diversity of attributes indicates that God is not *a se*. But this would only follow if those attributes (a) are in some sense prior to God, (b) are separable from God, (c) are less noble than God, or (d) make God dependent on the attribute. None of these follow.[74] (a) Does not follow because, as the eternal God, there is nothing before him. He has eternally existed in his unity and diversity (both in persons and attributes). As for (b), God cannot be separated from his attributes. While these attributes are really able to be distinguished, they cannot be separated from God's essence. As such, they are absolutely harmonious, mutually inclusive, and essential to God. As Frame says, "each attribute describes God's entire complexity, not just a part of it. So no attribute is separable from the others. Each attribute has all the attributes: God's love is eternal, just, and wise. his eternity is the eternal existence of a just and wise person."[75] In this light, to remove one attribute would be to remove all the attributes.

The third (c) is of significant importance. Aquinas struggled to maintain the Creator-creature distinction because of his analogy of being, whereby both Creator and creature shared a one level structure of reality.[76] As a consequence, God could be known through creation

---

[74] Aquinas gives another reason by saying, "things in themselves different cannot unite unless something causes them to unite." Here Aquinas is showing his methodology whereby he first knows by means of creation and then approaches revelation. In mankind, it is true, that things cannot be united unless someone unites them. However, if God is a unity in diversity (whereby every essential attribute he expresses is necessary for his existence), then it would not be required that someone unite such complexity, for he simply is essentially complex. Aquinas, *Summa Theologica*, 3.7.

[75] Frame, *The Doctrine of God*, 388.

[76] Frame notes that in Aquinas' one level of being "there is no hint of any doctrine of analogy, no suggestion that terms like essence and *esse* apply to God in any way other than univocally. So in Aquinas's treatment of essence, we

by deriving knowledge of the Creator from an attribute in a creature. This does not allow for proper separation between God's attributes and man's attributes. And as such, Aquinas was concerned that creaturely attributes would be attributable to God. However, if we maintain a two-level structure of being, whereby God does not create more *being* but created more *beings*, then we can maintain the majesty of God's attributes. While men analogically express God's attributes in an ectypal sense (as God has made man in his image), man's wisdom is never and could never be equal to God's wisdom. This is primarily because God's wisdom is unique being essentially his from all eternity.

Finally, (d) does not necessarily follow. Aquinas was concerned that any complexity in God's nature *requires* a dependent relationship.[77] Thomas Morris responds,

> What the simplicity theorist is concerned about is that, given the necessary goodness of God, for example, if goodness is thought of as a property distinct from God, then it is true that
>
> (1) If the property of goodness did not exist, then God would not exist.
>
> But this is just an expression of the idea that God's goodness is essential to him—that God is good in every circumstance in which he exists. But since, on the view we have been developing, it is also true that God exists necessarily, in every possible world, it can also be said of the property of goodness that it is essentially such that it is possessed by God. And this can be seen to support the truth of

---

lose the sense of divine transcendence that permeates his doctrine of analogy." Ibid., 224.

[77] Aquinas says, "Every composite is posterior to its component parts, and is dependent on them" Aquinas, *Summa Theologica*, 3.7.

(2) If God did not exist, then the property of goodness would not exist.

The simplicity theorist thinks that (1) expresses the dependence of God on the property of goodness. But if it did, (2) would express the dependence of the property of goodness on God. But, presumably, ontological dependence, dependence for being or existence, can only go in one direction—if my parents brought me into existence it cannot also be the case that I brought them into existence. Thus, the mere existence and truth of propositions like (1) and (2) cannot alone be taken to show ontological dependence. Their truth merely reflects the logical relation which holds between propositions about necessarily existent entities, and alone implies nothing about the ontological dependence or independence of those entities.[78]

As for Dolezal's second critique—i.e., that Frame's proposal emphasizes the *necessity* of the attributes, but the original intention of the doctrine of simplicity was to establish God as the sufficient reason for his attributes—we should note that Frame is not primarily interested in the reason simplicity was originally fashioned. He is chiefly concerned to maintain the aseity of God. Further, as much as we have shown Frame maintains the aseity of God, he has shown that God *is* the sufficient reason for his attributes.

Perichoretic-Simplicity Maintains Absolute Personality

A sixth way perichoresis can inform our understanding of simplicity is by providing a model for the *absolute personality* of the attributes.[79] That perichoresis is shot through with God's personality is

---

[78] Thomas V. Morris, *Our Idea of God: An Introduction to Philosophical Theology* (Vancouver, BC: Regent College, 2002), 116.

[79] Here we will focus only on the personality aspect, but both terms of *absolute personality* are important. Both perichoresis and simplicity guard God's

clear from its nature as the infinite interweaving of the three divine *persons*. But how is simplicity a fruit of personality? Frame explains, "The Christian is not devoted to some abstract philosophical goodness, but to the living Lord of heaven and earth."[80] In classical treatments of God's attributes, Frame contends that the attributes (and thus God himself) are sometimes presented as sterile, abstract, and impersonal monads without complexity. But God's absolute personality indicates that he is fully present in all of his attributes. The one (God) is fully expressed in all of the many (attributes). So Frame can conclude, "Those emerging from the murky waters of scholastic speculation may be surprised to find that the doctrine of simplicity is really fairly simple. It is a biblical way of reminding us that God's relationship with us is fully personal."[81]

Frame offers an example of how personalism provides the key for unity in God's complex nature:

> It is important to see the unity within this complexity. And to see it, we should remind ourselves that our covenant Lord is a person. What is God's 'goodness?' Is it something in God? It is more accurate, I think, to say, that 'divine goodness,' though it sounds like an abstract property, is really just a way of referring to everything God is. For everything God does is good, and everything he is is good. All his attributes are good. All his decrees are good. All his actions are good. There is nothing in God that is not good.

---

absoluteness. We have already noted how Trinitarian theology protects aseity by indicating that God's eternal attribute of love did not depend on the world or creatures; rather, in the Trinitarian communion, the Father, Son, and Spirit express an eternal love that is reflectively evidenced in creation. In a similar way, we have noted that a form of simplicity informed by perichoresis can protect aseity by indicating that there is no attribute, e.g., love, outside of God for which he is responsible for conforming to.

[80] Frame, *The Doctrine of God*, 230.
[81] Ibid.

To praise God's goodness is not to praise something other than God himself. It is not to praise something less than him, a part of him, so to speak. It is to praise him. God's goodness is not something that is intelligible in itself apart from everything else God is.

God's goodness is the standard of our goodness. We are to image God's goodness. Does that mean that we are to image some abstract property that is somehow attached to God or present in God somewhere? No; it means that we are to image God himself. Our moral standard is not an impersonal, abstract property. It is a person, the living God. The center of biblical morality is that we should be like him. As I argued earlier in this book, covenant lordship means personalism. The personal is prior to the impersonal. God's personal goodness defines any legitimate abstract concept of goodness.

God relates to us as a whole person, not as a collection of attributes. The attributes merely describe different things about that person. They are a kind of shorthand for talking about that person. Everything he says and does is good, right, true, eternal, wise, and so on.[82]

The same point can be noted by looking at a popular criticism of simplicity by the Plantinga brothers. Cornelius Plantinga argued that the strong account of simplicity reduces the persons to mere abstractions (*paternity, filiation, spiration*), and his brother Alvin Plantinga argued that the strong simplicity account of the attributes reduces God to a property.[83] But by noting that every distinguishable aspect of God represents the fullness of his being, Frame can maintain that none of them are impersonal. This is because "the ultimate

---

[82] Frame, *Systematic Theology*, 432.

[83] Cornelius Plantinga, "The Threeness/Oneness Problem of the Trinity," *Calvin Theological Journal* 23, 1 (April 1988): 48; Alvin Plantinga, *Does God Have a Nature?* (Milwaukee, WI: Marquette University Press, 1980).

identity of persons and relations means not that the persons are 'really' abstractions, but that the abstractions are 'really' personal."[84] And, in relation to the attributes, "To identify God with his attributes is not to say that he is an abstraction or a collection of abstract qualities. It is, rather, to insist that his attributes are fully personal."[85] By wedding the absolute interpenetration of all of God's qualities with his commitment to absolute personality, Frame can show that simplicity is a very practical doctrine.[86] It does not make God unknowable (the result of Aquinas's method), but rather makes him known through all of his attributes. When we address God as good, we are not saying something improper of him; rather, we are speaking of the fullness of the divine being from one focal perspective.

Frame believes Bavinck understood the distinctions of the attributes in perspectival fashion when the Dutchman said, "We are not able to conceive of the infinite fulness of God's essence unless it is revealed to us in this, then in another relation, now from this then from another angle."[87] In the same work, Bavinck refers to the multiplicity of names of God, indicating that "Every name refers to the same full divine being, but each time from a particular angle, the angle from which it reveals itself to us in his works."[88] These comments indicate that Bavinck understood the attributes and names of God as perspectives through which God has revealed himself to

---

[84] Frame, *Systematic Theology*, 487.

[85] Ibid., 487n34.

[86] Frame says, "I do believe in a doctrine of divine simplicity sufficient to justify the identity of the persons, their relations, and the whole divine nature. We may say, then, that the persons are identical to their relations; but on my view it is also true to say that the relations are identical to the persons. The doctrine of simplicity should not entail reductionism. The persons are identical to their relations, but they are not reducible to their relations; they are not mere relations. The persons are no more reducible to relations than the relations are reducible to the persons. The persons and the relations both exist together, both categories exhausting the divine nature, both expressing the complexity that exists as the divine nature." Frame, *The Doctrine of God*, 702–3.

[87] Ibid., 228n29.

[88] Bavinck, *Reformed Dogmatics*, 177.

man. These perspectives represent the "full divine being" and give epistemological access to God's essence.

Duns Scotus and Perichoretic-Simplicity

While we have argued that the present model is built upon theological themes present within scriptural revelation and within orthodox theology, we have not tried to historically locate proponents of the view. The task of locating proponents is difficult in that Aquinas's model has historically been dominantly assumed in orthodox theology.[89] However, there is a proponent of a view similar to the present model in the work of John Duns Scotus.[90] We will examine his views, showing in what ways they are consonant with the present model.

Scotus is heralded as a proponent of simplicity,[91] and while he did maintain the basic structure, he challenged some of the assumptions. Richard Cross summarizes Scotus's position on God's attributes in the following way: "God's attributes are real (constituents of God), that they are in some way distinct from each other, and that each one is in some way distinct from God too."[92] For those familiar with the classical statement of simplicity, these statements are clearly not in accord with the classical principle. Indeed, they appear to be exactly opposite. How can Scotus maintain these three positions and

---

[89] Aquinas did not invent the simplicity model, but he was the most able expositor of it, securing the model for years to come. Modern theology has moved away from the uniformity of confirming simplicity. Cornelius Plantinga, "Social Trinity and Tritheism," in *Trinity, Incarnation, and Atonement*, ed. Ronald J. Feenstra (Notre Dame, IN: Notre Dame Press, 1989), 21–47; Plantinga, *Does God Have a Nature?*

[90] Perhaps his willingness to differ with Aquinas' model derived from his closeness in time. Scotus was born (1265) near the end of Aquinas' life (1274), and before Aquinas' conclusions could take normative status.

[91] Dolezal lists him as a proponent, yet he does note the unique contribution of Scotus's theology in building the doctrine on infinity. Dolezal, "God without Parts," 9–10.

[92] Cross, *Duns Scotus on God*, 104.

yet preserve something close to Aquinas's notion of simplicity? In order to understand this quandary, we must understand the three types of *distinctions* in Scotus's epistemology.[93]

The three types of distinctions in Scotus's theology and philosophy are *real distinctions, rational distinctions, and formal distinctions*. First, *real distinctions* point to the separability between objects, indicating that at least one is not necessary for the existence of the other. Given in logical form, "A *real distinction* holds between two individuals [properties, etc.], x and y, if and only if it is logically possible either for x to exist without y or for y to exist without x."[94] For example, Snoopy's cape is not necessary for the existence of Snoopy, nor is Snoopy necessary for the existence of the cape. Therefore, the two maintain a *real distinction*. The same could be applied to personal properties (e.g., white hair, etc.).[95]

The second distinction, what Scotus calls a *rational distinction*, concerns the mind of the knower. These distinctions are not true in reality; rather, they are products of the knower's mind. In other words, these are merely mental creations without objective reality in the things known. Clark Kent and Superman present an excellent example. Though mentally imagined as different persons, in reality they are one. The difference is not in the thing, but it is a difference in the mind of the knower.

The final distinction, and the one most important for our purposes here, is the *formal distinction*. These are not *rational*, for they derive from the nature of things. However, they are not *real* because the qualities being distinguished are necessary for one another. In

---

[93] For a more detailed overview of the three distinctions see, Jeffrey Hause, "John Duns Scotus," *Internet Encyclopedia of Philosophy*, 2007, accessed June 20, 2014, http://www.iep.utm.edu/scotus/.

[94] Ibid.

[95] Scotus's notation that *only one* of the two needs to be non-necessary safeguards the distinction between the Creator and the creature. God is absolutely necessary for all that is in existence, but it is not true that God requires anything for his existence.

other words, it is not logically possible for x to exist without y or vice versa. Will and intellect, for example, are necessary for one another as expressed *in a person*.[96] The person cannot have a will without the intellect or vice versa. This example highlights an important aspect of the *formal distinction*—two things can be said to be *identical* if united by a third factor. This is because, for Scotus, "What unifies formally distinct finite attributes with each other is their unity with their suppositum. If, therefore, the attributes were abstracted from their suppositum, the cause of their real identity with each other would be lacking."[97] It is within the context of the *person*, then, that Scotus can maintain the simple identity of attributes while also maintaining their distinctiveness. Stated more fully, Cross says that Scotus believed his formal distinction

> is compatible with real identity, because the necessary properties of a thing are not themselves things, or separable from their subject.... Thus, what explains the real identity of my necessary properties with each other ... is just that they are properties of me. Considered in abstraction from their unity in me, they would not be unified with each other.[98]

If the attributes are identical as reflected in the person, what accounts for the diversity? In other words, how does he maintain the formal distinction? Jeffrey Hause helps us by indicating the three necessary aspects of a *formal distinction*: "According to Scotus, x and y are formally distinct if and only if (a) x and y are really the same [identical with one another through interrelation in a third uniting

---

[96] It is ironic that, having the view supplied here, Scotus would subordinate the intellect to the will as he does in God's nature. However, he is inconsistent on this point. For a summary, see Frame, *Spiritual Warfare*, chap. 4.

[97] Cross, *Duns Scotus on God*, 113.

[98] Richard Cross, "Duns Scotus: Ordinatio," in *Central Works of Philosophy: Ancient and Medieval*, ed. John Shand (Quebec: McGill-Queen's Press, 2005), 231.

factor] and (b) x has a different ratio (account or character) than y, and (c) neither ratio overlaps the other."[99] What is meant by *ratio*? Scotus has in mind a definitional distinction or, put differently, a distinction in the *function* of the two things being compared. Cross explains, "There are formal distinctions between the various divine perfections. The reason is that this intensional commonality *includes the basic definition of each perfection*, and the basic definitions of the various perfections are simply and irreducibly distinct."[100]

Before summarizing the results of maintaining the *formal distinction*, we might ask why Scotus believed the distinction was necessary. While Scotus may have wider philosophical reasons, our discussion will be confined to theological reasons. The primary motivation for the formal distinction was that Scotus believed the attribute distinctions among men were truly distinct, and, therefore, the distinctions among God must be as well.[101] The formal distinction provided a way to keep the integrity of the distinctions while also maintaining the principles motivating simplicity. But while other proponents of simplicity agree that the attribute distinctions among men are true distinctions, they refrain from necessitating such distinctions of God. So why does Scotus maintain that the attributes must function in the same way for God as for man? Ultimately, he believes that there must be some form of parallel between God's attributes and man's attributes, because *revelation assumes such a connection*.[102]

More specifically, Scotus believes that God's revelation truly reveals God, and, therefore, the medieval understanding of analogy must be reworked. This does not imply a *complete* univocism for Scotus. While he would maintain the necessity of univocal reasoning for true predication, he maintains that there remains a metaphysical divide between God and man. To understand how he can recast

---

[99] Hause, "John Duns Scotus."
[100] Cross, *Duns Scotus on God*, 109. Emphasis added.
[101] Ibid., 107–9.
[102] Ibid., 110–11.

analogical reasoning while maintaining some form of univocism, we must understand his central concept of infinity. The major distinction between God and man is that God has all of his attributes in infinity.[103] For Scotus, this is not the only distinction, for even when we speak of Socrates' wisdom and God's wisdom, the difference is not merely one of quantity. There are depths of God's wisdom (qualitative) that Socrates will never partake of, yet what we know in Socrates as wisdom is truly an image of the *same sort* of wisdom present in God—though quantitatively lacking.[104] As Cross notes, "Scotus's account of the extramental basis for univocally is ultimately the asymmetrical relationship of imitation. Hence, the reason why God's wisdom and Socrate's wisdom fall under the same concept is that Socrates imitates God."[105]

Taken as a whole, Scotus's *formal distinction* maintains both the primary motivations of simplicity and the integrity of revelation. While the attributes maintain a *formal distinction*, they are, when considered in the infinite person of the Godhead, identical.[106]

---

[103] Richard Cross, *Duns Scotus* (New York, NY: Oxford University Press, 1999), 33–39.

[104] As noted above, Scotus's argument for some measure of univocity is paralleled in Frame's writing. Frame says, "we need not be afraid of saying that some of our language about God is univocal or literal. God has given us language that literally applies to him. . . . the statement that 'God is good' uses the term *good* univocally. God's goodness is, of course, different from ours in important ways. But goodness on either divine or human levels can be defined by such concepts as justice, mercy, and kindness. The differences between God's nature and ours do not require that we use the term *good* in different senses." Frame, *The Doctrine of God*, 209n26.

[105] Scotus does make a distinction between pure univocity and a univocity expressed through imitation. This appears to broadly parallel Frame's understanding that while revelation gives true information about God, it does not exhaust the differences between God and man in any particular attribute. Cross, *Duns Scotus on God*, 111.

[106] Scotus shows an inconsistency at this point. While he maintains that attribute distinctions are formal, because they are identical when considered in the person, he argues later that this does not apply to God. For Scotus, it is unnecessary to posit such a relation in God because infinity already does the

Perichoretic-Simplicity

The similarities between the perichoretic-simplicity Model and Scotus's model can now be examined. First, both models emphasize the role of revelation in making distinctions. The distinctions expressed in Scripture about the Godhead are true distinctions, and they should not be eliminated by means of a philosophical program. Second, a parallel between simplicity and perichoresis exists in both systems. Both the persons of the Godhead and the multiplicity of the attributes are genuinely distinct.[107] Third, the difference

---

same job. That is, infinity of each attribute necessarily encompasses every other one. In sum, the identity of God's attributes is not a function of his person; rather, it is a function of the infinity of the attributes. In response, we would say that Scotus's caveat is unnecessary and problematic for two reasons. First, as much as infinity is an attribute, it likewise gains identity through relation of the person. It appears that Scotus's lack of a robust divine personality (as present in Van Til) is responsible for his inconsistency. Second, by arguing that we can view infinity in "ultimate abstraction" and derive all of the attributes of the Godhead from it, Scotus emphasizes infinity to the detriment of the persons of the Godhead. Such a construal understands the Godhead on the basis of infinity rather than understanding God's attributes (of which infinity is a part) on the revelation of the person in Scripture. Further, Cross notes that this understanding of infinity makes God "nothing more than a collection of really identical and formally distinct attributes," leading to the conclusion that "Scotus' one category [analysis of the divine essence] is entirely properties." In other words, God is simply a property. By abandoning the absolute personhood of God, this understanding falls directly to the attack of Alvin Plantinga. Ibid., 113; Plantinga, *Does God Have a Nature?*

[107] Scotus says, "The distinction of attribute-perfections is the basis in relation to the distinction of emanations. But the distinction of emanations is real, as is evident . . . therefore the distinction of attributes is not merely rational, but in some way real." Here Scotus argues that the processions are manifestations of various attributes of God (the Son being the intellect, and the Spirit being the will). Thus, the connection he draws is not based on the unity and diversity of the two (as in Frame), but on the derivation of the persons through means of distinct attributes. So whereas our model will argue that since the persons are distinct, so we can see that the attributes are distinct, Scotus's model would maintain that since the attributes are distinct, so we can see that the persons are distinct. Ioannis Duns Scoti, *Opera Omnia*, ed. C. Balić et al., vol. 4 (Città del Vaticano: Typis Polyglottis Vaticanis, 1956), 1.8.1.4n177 as translated in Cross, *Duns Scotus on God*, 106–8.

between attributes is definitional. Just as the perichoretic-simplicity model depends on the reality of the distinctions as can be expressed through definition of those qualities, so Scotus's model does the same.[108] Fourth, the identity of attributes is a function of their relationship *in the person*.

Having noted the similarities, we should say that there are certainly differences between Scotus and the present model. Particularly, the motivations for the doctrines appear to be distinct (as noted above). Nevertheless, our purpose here was to show the similarities, noting that some of the argumentation used by Frame has precedence in previous theological work.

Summary of the Perichoretic-Simplicity Model

Frame provides a brief summary of his overall position when he says,

> God is not simple in the sense of lacking all complexity, but in the sense that each of his necessary attributes exhausts his being. We saw that each necessary attribute is a way of looking at God's complete nature. Each attribute, indeed, includes all the others (his love is eternal, his mercy just, etc.) But this kind of mutual perspectivalism does not exclude, but presupposes, complexity in the Godhead. For it is true to say that God is merciful, just, and eternal. his being is so complex that these and all his other attributes truly characterize him. So we can now take a similar approach to the persons of the Trinity. Each exhausts the divine being; each bears all

---

[108] Scotus says, "There is therefore some formal non-identity between wisdom and goodness, inasmuch as there would be distinct definitions of them if they were definable. . . . A definition does not only indicate a concept caused by the intellect, but the quiddity of a thing: there is therefore formal non-identity." Scoti, *Opera Omnia*, 1.8.1.4 as translated in Cross, "Duns Scotus: Ordinatio," 231.

the divine attributes, and, indeed, each is in the other two (circumincessio). So when we encounter one person, we are encountering the Triune God.[109]

By suggesting such a model Frame does not believe he has done damage to the original intention of the doctrine of simplicity, for his model maintains aseity. But he does believe that he has moved the doctrine a step further by applying Van Til's foundational conception of absolute personality to bear on simplicity. By doing so, Frame is following his own advice that "as we build on Van Til's foundation, we should be even more explicitly personalistic."[110]

To summarize the main points of perichoretic-simplicity and to show how these are intimately related to perspectivalism, we will point out the implications of the model. First, in God there is no aspect or person (e.g., *love, the Son)* that could possibly conflict with another aspect of God (e.g., God's *justice, the Father)*, for these aspects are complementary ways of describing the *one* God. his love and justice are simply diverse descriptions of who he is eternally.

Second, we cannot discuss any characteristic or person of God in absolute distinction from his other characteristics or persons. By referring to God's love, one must not eliminate God's justice. Even in an earthly sense, love cannot exist without justice.[111] In God, however, we find a more substantial reason for their equality: Scripture describes God as both loving and just. Thus, our concept of God's love must, if it is to be understood fully, include the concept of God's justice. And, as it pertains to the triune persons, by referring to the

---

[109] Frame, *Systematic Theology*, 486.
[110] Frame, *Cornelius Van Til*, 60.
[111] For instance, we would not say that a father loves his children if he seeks no justice in their wrongful death. Indeed, the father who fails to seek out justice would be considered unloving. For a moving defense of the necessity of justice and wrath to complement love, see Miroslav Volf, *Free of Charge: Giving and Forgiving in a Culture Stripped of Grace* (Grand Rapids, MI: Zondervan, 2009), 138–39.

Son, we are led to the Father and Spirit, for we know the Father through the Son by the Spirit.

Third, and following from the second, a full understanding of one attribute or person will lead naturally to the other attributes and persons. In seeking to know God's exhaustive power, we also come to know his eternality, for omnipotence is impotent without eternality. While not every attribute will lead as clearly to every other attribute, none can be *fully* understood without the others. And when we fully know the Father, we know him through the Son and Spirit.

Fourth, because each of the attributes and persons is a full expression of God, each attribute and person fully relates to the others. To illustrate this process, we could add any attribute of God as an adjective to any other attribute as a noun. For illustrative purposes, let's examine God's justice. God has a loving, eternal, free, wrathful, merciful, and holy justice. Of course, some of the adjectives are more understandable on the surface than others, but all are ultimately complementary as multiple descriptions of God's person. As this relates to the persons, we would say that the Son is a Son because he is the Son of the Father, etc.

The fifth implication of God's perichoretic-simplicity is perhaps the most surprising: all of God's attributes and persons can be described as identical to God. As Frame succinctly notes, "God's attributes are not abstract qualities that God happens to exemplify. They are, rather identical to God himself. . . . Each describes the whole nature of God. So to talk of God's attributes is simply to talk about God himself, from various perspectives."[112] Similarly, the persons of the Godhead are identical to God in that they describe the whole nature of God from a unique perspective.

The sixth implication corrects a potential wrong view of the fifth. That is, some might believe perichoretic-simplicity eliminates

---

[112] John M. Frame, "Divine Aseity and Apologetics," in *Revelation and Reason*, ed. K. Scott Oliphint and Lane G. Tipton (Phillipsburg, NJ: P&R Publishing, 2007), 115–16.

all distinctions. However, if this were the case, humans could not speak of the love of God as distinct from God's omnipotence. Of course, it is clear that humans do distinguish these characteristics. Is this merely a human epistemological limitation? Frame argues that such a position provides a limitation on God's lordship such that he could not present himself as he really is. Further, this would imply that we do not really know God. Thus, Frame, following Scripture, argues that we must maintain both the ultimate identity as well as the ultimate diversity of God's attributes and persons. Because God has revealed himself as three persons, we would be wrong to argue for unity over diversity. And since God has revealed himself as a person with multiple (and distinguishable) attributes, we would be wrong to argue for unity over diversity. Further, this diversity is expressive of definitional distinctions. Love is different from wrath, because they are experienced, understood, and defined differently. The Father is distinct from the Son, because his acts (becoming incarnate, etc.) and procession (begotten of the Father) provide the resources to describe the difference in a definitional way.

A seventh implication of perichoretic-simplicity concerns the fullness of God's nature. Because God is eternally complete as one and many, no new attribute can be added that did not eternally exist.[113] Further, no attribute can be taken away. In the former case, God would either improve or worsen (both of which are impossible). In the latter case, to take away an attribute would be to destroy the whole. Similarly, no new person can be added or subtracted.

The eighth implication is that God is fully present in his persons and attributes. We never experience God's love as an abstract

---

[113] Attributes that God takes upon himself in creating the world (e.g., mercy, grace, etc.) are various manifestations of attributes that were eternally existent (e.g., love). Therefore, new circumstances may reflect more of God's inherent, eternal character. Further, because creation is a reflection of God's eternal plan, in eternity God is he who *if he decided to create* would be loving to those whom he created. Such an analysis seeks to retain the freedom of God's will and the necessary character of God.

quality; rather, we experience the fullness of God through knowing him as love. While we will never fully understand his love, we have a glimpse from that one *focal perspective* on the fullness of divinity. In the same way, when we know one of the persons of the Godhead, we know the fullness of the divine being through that person, who functions as a focal perspective. This implication is dependent on the preceding ones, being based on the fact that every attribute/person is inseparable, mutually penetrating, eternally complete, and identical to God. As such, each can function as a focal perspective.

A final implication of perichoretic-simplicity concerns priority. It is here that we find a major distinction between the persons and attributes. As it concerns the attributes, there is no priority, but as it concerns the persons, there is a priority evidenced through the processions. Frame and Poythress have not recognized this distinction in perspectival methodology. We will seek to address this concern in chapter eight.

Conclusion

We have sought to show in this chapter that Frame's perspectivalism is Trinitarian in that it is built upon the unity in diversity of the Godhead as exhibited in the persons (perichoresis) and the nature of God (simplicity). In order to show the connection to perspectivalism, it was necessary first to show the connection perichoresis and simplicity (or the persons and the divine nature) had to one another. The perichoretic-simplicity model was a fruit of that necessity and provides for us a framework for understanding perspectivalism. Also, it provides a model by which we may clarify and even modify some of the main points of perspectival methodology. Chapter eight will examine the influence that the perichoretic-simplicity model has on Frame's perspectivalism. For now, we will turn in the next chapter to show how the perichoretic-simplicity model provides a basis for the perspectival dynamics.

6

Triperspectivalism and the Trinity

In this chapter, we will continue to explore the Trinitarian foundations of perspectivalism. We will do so in three steps. First, we will seek to show why we have argued that creation reflects the Trinitarian nature of the Creator. Second, after having showed how God's nature is connected to his creation, we are finally in a place to develop the perspectival dynamics, showing how perichoresis and simplicity are imaged into various perspectival groups. Finally, we will seek to explain the various types of triads Frame and Poythress express in their writings. By classifying the triads according to their function, we will see both that not all triads are the same and that despite the differences their unity is derived from the fact that they all image God's triunity in some fashion.

Connection between God's Nature and Creation

One issue we have simply assumed up to this point should be examined more carefully. What is the connection between God's nature and creation as a whole? More explicitly, even if God's unity in diversity can be described according to the perichoretic-simplicity model, why would we assume God has created according to this model? Because perspectivalism is built upon the connection between created reality and God's nature, it is necessary to examine whether this connection is legitimate.

We will seek to express the connection between God's perichoretic-simplicity nature and creation by first noting a foundational belief of perspectivalism: *the world necessarily reflects its Trinitarian Creator*. Next, we will seek to defend that belief through (1) a proper understanding of God's nature as absolute, (2) the imaging of God in creation, and (3) the linguistic structure of created reality.

Foundational Belief of Perspectivalism

One of the basic beliefs of perspectivalism should be expressly stated here: creation necessarily reflects its Trinitarian Creator. This could be stated more broadly as *that which is created by an absolute being reflects the nature of him who created it*. Earlier, in our examination of general perspectivalism, we noted that the ultimate source of the multiple epistemological perspectives is the perspectival nature of God's own knowledge (i.e., his knowledge as Father, Son, and Spirit). Our knowledge is a reflection of God's knowledge, or, in other terms, our knowledge is an ectypal manifestation of God's archetypal knowledge. Poythress shows that ectypal reflection is not accidental or merely potential: "Ectypal knowledge *must inevitably show the stamp of its Trinitarian archetype*, because all knowledge, insofar as it is true knowledge at all, is knowledge of truth, and archetypal truth is God's truth, truth in his mind."[1]

Creation Necessarily Reflects Its Trinitarian Creator

Why is this ectypal manifestation *inevitably* related to the archetypal origin? There are three answers we will explore. First, God as absolute implies that any perichoretic-like relations in creation reflect God's original perichoretic nature. Second, God's imaging in creation implies that creation bears the marks of his Trinitarian nature. Finally, the linguistic structure of reality leads to the conclusion that creation is structured according to a Trinitarian pattern.

---

[1] Vern S. Poythress, "Multiperspectivalism and the Reformed Faith," in *Speaking the Truth in Love: The Theology of John M. Frame*, ed. John J. Hughes (Phillipsburg, NJ: P&R Publishing, 2009), 191. Emphasis added.

Triperspectivalism and the Trinity

God as Absolute Implies Trinitarian Reflection in Creation

God's nature as absolute requires that he be the ultimate explanation for all things in existence. The world, because created by an absolute God, draws its every origin back to God. As a result, when perichoretic-like relations are evident in creation, faithful subjects can properly draw the implication that these are a reflection of God's nature in creation.[2] Note again Poythress' ground for perspectivalism: "There can be *no other ultimate foundation* for perspectives than in God himself. God alone is absolute. Thus absoluteness . . . serves naturally as a key incentive for moving toward . . . a triperspectivalism that imitates the coinherence of the persons in the Trinity."[3] Reformed theology, with its emphasis on the biblical description of God as absolute, has emphasized this point more than other evangelical streams.[4] Frame, after defending the absolute nature of God in his treatise on the doctrine of God, appears to be making this argument implicitly as he speaks of traces of the Trinity in creation: "We have seen that the world as a whole reflects God's glory, and that glory is the glory of the Triune God. So the whole creation is a *vestigium trinitatis*."[5] Stated differently, according to God's absolute

---

[2] Gunton, in his *Bampton Lectures*, argued from perichoretic-like relations in creation to God's perichoretic inter-Trinitarian reality: "Because the one God is economically involved in the world in those various ways, it cannot be supposed other than that the action of the Father, Son and Spirit is a mutually involved personal dynamic. It would appear to follow that in eternity Father, Son and Spirit share a dynamic mutual reciprocity, interpenetration and inter animation." Colin E. Gunton, *The One, the Three and the Many: God, Creation and the Culture of Modernity* (New York, NY: Cambridge University Press, 1993), 163.

[3] Poythress, "Multiperspectivalism," 199. Emphasis added.

[4] As Van Til asserts, "Reformed theologians have made the concept of God as absolute in all his attributes determinative for the whole of their theology." Cornelius Van Til, "Review of Worship of God by James Vance," in *Reviews by Cornelius Van Til*, ed. Eric H. Sigward, Logos Digital Collection. (New York, NY: Labels Army Company, 1997).

[5] John M. Frame, *The Doctrine of God* (Phillipsburg, NJ: P&R Publishing, 2002), 726–27.

nature, if God's glory is to be abundantly reflected in creation, it must be a Trinitarian reflection.[6]

God's Work of Imaging Implies Trinitarian Reflection

A second way to relate the Trinitarian nature to creation is through the biblical concept of imaging. The *original* imaging pattern is the Son reflecting the Father. Colossians describes the Son as "the image of the invisible God," and Hebrews adds that he is "the radiance of the glory of God and the exact imprint of his [the Father's] nature" (Col. 1:15; Heb. 1:3). Genesis 1:26–28 extends this original imaging to the creation of man. So Poythress argues, "Adam was created not simply in the image of God, but after the pattern of the archetypal divine image, namely the Son, the second person of the Trinity."[7]

That Adam was created according to the divine ectypal image of the Son may not be obvious on the surface, but Poythress is following Ridderbos who argued, "The whole of the so-called hymn in [Colossians 1:15] speaks of creation. The expression Image of God is here clearly rooted in Genesis 1:27."[8] Ridderbos is arguing that Adam's creation in the image of God was actually his creation in the image of the divine ectype of the Son.[9] The patterning of the image originally existent in the intra-Trinitarian relations is now expressed in creation through the creation of man in the image of the Son.[10] While there are certainly distinctions to be made between

---

[6] Gunton agrees: "Because the trinitarian concepts reflect the being of God, we should be prepared to find them echoed in some way in human thought and in structures of the created world." Gunton, *The One, the Three and the Many*, 211.

[7] Poythress, "Multiperspectivalism," 193.

[8] Herman N. Ridderbos, *Paul: An Outline of His Theology* (Grand Rapids, MI: Eerdmans, 1997), 72.

[9] For his fuller treatment see, Ibid., 70–73.

[10] See also Kline's argument that Hebrews 1:3 is a direct reference to creation. Meredith G. Kline, *Images of the Spirit* (Eugene, OR: Wipf and Stock, 1999), 16.

the imaging of the Father in the Son and the imaging of man in the Son's image, the nature of image indicates that there are intentional and significant similarities.[11]

Adam, as a human ectypal manifestation of the Son (i.e., the Father's divine ectypal image), produced an ectypal manifestation of his own ectypal image: "[Adam] fathered a son in his own likeness, after his image" (Gen. 5:3). Imitating the Creator, humans reflect their own attributes into that which they create (i.e., into their image). Children are not an exact replica of their parents, but they do reflect the parent's nature (e.g., temperament, abilities, physical features, etc.). Analogously, man is not an exact replica of God, yet he does share many of God's characteristics through imaging.[12]

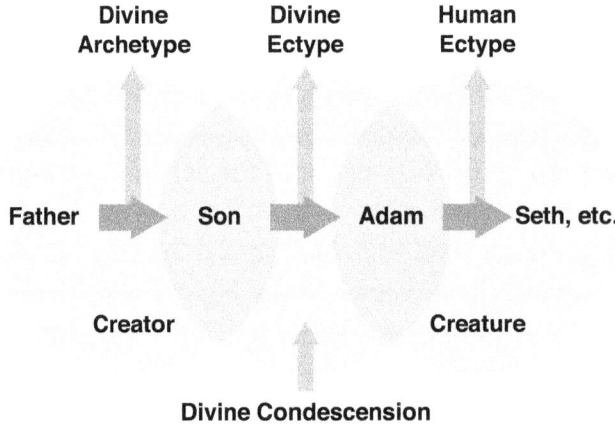

Fig. 6.1. Archetypal and Ectypal Imaging[13]

[11] Bavinck notes that the image of God "can be applied to humans but in an absolute sense it belongs to Christ." Herman Bavinck, *Reformed Dogmatics*, ed. John Bolt, trans. John Vriend (Grand Rapids, MI: Baker, 2003), 2.276.

[12] It would take us too far off topic to discuss the intricacies of what is communicated through divine condescension in the divine image. Our general point is merely to note that God's attributes are reflected in his image bearers. Because he is necessarily triune, it would not be surprising to find that some aspects of his triunity are reflected in man through that image.

[13] In figure 6.1, divine archetype refers to the imaging process itself. Thus,

The above analysis has dealt only with the creation of living, rational beings. The image of God is never *explicitly* related to the non-rational, so one may think that the image only relates to rational persons. Meredith Kline, however, has made a very strong case for the image relating to all of creation. Kline's work in *the Images of the Spirit* argues for God's theophanic presence throughout the Old Testament. Kline implies that every manifestation of God in the Old Testament (through cloud, pillar, thunder, fire, temple, etc.) is an *imaging* of the triune God through the Spirit. These images are dependent on the Glory-Spirit,[14] which is likewise the foundation for God making man in his own image. As a result, Kline concludes that the imaging present in creating man is the *same imaging* involved in the creation of all reality.[15] Therefore, *all of creation*—not just man—is made in the image of God. While Kline does maintain a special and unique status for man, he nevertheless indicates that God is covenantally imaged throughout all of creation.[16]

In sum, Kline's research suggests that creation, as a whole, is a covenantal image of God. Consider Isaiah 66:1: "Thus says the Lord: "Heaven is my throne, and the earth is my footstool; what is the house that you would build for me, and what is the place of my rest?" God is comparing the entire creation to a Temple in which he is covenantally present. In other words, the entire creation is the image of God as represented through the analogy of a temple (cf. Ps. 104:1–4). Poythress connects this theophanic language to Romans

---

the Father being imaged in the Son is the divine archetype by which the divine ectype (Son being imaged in Adam) is modeled. The Human ectype is then reflective of all imaging occurring in humanity from that point forward.

[14] The Glory-Spirit is the Spirit of God present in Genesis 1:2. See, Kline, *Images of the Spirit*, 13–16.

[15] So Kline says, "The theophanic Glory was an archetypal pattern for the cosmos and for man, the image of God." Ibid., 17.

[16] "The Glory functioning as a dynamic paradigm-power reproduced its own likeness at the *mundane level*, in the earth-cosmos." Ibid., 257. Emphasis added.

1:19–20,[17] where God indicates that all mankind knows him for "what can be known about God is *plain to them*, because God has shown it to them. For his invisible attributes, namely, his eternal power and *divine nature*, have been clearly perceived, ever since the creation of the world, in the things that have been made. So they are without excuse."

Four points of importance derive from the theophanic presence of God within creation as noted in Romans 1:18–20. First, this knowledge is exhaustively present throughout creation from the very beginning and remains today. Second, this knowledge is a product of God's absolute personality, whereby he is present in all of his works. Third, this knowledge comes by way of God's creation (i.e., *in the things that have been made*—ποιήμασιν). As God *images* himself throughout all creation, all existence reveals him.[18] Finally, Paul indicates that all men perceive God's *divine nature* (θειοτης) through this imaging.[19] Charles Hodge understands θειοτης in its widest sense to refer to a "collective term for all the divine perfections."[20] Because of the central nature of God's triunity, is it a stretch to believe it is one of the divine perfections? On this reading, one should expect that creation *would* reflect the Trinitarian nature of God.[21]

---

[17] Poythress, "Multiperspectivalism," 194.

[18] Oliphint describes this knowledge in personalistic/covenantal terms: "This is relational, *covenantal*, knowledge. It is knowledge that comes to us because, as creatures of God, we are always and everywhere confronted with God himself." K. Scott Oliphint, "The Irrationality of Unbelief: An Exegetical Study," in *Revelation and Reason: New Essays in Reformed Apologetics*, ed. K. Scott Oliphint and Lane G. Tipton (Phillipsburg, NJ: P&R Publishing, 2007), 67.

[19] This term is difficult to clearly define, because its noun form is only used here.

[20] Herny Morris and K. Scott Oliphint argue for a broad understanding of the term as well. Charles Hodge, *A Commentary on Romans* (Edinburgh, Scotland: Banner of Truth, 1972), 37; Leon Morris, *The Epistle to the Romans*, The Pillar New Testament Commentary (Grand Rapids, MI: Eerdmans, 1988), 81–82; Oliphint, "The Irrationality of Unbelief: An Exegetical Study," 66.

[21] A caveat should be made here. We are not suggesting that man through natural resources and by means of natural revelation could derive the Trinitarian

In sum, Scripture presents the whole creation as imaging God (theophany). Therefore, as a result of its inherent imaging and his nature as absolute, it also expresses his triune, divine nature. Poythress summarizes the connection between theophany and perspectivalism:

> Theophany, as we have seen, is innately Trinitarian and therefore perspectival. We see the Father in the Son. By implication, the creation itself displays the imprint of Trinitarian structure. Although man is the image of God in a unique sense, the created world 'images' God in a great variety of ways. It images the Trinitarian God. Therefore, it is rich with the potential for perspectival investigation.[22]

Through imaging, Poythress finds the connecting point between God's nature and creation. Because creation is fashioned after the likeness of God, it exemplifies God's attributes (Rom. 1:20).[23] These attributes include triunity and are related to one another in absolute unity and diversity through the perichoretic-simplicity model

---

nature independently of God's special revelation. A central argument in this passage is that the fallen creature will twist God's revelation. Oliphint makes this point powerfully: "We should be clear about Paul's emphasis. What Paul is concerned to deny in this context is that we, in our sins, as covenant-breakers in Adam, would ever, or could ever, produce or properly infer this truth that we have, this knowledge of God, in and of ourselves." Oliphint, "The Irrationality of Unbelief: An Exegetical Study," 65.

[22] Poythress, "Multiperspectivalism," 194.

[23] See also Gunton, who argues, "If God is God, he is the source of all being, meaning and truth. It would seem reasonable to suppose that all being, meaning and truth is, even as created and distinct from God, in some way marked by its relatedness to its creator." From this foundation, Gunton continues, "we should gladly affirm Paul's confession that 'Ever since the creation of the world [God's] invisible nature, namely his eternal power and deity has been clearly perceived.'" In light of this, Gunton says it is disappointing that man, as the image, has rarely been viewed through the lens of perichoretic imaging. Gunton, *The One, the Three and the Many*, 167–68.

previously described. By implication, creation itself shows perspectival relations.[24]

The Linguistic Character of Created Reality Implies Trinitarian Reflection

The third reason perspectivalism argues for Trinitarian reflection in creation is due to the linguistic nature of creation. Poythress states the argument in succinct fashion: "God creates with his Word. his Word is an expression of himself, and so his Word is Trinitarian. Since we are the creation of God's speech, then we are likewise one and many (along with all creation)."[25] In order to grasp his point, we will work through this statement step by step.

First, "God creates with his Word." This is a clear statement of the biblical principle given in Genesis 1:3; 1:6; 1:9; 1:11; 1:14; 1:20; 1:24, whereby God is said to have created through speech (cf. John 1:1; Heb. 11:3). Poythress notes the importance of this fact:

> If indeed God spoke to create the world, then the world from its beginning, and down to its roots, is *structured by God's language*. Language is not an alien imposition on the world but the very key to its being and its meaning. And if God governs the world even today through his word, then language, God's language, is also the deepest key to history and to the development of events.[26]

---

[24] In personal correspondence, Frame said, "I do believe that the triperspectival nature of God (the Trinity) is ontological. . . . Then when God contemplates and creates a world outside himself, the world is an image of his triadic nature. . . . all of the triads reflect his ontological nature, but they are refracted by the lens of creation into a form appropriate to the creation." Frame here shows that he agrees with the imaging from Poythress. He further reveals something Poythress implicitly maintains; namely, God's image is reflected in a way that is appropriate to creation. John M. Frame, e-mail message to the author, January 28, 2014.

[25] Vern S. Poythress, *Logic: A God-Centered Approach to the Foundation of Western Thought* (Wheaton, IL: Crossway, 2013), 145.

[26] Vern S. Poythress, *In the Beginning Was the Word: Language: A God-Centered*

Poythress is suggesting that the creation of the world through God's language is not an insignificant fact to be passed over. Rather, as the very structure through which the world is created, this vehicle must be comprehended as transformative of how we understand creation.

Poythress's second statement—that God's Word is an expression of himself, and so his Word is Trinitarian—should be understood in light of the absolute nature of God. Because God is absolute, when he speaks, such speech is expressive of himself. Further, because God is Trinitarian, his language bears the mark of his Trinitarian nature.[27] This fact gives massive import to the previous observation. Namely, if all of creation is structured upon God's linguistic expression, and if that linguistic expression is determinatively Trinitarian, then all of creation bears the marks of Trinity.

The last part of Poythress's quote is the conclusion of the previous points. Man and all of creation have been created according to divine speech. Therefore, it is not only man that bears the marks of Trinity, but all creation does as well. Poythress also develops this same point from a slightly different angle—because God's decrees are both Trinitarian and verbal in nature,[28] then all of history (as an unfolding of those decrees) bears the marks of Trinity.[29]

Poythress provides another rich approach to this truth by

Approach (Wheaton, IL: Crossway, 2009), 24. Emphasis added.

[27] While we do not have the space to develop all of the triads inherent in divine and human language, Poythress develops many of them in his *God-Centered Biblical Interpretation*. The following are representative: triad of meaning (sense, application, import), triad of archetypal communication (speaker, words spoken, listener), triad of ectypal communication (speaker, words spoken, vehicle of communication). Vern S. Poythress, *God-Centered Biblical Interpretation* (Phillipsburg, NJ: P&R Publishing, 1999).

[28] "If history matches God's verbal decrees, we would expect that events of history show a structure similar to what we have already found with respect to God's speech." Ibid., 146.

[29] God's decrees are a reflection of God's perspectival knowledge. Thus the world is Trinitarian because both the constitutive knowledge of that creation as well as the verbal expression of that knowledge is inherently Trinitarian.

aligning the three aspects of speech (speaker, words spoken, vehicle for the words) with the three persons of the Trinity according to Frame's lordship model:

> God the Father as speaker acts more like a planner. God the Son as the one associated with the speech itself is the one who puts the plan or thought into execution. The Holy Spirit as the breath of God is the one who brings the word in power to its destination, and works effects on those who hear. That is to say that he is the empowerer and consummator. Thus, God's actions in history express the speech of God, which has innately trinitarian structure.[30]

So, as we have argued, God's acts are linguistic in that all his acts originate from his creative speech. But additionally, Poythress shows that God's acts are also linguistic in that the aspects of speech naturally align with the persons of the Trinity. Thus, God's speech is reflective of his acts just as his acts are reflective of his speech. Ultimately, this unity derives from both being expressions of an absolute Trinitarian God.

Bavinck and Trinitarian Vestigia

Frame, in *Doctrine of God*, cites Herman Bavinck's work on the doctrine of God twenty-six times. The influence of Bavinck can be seen in numerous areas, but one obvious influence concerns the doctrine of the Trinity. More specifically, it concerns the presence of *vestigia trinitatis*. Here we will seek to develop the views of Bavinck, showing how Frame's work is dependent on this Dutch Reformed theologian.[31]

---

[30] Vern S. Poythress, *Redeeming Philosophy: A God-Centered Approach to the Big Questions* (Wheaton, IL: Crossway, 2014), 274.

[31] Because Van Til was also deeply influenced by Bavinck, we have the difficulty of discerning which man influenced Frame towards particular theological positions.

Bavinck is responsible for one of the foundational beliefs of perspectivalism we have noted above. Namely, Bavinck notes that everything within creation must be sourced out of the Trinity: "The Christian mind remains unsatisfied until all of existence is referred back to the triune God."[32] This quote derives from a larger context in which Bavinck is arguing that the Trinitarian nature of God must be the centerpiece of a proper theological system:

> The thinking mind situates the doctrine of the Trinity squarely amid the full-orbed life of nature and humanity. A Christian's confession is not an island in the ocean but a high mountaintop from which the whole creation can be surveyed. And it is the task of Christian theologians to present clearly the connectedness of God's revelation with, and its significance for, all of life. The Christian mind remains unsatisfied until all of existence is referred back to the triune God, and until the confession of God's Trinity functions at the center of our thought and life.[33]

Latent within this quote are several critical ideas Van Til and Frame develop. When Bavinck discusses the island and mountain metaphor, he is suggesting that the revelation of the Trinity is not unconnected to the rest of creation like an isolated island, but is rather the vantage point from which all else is understood. For this reason, Bavinck is fundamental to understanding Van Til's development of the transcendental argument from a triune God.[34]

[32] Bavinck, *Reformed Dogmatics*, 2.330.
[33] Ibid.
[34] Mattson indicates that Bavinck's central purpose was formulating a transcendental expression of the Trinity. However, Mattson indicates that Bavinck is only successful in creating a *quasi*-transcendental argument, since Bavinck fails to show how *only* a triune God could be responsible for the world. Bosserman also critiques Van Til who, following Bavinck, does not explicitly show why *only* a triune God is the necessary transcendental for creation. Brian G. Mattson, *Restored to Our Destiny: Eschatology and the Image of God in Herman*

Frame, embracing the transcendental thrust of Bavinck's theology, seeks to develop another aspect of such a transcendental conclusion; an aspect that Bavinck explicitly notes, but does not develop at length. Namely, Bavinck believed that a transcendental outlook intimated the existence of *vestigia trinitatis*. As James Englinton notes, "At the core of Bavinck's methodology is the principle that an essential coherence exists between Creator and creation. When properly understood, the cosmos will bear the inevitable marks of its triune Maker whose special revelation will also reflect his own being and nature." As a result, Bavinck believes that, "In the Trinity's cosmos, *vestigial trinitatis* will abound."[35] This core principle appears to be an implication of Bavinck's transcendental reflection that all things come from and are therefore reflective of the Trinitarian God.[36] Consequently, Bavinck says, "There is much truth in the belief that creation everywhere displays to us vestiges of the Trinity."[37]

Bavinck was a student of Reformed Theology and was aware that Calvin and the Reformers were reluctant to embrace analogies or vestiges of the Trinity.[38] The problem, as Bavinck saw it, concerned whether one used such analogies or examples as *proof* for the doctrine of the Trinity. Such use Bavinck explicitly denied. Nevertheless, Bavinck was willing to say that despite how "the revelation

---

Bavinck's Reformed Dogmatics (Boston, MA: Brill, 2011), 43; Brant Bosserman, "The Trinity and the Vindication of Christian Paradox: An Interpretation and Refinement of the Theological Apologetic of Cornelius Van Til" (PhD Diss., University of Bangor, 2011).

[35] James Eglinton, *Trinity and Organism: Towards a New Reading of Herman Bavinck's Organic Motif* (London: T&T Clark, 2012), 101.

[36] Bavinck confirms this position when, after arguing against the use of Trinitarian images in proving the Trinity, he says, "Nevertheless, the arguments advanced to shed light on the dogma of the Trinity are not devoid of all value . . . Scripture itself gives us the freedom to use them when it says that the entire creation and especially humankind is a work of the triune God." Bavinck, *Reformed Dogmatics*, 2.329. Emphasis added.

[37] Ibid., 2.333.

[38] Ibid., 2.329.

of God in his works has been shrouded and our mind's eye has been darkened by sin, it cannot a priori be denied that the mind, *illumined by revelation*, can discover in nature the imprints of the God whom it has come to know from Scripture as triune in his mode of existence and actions."[39] Here Bavinck follows Calvin's view of evidences, wherein Calvin argued that natural evidences were not sufficient to produce belief, but they were helpful as aids after regeneration.[40] In a similar light, Bavinck uses the *vestiges* not to prove the Trinity, but rather to view all of creation from the mountain peak of Trinitarian revelation.

Eglinton remarks on this tension between Bavinck and his tradition: "Bavinck shows that one can be wholly against natural theology *and* wholly for the *vestigial trinitatis*." The key to maintaining both is Bavinck's unique "understanding of Trinity and cosmos, *The Trinity is wholly unlike anything else, but everything else is like the Trinity*."[41] Eglinton is indicating that while natural theology would never lead to a proper view of the Trinity, once a proper view has been understood through revelation, that new view casts a revealing light on all creation. Bavinck mentions several ways in which Trinitarian reflection might be seen in creation as evidenced in historical theology. First, he develops the prominence of the number three in Scripture, other literature, and throughout creation.[42] Second, he notes the logical analogies of the Trinity such as the three branches of philosophy, the three aspects of grammar, and the triad of being.[43]

---

[39] Ibid., 2.330.

[40] John Calvin, *Institutes of the Christian Religion: 1536 Edition*, trans. Ford Battles (Grand Rapids, MI: Eerdmans, 1995), 1.8.1, 15.

[41] Eglinton, *Trinity and Organism*, 89.

[42] It is from Bavinck that some of Frame's triads derive. For instance, Bavinck notes the family unit of father, mother, and child—a triad Frame will later use. Other examples include the triadic harmony in music, colors on the spectrum, and the dimensions of space. Bavinck, *Reformed Dogmatics*, 2.322–23; Frame, *The Doctrine of God*, 743–50.

[43] The triad of being is nearly identical to Poythress's ontological triad of classificational, instantational, and associational. Bavinck, *Reformed Dogmatics*,

Finally, Bavinck speaks explicitly about Augustine who believed that "the entire creation is a mirror of God."[44] And, as Bavinck notes approvingly, Augustine sought analogy of the Trinity not only on the basis of the number three but further in that a "triad consists in the fact that all three are one and equal, that each of the three is present in the two others, and that these two in turn are present in one another and thus 'all are in all.'"[45] Such triads go deeper than mere numerical reflection by imaging the nature of the three persons of the Godhead.

Bavinck's Contribution to Vestigia

After having surveyed the field of *vestigia* in theology, Bavinck turns to his own contribution. While others have found analogy to the Trinity in triadic forms, Bavinck proposes the universal concept of unity in diversity as a *vestigie*.[46] In the Trinity we find "absolute unity as well as absolute diversity."[47] And while we do not expect the world to exhibit the Trinitarian relation perfectly or absolutely, we should not be surprised that unity in diversity is reflected throughout

---

2.323–24; Poythress, *God-Centered Biblical Interpretation*, 142–43.

[44] Bavinck, *Reformed Dogmatics*, 2.325.

[45] Ibid., 2.325–26.

[46] Eglinton says that for Bavinck, the "key development within the idea of the *vestigial trinitatis* . . . lies in the establishment of the non-numerical paradigm of unity in diversity (rather than the medieval triad form) as the norm in terms of triniform hallmarks." Eglinton further argues that Bavinck moved away from triads as he developed the Trinitarian pattern of unity in diversity. However, Eglinton never explains why Bavinck spends so much time positively speaking of the contributions of past theologians towards the triadic forms. A better reading is to note that Bavinck is not detracting from useful triads but is rather enhancing *vestigia* awareness by emphasizing *another* pattern that is reflected into creation. The only hesitancy Bavinck shows concerning *vestigia* is with supposed natural theological implications. He shows no hesitancy with triadic forms. Indeed, even as Eglinton notes, Bavinck develops his entire dogmatics on the basis of a triad (Father in creation, Son in salvation, and Spirit in consummation). Eglinton, *Trinity and Organism*, 86, 88, 94.

[47] Bavinck, *Reformed Dogmatics*, 2.332.

creation: "Just as God is one in essence and distinct in persons, so also the work of creation is one and undivided, while in its unity it is still rich in diversity."[48] But Bavinck, like Frame, also recognizes the unity and diversity in the attributes as well:

> The diversity of attributes . . . does not clash with God's simplicity. For that simplicity does not describe God as an abstract and general kind of being; on the contrary, it speaks of him as the absolute fullness of life. It is for this very reason that God reveals himself to finite creatures by many names. The divine essence is so infinitely and profusely rich that no creature can grasp it all at once. Just as a child cannot picture the worth of a coin of great value but only gains some sense of it when it is counted out in smaller coins, so we too cannot possibly form a picture of the infinite fullness of God's essence unless it is displayed to us now in one relationship, then in another, and now from one angle, then from another.[49]

Eglinton shows that such unity and diversity is the "centerpiece" of the "most important section in Bavinck's entire Dogmatics."[50] Mattson agrees, noting that unity in diversity "may not on the surface appear to be a major theme in Bavinck's *Dogmatics*, but it underlies a variety of his theological formulations."[51] In other words, having recognized the centrality of unity in diversity from God's Trinitarian nature, Bavinck seeks to understand creation from that mountain peak.

At this point a summary will help. First, Bavinck has argued that Trinitarian revelation is the mountain peak from which Christians must begin their examination of the world. Second, the world

---

[48] Ibid., 2.422.

[49] Frame indicates that Bavinck's language "approaches a perspectival formulation." Ibid., 2.127; Frame, *The Doctrine of God*, 228n29.

[50] Eglinton, *Trinity and Organism*, 104.

[51] Mattson, *Restored to Our Destiny*, 45.

is necessarily reflective of God's Trinitarian nature, providing *vestigia trinitatis* throughout. Third, one key element of God's Trinitarian nature is his unity in diversity. These three observations, when brought together, lead Bavinck to argue for the *organic* nature of the world: "The world can, metaphorically, be called an organism, in which all the parts are connected with each other reciprocally."[52] Ultimately, the world is one large functioning organism, because "Trinity *ad intra* leads to organism *ad extra*."[53]

What Bavinck means by organism has been debated, but two recent studies have sought to ground Bavinck's use of the term in his own writings rather than in the way the term was used in idealist philosophy.[54] As a result of extensive research within Bavinck's corpus, Eglinton concluded that Bavinck's use of organic included four concepts:

1. Organisms exhibit both simultaneous unity and diversity.
2. In an organism, unity precedes diversity.
3. Organisms operate harmoniously.
4. Organisms have a united goal, which is to glorify God.[55]

By calling the world an organism, Bavinck shows that he believed the entire world is an image of the triune God. Everywhere within this organism are smaller organisms,[56] working together for God's glory.

---

[52] Bavinck, *Reformed Dogmatics*, 2.436.

[53] Eglinton, *Trinity and Organism*, 81.

[54] Mattson, *Restored to Our Destiny*; Eglinton, *Trinity and Organism*.

[55] James Eglinton, "Bavinck's Organic Motif: Questions Seeking Answers," *Calvin Theological Journal* 45, 1 (April 2010): 63–64.

[56] Bavinck intimates that there are organisms within organisms (or *vestigie in vestigie*): "Naturally just as the cosmos is an organism and reveals God's attributes more clearly in some than in other creatures, so also in man as an organism the image of God comes out more clearly in one part than another, more in the soul than the body, more in the ethical virtues than in the physical powers. None of this, however, detracts in the least from the truth that the whole person is the image of God." Bavinck, *Reformed Dogmatics*, 2.555.

So captivating was this paradigm for Bavinck that he developed the rest of his Dogmatics on its foundation. As Eglinton again notes,

> Bavinck's most rudimentary characterization of God is as a being of immense diversity and profound unity. This fact exerts a controlling influence on Bavinck's understanding and appropriation of all created reality. It also sets the parameters within which he grasps the overarching scheme of Father as Creator (RD 2), Son as Saviour (RD 3), and Spirit as Consummator (RD 4).[57]

As another example of his use of organism as a reflection of the Trinity, Bavinck suggests that epistemology and ethics are two aspects of one organism: "Dogmatics is the system of the knowledge of God; ethics is that of the service of God. The two disciplines, far from facing each other as two independent entities, together form a single system; they are related members of a single organism."[58]

Other Forms of Vestigia in Bavinck's Work

So it is clear that Bavinck recognizes macroscopic and microscopic *vestigia* in creation by means of the organic motif. But another Trinitarian *vestigie* present in perspectivalism may derive from Bavinck as well. Namely, Poythress's observation concerning the imaging of God through language is evident in Bavinck's work as well. Notice how Bavinck connects the archetypal intra-Trinitarian relations to ectypal human communication: "The most striking analogy of divine generation is thought and speech, and Scripture suggests this when it calls the Son 'Logos.'"[59] Further, "Just as the human mind objectivizes itself in words, so God expresses his entire being in the Logos. For God to beget is to speak, and his speaking

---

[57] Eglinton, *Trinity and Organism*, 104.
[58] Bavinck, *Reformed Dogmatics*, 1.58.
[59] Ibid., 2.309.

is eternal."⁶⁰ Bavinck's belief that all things necessarily trace back to the Trinity allows him to connect the line between God's eternal self-communication and creation: "The dogma of the trinity . . . tells us that God can reveal himself in an absolute sense to the Son and the Spirit, and hence, in a relative sense also to the world. For, as Augustine teaches us, the self-communication that takes place within the divine being is archetypal for God's work in creation."⁶¹ According to Bavinck, human language is an ectypal image of God's eternal archetypal relations. It is these Trinitarian reflections that Poythress develops throughout his major works on interpretation.

An additional way Bavinck shows *vestigia* of the Trinity is through absolute personality. Van Til and Frame derive their emphasis on absolute personality from Bavinck, who observes, "in Scripture the personality and the absoluteness of God go hand in hand."⁶² In context, Bavinck is noting that God's ontological character is revealed by means of his economic manifestation. Thus, we know the absoluteness of God only in communion with his revealed personality. Bavinck further notes, "The 'ontological' Trinity is mirrored in the 'economic' Trinity. For that reason special properties and works are attributed to each of the three persons . . . in such a way that the order present between the persons in the ontological Trinity is revealed."⁶³ Such revelation is both analogical and yet truly revelatory of who God is, or to put it in Bavinck's words, "As God reveals himself so is he."⁶⁴

---

⁶⁰ Ibid., 2.259.
⁶¹ Ibid., 2.333.
⁶² Ibid., 2.34.
⁶³ Ibid., 2.318.
⁶⁴ Scripture, Bavinck says, "posits no split, much less a contrast, between God's ontological existence and his 'economic' self-revelation. As God reveals himself so is he; in his names he himself becomes knowable to us. Though he is indeed infinitely superior to all his creatures—so that we can possess only an analogical knowledge of him not an exhaustive (adequate) knowledge—yet his several attributes, attributes that come through in his revelation, bring to our mind, each time from a special perspective, the fullness of his being." Ibid.,

What does the economic reveal about the ontological? Or what do we see in the tri-personality of God that helps us recognize concerning the nature of God? Bavinck says,

> Distinctions interior to the divine essence are also revealed outwardly. To be sure, outgoing works are works of the Divine Being as a whole. Nevertheless, some of these works are more particularly ascribed to one person, and others more especially to another; creation to the Father, redemption to the Son, sanctification to the Holy Spirit. Similarly, in the order of revelation the Father is first, the Son second, and the Holy Spirit third. Thus, the order of subsistence in the ontological trinity is beautifully reflected in the order and manifestation in the economical trinity.[65]

A few important points can be derived from this text and its surrounding context. First, as we have seen, it is on this triadic basis that Bavinck develops his *Reformed Dogmatics*: the Father is the creator (RD 2); the Son is the redeemer (RD 3); and the Spirit is the consummator (RD 4). Second, Bavinck indicates in the broader context that these activities are sourced out of the ontological Trinity, and are not merely the economical.[66] Third, Bavinck shows that his division

---

2.111. And also, "There is no knowledge of God apart from his revelation in his creatures, hence always analogical and ectypal, but by that revelation we do have true and authentic knowledge of God's incomprehensible and adorable being!" Ibid., 2.137.

[65] Herman Bavinck, *The Doctrine of God*, ed. William Hendriksen, trans. William Hendriksen (Edinburgh, Scotland: Banner of Truth, 1977), 317.

[66] "The diversity of the subjects who act side by side in divine revelation, in creation and in re-creation, arises from the diversity that exists among the three persons in the divine being. There could be no distinction *ad extra* in the unity of the divine being, if there were no distinction *ad intra*." Bavinck, *Reformed Dogmatics*, 2.332. Bavinck also says, "We also find 'economic' distinctions in the works *ad extra*. All of these works are accomplished by the one God, yet in each of the three persons fulfills the role that corresponds to the order of his existence in the divine being." Ibid., 2.319.

of labor is consonant with past historical reflection on the Trinity.[67] Finally, what is most significant about the paragraph is the organic relationship Bavinck finds in the activity of the Trinitarian persons. We have already noted that he derives the organic relationship from the Trinitarian persons and the attributes of God, but additionally we find that he also perceives a unity and diversity among God's *acts*.

Notably, Frame develops his most versatile triad of lordship from the unity and diversity of God's acts. Indeed, Frame's development of triadic ectypes on the basis of the three persons gets much support from Bavinck, who says,

> The names Father, Son . . . and Spirit most certainly denote immanent relationships, but they are also mirrored in the interpersonal relations present in the works of God *ad extra*. All things come from the Father; the 'ideas' of all existent things are present in the Son; the first principles of all life are in the Spirit. Generation and procession in the divine being are the immanent acts of God, which make possible the outward works of creation and revelation. Finally, this also explains why all the works of God *ad extra* are only adequately known when their Trinitarian existence is recognized. . . . There is much truth in the belief that creation everywhere displays to us vestiges of the Trinity.[68]

Summary of Bavinck and Vestigia

In summary, Frame is emboldened to find *vestigia* throughout creation from the transcendental thrust of Bavinck's thought. Because the world is necessarily the product of a Trinitarian God, and because God's handiwork necessarily reflects his nature, it is natural to seek and find *vestigia* in creation. While Bavinck approvingly cites many historical expressions of *vestigia*, he is careful to avoid any indication

---

[67] Bavinck, *Reformed Dogmatics*, 2.318–22.
[68] Ibid., 2.333.

that the *vestigia* should be used in a natural theology program. For this reason, he can agree with the caution towards *vestigia* that his Reformed predecessors showed while also embracing the existence of *vestigia*. Bavinck's most notable contribution to the field is his development of unity in diversity archetypally present in the triune God and ectypally manifested in the organisms of creation. Bavinck's work is also congenial to other *vestigia* by noting the origins of language in the triune activity of God, and by showing that God's acts are a unity in diversity, providing a basis for recognizing *vestigia* which correlate according to the pattern originally found in the triune persons.

Perspectival Dynamics

Perspectivalism is chiefly concerned with showing how the Trinitarian nature of God is expressed in creation. In that light, we are now ready to turn to develop the *perspectival dynamics*, i.e., those characteristics determinative of perspectival groups. We will see that the perspectival dynamics are ectypally reflective of perichoretic-simplicity, which we have developed in previous chapters.

Interdependence, Inclusivity, and Identity

The major characteristics of perspectival dynamics can be summarized under three main headings: interdependence, inclusivity, and identity.[69] These same dynamics are evident in God's knowledge, attributes, and persons. Therefore, the same characteristics noted in relation to simplicity and perichoresis apply to perspectivalism as well. Here we will summarize these relationships by giving them expression in relation to the ultimate triad, the Trinity.[70]

---

[69] John Hughes appears to be the first to coin the term, *triad dynamics*. By calling them perspectival dynamics, we are broadening the designation to reflect both triperspectivalism and multiperspectivalism. John J. Hughes, "The Heart of John Frame's Theology," in *Speaking the Truth in Love: The Theology of John M. Frame*, ed. John J. Hughes (Phillipsburg, NJ: P&R Publishing, 2009), 41.

[70] We must keep in the forefront Frame's concern that while the Trinity is

Perspectival Dynamics

Interdependence, inclusivity, and identity imply the following perspectival dynamics. First, *no one perspective can be fully understood without the others*. In terms of God's triunity, one cannot fully know the Father without knowing the Son (John 14:6).[71] The reverse is also true (Matt. 11:27). Further, one comes to know the Father through the Son by the Spirit (1 Cor. 2:14). No one can know the Father or the Son except by the Spirit. What applies epistemologically is true ontologically as well. The Father, Son, and Spirit exist inseparably in relation to one another.

That each perspective *implies all the other perspectives* is a second perspectival dynamic. Applied to the Trinity, this shows that a full understanding of the Son implies and leads naturally to understanding the Father and Spirit. In the same way, a full understanding of the Spirit implies both the knowledge of the Father and the Son. Again, this is true both epistemologically and ontologically. The Father cannot be *known* as the Father without the Son, but he also cannot be *Father* without a Son.

The mutual implication of the persons leads to a third perspectival dynamic: *perspectives can be derived from one another*. Poythress has developed this point in relation to the attributes of God arguing, "On a human level, we can derive any attribute from any other. We just have to expand or stretch our conception of the starting attribute, and we will find that it involves or implies the derived

---

perspectival, the persons are not *merely* perspectival. John M. Frame, "A Primer on Perspectivalism," in *John Frame's Selected Shorter Writings* (Phillipsburg, NJ: P&R Publishing, 2014), 9–10.

[71] The concern that the Old Testament did not explicitly present God as triune does not concern us here. Clearly, the revelation of God was of the Father, Son, and Spirit. In one sense, we could say that the revelation of God as unity in the Old Testament serves to complement the argument here. In knowing the work (and person) of the Son, we know the work (and person) of the others. Thus, we can speak of them as a unity (as emphasized in the Old Testament) and as a diversity (as emphasized in the New Testament).

attribute."[72] There are limitations to this process, however. First, in order to derive perspectives from one another, there needs to be robust knowledge. That is, *limited knowledge* of one perspective does not necessarily lead to other perspectives. Nevertheless, when a particular perspective is *fully* known, the others can be derived from it. In relation to the Trinity, it is not suggested that knowledge of the Son could be derived from the knowledge of the Father from *only* one specific text (e.g., Gen. 1:1) or even a grouping of texts. Nevertheless, if Genesis 1:1 and the Father are known in full, then the knowledge of the Son and Spirit is included in that *full* knowledge.[73] A second limitation is that, since our perspective is never exhaustive, our derivations must always be up for emendation to Scripture. Poythress is aware of this limitation and warns the reader, "Such ways of speaking, of course, can lead to incorrect deductions about God, in which we might use a distorted human conception. . . . We might wrongly claim that those deductions gave us more ultimate insight than biblical statements about God's other attributes."[74] These limitations, however, are limitations for creatures and not God. Because he has exhaustive knowledge, his exhaustive perspectives always lead to and, therefore, can be derived from every other perspective.

Because each perspective, when fully informed, includes all others, *perspectives are epistemologically identical*. In their writings, Frame and Poythress define this fourth perspectival dynamic in different ways—having the same concept, covering the same material, overlapping, intersecting, and being identical. Poythress's analogy of a multi-faceted jewel is illustrative.[75] A jewel has many facets, yet it

---

[72] Vern S. Poythress, *Symphonic Theology* (Grand Rapids, MI: Zondervan, 1987), 83.

[73] But as Frame argues, the context of Genesis 1:1 is the entirety of Scripture (and beyond). See, John M. Frame, "Contexts," in *John Frame's Selected Shorter Writings* (Phillipsburg, NJ: P&R Publishing, 2014), 52–58.

[74] Poythress, *Symphonic Theology*, 38.

[75] Ibid., 37.

is essentially one. Looking through one facet will give all the knowledge contained in every other facet. In a similar way, knowledge of the Father, if it is complete, will include *all* knowledge of the Son. Further, knowledge of the Son, if it is complete, will include the full knowledge of the Father. Thus, in an important way, all of the perspectives contain all of the same truth.

The epistemological identity of the perspectives does not eliminate the diversity of perspectives, however. In order to prevent a misunderstanding, a fifth perspectival dynamic should be stressed—*each perspective has a different entry point for knowledge*. Poythress's analogy of a multi-faceted jewel is again illustrative. While the entire jewel can be seen from any one facet (if examined with enough care), nevertheless "not everything can be seen equally easily through only one facet."[76] Each facet remains only a facet, but it does give entrance into the whole jewel. This can be seen from the persons in the Trinity. Metaphysically, there is an identity among the three persons in the essence, yet this identity does not eliminate the diversity of their persons. Epistemologically, by knowing the Son we know the Father; nevertheless, the knowledge gained in this way remains a knowledge viewed through the facet of the Son.

In God's knowledge, the Father has a view of the Son's knowledge. Also, the Son has a view of the Father's knowledge of the Son. Of course, this implies that the Father has knowledge of the Son's view of the Father's view of the Son's view of the Father's knowledge of the Son. This infinite chain leads to the conclusion that *perspectives are infinitely interrelated*. Frame illustrates this relationship within his lordship triad, which provides the overall structure for his *Doctrine of the Knowledge of God*. There he argues that the book could be "further subdivided into existential-normative-normative, existential-normative-situational, and so forth, *ad infinitum*."[77] Since

---

[76] Ibid.

[77] John M. Frame, *The Doctrine of the Knowledge of God* (Phillipsburg, NJ: Presbyterian and Reformed, 1987), 167n1.

each perspective provides a window through which the other perspectives may be viewed, and since all of the perspectives are united under God's comprehensive plan, then all of the perspectives can be viewed in ever-deepening relationship. This replicates on the mundane level what is inherently related on the divine level. In perichoresis, the persons of the Trinity infinitely relate. Thus, in harmony with perichoresis, the perspectives infinitely relate as well. The truth is exhaustive and infinite, showing that man can never embrace the depth of God's revelation.[78]

The seventh and final perspectival dynamic shows that *perspectives are equally ultimate*. Said alternatively, perspectives show no *ultimate* priority. Frame relates this to both the persons and attributes of God: "None of the persons is 'prior to' the others; all are equally eternal, ultimate, absolute, glorious. None of the attributes is 'prior to' any of the others; each is equally divine, inalienable, and necessary to God's deity."[79] However, we will argue in a future chapter that since the divine persons show priority and order, some of the triads reflect this pattern. In this light, the seventh dynamic should be remodeled. In the unity of the perspectives, they are equally ultimate (just as the persons are equally ultimate in the essence); however, in their diversity some of the perspectives show order and priority (just as the persons truly represent order and priority in their diversity).

---

[78] This perspectival dynamic is chiefly responsible for the flexibility of the perspectival system. Is the Father the authority or the Son? Well, both have authority, so there is overlap. What is the exact distinction between God's love, mercy, and grace? While they can be defined differently, in practical application, they are infinitely interrelated, so that they cannot be easily separated. This interrelation can cause difficulty for the neophyte perspectivalist, who believes that the elements within a perspectival triad must be entirely distinct. But as Frame notes, "I am consoled by the fact that the three perspectives are, after all, perspectives, which means that anything we say about God can be said under any of the three categories." Frame, *The Doctrine of God*, 287n17.

[79] Frame, *The Doctrine of the Knowledge of God*, 192.

Table 1. Perspectival Dynamics

	Perspectival Dynamics
1	Perspectives do not make full sense without one another
2	Perspectives imply all the other perspectives
3	Perspectives can be derived from one another
4	Perspectives are epistemologically identical
5	Perspectives have a distinct entry point for the knowledge they share
6	Perspectives are infinitely interrelated
7	Perspectives are equally ultimate in their unity

Clarification of Identity

Frame often calls elements within perspectival groups *identical* with one another. For instance, when speaking of the sources of knowledge, Frame says, "the knowledge of God's law, the world and the self are interdependent and ultimately identical."[80] Such language has been the source of confusion for some of Frame's critics.[81] Two

---

[80] Ibid., 89.

[81] Greg Bahnsen, referring to Frame's correlation of presuppositions and evidences as identical, demurs, "The evidences that go with the presuppositions and the presuppositions make the evidences intelligible are one. But to say that they are identical on the other hand I think would be mistaken." Scrivener also argues that the idea of identity derives from a mistaken view of simplicity. Finally, James Anderson calls Frame's correlation of the identity of the elements of knowledge a "confusing claim" that may "erode their distinctiveness." Greg Bahnsen, "The Place of Evidence in Apologetics," January 17, 1986, accessed June 27, 2014, http://www.cmfnow.com/theplaceofevidencein-apologetics.aspx; Glen Scrivener, "How Frame's Doctrine of the Knowledge of God Might Shape and Inform the Christian Study of Ethics" (Bth Paper, Oak Hill Theological College, 2006), http://www.christthetruth.org.uk/Frame.htm; James N. Anderson, "Presuppositionalism and Frame's Epistemology," in

points should be emphasized in light of these critiques. First, critics often confuse epistemological claims with ontological claims.[82] Frame responds, making explicit the epistemological-ontological distinction: "Someone might look at this reasoning and say that in the end it makes Scripture, the world, and the self identical.... And I say no. These three are not identical. But the *knowledge of them is identical*. You can't know one apart from knowing the others."[83] When speaking of metaphysical identity, Frame explicitly denies identity among the sources of knowledge: "The Christian, though, knows that however inseparable these elements are in our knowledge, they are not identical."[84] If the ontological-epistemological distinction is maintained, much of the criticism of Frame's language is circumvented.[85]

A second way of responding to the critiques against identity

Speaking the Truth in Love: The Theology of John M. Frame, ed. John J. Hughes (Phillipsburg, NJ: P&R Publishing, 2009), 439n21.

[82] Frame anticipated this confusion, providing "an ontological clarification" as a partial explanation. Frame, *The Doctrine of the Knowledge of God*, 401.

[83] As quoted from e-mail correspondence in John Barber, "John Frame's Theology in the Present Cultural Context," in *Speaking the Truth in Love: The Theology of John M. Frame*, ed. John J. Hughes (Phillipsburg, NJ: P&R Publishing, 2009), 900n51.

[84] He continues, "I am not the world, nor vice versa.... Nor is God's word identical with the world or with myself." John M. Frame, "The Spirit and the Scriptures," in *Hermeneutics, Authority, and Canon*, ed. D. A. Carson and John D. Woodbridge (Grand Rapids, MI: Zondervan, 1986), 230.

[85] Having argued that much of the confusion over the language of identity is a categorization error, we should indicate that at times Frame does present *some* perspectival relationships ontologically. For example, Frame says, "Our *knowledge* of the work of the three persons [of the Trinity] is perspectival. In a sense, these divine works are also perspectival in their *nature*." He continues, "Although they are distinguishable, it is important to realize that the divine plan includes the atonement and its application; the atonement is the outworking of the plan and the event to be applied; and the application is the application of the plan and the atonement. As the Trinity itself, these divine acts are mysteriously one and many." Frame, "A Primer on Perspectivalism," 11.

language more directly pertains to our discussion of the perichoretic-simplicity model. Perichoresis provides us with two functions—one of interrelation and one of identity with distinction. Both are necessary to understand Frame's epistemological point about the identity of knowledge elements. On the one hand, the identity of the aspects of knowledge is a function of their interrelatedness. Because each covers the same territory as the others, they contain the same information.[86] So there is unity, but they also remain diverse according to the second function of Perichoresis. Just as the members of the Trinity are identical to the essence of God yet remain distinct persons, so the three aspects of man's knowledge remain distinct yet are identical as considered in the human knower *as a person* (figure 6.2). Metaphysically, the law is distinct from both the situation and person in which and to which it is applied. Nevertheless, as brought together *in the person*, these three forms of distinct knowledge gain what Frame calls identity. Again, this is not to say the human knower could not distinguish the three elements of knowledge in his or her mind; rather, when the subject seeks to know, he or she must integrate all three together in order to have any knowledge. Each aspect encompasses and includes the others.[87]

---

[86] Poythress pointed to the interrelatedness of the perspectives as the motivation for Frame's use of identical language: "I do avoid the language of identity. But I think Frame's point with this strong language is that when used faithfully and in the long run, the perspectives all give you 'the same thing' in the sense that they lead to covering the whole field. That is, each perspective actually encompasses the others—when actually engaged in expansively and explored in the effort to cover the whole field." Vern S. Poythress, e-mail message to the author, January 29, 2014.

[87] Anderson argued this same point from a different angle: "Perhaps this tension can be resolved by following Gottlob Frege's distinction between sense and referent. 'Clark Kent,' 'Superman,' and 'the last survivor of the planet Krypton' have distinct senses but identical referents." Frame agreed with his sense/referent distinction, but it does not seem to be the entirety of the answer. If so, it would seem to lead to modalism. Anderson, "Presuppositionalism and Frame's Epistemology," 439n21; John M. Frame, "Responses to Some Articles," in *Speaking the Truth in Love: The Theology of John M. Frame*, ed. John J.

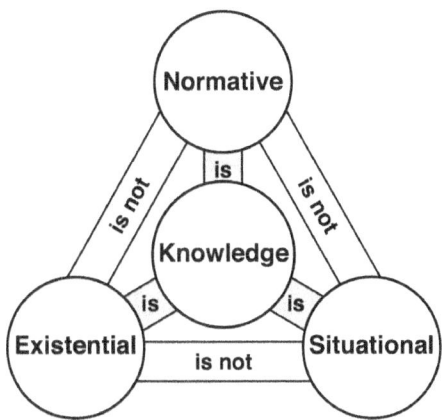

Fig. 6.2. Lordship Triad

In light of this clarification, it can be quite confusing to those uninitiated in perspectivalism to hear Frame use the language of identity. Generally, identical means identical in *every sense*, but this is clearly not what Frame means.[88] Just as Frame indicates that the Trinitarian persons are not identical in every sense, he maintains the same here. Thus, for Frame, identity is reserved for the absolute harmonization of groups in perichoretic interpenetration within the knowing subject. Such a position provides the needed resources to maintain both the unity and diversity of human knowledge.[89]

Hughes (Phillipsburg, NJ: P&R Publishing, 2009), 961.

[88] Again, in reference to the Trinity, Frame says, "Generally, we say that things identical to the same thing (here, Jesus and the Spirit to Yahweh) are identical to each other (so the Lord is the Spirit). . . . But we know from other Scriptures that that is not the whole story, and the 'identity' here is not an identity in every sense, but an identity of nature or essence." Frame, *The Doctrine of God*, 692–93.

[89] That Frame uses the language of identity so frequently without explicit clarification is ironic in light of both his critique of Van Til's difficult terminology as well as his otherwise lucid writing. Perhaps his insistence on using the

Types of Triads

In the next chapter we will detail the lordship triad and how many of Frame's other triads derive from it. It would be a mistake to believe, however, that all of the triads derive only from the lordship triad. So what is the organizing motif? What is the fundamental system by which the triads are recognized? Bosserman has pointed to this as a major flaw in perspectivalism, noting that "Little effort has been made to demonstrate whether and how at least several of these triadic perspectives can be organized into a single system."[90] He further argues that, when analyzed, the perspectives offered by both Frame and Poythress are arbitrary, haphazard, and prone to relativism.[91]

The lack of an explicit method for determining triads is also responsible for the apparent impenetrability of the perspectival method. As R. Scott Clark has argued, the perspectival game seems rigged. The only people who know how to play are Frame and Poythress, and they get to set the rules.[92]

Clearly, a model for deriving triads would be helpful for the future of perspectivalism, but is it possible to find such a model?

---

term is reflective of the emphasis he believes the perichoretic-like relationship should have (and historically has not had).

[90] Bosserman, "The Trinity and Christian Paradox," §156.

[91] DeYoung shares some of the concerns, noting, "It's not immediately clear that the categories [in a triad] have to line up the way they do." Ibid., §152–53; Kevin DeYoung, "Review of Systematic Theology by John Frame," *The Gospel Coalition*, last modified November 14, 2013, accessed November 21, 2013, http://thegospelcoalition.org/blogs/kevindeyoung/2013/11/14/book-review-systematic-theology-by-john-frame/.

[92] "In my experience, debates with [triperspectivalists] always collapse because the [triperspectivalist] gets to say who gets to participate in the discussion, what the rules are, and who wins and no one else really understands the game." R. Scott Clark, "Peace (with Evangelicalism) in Our Time," *The Heidelblog*, last modified October 7, 2009, accessed October 2, 2013, http://heidelblog.net/2009/10/subjectivism-and-peace-with-evangelicalism-tim-keller/.

When asked about whether the perspectival method has been used inappropriately in the past, Frame said,

> Well, yes. Sometimes I go back and look at my own triads and think, 'Oh, that was too much.' Like 'red, green, and blue' (*DG*, 747) or 'yolk, white, and shell.' But you never know. Sometimes one just gets a feeling about something. There is no mathematical formula here. And since the perspectives are perspectives on anything, then in principle anything can be brought into a triad.[93]

One might think that since there is "no mathematical formula" the prospect of forming a model for the derivation of perspectival triads is doomed to failure. It appears that Frame's concern in the above quote is to maintain the infinity of ways in which God can reveal himself through creation. To propose a strict, standardized model would seek to show that we have fully grasped all the ways God's Trinitarian nature is reflected in creation.[94] Thus, it appears that the combination of God's absoluteness and infinity provide a level of humility in Frame's theology, whereby Frame will not place limitations on God's Trinitarian revelation in creation.

But it appears that we can maintain the infinity of God's reflection in creation while also providing a model for deriving triads. Stated differently, we can organize Frame's and Poythress's triads according to various patterns the triads follow. Whether these patterns are exhaustive of the patterns of triunity in creation is not the question we are seeking to answer. Perhaps more ways will be

---

[93] John M. Frame, e-mail message to the author, January 28, 2014.

[94] Poythress agrees, arguing, "In a Christian or biblical world view, God himself is the only truly ultimate explanation for anything. If one category could serve as a tool for obtaining an ultimate analysis, it could only be the 'category' of God. And as we have seen, God always remains mysterious for us." Poythress, *Symphonic Theology*, 83.

shown in the future. The purpose at hand is to show the various ways Frame and Poythress have derived triads. In this way we can maintain the infinity and absoluteness of God's revelation while also providing a channel by which we may show that the triads are not haphazard, arbitrary, or relativistic.

In light of the above, we will seek to show, first, that not all triads derive directly from the lordship triad. Next, we will show the patterns for triads Frame and Poythress have discovered in creation. Third, we will show how the diverse types of triads are reflective of the Trinity in different ways. Finally, we will try to relate the various types of triads together.

Triads and the Lordship Triad

Frame's *Doctrine of God*, which lists 111 triads, shows that not all the triads are directly derived from the lordship triad. This extensive list ranges from some of the foundational triads used throughout Frame's work to some more abstruse ones. As for the latter, note the following triads: husband, wife, and child; circulation, respiration, and brain-nervous system; root, trunk, and branches; yolk, white, and shell; red, green, and blue.[95] Do these triads align with the lordship characteristics? While Frame jokingly suggests that he can relate the three primary colors along lordship lines,[96] it is clear that he does not actually have a decisive way of doing so.[97]

Frame's list clearly indicates that there are various *types* of triads in Frame's methodology. In the introduction to his extensive

---

[95] Earlier in the text, Frame admitted that some of his triads in the appendix are "far-fetched." Frame, *The Doctrine of God*, 727.

[96] "I have said (rather tongue in cheek) of the first triad that blue is the sky (normative), green the earth (situational), and red the interior of the body (existential)." Ibid., 747.

[97] Despite not having a *direct* way of aligning lordship with all of his triads, Frame would contend that all things are created in light of God's lordship. Thus, red, green, and blue are products of God's lordship. They show God's power, authority, and control.

list, Frame does not suggest that all the triads are *directly* reflective of lordship. Instead, he merely suggests that the characterization of the world into categories of three *may* reflect a Trinitarian God standing behind the creation. As we have shown above, Frame's belief that triads are reflective of the Trinity follows from both the formative influence of Herman Bavinck and Frame's understanding of the covenantal relation of creation to God.[98] Because God is reflected in creation, the creation may exhibit tripartite schemes. Consequently, Frame does not believe every aspect of creation exhibits God's nature in the same way. Instead, he seems to follow in a more cautious line of reasoning which suggests that the world exhibits the character of God *to the extent that it is capable of doing so*. The triads mentioned in the last paragraph are one in many and thus reflect the Trinity. However, they fall short of some other triads, which are capable of not only showing a one and many relationship but also reveal more explicitly a dynamic, perichoretic unity in diversity.[99]

Ways of Discovering Triads

In perspectivalism there are multiple ways of identifying triads. We will first examine Frame's list of five ways before turning to add

---

[98] Frame says, "If all of creation reflects God's invisible nature, his power and glory, is there any way in which creation reflects the Trinity as such? Certainly there are many phenomena that are three in one sense, one in another (or, more broadly, one-and-many)." John M. Frame, "Trinitarian Analogies," *The Works of John Frame and Vern Poythress*, last modified 1999, accessed September 4, 2013, http://www.frame-poythress.org/trinitarian-analogies/.

[99] Frame would maintain that because all of creation—from the largest categories to the smallest—displays the problem of the one and many, it likewise displays the Trinitarian nature. Nevertheless, Frame believes that some expressions of the Trinity are more explicit than others. So Frame says, "there are many phenomena that are three in one sense, one in another (or, more broadly, one-and-many). . . . But are there phenomena that can be more specifically related, in edifying ways, to the Trinitarian unity and diversity?" Frame answers in the affirmative. Frame, *The Doctrine of God*, 727.

another from Poythress's work. Finally, we will summarize the six ways, showing how each is dependent on the Trinity.

Frame's Five Ways of Discovering Triads

After Frame acknowledges that "the covenant structure of Scripture reveals many analogies of the Trinity," he points to the following five ways to recognize triads in God's covenantal revelation:

A1. Where beginning moves to accomplishment and then to application-consummation,
A2. Where categories in a group (especially a group of three) coinhere,
A3. Where there are significant analogies to the lordship attributes or the three perspectives that emerge out of them,
A4. When three categories exhaust their universe of discourse
A5. When there seems to be an emphatic, intentional repeating of the number three as often in biblical law, narrative, and theology.[100]

Naturally, by seeking to cultivate a *theology of lordship*, the focus of his most developed triads relates to the lordship triad (#3 above). Nevertheless, from the list above, we can see that Frame does not believe all triads are of the same variety.

The first way of discovering triads (#1 above) can be shown through the example of biblical history. Frame organizes biblical history into three parts.[101] The first (roughly correlated with the Old Testament) was a period in which God made manifest (through covenants) his eternal plan. Jesus' incarnation, life, death and resurrection, the second period of biblical history, encompassed the accomplishing of his plan. Finally, the last period is the application of this salvific plan from Pentecost to the consummation. Bavinck

---

[100] Ibid., 728.
[101] Ibid., 744.

suggests that each of these periods is associated with the work of one of the members of the Trinity: "In the history of revelation, the economy of the Father was especially that of the Old Testament, that of the Son began with the incarnation, and that of the Holy Spirit began at the day of Pentecost."[102] While each period remains distinct from one another, in their unity as God's comprehensive plan for salvation, they are ultimately one.

An example of the second way of discovering triads comes by way of "the transcendentals of being" in Greek and Scholastic philosophy. The most popular categorical triad consisted of the transcendentals of the good, true, and beautiful.[103] These were not considered separable; rather, they were thoroughly expressive of one another. That the Greeks categorized creation according to this trifold scheme is consonant with the revelation of God to all men of his divine nature (Rom 1:18–20).[104]

Because we will develop the third way (lordship attributes) of discovering triads in the next chapter, we will turn to the fourth. Examples include the following: time consisting of past, present, and future; space consisting of height, width, and length; states of being consisting of liquid, solid, gas; processes consisting of beginning, middle, and end; worldliness defined as lust of the flesh, lust of the eyes, and the pride of life (John 2:16); and the three categories of philosophy consisting of metaphysics, epistemology, and axiology. What other element could be added to these triads? Each grouping appears to exhaust their universe of discourse. Yet does exhausting the universe of discourse *necessarily* imply perspectival relationship? It does not appear that Frame would say so. Like the fifth way we are turning to next, these triads may reflect the Trinity in a triadic but not perspectival way.

---

[102] Bavinck, *Reformed Dogmatics*, 2.259–60.

[103] Frame does recognize other categories of transcendentals in Greek philosophy. Frame, *The Doctrine of God*, 746.

[104] Of course, Frame is not arguing that they understood the Trinitarian reflections in the transcendentals.

Frame's final way of discovering triads can be seen from the following examples he gives from Scripture:

> three stories in ark, three sendings of birds after the flood, three sons of Noah, three visitors to Abraham, three patriarchs, three divisions of the tabernacle, three feast-periods, three offerings. Cleansing of a leper by blood, water, and oil on the ear, thumb, toe (Lev. 14:1–20). Three years in Jesus' ministry, three temptations, three crosses.[105]

Clearly Frame does not believe the profusion of the number three is accidental. But Frame is careful to warn the reader not to "see a rigid and unvarying pattern here." Instead, Frame openly accepts that there are "twofold distinctions in Scripture . . . as well as four-fold, sevenfold, tenfold, etc." But the prominence of the threefold pattern leads Frame to conclude, "the threefold distinctions nevertheless are strangely pervasive, and they hold special interest for our present discussion."[106] That these triads are in some way a reflection of the Trinity, Frame would argue positively, but it is not clear that he would argue for them being *perspectival* triads. That is, while he would recognize a vestige of the Trinity in these triads, he does not argue for these types of triads as having perichoretic-simplicity relations. This serves to show a confusion that could potentially sidetrack a reader of Frame's theology. Not all triads are alike. They all share in revealing God as he is (triune), but they do not all do so in the same way. In other words, readers need to note that Frame's lists of triads are not always perspectival triads. Commenting on this fifth way of discovering triads, Poythress argues that in perspectival triads "I want to see more than just the number three. I want to see something like coinherence."[107]

---

[105] Frame, *The Doctrine of God*, 744.
[106] Ibid., 750n19.
[107] Vern S. Poythress, e-mail message to the author, April 2, 2014.

Poythress's Sixth Way of Discovering Triads[108]

To the previous five ways of recognizing triads, Poythress adds a sixth:[109] (A6) *a triad is present when something original is reflected in a second entity and the two are inseparably associated.*[110] Poythress argues that this pattern is foundational in Scripture.[111] John 1 argues

---

[108] In light of the sixth and final way of discovering triads, we can present a mapping of Frame's triads from Appendix A in *The Doctrine of God*. The following list correlates Frame's extensive triad list into the categories above:
Table 2. Frame's Triads

Ways of Discovering Triads	Important, or Exceptionally Clear Examples	Other Examples
A1	27	2, 7, 23, 24, 26, 27, 31, 51, 109–112
A2	48, 77	71, 96
A3	34, 35, 37	4, 6, 14–19, 22, 25, 28, 32, 33, 36, 39–41, 43, 49, 50, 52–55, 57, 60, 61, 63, 64, 68, 80, 85, 91, 93, 95, 105–107
A4	65, 92	3, 5, 8, 20, 21, 47, 56, 58, 59, 66, 67, 70, 72–79, 81–83, 86–89, 94, 97–103
A5	29, 38	13, 30
A6	42, 45	46, 62, 90, 104, 108

[109] In personal correspondence, Poythress indicated that this sixth way could be classified under Frame's second category. Here we have kept it separate, because though all of the ways of discovering perspectival triads could be generally classified under the second category, some of them are more specifically aligned with this sixth way. By keeping this category separate, we are interested in being as specific as possible in showing how to discover triads. Vern S. Poythress, e-mail message to the author, April 4, 2014.

[110] As will be shown below, Frame argues for this pattern even though he does not list it among the ways of discovering triads. On the basis of his list of triads in *The Doctrine of* God, it appears that Frame believes this sixth pattern is closely aligned with the first. But while there are similarities (apparent development), there are differences as well. The notable difference is that the third element in the first seeks to bring application to the plan that was accomplished, while the third element of the sixth seeks to bring harmony to the various manifestations of an original theme. On the whole, it seems better to express this as a distinct way.

[111] Some of Poythress's most significant triads derive from this pattern. As much as the lordship triad provides the basis for most of Frame's triads, so this

that Jesus was the spoken Word through whom creation was made (Gen. 1). This analogy indicates that we are to understand God's Word through the relation of the Father to the Son:

> The coinherence of the Persons of the Trinity [through the Spirit] provides a background for understanding the character of God's word. The Persons of the Trinity are present to one another. The Word is 'with God' according to John 1:1. He is 'at the Father's side' (NIV) or 'in the bosom of the Father' (RSV, KJV) according to John 1:18. This coinherence provides the archetype. In an ectypal way, God is present in all his words with respect to creation. The Father is 'in' the Son (John 14:10) without being identical with the Son (the two are distinct Persons). Similarly, the Father is present in his words without being identical with those words. Since the Son is in the Father, the Son also is present in all the words of God. The eternal Word of John 1:1 is present in the particular words. Thus, there is a unity of being to all the words. All the words of God are not only words from God as speaker. They are words that manifest the presence of the eternal Word. They are expressions and manifestations of that one Word.[112]

Poythress calls this the triad of imaging: Originary, Manifestational, and Concurrent.

We can give both the Trinity and God's Word as examples of this triadic process. As for the Trinity, in the originary perspective we see the unity of God's being (i.e., Trinity). In the manifestational perspective, we see a particular expression of the triune God (e.g.,

---

pattern appears to be the basis for many of Poythress's triads. As noted above, Frame praises Poythress's work even though Frame does not use these triads as frequently. This apparent conflict may be explained by noting the distinct fields Poythress and Frame have dedicated their life work towards.

[112] Poythress, *God-Centered Biblical Interpretation*, 37.

the Son). In the concurrent perspective, we see the infinite interrelatedness (i.e., perichoresis) between the original and manifestation, or the one and the many. The triad also relates to God's Word. The originary perspective describes God's eternal united decree. However, God's decree is expressed in a multiplicity of ways. Thus, the manifestational perspective aligns with one of the historic ways that God has expressed his eternal decree (through events, through Scripture, through his Son, etc.). The concurrent perspective focuses on the relation between the originary and the manifestational. As Poythress says, "The originary aspect is concurrent with the manifestational aspect, in that the two are present in one another. The original plan is in the particular manifestation and is expressed in the manifestation."[113]

Poythress aligns this triad with the Trinity by arguing that the Father is representative of the originary perspective. The Son is representative of the manifestational for the same reason the Father is representative of the originary—the Son is the imprint of the image of God (Col. 1:23; Heb. 1:3). Finally, the Spirit is representative of the concurrent aspect.[114] Poythress explains why the Spirit most naturally fills this role:

> The Spirit is the Father's gift to the Son. As such, he is the expression of the Father's love: 'the Father loves the Son and has placed everything in his hands' (John 3:35). We know that the Spirit is given to us to express the Father's love for us (John 14:23–27). Through the Spirit, both the Father and the Son dwell in us (John 14:23). The Son's dwelling in us is analogous to the Father's dwelling in the Son (John 17:21–23). In other words, God's dwelling in us

---

[113] Ibid., 38.

[114] Poythress does warn, "we oversimplify if we say that therefore the aspects correlate *exclusively* with only one Person. The aspects are inseparable, and in fact belong to all three Persons of the Trinity. Precisely because the Persons dwell in one another, we cannot penetrate this ultimate mystery." Ibid., 40–41.

is an ectype, an image, of God's dwelling in God. The Father dwells in the Son and the Son in the Father. This indwelling takes place through their mutual love, which is the gift of the Spirit.[115]

The triad of imaging leads Poythress to develop the ontological triad: classificational, instantational, and associational. This second triad merely displays a different emphasis on the truths presented in the imaging triad. Classificational refers to the unity of a class. The instantiation refers to one of the diverse manifestations of the class. Finally, the associational refers to the harmonious relation between the classificational and instantational. Applied archetypally to the Trinity, the classificational would refer to the class *Godhead*. The instantational would refer to one of the three personal manifestations of the Godhead (e.g., the Son). The associational would refer to the infinite interrelatedness between the classification (Godhead) and the instantiation (Son).

Poythress again relates these three to the persons of the Trinity. The Father is most aligned with the classificational because he remains most unchanged in light of the incarnation of the Son and the coming of the Spirit at Pentecost.[116] Because of the Son's explicit revelation in flesh to man, Jesus is the most expressly aligned with the instantational perspective. Finally, because the Spirit is the

---

[115] Poythress concludes the section with this helpful summary: "This coinherence is only one instance of coinherence that God expresses in all his works. He manifests coinherence in each particular kind of work, because he is himself eternally coinherent in the being of the Trinity. He acts toward us in a way that manifests who he is in himself. The most fundamental coinherence is the coinherence of the Persons of the Trinity. But we see derivative coinherence in the perspectives in which he manifests himself. One such triad consists in the originary, manifestational, and concurrent perspectives." Ibid., 40.

[116] Poythress confirms an orthodox position by asserting, "Of course all three Persons of the Godhead remain the same through all history. But it is preeminently the Father who remains the same, through the diversities of the coming of the Word in flesh and the pouring out of the Spirit at Pentecost." Ibid., 71.

source of mutual indwelling, he is most properly aligned with the associational perspective.[117]

The payout for the ontological triad is that it shows how *all of creation* manifests perspectivalism. That is, everything within creation falls under a classification and is an instantiation of that classification. Further, these categories are interminably pervasive within creation. For example, a poodle is an instantiation of many classifications including animal, mammal, carnivore, dog, and pet. The number of classifications is as wide as creation itself. The ontological triad ably describes the pattern of organization of an instantiation within a classification in holistic harmony. Our minds are created to think this way, and Poythress seeks to show the ontological basis for this in the Trinity. In emphasizing the perspectival relation of all creation through one and many, both Frame and Poythress are united. As Frame notes, "We never experience the 'one' without the 'many,' because in God one and many are inseparable, and he has made the universe to reflect his Trinitarian mystery."[118]

In sum, the ontological triad, which Poythress derives from John 1:1, furnishes the foundation for understanding the unity and diversity (one and many) of created reality. The archetypal classificational, instantational, associational in the Trinity is the source of the ectypal triad represented throughout all of creation. It is this insight that led to Poythress's article, *Reforming Ontology and Logic in Light of the Trinity*, and later book, *Logic: A God-Centered Approach to the Foundation of Western Thought*.[119] Within these works, Poythress argues that God is the source of all reality, and, therefore,

---

[117] Ibid., 38.

[118] John M. Frame, *A History of Western Philosophy and Theology* (Phillipsburg, NJ: P&R Publishing, 2015), chap. 12.

[119] Having argued for the ontological triad from John 1:1, Poythress suggests, "Reflection on John 1:1 can lead us in reforming our conceptions of fundamental philosophical categories and logic." Vern S. Poythress, "Reforming Ontology and Logic in the Light of the Trinity: An Application of Van Til's Idea of Analogy," *Westminster Theological Journal* 57, 1 (Spring 1995): 187–219; Poythress, *Logic*.

all manifestations of reality must be reflective of that which is originally present in the Creator. The ontological triad provides the way of understanding both how we think and how we communicate.[120]

Types of Triads and the Trinity

These six ways of fashioning triads could be a potential source of confusion for those just introduced to perspectivalism. Because, as noted above, our minds are made to think categorically, there is often a search for the uniting factor bringing the perspectives together. Because of the preponderance of the lordship theme in Frame's work, one might mistake lordship as the uniting factor. However, the lordship attributes do not express the fullness of the triads present in reality. Lordship is only one of six ways to recognize the triads. So what is this uniting factor? Ultimately, *it is the Trinity*. Again, Poythress notes this powerfully: "In a Christian or biblical world view, God himself is the only truly ultimate explanation for anything. If one category could serve as a tool for obtaining an ultimate analysis, it could only be the category of *God*."[121] In order to show how all six types relate to the Trinity, we will reorder and repeat them here:

B1. When something original is reflected in a secondary entity and the two are inseparably associated,
B2. Where categories in a groupcohere,
B3. When three categories exhaust their universe of discourse,
B4. Where beginning moves to accomplishment and then to application-consummation,
B5. Where there are significant analogies to the lordship attributes or the three perspectives that emerge out of them,

---

[120] Poythress has an earned doctorate in both New Testament and Mathematics. These dual interests have aided him in seeing the connections between language and the sciences. The broadest connection is in the problem of relating the one to the many, which is exactly the problem the ontological triad is designed to aid in understanding.

[121] Poythress, *Symphonic Theology*, 83.

B6. When there seems to be an emphatic, intentional repeating of the number three as often in biblical law, narrative, and theology.

The first three ways of deriving triads are based on God's eternal nature. According to the first, the Son is eternally the image of the Father infinitely related through the Spirit. Thus, anything in creation that reflects this eternal pattern is perspectivally triadic. The second way of discovering triads is also based on God's nature in that whenever a group of three coinherently relate, that relationship is based upon God's perichoretic interrelatedness. Finally, the third, while not necessarily leading to perspectival triads, is based on God's nature in that the triune God is exhaustive of all things. When three things can be said to exhaust all things, they are reflecting God's unity in diversity exhaustiveness.

The last three ways of deriving triads are reflective of God's activities in relation to creation.[122] The fourth is reflective of God's eternal salvific decree. In the triune Godhead, the Father eternally *planned* that he would save a people through the *accomplishment* of the Son so that the Spirit might *apply* the redemption to the elect.[123] Every historic process that follows the *plan, accomplish*, and *apply* paradigm follows in the pattern first established in the Trinity. The fifth way is Frame's most prolific. As noted above, the lordship attributes both reflect the eternal attributes of God and reflect God's actions towards his creatures. And since all of creation is the activity of the Lord, all of it bears the reflection of his lordship. Finally, the sixth way to derive triads is the most general and does not necessarily lead to *perspectival* triads. Frame notes, "The number three seems omnipresent in Scripture, nature, philosophy, and religion."[124] Is the preponderance of the number three accidental? For Frame, it is more

---

[122] Indeed, God's acts are reflective of his nature, which points to another triad: God's nature, acts, and persons are all interrelated.

[123] Frame, "A Primer on Perspectivalism," 14.

[124] Frame, *The Doctrine of God*, 727.

likely that God, being triune, intentionally creates groups of three within creation as a vestige of his eternal nature: "the world as a whole reflects God's glory, and that glory is the glory of the Triune God. So the whole creation is a *vestigium trinitatis*."[125]

Because we are specifically concerned for perspectival triads, we can bring the six ways of deriving triads down to three. The third and sixth will be eliminated because while they may lead to triads, they do not necessarily lead to perspectival triads. The second will be eliminated because it is simply descriptive of the relations present within the other three. That is, number two can be understood as a catchall, encompassing the similarity of the other three (i.e., that they all coinhere).[126] Thus, we are left with the following three ways in which Frame and Poythress derive their perspectival triads:

C1. When something original is reflected in a secondary entity and the two are inseparably associated (based on God's persons).
C2. Where beginning moves to accomplishment and then to application-consummation (based on God's eternal decree).
C3. Where there are significant analogies to the lordship attributes or the three perspectives that emerge out of them (based on God's eternal character).

In sum, the only organizing motif of the triads is the *Trinity*. This follows from the belief that everything has its origins in God himself. There can be nothing more foundational. Thus, though we could say that all of the perspectives share a relationship of one and many to some degree, this is merely a reflection of their reliance on the Trinitarian unity in diversity. How then do the perspectival triads derived from the Trinity through alternative paths relate to one another? That is the question we will turn to next.

---

[125] Ibid., 726–27.
[126] This is the primary way of discovering general perspectival groups.

Relationships among the Triads

Frame's most prolific triad in his writings is the lordship triad (C3 above). Poythress seems to focus his attention (though certainly not exclusively) on the Imaging and Process triads (C1 & C2 above). In examining these significant triads, we might ask, does Poythress's imaging triad correspond in any way to Frame's lordship triad? Poythress believes it does, and this provides a good opportunity to express how triads relate with one another. Overall, Poythress suggests that when we compare triads we should "expect coinherence without mere mathematical identity."[127] Each triad is a representation of reality from a distinct vantage point.[128]

The relations among the triads leads to a parallelism amongst the triads. Poythress shows how one of the attributes in the lordship triad—that of control—relates to the three attributes in the imaging triad by arguing that "control involves an originary aspect, consisting in God's attribute of omnipotence. God's control involves a manifestational aspect, consisting of actual acts of control over what he has made. God's control involves a concurrent aspect, in that the acts of control are in harmony with who God is in his omnipotence."[129] Of course, the process could be continued with the other attributes from each side.

Since many of the attributes in the triads show an affinity to one of the persons in the Trinity, these same attributes can also show affinity towards one of the attributes in another triad. For instance, the originary perspective was aligned most closely with the Father. In the lordship triad, the attribute of authority is most aligned with the Father. Poythress recognizes a kinship between these two by

---

[127] Poythress, *God-Centered Biblical Interpretation*, 55.
[128] Poythress explains, describing the relation between two triads he uses in his work: "The two triads are not merely two names for exactly the same thing. Rather, the triad of imaging focuses on God's representation of himself, while the triad of purposes [analogous to Frame's lordship triad] focuses on God's carrying out purposes." Ibid.
[129] Ibid.

saying, "God's meaning exists even before it is manifested, which is closely related to the originary perspective."[130]

In sum, the various triads relate to one another in a coherent fashion. They express the same material, but they approach it from a different angle.

Asymmetrical and Symmetrical Triads

Another important distinction in the types of triads is between asymmetrical and symmetrical triads. Poythress first noted this distinction as he considered the difference between one of his major triads and one of Frame's major triads: "The two sets of perspectives are not completely the same. My triad of perspectives applies archetypally to God and ectypally to creatures. By contrast, Frame's triad is asymmetric."[131]

Asymmetrical Triads

That Frame's triad of normative, situational, and existential is asymmetrical is not intended to communicate, as might be suggested by the terminology, that Frame's triad fails to cohere. Rather, it indicates that one aspect of the triad is distinct from the other two. This distinction is in the ultimate referent. The normative perspective, differing from the situational and existential, is divine. As Frame argues, "God's law . . . is divine—divine in authority, power, and ultimacy. We cannot know God without knowing him as law. God's law, then, is God himself."[132] In the same section, Frame aligns God's law with God's authority, the normative perspective.[133] In other

---

[130] As noted in an earlier chapter, Poythress defines God's *authority* as *meaning* for the sake of his theological purposes. He does note that these align with Frame's lordship attributes. Ibid., 61n1.

[131] Poythress, *Logic*, 688n10.

[132] Frame, *The Doctrine of the Knowledge of God*, 63.

[133] While Frame does not equate the normative with the Scripture or God, the analogous relationship is present here. Indeed, Poythress recognizes it as such by calling the triad asymmetrical.

Triperspectivalism and the Trinity

words, the normative perspective reaches outside of created reality to the Creator.[134] The other two aspects of the triad—the situational and existential—are aspects of created reality (figure 6.3).

We must remember, however, that the perspectives are perichoretically related. In man's experience, there is no situational without the normative, and thus the situational can be revelatory of the normative. After noting that the law is divine, Frame continues, "that law is also revealed to us through creaturely media: nature, history, conscience, theophany, prophecy, Scripture. The law in these forms is no less divine than in its essential identity with God."[135] This does not suggest that all of reality is divine; instead, it argues that all of reality reflects the normative, or divine, perspective. The identity is one of epistemological reflection and not ontological identity.

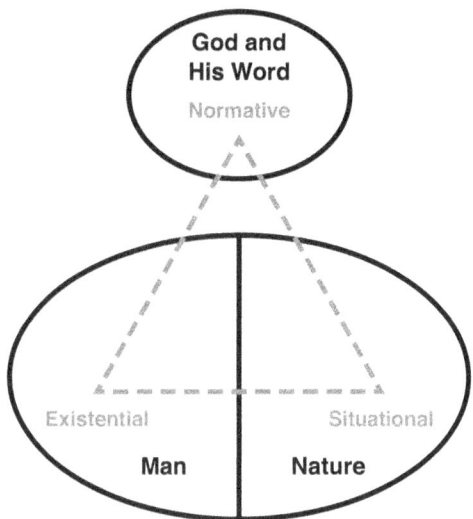

Fig. 6.3. Asymmetrical Triad[136]

---

[134] While it was not mentioned earlier, one of the motivations for perichoretic triperspectivalism is the asymmetry of Frame's triad. If the normative is more appropriately connected to the divine, as Poythress suggests, then the normative must display some form of primacy.

[135] Frame, *The Doctrine of the Knowledge of God*, 63.

[136] Reproduced by permission from Brant Bosserman, "The Trinity and

Symmetrical Triads

While Poythress does not explicilty name his own triad as symmetrical, by calling Frame's assymmetrical he has indicated that his own is symmetrical. The symmetry denotes that all three aspects relate to the same created reality. Poythress's classificational, instantiational, and associational can be used to illustrate this point. While the ultimate basis of this triad, as argued above, is divine, the replication of the divine is within creation. That is, there is a distinct divine archetype (God as expressed through the Son in unity in diversity) which produces an ectypal manifestation (mammal as expressed through a dog in unity in diversity). Thus, while Frame's triad reaches into both sides of the Creator/creature divide, Poythress's triad seeks to show how one side (creature) replicates the other side (Creator: See figure 2).

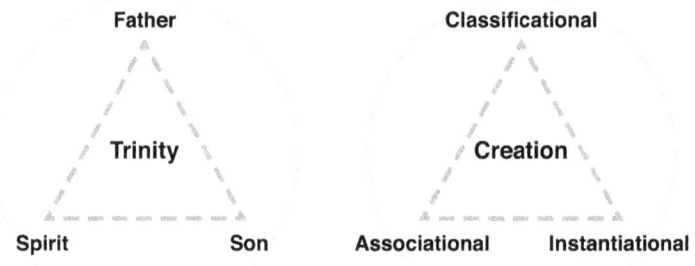

Fig. 6.4. Symmetrical Triad[137]

Relationship between the Asymmetrical and Symmetrical

Brant Bosserman notes the potential problem caused by having these two types of triads: "This raises the question of whether the symmetrical model, the asymmetrical model, or neither model

---

Christian Paradox," fig. 27. © 2011 by Brant Bosserman.

[137] Reproduced by permission from Brant Bosserman, "The Trinity and Christian Paradox," fig. 28. © 2011 by Brant Bosserman.

is more accurate than the other." He concludes by asking, "If both are true at once, does this suggest that human thought always has at its base a fourfold referent, including three that reflect God and a fourth that is based directly on the Word of God?"[138] We will argue that present within the text Bosserman was critiquing is a sufficient answer to this question; namely, Poythress affirmed, "Frame's triad is . . . an analogical image of mine."[139]

What does Poythress mean by analogical image? In other words, how does the symmetrical relate to the asymmetrical? As noted above, there are various manifestations of perspectivalism. While they ultimately derive from the Trinity, they are different manifestations of his presence in that which he has created. The asymmetrical stresses God's intimate, covenantal relationship to creation. Because everything is reflective of God's lordship, everything displays God's authority, or divine law. Thus, God himself is present everywhere within creation.[140] The symmetrical stresses the ontological foundation of reality in God. In this way it is likewise covenantal, yet it stresses a different aspect of God's relationship to creation. By focusing on imaging, the symmetrical triads show the presence of God as the foundation for all existence (most exemplified in the one and many relationships pervasive in creation). So the diversity of ways God has imaged his Triunity in creation accounts for both the asymmetrical and symmetrical triads.

Further, while the normative perspective has its origin in God, that perspective is not God. Instead, it is an ectypal image of his authority, but it still bears his authority. In other words, what is experienced in creation is an ectypal manifestation of God's archetypal norms, which carry all of the authority of the original norms. Again, Frame says that the norms are "revealed to us through

---

[138] Bosserman, "The Trinity and Christian Paradox," §156.
[139] Poythress, *Logic*, 688n10.
[140] So Poythress says of asymmetrical triads, "I believe that Frame's approach remains useful in emphasizing the interrelatedness of norm, world, and self in people's practical, concrete reception of the word of God." Ibid.

creaturely media: nature, history, conscience, theophany, prophecy, Scripture. The law in these 'forms' is no less divine than in its essential identity with God."[141] As such, Frame's triad is *also* symmetrical, for the norms are imaged norms. Going further, we could also say that the situational and existential are also imaged, because they are reflective of the eternal plan of God (figure 6.5). It is in this light that Poythress can argue for a similarity between his triad and Frame's triad.[142]

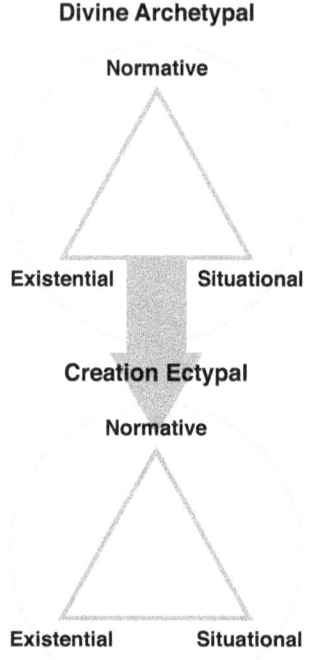

Fig. 6.5. Symmetrical Expression of the Lordship Triad

[141] Frame, *The Doctrine of the Knowledge of God*, 63.
[142] Poythress uses the communicative triad to make the same point. God's speech is informational, productive, and expressive. Informational indicates that there is a substance (question, assertion, etc.) to what is being communicated. Productive indicates that this communication has an effect on the

Summary of the Trinitarian Roots

At its core, perspectivalism of both varieties (general perspectivalism and triperspectivalism) is built upon the revelation of the Trinity. While there are various ways of deriving the perspectival triads, the unifying factor is the person and work of the triune God. Because of his absolute personhood and in union with his covenantal relation with creation, God is expressive in all that he creates. Further, because of his nature as the Creator, he must be the ontological basis of all that is in creation. The perspectival triads are merely a human recognition of the ways that God has revealed himself in creation. Said differently, perspectivalism has taken seriously that God has "revealed his divine nature" (Rom. 1:20) through creation.

God's triune nature is seen most clearly in symmetrical triads, which show how God has ectypally manifested his archetypal triune nature. God's triune nature is also seen through his covenantally conditioned asymmetrical triads. The lordship attributes display to the world God's eternal nature as the one who is in authority, in control, and in presence. These lordship attributes are reflective of God's eternal nature both in his attributes (aligning with omniscience, omnipotence, and omnipresence) and in the work of his

---

one listening (convince, amuse, etc.). Expressive indicates that something of the speaker (desires, feelings, etc.) is communicated with the message. This pattern can be seen archetypally in the speech of the Son to the Father in John 17. The communicative triad is ectypally reflected in man's language. Just as God's speech has informational, productive, and expressive aspects, so does man's speech. The importance of this triad is seen in that it is analogous to Frame's symmetrical lordship triad—the normative aligns with the informational perspective, the situational aligns with the productive, and the existential aligns with the expressive. It is because of the analogous relationship between Poythress's triad and Frame's triad that Poythress can say that Frame's triad is analogical of his own. Vern S. Poythress, "Canon and Speech Act: Limitations in Speech-Act Theory, with Implications for a Putative Theory of Canonical Speech Acts," *Westminster Theological Journal* 70, 2 (Fall 2008): 337–54; William P. Alston, *Illocutionary Acts and Sentence Meaning* (Ithaca, NY: Cornell University Press, 2000).

person (Father as authority, Son as controller, and Spirit as personal presence). Both the asymmetrical and symmetrical triads display a unity in diversity reflective of the simple and perichoretic relation in the archetypal triune nature.

7

Lordship, Trinity, and Perspectivalism

Theologians sometimes have a central motif (or focal perspective) through which they view theology. For Frame that motif is God's lordship, and it is from meditation on lordship that Frame derives his most used perspectival triad of *control, authority, and presence*. Not only is this triad foundational for understanding Frame's triperspectivalism, but it is also the model from which many of Frame's other triads derive.[1] For this reason, we will develop the concept of lordship at some length, noting how Frame derives the three aspects theologically and exegetically, how the three function together in absolute harmony, and how this triad serves as a foundation for many of Frame's other triads.

The Centrality of Lordship

Frame has heavily invested in lordship as a central theological paradigm. But is lordship *the* central teaching of Scripture? In answer to that question, Frame asks us to consider the following: *Lord* occurs in its various forms over 7,776 times in Scripture.[2]

---

[1] Frame says, "Readers familiar with my previous books know that I use quite a number of triangular perspectival diagrams. Usually they form a pattern derived from God's lordship attributes." John M. Frame, *A History of Western Philosophy and Theology* (Phillipsburg, NJ: P&R Publishing, 2015), chap. 1n21.

[2] John M. Frame, *Systematic Theology: An Introduction to Christian Belief*

Frame further highlights that the first time God names himself in Scripture (Ex. 3:14), he tells Moses that he is Lord (*Yahweh*), a name he wants to be identified by forever. Frame also compiles a hefty list of passages where God says that he acts in order that people will "know that I am Lord."[3] In a terse summary of Scripture, Frame says, "The basic message of the OT is 'God is Lord,' and the basic message of the NT is 'Jesus Christ is Lord.'"[4] In light of the above, Frame has no problem describing lordship as central to Scripture. In fact, his lordship series is the direct result of his recognition that there has been a lack of theological works centered on lordship.[5]

While one might naturally believe that embracing lordship as a central theme would exclude other themes from the center, this is not the case in Frame's theology. Frame has a theological aversion to exclusive centers, believing instead that the themes of Scripture are perspectivally related.[6] That is, they are focal points from which the entirety of theology may be viewed. So while lordship is essential to any view of Scripture, he refrains from excluding other centers on its account. Any theme may be described as central, because all of them can express the full Christian worldview. Of course, as with all focal perspectives, some approach the truth from a more helpful angle than others. So while Frame would not exclude other centers, he would argue that lordship is *one* perspective through which every Christian should view the Bible, the world, and the self.

(Phillipsburg, NJ: P&R Publishing, 2013), 15.

[3] He cites the following: "Ex. 14:4, compare 6:7; 7:5, 17; 8:22; 10:2; 14:18; 16:6, 12; 29:46; 31:13; Deut. 4:35; 29:6; 1 Kings 8:43, 60; 18:37; 20:13, 28; 2 Kings 19:19; Ps. 83:18, Isa. 37:20 Jer. 16:21; 24:7; Ezek. 6:7, 10, 13, 14; 7:4, 9, 27; 11:10, etc." Ibid., 15–16.

[4] John M. Frame, "A Primer on Perspectivalism," in *John Frame's Selected Shorter Writings* (Phillipsburg, NJ: P&R Publishing, 2014), 11.

[5] "I started wondering why nobody had employed God's lordship as a central theological theme. Certainly God himself is central to the biblical story, and he indicates in many contexts that he wants to be known as the Lord." Frame, *Systematic Theology*, 15.

[6] Ibid., 14–16.

Lordship as Control, Authority, and Presence

We will seek to show why Frame has described lordship as *control*, *authority*, and *presence* by first examining his clarification of the language of transcendence and immanence in light of God's lordship. Next, we will seek to set forth Frame's case for this triadic characterization by examining his exegetical basis in covenant, God's acts, and the biblical descriptions of God in Scripture.

Transcendence and Immanence Expressed by Lordship

What does lordship mean? Frame seeks to build theology on exegesis. For this reason, Frame was dissatisfied with the description of God as transcendent and immanent. While these two categories have been substantial in the history of theology, Frame does not believe they express the truth clearly. The language is certainly not self-explanatory, but Anderson shows a more serious concern of Frame's: "These technical terms can . . . lead us astray . . . the casualties of which are strewn across the battlegrounds of twentieth-century theology."[7] A final, and perhaps more substantial, reason Frame is dissatisfied with the transcendence/immanence model is that it uses language foreign to Scripture.[8] For Frame, this is not necessarily wrong, but if there are better descriptive words that God uses of himself, these would be preferable.

Believing the two-category structure of transcendence and immanence was unclear and potentially misleading, Frame believed a change would be helpful. As an alternative, Frame offered a three-fold structure of control, authority, and presence. First, God exhaustively *controls* everything within creation. Second, God has

---

[7] James N Anderson, "Presuppositionalism and Frame's Epistemology," in *Speaking the Truth in Love: The Theology of John M. Frame* (Phillipsburg, NJ: P&R Publishing, 2009), 434.

[8] "Transcendence and immanence . . . are not biblical terms, so we must exercise some care in relating them to the teachings of Scripture." John M. Frame, *The Doctrine of God* (Phillipsburg, NJ: P&R Publishing, 2002), 103.

authority over everything within creation. Finally, God is *present* throughout all creation. Not only are these three, for the most part, self-explanatory, they also derive more directly from biblical statements about God. While no one text *explicitly* mentions control, authority, and presence as defining lordship, Frame believes these three attributes are a good and necessary consequence of many biblical statements and themes concerning God's lordship. In sum, Frame acknowledges that he knows "of no better way to summarize the biblical concept of divine lordship" than through these three attributes.[9] A full exposition and exegetical defense of Frame's preference for his three-fold pattern is not possible here,[10] but we can summarize the foundations of his choice of the three-fold pattern from Frame's understanding of covenant, God's acts, and biblical descriptions of God.

Lordship in Covenant

The first substantial basis for Frame's three-fold pattern derives from the concept of covenant. Lordship and covenant are two concepts that cannot be separated.[11] God is Lord because (though not only because) he is Lord of the covenants he has established.[12] After citing Isaiah 66:1, "heaven is my throne, and the earth is my footstool," Frame argues, "God rules over all things

---

[9] John M. Frame, *The Doctrine of the Knowledge of God* (Phillipsburg, NJ: Presbyterian and Reformed, 1987), 17. Emphasis added.

[10] For Frame's most developed defense see, Frame, *The Doctrine of God*, 1–103.

[11] "'Lord' denotes the relation of a covenant head to his vassals. So lordship and covenant go together." Frame, "A Primer on Perspectivalism," 12n14.

[12] The connection between the nature of God and covenants is so explicit for Frame that, in correspondence with Howard Griffith, he argued, "Covenant can function as a model for the creator-creature distinction. Essentially, God is the Lord, and the world is his covenant vassal." Howard Griffith, "Frame as a Reformed Theologian," in *Speaking the Truth in Love: The Theology of John M. Frame*, ed. John J. Hughes (Phillipsburg, NJ: P&R Publishing, 2009), 308.

as lord of a covenant . . . even before his covenant with Adam and Eve. So God's sovereignty over everything he has made is a covenantal lordship."[13]

Covenants, which were prolific in the Ancient Near East,[14] took one of two forms. The *Parity Covenant* exitsed between two equal parties. The *Suzerainty Covenant*, however, was between a person of a higher rank and a person of a lower rank. This latter treaty was unilateral, demanding obedience from the lower ranking party. Historical documents reveal a *treaty form* that was typically followed in suzerainty treaties. The following elements would ordinarily be involved in these treaties: (1) the identity of the author of the treaty (the suzerain), (2) a *historical prologue* which catalogued the actions of the suzerain on behalf of the vassals, (3) the *stipulations* including a general command to be loyal to the suzerain and more specific stipulations concerning particular actions required, (4) the *sanctions* which would reveal both the blessings for obedience and the curses for disobedience, and (5) the *continuity* section, detailing how the provisions were to be remembered by periodic reading.[15]

Frame indicates how covenant relates to lordship and the lordship attributes:

> 'Lord' names the head of a covenant. his essential relation to us is that of a great king who has delivered us from death and calls us to serve him by obeying his written word.

---

[13] Frame, *Systematic Theology*, 19. For a more extended definition of the covenant of creation, see Michael D. Williams, *Far as the Curse Is Found: The Covenant Story of Redemption* (Phillipsburg, NJ: P&R Publishing, 2005), 46–52; O. Palmer Robertson, *The Christ of the Covenants* (Grand Rapids, MI: Baker, 1980), 19–21.

[14] Frame's understanding of covenants derives from Kline's work on Ancient Near East Covenants. Meredith G. Kline, *The Structure of Biblical Authority* (Eugene, OR: Wipf and Stock, 1997).

[15] Frame, *Systematic Theology*, 20.

> But within this covenant relationship, how should we understand the nature and role of the Lord? There are a number of passages in Scripture that focus on the nature of God's lordship, and in these passages are three recurring themes, control, authority, and presence. I shall call these the 'lordship attributes.'
>
> We see these in the main body of the suzerainty treaty form: the historical prologue, the stipulations (commands) and the sanctions (blessings and curses). In the historical prologue, the Lord declares that he has exercised his great *power* in rescuing the vassal: 'who brought you out of the land of Egypt, out of the house of slavery' (Ex. 20:2). His power *controlled* the situation for the vassal's benefit. In the stipulations, he indicates his *authority* to command: 'You shall have no other gods before me' (verse 3). In the sanctions (blessings and curses) he indicates that he will be aware of what the vassal is doing and will be *present* to bless or judge: 'I the Lord your God am a jealous God, visiting the iniquity of the fathers upon the children . . . but showing steadfast love to thousands of those who love me . . .' (verses 5–6).[16]

In sum, Frame argues that the suzerainty treaties emphasized three aspects of the suzerain over the vassal: control, authority, and presence. Thus, the treaties of the Ancient Near East and the biblical covenants indicate that Frame's triad is descriptive of what it means to be Lord.

Lordship in God's Acts

A second substantial reason Frame embraced the triad model of control, authority, and presence pertains to the actions of the triune God:

[16] Ibid.

There seems to be a general division of labor among the persons in the work of redemption. The Father establishes the eternal plan of salvation; the Son executes it, and the Spirit applies it to people. It was the Father who sent the Son to redeem us, the Son who accomplished redemption, and the Spirit who applies the benefits of Christ's atonement to believers.[17]

This division of labor is a major motivation for Frame's lordship attributes. In these, Frame finds a three-fold pattern that summarizes what it means for God to be Lord. Notice the direct connection he makes concerning the activities of God and the lordship attributes: "Scripture does present a rough division of labor among [the Trinity]: the Father devises the eternal plan, the Son executes that plan, and the Spirit applies it. *So emerges the pattern authority, control, and presence.*"[18]

The Father's works exhibit to a higher degree the authority of God (planning, decreeing, etc.), while the Son's work expresses the control (executing, completing, controlling, etc.), and the Spirit the presence of God (application, conviction, etc.).[19] While each member of the Trinity shares in each of these functions (e.g., the Son has authority, control, and presence), nevertheless, there is a sense in which each attribute is connected to an individual member of the triune Godhead.

---

[17] Frame, "A Primer on Perspectivalism," 10.

[18] John M. Frame, "Directory of Frame's Major Ideas," in *Speaking the Truth in Love: The Theology of John M. Frame*, ed. John J. Hughes (Phillipsburg, NJ: P&R Publishing, 2009), 977. Emphasis added.

[19] Within the acts of redemption there is another argument for processional triperspectivalism. As much as the Son fulfilled the plan of the Father, and as much as he with the Father sent the Spirit, so there appears to be a procession from the plan of redemption to the work of redemption and the application of that redemption. In one sense, these are all necessary for the reality of redemption (and they are thus united), yet there is an order and structure that cannot be compromised.

In sum, by combining the exegetical prominence of the concept *Lord* in Scripture with the descriptions of God's acts, Frame was led to define lordship according to these three categories.[20]

Lordship in Biblical Descriptions of God

The third foundation for Frame's describing lordship in his triad derives from the descriptions of God in Scripture. Here we will consider biblical descriptions that lead to a tripartite definition of lordship.

Covenant Head

One primary description of God is *covenant head*. Both elements of covenant head are important. As covenant *head*, God has power and authority, and as *covenant* head, God is present with his people to curse and to bless. We will examine the following three descriptions of God as more specific elements of his covenant headship.

Description of God as One in Authority

In harmony with the Reformed tradition, Frame maintains that God is the ultimate authority over all things. This is implied in all of his relationships with creatures (and creation itself) because he is the covenant head. Authority is also implied in God's essential nature, because lordship is an attribute of God. That is, God could be nothing less than the covenant head in relation to creation. Frame recognizes that lordship is different from some other attributes of God in that the attribute of lordship is only evident when there are covenant servants. In other words, the attribute of

---

[20] Frame notes that in passages stressing the lordship of God "three themes appear prominently: the Lord is (1) the one who controls all things by his mighty power; (2) the one who speaks with absolute authority, rightly requiring all to obey, and (3) the one who gives himself to his people in covenant intimacy." Frame, "A Primer on Perspectivalism," 12.

lordship is only descriptive of God in relationship with his creation. But Frame argues, "Lordship is an essential attribute of God in that it is the quality of his nature by which he necessarily is Lord to any creature."[21] As Creator of all, God is the Sovereign Potter, who has authority over the clay to do as he desires.

Scripture presents God as ultimate authority by showing that loyalty to him transcends all other responsibilities (Ex. 20:3; Luke 14:26), loyalty to him touches every aspect of life (1 Cor. 10:31; Rom. 14:23), and the extent of required loyalty to him implies that he cannot be questioned (Rom. 9:20; Job 40:1–5).[22]

That God is absolute also implies his authority. All that exists comes from him and exists because of his decree. Even if all of creation refused to recognize it, God's authority would still remain because he is the one who has created all things (Col. 1:17), and he is the sustainer of all that exists (Col. 1:17; Heb. 1:3).

---

[21] His full explanation is as follows: "I realize, of course, that lordship and the lordship attributes are relational attributes, attributes that characterize God's relationship with creatures. It might be argued, therefore, that these are not part of God's essence. Had God determined not to create the world—and he was free to make that choice—he would not have been Lord. True. But the essence of God is such that in his creation, in relation to his creatures, he cannot be anything other than Lord. So the lordship attributes, though not necessary in themselves, are grounded in God's essential nature. We can say that lordship is an essential attribute of God in that it is the quality of his nature by which he necessarily is Lord to any creature." Frame, *The Doctrine of God*, 228n30. Frame's response may not satisfy the critic who believes that Frame is still confusing essential attributes with those attributes God takes on in creation. An analogy might help. A man does not have the characteristic of *being a father* until he has a child. Nevertheless, he is such that *if* he has a child, he will have the characteristic of *being a father*. The change is not in the man but in the relations of the man. In the same way, God does not have the relational characteristic of Lord unless he has created. This introduces no *new* characteristic in God's nature; rather, it relationally exemplifies the eternal character of God.

[22] John M. Frame, "The Lord's Authority," *The Works of John Frame and Vern Poythress*, October 2000, accessed March 25, 2014, http://www.frame-poythress.org/the-lords-authority/.

Description of God as One in Control

The previous comments also show that as the absolute *authority*, God is the absolute *controller*. Frame follows his Reformed brethren in upholding the absolute sovereignty of God over all of creation. Absolute control is an implication of absolute authority in that God could not have *absolute* authority without *absolute* control.[23] Absolute control is also an implication of God's omnipotence. Whatever God decrees necessarily comes to pass. Frame maintains the mystery of God's execution of his comprehensive plan, yet Frame never questions that God does all that he has eternally decreed to do.[24] The absoluteness of God is expressed in control as well. Because all comes from God's eternal constitutive knowledge, God controls all things to accomplish his eternal decrees.

Scripture's descriptions of God defend his ultimate control over creation. First, the Bible indicates that nothing is impossible for God (Jer. 32:27; Matt. 19:26; Luke 1:37). Second, implied in the concept of creation *ex nihilo* (Gen. 1:1) is that nothing stands outside the power of God.[25] The descriptions of God's actions within creation also show that he has exhaustive control over life events—even those for which are thought random or accidental (Ex. 21:13; Prov. 16:33; Jonah 1:7). Finally, even evil is said to be in God's control (Gen. 45:5–8). If the most evil event ever perpetuated on the earth (i.e., the crucifixion of the Son) is in the control of God, the implication is that all events—whether good or evil—are ultimately in God's control (Acts 2:23).

---

[23] In creation we can imagine someone who has "authority" without control. For instance, a representative of the government may have authority during a riot, but he has little control. In God, however, authority and control are tied to his metaphysical existence as Creator. Thus, the analogy between human rulers fails, since humans never have *absolute* authority and control.

[24] Frame, *The Doctrine of God*, 47–79.

[25] Omnipotence is understood in light of God's other characteristics. In this way, each of God's attributes is a limiting concept to every other attribute. This does not negate God's omnipotence; rather it provides the bounds by which

Description of God as One Present

God's *control* leads us to consider the third lordship attribute, God's *presence*. Poythress shows how Frame relates these themes: "[God's] absoluteness implies his ability to make himself accessible . . . if God controls all things, including his relation to us, he can make himself present and available to us. Within a Christian framework, transcendence (control) undergirds immanence (presence), rather than being in tension with it."[26] The absolute authority of God also points to God's personal presence. As Creator and sustainer of all that exists, God is necessarily present throughout his creation. Further, because his thought is constitutive of reality, there can be nothing in all of creation that is not both known by God and expressive of God (Ps. 119; Rom. 1:18–20).[27] Finally, as covenantal head, God is present to all creation for both blessing and cursing.

Another way of expressing the attribute of Presence is through an understanding of God's exhaustive presence in creation. Everything within creation is covenantally conditioned, being created for the purpose of God's revealing himself to his covenantal creatures. Further, everything is exhaustively representational of God, such that nothing can be explained without reference to him. This is what is meant by Paul in Romans 1:20: "For his invisible attributes, namely, *his eternal power and divine nature*, have been clearly perceived, ever

---

the concept should be described. See, Cornelius Van Til, *Common Grace and the Gospel* (Nutley, NJ: Presbyterian and Reformed, 1972), 11–13.

[26] Vern S. Poythress, "Multiperspectivalism and the Reformed Faith," in *Speaking the Truth in Love: The Theology of John M. Frame*, ed. John J. Hughes (Phillipsburg, NJ: P&R Publishing, 2009), 198.

[27] Frame shows how intimately present God is with every fact in creation by paralleling it with the self: "On the one hand, if we merely listed the 'facts' that appear in our sense experience, we would not list the self, for the self is neither seen nor heard. The same is true of God . . . On the other hand, *God is so intimately involved with the facts that no fact can be accounted for apart from him*. And the same is true of the self. This is, I believe, part of the likeness between God and man." Frame, *The Doctrine of the Knowledge of God*, 70. Emphasis added.

since the creation of the world, *in the things that have been made. So they are without excuse.*" Tying this text together with the doctrine of the covenants, Frame says, "The covenant presence of God implies that we cannot escape knowing him, for we cannot know anything else apart from him."[28]

We could describe God as *he for whom we ought to be in communion*. Adam and Eve in the Garden of Eden were designed to walk and talk with God (implied by Gen. 3:8). Their sin separated them from the Garden and from the *blessed* immediacy of God's presence (Gen. 3:23). The entirety of Scripture can be described as an expression of how that blessed presence may once more be experienced. While Adam and Eve lost the *blessing* of God's presence, they immediately knew the *curse* of God's presence (e.g., shame). Their attempts to hide from his presence were futile (Gen. 3:8). The redeemed have been granted the blessing of God's loving presence once more through Christ (e.g., in the Tabernacle, Temple, incarnation, and indwelling of the Spirit, etc.). The lost have maintained the presence of God in judgment (Rom. 1:32). In both cases, Scripture clearly presents that, as Lord, God is present to his creatures.

Paul's Description of God to the Athenians

Another way Scripture describes God as Lord according to these three categories is expressed in Acts 17:22–34. In his presentation to the pagans, Paul summarily expressed three attributes of God. First, Paul presented God as the *Authority*. Covenantal language was used to express this fact, indicating that God is "*Lord* of heaven and earth" (v. 24). Later in the speech, Paul connected God's lordship to his creation of man in his image (v. 29), indicating that this lordship gives God the right to judge the world (v. 31) and to demand repentance (v. 30).

After establishing God's *Authority*, Paul rhetorically asked what the Creator of everything in the cosmos would need from

---

[28] Frame, *The Doctrine of God*, 110.

man. This leads naturally to Paul's second characteristic of the Lord—*Control*. As Creator of everything, God does not need anything from man, whether a temple or physical sustenance (v. 24). Further, God is not only responsible for the objects in existence, but he is also responsible for the creation of all living things (v. 25). Most importantly, God controls every man's life, such that God has "determined the times before appointed, and the bounds of their habitation" (v. 26).

God's exhaustive *Control* leads Paul naturally to consider the third attribute of the true God, God's *Presence*. God's control has placed man in the ideal situation to seek after God, for God "is actually not far from each one of us" (v. 27). Paul clarified what he meant by citing a Greek poet, who argued, "In him we live and move and have our being" (v. 28). In other words, God is present both (1) because he controls when and where people are born and (2) because he is covenantally present in all of creation.[29] To these two expressions of God's covenantal presence, Paul adds a third: (3) "we are indeed his offspring" (v. 28). Finally, Paul's emphasis on God's covenantal presence through the *imago dei* leads him naturally back to consider God's lordship in demanding repentance (v. 30) and judging the world (v. 31).

Acts 17 is an important text because it is one of the rare glimpses Scripture gives of apologetics to the Gentiles. How should evangelism towards those who do not share a Judeo-Christian conception of God proceed? Paul's answer indicates that we must preach God's lordship. Because God is the ultimate authority, who has with his control placed man in the present position, man is responsible in God's presence to respond positively to God's free offer of grace. Thus, as Acts 17 demonstrates, control, authority, and presence is a

---

[29] Undoubtedly, Paul's reference in verse 28 is to God's covenantal presence in creation. It is not a pantheistic presence, as the quote may have originally meant; rather, it is a lordship presence as Paul has already developed at the beginning of the speech. See, Eckhard J. Schnabel, *Acts*, Exegetical Commentary on the New Testament (Grand Rapids, MI: Zondervan, 2012), 736–37.

beneficial way of describing the biblical God to his rebellious covenantal subjects.

The Bible's Description of the Offices of Christ

Both the wider analysis of the descriptions of God in Scripture and the more confined description in Acts 17 have led to the tri-fold categorization Frame has suggested. One more expression of Frame's three-fold pattern will be suggested before moving to show the connection between lordship and triperspectivalism. The Westminster Confession of Faith describes three offices of Christ: "It pleased God, in his eternal purpose, to choose and ordain the Lord Jesus . . . the *Prophet, Priest, and King*."[30] Frame finds an analogy between these three offices and the lordship attributes: "These three offices fit right in with [the lordship] triad. As prophet, Jesus displays especially the lordship attribute of authority; as priest, the lordship attribute of presence; and, as king, the lordship attribute of control."[31] These three offices, so dominantly displayed throughout the Old Testament, were a shadow of the lordship of Christ, which was to be revealed in the New Testament.[32] That they align so well with Frame's three attributes of lordship may indicate that Frame has correctly grasped the central components of lordship.

Lordship and Perspectivalism

Having examined the basis for the lordship characteristics through covenant, God's acts, and biblical descriptions of God, we are now in a position to answer the question of greatest importance

---

[30] "Westminster Confession of Faith," 1646, 8.1, accessed December 9, 2009, http://reformed.org/documents/wcf_with_proofs/.

[31] John M. Frame, *Salvation Belongs to the Lord: An Introduction to Systematic Theology* (Phillipsburg, NJ: P&R Publishing, 2006), 146–47.

[32] For a fuller treatment of the correlation between the three offices and the lordship attributes see, Ibid., 146–58.

for this study—how does the lordship triad relate to triperspectivalism? We will answer this question by first showing how Frame and Poythress align the lordship attributes with perichoresis and simplicity. Second, we will seek to show how the lordship triad, founded on perichoretic-simplicity, operates within the created world.

Lordship Attributes and the Triune God

So how do the lordship attributes relate to perspectivalism? Frame answers,

> It is important that we see the three lordship characteristics as forming a unit, not as separate from one another. God is 'simple' in the theological sense (not compounded of parts), so there is a sense in which if you have one attribute you have them all. All of God's attributes involve one another, and that is definitely the case with the lordship triad. God's control, according to Scripture involves authority, for God controls even the structure of truth and rightness. Control involves presence, for God's power is so pervasive that it brings us face to face with him in every experience. Authority involves control, for God's commands presuppose his full ability to enforce them. Authority involves presence, for God's commands are clearly revealed and are the means by which God acts in our midst to bless and curse. Presence involves control, lest anything in heaven or earth should keep us from God or him from us (John 19; Rom. 8). Presence involves authority, for God is never present apart from his Word.[33]

By coordinating the lordship triad as attributes of God, Frame aligns lordship along simplicity-relational terms. That is, because every characteristic of God is inclusive of every other characteristic,

---

[33] Frame, *The Doctrine of the Knowledge of God*, 17–18.

lordship itself (as an attribute) must relate simplistically with the others.[34] Control, authority, and presence are inclusive and interdependent, having perichoretic-like relations because they are the unfolding expression of God's essential nature, which is ontologically one and many.

Poythress aligns the three more directly with perichoresis:

> These three aspects of the word of God, namely, its meaning [i.e., Frame's authority], control, and presence, are coinherent. They are not neatly separable, as though some parts of his word have meaning [i.e., authority], other parts exert control, and still other parts exhibit God's presence. Rather, all three aspects are there in everything that God speaks. They are coinherent because they reflect the coinherence or mutual indwelling of the three persons of the Trinity.
>
> We can also see that the three aspects of the word of God are coinherent by remembering that the three aspects are related to attributes of God—omniscience, omnipotence, and omnipresence.[35]

Poythress not only relates the three along perichoretic lines, but he also argues that the three lordship characteristics are directly related

---

[34] The opposite is the case as well. Simplicity can be defined along lordship lines: "So the simplicity of God, like all his attributes, sets forth his covenant lordship. It reminds us of the unity of our covenant Lord, and the unity that he brings into our lives as we seek to honor him and him alone. The Christian is not devoted to some abstract philosophical goodness, but to the living Lord of heaven and earth." By showing the relationship between these two, Frame makes simplicity a very practical and useful theological expression. Frame, *Systematic Theology*, 433.

[35] In this passage Poythress is referring to the Word of God, which is an expression of the acts of God (God's speech). Thus, Poythress's *meaning* is analogous to Frame's *authority*. Vern S. Poythress, *In the Beginning Was the Word: Language: A God-Centered Approach* (Wheaton, IL: Crossway, 2009), 26.

to omniscience, omnipotence, and omnipresence. Because the characteristics are inclusive and interdependent, it should be no surprise that the lordship attributes can be aligned with other of God's essential attributes.[36]

The Lordship Attributes as Expressed in Creation

The lordship attributes demonstrate the connection that exists between God's essential nature, his acts, and creation. In summary we can say that because God is ontologically one in many, God's acts are reflectively one in many. In lordship terms, this truth will be worked out in the following way: because lordship is one of God's essential attributes, he necessarily relates to creation as covenant head. As covenant head, he relates to all of creation with authority, control, and presence. All of his acts are reflective of these attributes, since the attributes are essential to his nature as Creator. These three, as essential attributes (aligning with omniscience, omnipotence, and omnipresence),[37] cohere. This coinherence is reflective of the

---

[36] Frame also argues that divine aseity, as an attribute of God, points towards lordship: "Aseity also applies in one sense to God's relationships with the creation, particularly his lordship, which I have defined as his control over the world, his authority over the world, and his presence in the world. . . . So, considering the three attributes of lordship noted above, we may describe God's control as self-sufficient, his authority as self-justifying. His presence in the world is an implication of his universal power and authority. Wherever we go, we cannot escape from him (Psm. 139:7–12, Jer. 23:24). God's presence is inescapable, unavoidable, and therefore not dependent on the will of creatures. This is to say that God's lordship is *a se*." John M Frame, "Divine Aseity and Apologetics," in *Revelation and Reason: New Essays in Reformed Apologetics*, ed. K. Scott Oliphint and Lane G Tipton (Phillipsburg, NJ: P&R Publishing, 2007), 116–17.

[37] Frame says, "God's lordship is grounded in his nature. He acts as Lord because it is his nature to act that way with his creatures. Indeed, he would not be God if he did not control everything he made, rule it with supreme authority, and pervade all creation with his presence." Such an analysis leads him to conclude, "So in a certain sense, lordship is an essential attribute of God's nature. Or, perhaps better: *God's lordship is grounded in essential attributes of God's nature*." Frame, *The Doctrine of God*, 389. Emphasis added.

coinherence present in the one in many of the triune persons. Thus, in all of God's acts towards man and creation, he relates as Lord and therefore as harmoniously one in many. The created reality, imaging its Creator, inheres these lordship characteristics and reflects them throughout all of creation. This can be seen metaphysically, epistemologically, and axiologically.

The Lordship Attributes and Metaphysics

The created world is established through God's lordship: God, through his *authority*, creates and sustains the laws (the *norms*) of creation; God, through his *control*, governs the details of the created world (the *situation*); and God, through his *presence*, aligns the norms and situations to be in harmony for human flourishing (the personal or *existential*). Thus, from the lordship triad comes an understanding of creation as a whole. Poythress summarizes the benefit of embracing God's lordship over creation: "Because God is Lord of all, these perspectives harmonize in principle. God promulgates the norms; God controls the situation; God created the human persons in his image."[38] In other words, the harmony of the attributes provides the basis for the harmony of norm, situation, and the person.

While we cannot develop it at length here, perspectivalism helps the believer to understand the relationship of the one and the many.[39] This classic problem in the history of philosophy expresses the human struggle to understand how the one (for instance the category *dog*) embraces the many (Fluffy, Rover, and Lassie) without capitulating either to one another. God has made creation after his image to be a unity in diversity: God's control has created the

---

[38] Poythress, "Multiperspectivalism," 175.
[39] For a helpful overview see, Brian Weatherson, "The Problem of the Many," in *The Stanford Encyclopedia of Philosophy*, ed. Edward N. Zalta, 2014, accessed September 30, 2014, http://plato.stanford.edu/archives/fall2014/entries/problem-of-many/.

many, his authority has established the unity amidst the diversity, and God's faithful presence has guaranteed the harmony between the unity and diversity.[40]

The Lordship Attributes and Epistemology

The metaphysical harmony of creation as expressed through the lordship attributes has epistemological ramifications. Because God is Lord, he can make creation understandable. Frame expresses the connection between epistemology and lordship by showing that God's lordship is the *sine qua non* of epistemology:

> So the three aspects of knowledge correspond to the attributes of God's lordship. The object is the world as God's control has made it and maintained it. The norm is God's authority for human knowledge. And the subject is the knower, standing in the presence of God.
>
> These three aspects of knowledge are perspectival. You can't have one without the others, and with each, you will have the others. Every item of true human knowledge is the application of God's authoritative norm to a fact of creation, by a person in God's image. Take away one of those, and there is no knowledge at all.[41]

---

[40] Frame says, "God's plan is a personal one and many, because his nature is one and many. The 'manifoldness' of God is seen in the diversity of his attributes, his thoughts, and his plans. But it is seen pre-eminently in the three persons of the Trinity. There is nothing in the persons that is not in the divine unity, and there is nothing in the divine unity that is not fully expressed in the persons. In God, all particularities are fully united, and all unity is fully expressed in detail. Indeed, God's oneness is a unity of the richness of his nature, and God's richness is his 'self-contained fullness,' the richness of his uniform character." John M. Frame, *Cornelius Van Til: An Analysis of His Thought* (Phillipsburg, NJ: P&R Publishing, 1995), 75.

[41] Frame, "A Primer on Perspectivalism," 15.

Because of the centrality of the lordship triad in his epistemology, Frame actually calls his perspectivalism "an exegetically based epistemology."[42] Indeed, as Frame shows, "The Trinitarian distinctions and the lordship attributes generate three perspectives under which *anything can be viewed.*"[43]

As with metaphysics, epistemology is also helpfully directed by a proper understanding of God's essential nature and its perspectival reflection in the created reality. Hope for knowledge is lost if there is no way of relating unity and diversity in a harmonious fashion.

The Lordship Attributes and Axiology

There is a strong connection between epistemology and ethics in Frame's theology.[44] *Norms* are the expression of God's *authority* for human knowledge, indicating what God authoritatively wills us to do with the facts we encounter. The *situation* is the world as *controlled* by God, who faithfully correlates the norms with his creation. The existential aspect is God's *presence* among men whereby we must faithfully replicate God's knowledge by correctly correlating the norms to the situation.[45] Thus, man is a covenantal subject, standing

---

[42] John M. Frame, "Systematic Theology and Apologetics at the Westminster Seminaries," in *The Pattern of Sound Doctrine*, ed. David Van Drunen (Phillipsburg, NJ: P&R Publishing, 2004), 92.

[43] He delineates these perspectives as "the normative (showing how anything functions as divine revelation), the situational (showing how it functions as an object in the world), and the existential (showing how it functions as part of our subjective experience)." Frame, "Directory of Frame's Major Ideas," 978.

[44] Frame shows this connection in his address to Trinity Evangelical Divinity School: "I developed the threefold scheme in ethics before applying it to epistemology. Ethics is its natural home, and I think the ethical applications of it are more easily understood than the applications to epistemological theory. Indeed the point of my epistemology is that epistemology can be fruitfully understood as a subdivision of ethics and thus can be fruitfully analyzed by the use of my metaethic." John M. Frame, *Perspectives on the Word of God: An Introduction to Ethics* (Phillipsburg, NJ: Presbyterian and Reformed, 1990), 40.

[45] Frame speaks of mankind as "creators" of the world they live in. What

in the presence of God, required to think God's thoughts after him. Because God is the source of all existence, is present within all existence, and is authoritative in all his relations, even our knowledge is ethical.[46]

In every ethical situation, there is a norm (God's law) that should be faithfully used to understand God's world (God's facts) by a person made in God's image (God's covenantal servant). Contemplation of these lordship facts led Frame to consider what was necessary for proper ethics:

> There are three necessary and sufficient conditions of good works: right motive, right standard, and right goal. Right motive corresponds to the lordship attribute of covenant presence: for it is God's Spirit dwelling in us who places faith and love in our hearts. Right standard corresponds, obviously, to God's lordship attribute of authority. And right goal corresponds to the lordship attribute of control, for it is God's creation and providence that determines what acts will and will not lead to God's glory. God determines the consequences of our actions, and he determines which actions lead to our summum bonum.[47]

Frame is suggesting is that our knowledge, like God's, is analogously constitutive of the world we live in. Frame is not suggesting that each person has a distinct metaphysical reality; rather, he is arguing that the failure to appropriate God's knowledge leads to living in an epistemological fantasy world. Frame, *The Doctrine of the Knowledge of God*, 100.

[46] The naturalistic fallacy is illegitimately deriving *is* from *ought*. In Christianity, we *must* derive *is* from *ought*, because God's lordship includes both the *is* and the *ought*. Frame says that Christians do not commit the naturalistic fallacy because the Christian premise (the *is*) is inherently moral. See, John M. Frame, *The Doctrine of the Christian Life* (Phillipsburg, NJ: P&R Publishing, 2008), 60–63.

[47] Frame admits that his three-fold analysis is not original to him. He derived it from Van Til who derived it from the Westminster divines. Ibid., 28–29.

In his work on ethics, Frame shows how each of the world's ethical theories builds on one or more than one of the three necessary and sufficient conditions. The Christian, however, can base his ethic on the correlation of all three in perfect harmony. He can do this because ethics is ultimately based on the perichoretic harmony originally present in the persons of the Trinity.

Summary of Lordship and Perspectivalism

In sum, we may say that triperspectivalism finds its ultimate roots in the unity and diversity of Trinitarian persons (perichoresis) and attributes (relations implicit in simplicity). This unity in diversity is found in all of God's attributes, including the lordship attributes. Because God is an absolutely personal being, he is absolutely present in all of his acts. Thus, these acts are necessarily reflective of his lordship (as expressed in the lordship attributes). Through the lens of the lordship triad, mankind can view the perichoretic-like relations of much of creation (i.e., by viewing them as normative, situational, and existential). In this way, all of creation, which images God, also shares in perichoretic-like relations (i.e., perspectival relations).[48]

Put differently, Frame's triperspectivalism seeks to understand what it means for God to be *Covenantal Lord*. He summarizes *lordship* as Authority, Control, and Presence. He summarizes *Covenant* to mean that God is image-represented in creation. Combining these ideas, Frame finds that the world can be understood according to three perspectives: normative (stressing God's authority), situational (stressing God's control), and existential (stressing God's presence). Further, these attributes not only reflect God in their metaphysical expression but also in their perichoretic-like relations. Here Frame finds that each of the three persons of the Trinity naturally align

---

[48] The most extensive list appears in Frame's *Systematic Theology*, where he organizes 112 triads according to the lordship pattern. Frame, *Systematic Theology*, 1117–124.

with one of the lordship attributes: Father as normative (stressing God's authority), Son as situational (stressing God's control), and Spirit as existential (stressing God's presence).[49] Thus, all aspects of life—metaphysical reality, epistemological perspective, and ethical duty—are reflective of God's lordship. Indeed, the categories of metaphysics, epistemology, and axiology are themselves reflective of lordship.[50]

---

[49] Poythress offers an alternative way of understanding this through language: "Speaking is a perspective on everything that God does. We can say that he does everything by speaking. In this speaking, God the Father as speaker acts more like a planner. God the Son as the one associated with the speech itself is the one who puts the plan or thought into execution. The Holy Spirit as the breath of God is the one who brings the word in power to its destination, and works effects on those who hear. That is to say that he is the empowerer and consummator. Thus, God's actions in history express the speech of God, which has innately trinitarian structure." Vern S. Poythress, *Redeeming Philosophy: A God-Centered Approach to the Big Questions* (Wheaton, IL: Crossway, 2014), 274.

[50] Metaphysics relates to the normative, because God's being (the ultimate metaphysical reality) provides the norms by which the world is fashioned. Epistemology relates to the situational, because what can be known is a part of the situation. Finally, axiology relates to the existential, because only persons can have value.

8

Processional Triperspectivalism[1]

This dissertation has been dedicated to showing the Trinitarian foundations of perspectivalism. This chapter will contribute to that goal in a critical way by showing that while triperspectivalism is Trinitarian, it is not yet sufficiently Trinitarian. A model that reflects the Trinitarian persons into creation should reflect not only the interrelation of the three persons but also their priority and order.

The Need for Processional Triperspectivalism

Frame's perspectivalism is famous for its elimination of both order and priority in the fields to which it has been applied. But as much as Frame's perspectivalism is based upon the persons of God in perichoresis, it will have a difficult time eliminating *all* order and priority. In the original triad, the Father begets the Son, and the Son submits to the Father. The procession is not reversible. These facts indicate that the perichoretic relationship includes both *order* and

---

[1] The idea for Processional Perspectivalism derives from Nathan Wood's work, *The Secret of the Universe*. While his work predates Frame's by four decades, they share quite a few foundational principles. In his work, Wood attempts to show how various aspects of creation show affinity to the Trinity in what Frame would call perspectival relation. Nathan Wood, *The Secret of the Universe*, 6th ed. (Boston, MA: Warwick Press, 1936).

priority.[2] As Frame argues, "That the Father has some sort of *primacy* is implicit in the name Father in distinction from Son and Spirit . . . the Father has some sort of unique 'originative' role. So the church has generally spoken of the persons as '*first, second, and third.*'"[3]

While we have been emphasizing the similarities between the persons and the nature of God, they are distinct in that perichoresis uniquely includes order and priority. Scripture provides no basis, however, for order or priority among God's attributes.[4] This foundational distinction between simplicity and perichoresis may serve as a foundation for two types of perspectivalism: one type that is structured by order and priority and another that is structured by mutual ultimacy. In order to introduce these types, we need to provide a stronger distinction between general perspectivalism and triperspectivalism.

While neither Frame nor Poythress have explicitly made this connection, it appears that general perspectivalism gets its most worthy analogy in simplicity (i.e., the relationship of unity in diversity among the attributes of the Divine Nature) while triperspectivalism gets its most worthy analogy in perichoresis (i.e., the unity in diversity present in the triune persons). The former would encompass relationships that include a multiplicity of perspectives that find their ultimate unity in the comprehensive plan of God, while the latter would include those examples that relate in triads that find their

---

[2] Scrivener agrees: "Perichoresis upholds the need for a *starting point* and a *structure*. With perichoresis there is a *Beginning* and a *Way*. And you have to get the Beginning right (you can't start just anywhere). And you have to continue according to the Way (you can't proceed any old how)." Glen Scrivener, "How Frame's Doctrine of the Knowledge of God Might Shape and Inform the Christian Study of Ethics" (Bth Paper, Oak Hill Theological College, 2006), http://www.christthetruth.org.uk/Frame.htm.

[3] John M. Frame, *Systematic Theology: An Introduction to Christian Belief* (Phillipsburg, NJ: P&R Publishing, 2013), 501. Emphasis added.

[4] Theologians have sometimes attempted to establish an order for the attributes on the basis of a master attribute (infinity, aseity, etc.). Nevertheless, Scripture does not provide a model whereby such an attempt could be made.

unity and relational analogy in the persons of the Trinity. In sum, we will propose that general perspectivalism represents mutual implication *without order or priority*, while triperspectivalism represents mutual implication *with order and priority*. We might call this latter form, *processional triperspectivalism*.

Processional triperspectivalism would have an originary perspective (analogous to the Father), a perspective proceeding from the originary perspective (analogous to the Son), and a third perspective flowing from both preceding perspectives (analogous to the Spirit).[5] In personal correspondence, Vern Poythress noted how such a model might integrate with Frame's system: "You could argue that, since there is an 'order' to Father, Son, and Spirit, there is also suggested, derivatively, that there would be an 'order' to the normative, situational, and existential perspectives that Frame thinks are analogical to the three persons, in that order. Similarly for authority, control, and presence."[6] As we will see below, Frame and Poythress organize many of their triads according to Trinitarian persons. As such, there is potential for applying order and priority to many such triads.

The Concern over Persons and Priority

Before giving an example of Processional Perspectivalism, we should address a potential critique. Many theologians argue that the order and priority of the persons is not ontological but is merely economical. That is, there *really* is no order and priority in the

---

[5] While it is not the direct purpose of perspectivalism to provide evidence for the Trinity, it may be a result of the method. In the same way, while it is not the purpose of processional triperspectivalism to provide evidence for the *fililoque* doctrine, it may be the result of the method.

[6] Frame agrees that a processional model may be possible: "if you want to talk of hierarchy here in some sense (not ontological, of course) it would have to be that the normative is in some sense primary, and the situational and existential are in SOME sense subordinate." John M. Frame, e-mail message to the author, January 28, 2014.

divine persons; what is seen in creation is economic role-playing. If so, perhaps triads should not reflect order and priority, because ontologically the persons of the Godhead do not display order and priority.

We would provide two answers. First, even if the order and priority of the persons is merely economic, this does not preclude God's revelation from functioning according to the economical model.

Second, *economical processions indicate something about the ontological Trinity*. While dismissing Karl Rahner's identification of the economic Trinity with the ontological Trinity, Frame suggests that theologians like Rahner and Barth were right to emphasize the following three points:

1. God reveals himself as he really and truly is. His economic dealings with us, particularly his revelation in Scripture, do not distort his true nature.
2. The incarnate life of Jesus is itself an aspect of the life of Jesus as eternal Son of God. The actions and experiences of Jesus in time are actions and experiences of God.
3. The economic roles played by the three persons must be roles appropriate to their natures. That the Son, rather than the Father or the Spirit, became incarnate, was a free decision among the persons of the Trinity, but not an arbitrary one.[7]

So according to Frame, when God reveals himself in the economical processions, these revelations are indicative of who God is ontologically. That is, because God reveals himself truly in his revelation (not being limited by human language), then the economic manifestations of the processions are related to who God is ontologically. In this he is following Van Til who said, "Now as God is, so he works. This ontological Trinity forms the basis of the

---

[7] Frame, *Systematic Theology*, 490.

economical Trinity."[8] And he is also following Bavinck who said, "The diversity of the subjects who act side by side in divine revelation, in creation and in re-creation, arises from the diversity that exists among the three persons in the divine being. There could be no distinction ad extra in the unity of the divine being, if there were no distinction ad intra."[9]

Frame makes this connection clear as he discusses what it means for the Son to be eternally generated.[10] Having shown that it cannot mean that Jesus was created, was physically progenated, or simply takes on the name Son,[11] Frame offers another alternative. Rather than revealing something about what *happened to the Second member of the Trinity*, perhaps the name is a revelation of something *about the Second member of the Trinity*:

> The fact that Jesus was begotten and born in history does give us some hints as to his eternal nature. His earthly begetting images something of his eternal relationship with the Father. I would suggest that perhaps the phrase 'eternal generation' could be taken to designate that parallel. To say that

---

[8] In context, Van Til is expressing the covenantal relation of the triune persons to all of creation. Cornelius Van Til, "The Will in Its Theological Relations," in *Unpublished Manuscripts of Cornelius Van Til*, ed. Eric H. Sigward, Logos Digital Collection. (New York, NY: Labels Army Company, 1997).

[9] Herman Bavinck, *Reformed Dogmatics*, ed. John Bolt, trans. John Vriend (Grand Rapids, MI: Baker, 2003), 2.332. See also Bavinck's comment that "The 'ontological' Trinity is mirrored in the 'economic' Trinity. For that reason special properties and works are attributed to each of the three persons…in such a way that the order present between the persons in the ontological Trinity is revealed." Ibid., 2.318.

[10] We will assume the doctrines of the eternal generation of the Son and the eternal procession of the Spirit, as reflected in the Westminster Confession: "The Son is eternally begotten of the Father; the Holy Ghost eternally proceeding from the Father and the Son." "Westminster Confession of Faith," 1646, 2.3, accessed December 9, 2009, http://reformed.org/documents/wcf_with_proofs/.

[11] Frame, *Systematic Theology*, 490–94.

the Son is eternally generated from the Father is to say that something about his eternal nature makes it appropriate for him to be begotten in time.[12]

Likewise, Frame defines eternal procession as "that quality of the Spirit that makes it appropriate for him to receive . . . missions from the Father and Son and to proceed as he does in the temporal world."[13]

But if we accept that the Second member of the Trinity is eternally subordinate in role to the First member,[14] doesn't this indicate a lack in the Son? Frame countenances this understanding by suggesting the following points:

1. There is no subordination *within the divine nature* that is shared among the persons: the three are equally God.
2. There is subordination of role among the persons, which constitutes part of the distinctiveness of each.
3. Because of (2), the persons subordinate themselves to one another in their economic relationships within creation.[15]

So, when considered in the unity of the divine nature, there is absolute equality and identity. When considered in the diversity of persons, there is order and priority. The latter cannot bring the former into disrepute, because there is an equal ultimacy of the one and many.[16]

---

[12] Ibid., 494.

[13] Ibid., 497.

[14] Eternal subordination appears to be an implication of eternal generation, but for more exegetical and theological defense, see Wayne Grudem, "Biblical Evidence for the Eternal Submission of the Son to the Father," in *The New Evangelical Subordinationism*, ed. Dennis Jowers and Wayne House (Eugene, OR: Pickwick, 2012), 223–61; John Dahms, "The Subordination of the Son," *Journal of the Evangelical Theological Society* 37, 3 (September 1994): 351–64.

[15] Frame, *Systematic Theology*, 501.

[16] Frame suggests that this account of the eternal subordination of the Son

But if the economic processions indicate something more fundamental about God's ontological existence, the argument for a processional triperspectivalism is strengthened. Indeed, on the basis of Frame's own statement, that "the economic activities of the persons present clues to, or analogies of, their eternal relationships,"[17] then the activities of the Godhead presented through the lordship triad should likewise show such an order and structure.

In fact, Frame himself comes close to suggesting the need for something like a processional triperspectivalism. After having argued that the Father is the exemplar of authority, the Son of controller, and the Spirit of presence, Frame says, "Or should we say, rather, that the Father is the controller, the Son the authority (because he is the Word), and the Spirit the presence? I am somewhat torn between the two models, but I now prefer the first, since it *better fits the patterns of mutual glorification and eternal role-subordination we have seen in the Trinity.*"[18] In other words, Frame is arguing that the roles of the Trinity are refracted in their works, and as much as perspectivalism is based on that refracting, the image should share the characteristics of the original.

Before turning to a few examples of how processional perspectivalism will benefit perspectival methodology, we should emphasize the type of order and priority being suggested here. We would not expect to find chronological order, for the triune persons are not chronologically ordered. Further, the priority is not one of importance; rather, it is one of function. Thus, as it pertains to the lordship triad, we should expect to find a functional priority of the normative

---

and Spirit provides a hierarchy of role that "does not compromise their equality of nature, glory, and honor." Further, the Trinitarian hierarchy with equal glory may also be refracted into creation: "So hierarchies of role in human society, even those based on gender, do not demean those who are subordinate to higher authorities." Ibid., 502.

[17] Ibid., 501.

[18] John M. Frame, *The Doctrine of God* (Phillipsburg, NJ: P&R Publishing, 2002), 727. Emphasis added.

over the situational and existential. Further, we should find a functional priority of the normative and situational over the existential. Additionally, because the triune persons are ordered in an unvarying pattern, we should find that the existential flows out of the normative and that the existential flows out of the normative and situational together. We will seek to demonstrate the order and priority through the following two examples.

Knowledge Triad: Processional Triperspectivalism

The following examples will serve both to illustrate the potential of a processional triperspectivalism and also to answer some of the more significant critiques posed against perspectival methodology. We will proceed by reintroducing the knowledge triad, examining the critiques of that triad, and then showing how a processional triperspectivalism serves to alleviate the concerns of the critics.

Frame's Knowledge Triad

According to Frame, there are three main perspectives on knowledge: the normative perspective is reflective of the law which needs to be applied; the situational is reflective of the context in which that law is applied; and the existential is reflective of the person, who correlates the law and situation to make a decision. These three perspectives coordinate with Frame's lordship triad, aligning the Father with the norm, the Son with the situation, and the Spirit with the existential. Moreover, Frame suggests that these three align with the three sources of revelation (God, world, man) in the following way: the normative is most clearly analogous to God's Word, the situational is most clearly aligned with God's world, and the existential is most clearly aligned with man made in God's image.

In Frame's system, the three sources of revelation are epistemologically identical. In other words, the knowledge of God comes to the knower through creation and personal experience, even while the knowledge of the world cannot be abstracted from the knowledge of

God (Rom. 1:18–20) and the knowledge of self, etc.[19] Further, special revelation is intimately connected to general revelation in such a way that one cannot understand special revelation without general revelation. These epistemological insights have led to some serious criticisms. We will now examine these criticisms before showing how processional triperspectivalism provides the needed resources to answer these criticisms.

Critiques of Frame's Knowledge Triad

Perhaps the most serious critique of Frame's perspectivalism is that it minimizes the Scripture to a perspective equal with both creation and man's constitution. Indeed, if one views the Scripture as the ultimate norm, the created world as the ultimate situation, and man as the existential person, Frame sounds anti-biblical when he says no perspective takes priority. Mark Karlberg reads Frame in exactly this way, arguing, "What [Frame's method] does is to place Scripture on a par with the human situation (including both the

---

[19] Notice how Frame aligns them: "The triad 'Scripture, world and self' corresponds roughly, not perfectly, to the epistemological triad, 'law, object and subject.' The correlation is imperfect, because, as we have seen, we discover laws (of thought and life) by correlating Scripture, world and self; and we learn of objects and subjects similarly. Indeed, every item of experience functions in all three ways, as law, object and subject: everything has a law-function, since any such item may be involved in an application of Scripture to a situation (God expects us to take account of, and thus to be governed by, all that is, to the extent that this is possible for us); everything has an object-function, since everything (in experience, again) is a possible object of knowledge; and everything in experience has a subject function, because it is my experience, part of my inner life. Items of experience, then, can be seen from what I would call 'normative, situational and existential perspectives.' But no item functions in only one or two perspectives; each functions in all three. Without normativity, an item cannot be understood; without objectivity, it cannot be real; without subjectivity, it cannot be known." John M. Frame, "Rationality and Scripture," in *Rationality and the Calvinian Tradition*, ed. Nicholas Wolterstorff, Hendrik Hart, and Johan Van Der Hoeven (Lanham, MD: University Press of America, 1983), 296, accessed September 3, 2013, http://www.frame-poythress.org/rationality-and-scripture/.

situational and existential factors)."[20] Tom Chantry also reads Frame in this light:

> When asked if at least we ought to give precedence to the one source of truth which is not corrupted by human sin, he passionately insists that no perspective is to be elevated above another. . . . Personality and circumstances are meant to effect our understanding of truth *in the same manner* and *to the same degree* as do the Scriptures![21]

R. Scott Clark agrees, but he takes the critique a step further. Sinful humanity always desires to fashion God's revelation according to its own whims, and Clark argues that Frame's method gives approval to such a program. Thus, the perspectival methodology makes mankind the "creators of theology" and allows mankind to "norm the word."[22]

The central concern of these critiques is to maintain the priority of God's special revelation. If the Scriptures are merely one of three equal perspectives, then the situational and existential must determine the meaning and import of Scripture. The result, it is claimed, is not only a denigration of God's unique revelation, but it is also capitulation to relativism.[23]

---

[20] Mark W. Karlberg, "On the Theological Correlation of Divine and Human Language," *Journal of the Evangelical Theological Society* 32, 1 (March 1989): 100.

[21] Tom Chantry, comment, February 14, 2008 (6:49 A.M., CST), on "New Appreciation: John Frame," Dan Phillips (blog), *Biblical Christianity*, February 12, 2008, accessed June 16, 2014, http://bibchr.blogspot.com/2008/02/new-appreciation-john-frame.html

[22] R. Scott Clark, "Peace (with Evangelicalism) in Our Time," *The Heidelblog*, last modified October 7, 2009, accessed October 2, 2013, http://heidelblog.net/2009/10/subjectivism-and-peace-with-evangelicalism-tim-keller/.

[23] Tom Chantry, "Re-Framing Reformed Baptist Doctrine," *Chantry Notes (blog)*, February 17, 2014, accessed June 16, 2014, http://chantrynotes.wordpress.com/2014/02/17/re-framing-reformed-baptist-doctrine/.

Greg Bahnsen also showed concern over Frame's epistemological triad. While Chantry and Clark focus on Frame's correlation of the three in a system, Bahnsen focuses more explicitly on the lack of priority in Frame's triad.[24] Bahnsen was worried that Frame's system, by excluding any sort of priority, would lead to future problems. Bahnsen does not go as far as Chantry and Clark in arguing that Frame's method embraces an anti-biblical stance; rather, Bahnsen merely seeks to warn that priority is necessary to maintain the primacy of Scripture. In fact, Bahnsen claims that Frame believes in priority in *practice*, even while he appears to deny it in is his explicit statements.[25]

Bahnsen's arguments for priority come from three different angles.[26] First, he argues that the language of *presupposition* requires priority.[27] Thus, if Frame aligns the normative with the presuppositional, the normative must have priority.[28] Second, because Frame aligns God's Word with the normative (under rationalism), general revelation with the situational (under evidentialism), and God's internal witness with the existential (under subjectivism), the correlation necessarily includes priority. Third, Frame's meta-perspectival discussion requires the priority of the normative. That is, because Frame says he has a "presupposition,

---

[24] Greg Bahnsen, "The Place of Evidence in Apologetics," January 17, 1986, accessed June 27, 2014, http://www.cmfnow.com/theplaceofevidencein apologetics.aspx.

[25] After quoting Frame's statement that none of the perspectives has an ultimate priority, Bahnsen says, "Upon analysis, I'm not sure that I would agree with that. I'm not even sure the author would agree with that either." Ibid.

[26] Ibid.

[27] Frame's definition of presupposition clearly includes priority: "A presupposition is a belief that takes precedence over another and therefore serves as a criterion for another. An ultimate presupposition is a belief over which no other takes precedence." Frame, *Systematic Theology*, 707.

[28] Frame makes this analogy. See John M. Frame, "Epistemological Perspectives and Evangelical Apologetics" (presented at the Evangelical Theological Society, Biola University, CA, 1982), accessed September 3, 2013, http://www.frame-poythress.org/epistemological-perspectives-and-evangelical-apologetics/.

derived from Scripture, that each perspective brings us into contact with God's truth,"[29] Frame must be analyzing the three perspectives from a pre-perspective (or at least priority) commitment to the harmony of the three.

Frame's Answers to the Critics

From his earliest writings, Frame anticipated such criticism: "To say as I have that none of the perspectives is infallible and that none is ultimate has relativistic overtones."[30] So how does Frame answer his critics? We will see that Frame has sought to explain how he can maintain the primacy of Scripture without giving priority to the normative perspective.

First, Frame argues that Scripture clearly indicates that we are creatures designed to gain knowledge in a sin-laden world by means of correlating Scripture with our world and other persons in existential experience. To illustrate Frame's point, we will look at another aspect of Chantry's critique mentioned earlier. While admitting that human knowers must necessarily gain knowledge as persons in a situation, Chantry laments, "The Reformed thinker, then, may acknowledge that his personality and his context play a role in his reading of Scripture, but he views this as a *shameful fact*, a result of his fallen nature and continuing sin—something to be *fought against* with all the power of the Spirit."[31]

Chantry's position is clearly opposite of Frame. Indeed, Frame would argue that Chantry's position is lacking in that it denigrates the personal and situational aspects of knowledge. Chantry is seeking knowledge abstracted from his situation and existential awareness, but a proper understanding of God's knowledge shows that Chantry's goal is futile. God's knowledge is inherently tri-personal and is foundational to the created situation he has foreordained. Clearly

---

[29] Ibid.
[30] Ibid.
[31] Chantry, "Re-Framing Reformed Baptist Doctrine." Emphasis added.

the ways in which existential and situational factors influence God's knowledge and man's knowledge are distinct. God knows and then creates the situation. The opposite is the case with creatures; they first experience the situation and then mentally fashion the knowledge of it. This is summarily stated in that creation is first in God's mind and then in created reality, but for man created reality is first experienced and then imaged in man's mind. This is what it means to think God's thoughts after him. To seek knowledge without situational factors is to seek an escape from creaturehood. The same can be said of seeking to escape personality in gaining knowledge. While sin does *strain* the accumulation of knowledge by means of personality, the accumulation of knowledge by means of personality is not the *product* of sin. It is ultimately the product of being an image of the tri-personal God.

Frame's second response to his critics concerns the content of the normative perspective. Frame laments that nearly all of his critics on this point fail to distinguish between the Scripture and the normative perspective. He says, "The normative perspective is not the Bible; it is my understanding of the Bible in its relations to me and all creation."[32] From this he concludes, "So understood, the normative perspective is certainly important, but it is not the Bible, and the primacy of Scripture does not of itself entail the primacy of the normative perspective."[33]

Frame's third response follows closely with the second; namely, the Scripture is not limited to the normative perspective. Instead, the Scripture is the chief element in every perspective. While it is the ultimate giver of norms (normative), it is also the ultimate object in the world (situational), and is the ultimate object of our experience (existential). In Frame's own words, "the Bible is the covenant constitution of the people of God, the highest authority . . . it is

---

[32] John M. Frame, *The Doctrine of the Knowledge of God* (Phillipsburg, NJ: Presbyterian and Reformed, 1987), 163.
[33] Ibid.

natural to consider it part of the normative perspective. But it is also part of our situation (the fact that illumines all other facts) and of our experience (the experience that illumines all others)."[34]

The previous two responses highlight the distinction that should be made between the Scripture and the normative perspective. While the Scripture is certainly normative, it is not *only* normative. And while the normative perspective most appropriately draws from the Scripture, it does not do so exclusively. God also reveals his divine norms through creation (Rom. 1) and the constitution of the creature (Rom. 2).

Having shown the confusion that is usually associated with the critiques of his position, Frame turns to a positive statement, further clarifying clarify the position. Thus, his fourth response is to highlight the "covenantal primacy" of Scripture. Frame describes this as the dominance Scripture has over each of the perspectives:

> *From one point of view, Scripture is a rather small 'item.'* From the normative perspective, it is only part of the 'organism of revelation' by which we determine our obligations. From the situational perspective, it is only one part of creation. Prom the existential perspective, it is only one item of our subjective experience. *Yet it is, in each case, the definitive part.*[35]

God's Word is not merely present as or in one of those perspectives; it is the definitive aspect to all three. When seen in this light, Frame is not seeking to denigrate Scripture; he is trying to maintain its ultimacy over all knowledge.[36]

A final response is offered in an appendix to Frame's first book

---

[34] John M. Frame, "A Primer on Perspectivalism," in *John Frame's Selected Shorter Writings* (Phillipsburg, NJ: P&R Publishing, 2014), 16.

[35] Frame, "Rationality and Scripture," 308.

[36] This observation serves to partially answer Bahnsen's critique concerning meta-perspectival analysis. Because God's Word stands above the perspectives, it can give a meta-analysis of the program.

on perspectivalism. Having reread his manuscript, Frame recognized that his claim that the three aspects of knowledge are both "ultimately identical" and "distinct" could cause confusion.[37] This confusion is particularly problematic due to aligning normative with special revelation, situational with general revelation, and existential with subjective revelation. Frame's solution is to speak of a *hierarchy of norms*:

> We can generalize by saying that all reality imposes demands on us but that some forms of revelation take precedence over others. The reason for this is not that natural revelation is in itself less authoritative than special but because our perception of natural revelation is obscured by sin, and special revelation is precisely the means God uses to correct our sinful misunderstandings of nature.
>
> Thus we need never confuse God's Word with nature or with our own subjectivity. Although 'everything is normative,' the hierarchy of norms enables us to distinguish clearly between God's Word and the promptings of our own hearts. It is this distinction that leads us to say that 'norm' is *not* the same thing as 'object' and/or 'subject.' The difference between norm and subject is the difference between levels of normativity on the hierarchy.
>
> And it is also a difference in *function*. 'Norm,' 'object,' and 'subject' all refer to the same reality; they cover the same territory. But each attributes a different function to reality. 'Norm' attributes to reality the capacity to govern intelligent subjects. 'Object' attributes to reality the property of being *knowable* by intelligent subjects. 'Subject' indicates that reality is inseparable from the subject himself and is to be found in and through his own experience.[38]

---

[37] Frame, *The Doctrine of the Knowledge of God*, 401–2.
[38] Ibid., 402.

Frame suggests that there is a unity and diversity to the three aspects of knowledge. Their unity is a function of their mutual expression of the same material (albeit from different perspectives). The diversity is indicated through function. Each of the three maintains a distinct role in knowledge. We could illustrate this with the diagram we used earlier in reference to the Trinity. The three aspects remain distinct from one another while at the same time having identity (epistemologically, in the knower) through mutual implication.

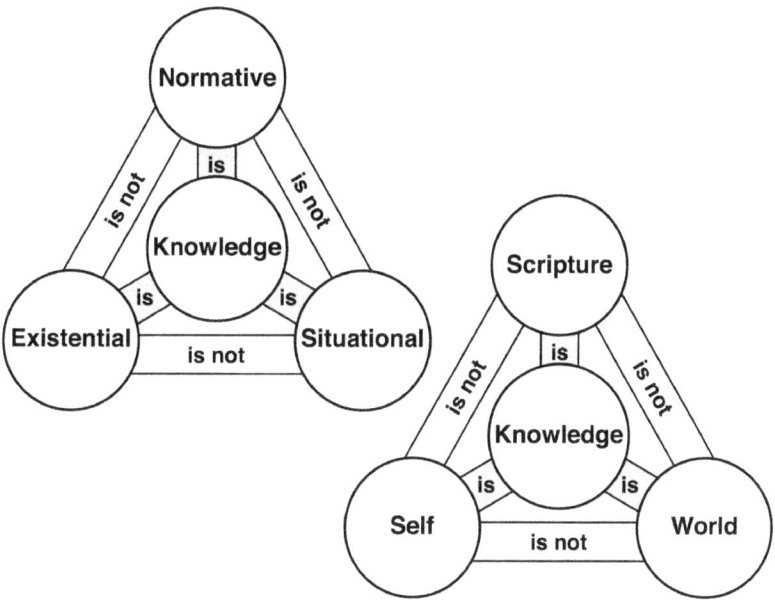

Fig. 8.1. Epistemological Identity through Mutual Implication

Processional Perspectivalism as a More Developed Answer

Frame's response to his critics has provided much needed clarity. However, one element still appears to be unresolved; namely, if Frame aligns Scripture with the normative, the world with the situational, and the self with the existential, one has to wonder why there would be a priority in one (Scripture, world, self) and not the other (norm, situation, existential). The only response appears to be that the incongruity is necessary to maintain the distinctiveness of revelation, yet this answer risks the harmony of his system.

The same problem can be described in another way. Frame often aligns the normative directly with the Scripture, implying—whether intended or not—that the normative perspective is more aptly descriptive of Scripture than the others. For instance, responding to Chantry's critique Frame said, "Within the normative perspective, Scripture plays a unique role: the covenant document (and therefore supreme authority) for God's people."[39] Earlier, Frame indicated that the covenant document aspect of Scripture stood outside of the three perspectives. Here he indicates that it is when considered in the "normative role." These descriptions are not mutually exclusive, but they do indicate (as many of Frame's critics want to stress) that the Scripture is most understandably described in the normative role. This is not to say that it cannot be described accurately and helpfully within the other perspectives; it is merely to indicate that there is something appropriate about aligning God's Word with the normative perspective.

The congruence of the normative perspective with Scripture is further strengthened by Frame's description of the normative function as "my *understanding* of the Bible in its relations to me and all creation," and as the process whereby "I examine all of my knowledge, *focusing* on Scripture."[40] We are not suggesting that the normative perspective (which is an epistemological reflection of the knowledge of the creature) is ontologically Scripture (a metaphysical reality). We are saying that there is an analogous relationship between the two that is appropriate.

Even if we say that the normative is broader than just the Scripture, e.g., by saying, "The normative perspective is not identical

---

[39] John M. Frame, comment, February 15, 2008 (8:17 A.M., CST), on "New Appreciation: John Frame," Dan Phillips (blog), *Biblical Christianity*, February 12, 2008, accessed June 16, 2014, http://bibchr.blogspot.com/2008/02/new-appreciation-john-frame.html

[40] Frame, *The Doctrine of the Knowledge of God*, 163.

with Scripture. It is, rather, the sum total of divine revelation, in Scripture, nature, and in ourselves as the image of God."[41] We still run into the same problem. If the normative perspective is "the sum total of divine revelation," how can it not have *some form* of priority?

We can resolve this dilemma through processional triperspectivalism in the following way: just as the triune persons proceed in both order and priority, so the three aspects of knowledge (built according to the Trinitarian model) do as well (figure 8.2). Thus, the normative (reflective of the Father) provides the order and structure by which the facts of the situation (reflective of the Son) are constituted, and both the normative and situational work together to be existentially (reflective of the Spirit) revelatory to the creature. And just as the Son, having been begotten of the Father, points back to the Father, so the situation, having been constituted according to the normative (i.e., plan of the Father), points back to the normative. Likewise, existential revelation, dependent on both the original plan (normative) and the created world (situation), points back to its dual origin. In this way, one may say the knowledge gained through these perspectives is interrelated and, in Frame's terminology, identical (i.e., having the same content).[42]

The epistemological conclusions are clear. There is a non-temporal priority for the normative,[43] because it is foundational to

---

[41] John M. Frame, comment, February 15, 2008 (8:17 A.M., CST), on "New Appreciation: John Frame," Dan Phillips (blog), *Biblical Christianity*, February 12, 2008, accessed June 16, 2014, http://bibchr.blogspot.com/2008/02/new-appreciation-john-frame.html

[42] More specifically, we can say that the normative points forward to the way God will accomplish in time (situational) what he wills for his creatures (existential). Thus, the normative contains the situational and existential. On the opposite end of the spectrum, we only know the normative by means of the norms being situated; consequently, the existential awareness is never without normative and situational dimensions.

[43] Non-temporal is a key modifier indicating that the priority here is a priority in *function*. The priority of the Trinitarian persons is not temporal, but it is clearly functional.

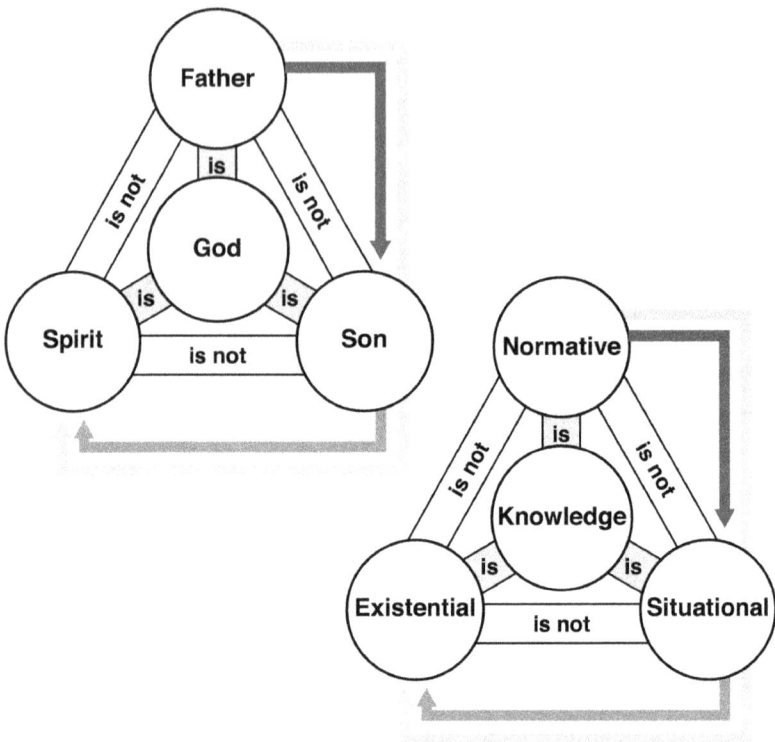

Fig. 8.2. Non-temporal Priority in Triads

all of knowledge (it is the law-like description of possibility under which the situational and existential function). Further, in connection with the normative, the situational (the context in which the law-like descriptions make sense of both the external and internal knowledge supplied by God, e.g., Rom. 1:18–20) has priority over the existential.

Such a model is warranted for the following reasons. First, it answers Bahnsen's concern as to how Frame could use the language of presupposition. The presuppositional, analogous to the normative, provides the structure and foundation upon which an understanding of the facts (situation) of personal experience (existential) make sense. Second, it more carefully seeks to align epistemology according to its Trinitarian foundations by introducing order and priority according to the analogies of the three persons.

Third, it provides a way to alleviate the apparent incompatibility between the analogies used (e.g., normative, situational, existential and special revelation, general revelation, and existential revelation). In other words, it alleviates some of the tension by suggesting that the Scripture (most often thought of as the ultimate norm), the world (most often thought of as the ultimate situation), and the self (most often thought of as the ultimate existential element), proceed in proper order. Scripture (normative) has priority over whatever may be thought to be revealed in a sin-cursed world (situation). Further, what is understood through Scripture (normative) and a *scripturally understood* sin-cursed world (situation) has priority over what is thought to be revealed through personal subjectivity (existential).

Apologetics: Processional Triperspectivalism

One of the most distinctive elements of Van Til's work is his development of presuppositional apologetics.[44] In this light, it is ironic that Frame believes both that perspectivalism derives from Van Til and also that perspectivalism leads towards a method of apologetics that minimizes the distinctiveness of Van Til's method.[45] We will seek to show that processional triperspectivalism can maintain the distinctiveness of Van Til's apologetic approach, allowing for the congruity of perspectivalism and presuppositional apologetics.

---

[44] "Covenantal Apologetics" has recently been suggested as a more beautiful and descriptive term for presuppositional apologetics. While we agree with the clarity of the name change, we do not follow that designation here because all of the primary sources use *presuppositional apologetics*. For a defense of the name change see K. Scott Oliphint, *Covenantal Apologetics: Principles and Practice in Defense of Our Faith* (Wheaton, IL: Crossway, 2013).

[45] Frame often cites Van Til as the inspiration for perspectivalism. For example, Frame says, "Van Til's discussion [of ethics] was the seed through

Frame's Apologetic Method

It is popularly argued that Frame's apologetic approach diverges from Van Til's approach. When Frame was asked to defend presuppositional apologetics in a multi-author work on apologetic methodology, the other authors were surprised to find that Frame dulled the edges of Van Til's approach. Gary Habermas noted that Frame moved "Van Tillian apologetics closer to its traditional cousins."[46] Kelly James Clark agreed, rhetorically asking, "I wonder how much of classical presuppositionalism remains in his views?"[47] William Lane Craig offered the most critical note, suggesting that in practice Frame "completely abandoned presuppositionalism . . . and launches into a straight evidentialist apologetic that would delight the heart of any theological rationalist!"[48]

To be fair, Frame does claim to hold to a *modified* presuppositional apologetic. Frame's presuppositionalism is understood in light of his perspectival methodology, resulting in a modification that challenges the historic distinctions between presuppositionalism and the other methods. Note how Frame aligns the apologetic methods according to perspectivalism:

> The presuppositionalist looks at apologetics from the normative perspective, insisting that when we argue with the unbeliever, we must above all obey God's laws of thought, we must be faithful to the Lord. In that respect, I am emphatically a presuppositionalist. But the evidentialist has a point to make also, from the situational perspective. He says that we must offer evidence; we must be willing and able to show a correspondence between our theology and the real

---

for all my triadic thinking." John M. Frame, *The Doctrine of the Christian Life* (Phillipsburg, NJ: P&R Publishing, 2008), 28.

[46] Steven Cowan et al., *Five Views on Apologetics* (Grand Rapids, MI: Zondervan, 2000), 237.

[47] Ibid., 255.

[48] Ibid., 233.

world. I gladly acknowledge that point, so you can call me an evidentialist as well as a presuppositionalist! But I do not think those two insights are incompatible. On the contrary, I believe that they are both true and that they are both important to apologetics. They appear incompatible to some, *because some people do not see the perspectival relation between the norm and the situation.* And so I can also find some value in the 'subjectivist' apologetics found in Pascal, Kierkegaard and others, writers who tend to look at knowledge from the 'existential perspective.'[49]

According to this paragraph, presuppositionalism aligns with the normative perspective, evidentialism aligns with the situational perspective, and subjectivist apologetics aligns with the existential perspective. Torres notes that by means of this analysis, Frame seeks to "transcend aspects of the methodological debate between presuppositionalists and evidentialists."[50]

Indeed Frame believes he is carrying presuppositionalism a step forward by building on Van Til's foundation. For, as Frame notes, "Cornelius Van Til had suggested that presuppositional apologetics can employ traditional arguments and uses of evidence." It was left to Frame and others to "show in general how that is possible."[51] Frame's development of an answer comes by way of a triad: "Evidences and psychological appeals represent the situational and existential perspectives within the broadly circular transcendental argument that represents the normative perspective."[52]

---

[49] John M. Frame, *Perspectives on the Word of God: An Introduction to Ethics* (Phillipsburg, NJ: Presbyterian and Reformed, 1990), 7–8. Emphasis added.

[50] Joseph Emmanuel Torres, "Perspectives on Perspectivalism," in *Speaking the Truth in Love: The Theology of John M. Frame*, ed. John J. Hughes (Phillipsburg, NJ: P&R Publishing, 2009), 111.

[51] John M. Frame, "My Books: Their Genesis and Main Ideas," in *Speaking the Truth in Love: The Theology of John M. Frame*, ed. John J. Hughes (Phillipsburg, NJ: P&R Publishing, 2009), 6.

[52] Ibid.

Table 3. Perspectivalism and Apologetics

Perspectives	Apologetic Methods	Apologetic Foundations	Apologetic Arguments
Normative	Presuppositionalism	Presuppositions/Laws	Transcendental Argumentation
Situational	Evidentialism	Facts/Evidences	Evidential Argumentation
Existential	Subjectivism	Psychological Experience	Psychological Argumentation

By arguing that the three competing methods of apologetics are perspectival, Frame is suggesting that they are different ways of viewing the *one* apologetic task. This does not eliminate all of the sharp edges of controversy, for Frame still believes that some apologetic methods may not honor the lordship of Christ.[53] Nevertheless, those who once were thought to be opposed, Frame believes, are actually in agreement. Even Aquinas, according to Frame, may not have been wrong in his use of evidence if he was subjectively submitting to the lordship of Christ as he presented the evidences.[54] The key is that one must be a *presuppositionalist of the heart*, meaning that one submits to the lordship of Christ throughout his apologetic method. On Frame's system, the difference between a presuppositionalist of the heart and a merely evidentialist apologist may or may not be reflected in external apologetic engagement.

---

[53] John M. Frame, *Apologetics to the Glory of God: An Introduction* (Phillipsburg, NJ: P&R Publishing, 1994), 4–6.

[54] By speaking of submission to the lordship of Christ, Frame is chiefly concerned to keep God as the presupposition of all thought, meaning that the apologist never assumes that anything can be intelligible or existent without the triune God of Scripture. John M. Frame, "Reply to Don Collett on Transcendental Argument," *Westminster Theological Journal* 65, 2 (Fall 2003): 307–9; Donald Collett, "Van Til and Transcendental Argument," *Westminster Theological Journal* 65, 2 (Fall 2003): 289n46.

There are two key elements to understanding Frame's apologetics, and both are reflective of perspectivalism. First, Frame believes that evidences and presuppositions (or facts and laws) are perspectivally related. Second, Frame believes that the different forms of theistic arguments are perspectivally related. We will deal with each of these in turn.

Thom Notaro, following Frame, notes, "presuppositions and evidences—at their base—are one."[55] In other words, they are perspectival, meaning that they cover the same territory from different vantage points. Greg Bahnsen substantially agreed, "Observations and presuppositions stand together. . . . In this sense, we might say that evidence and presuppositions are like distinct but inseparable perspectives on the truth about God."[56] Poythress adds that "Each fact contains implicitly a demand that we acknowledge it, take it into account, believe that it is so, live by it, and see it as exhibiting God's power and deity. Thus any particular fact implies law (standard) and is a fact-for-our-consciousness, something that I must acknowledge."[57] The intricate connection between facts and laws leads Frame to say,

> On this triperspectival approach . . . we can start anywhere; indeed, we start where we are, confident that all truth is God's truth. True facts [i.e., evidences], for example, will lead to true norms [i.e., presuppositions], and vice versa. Indeed, true facts are true norms, from a particular perspective; for God wants us to live according to all the truth he grants us. And of course true norms are also factual. And our inner responses are factual and, rightly evaluated, normative.[58]

---

[55] Thom Notaro, *Van Til & the Use of Evidence* (Phillipsburg, NJ: Presbyterian and Reformed, 1980), 92.

[56] Bahnsen, "The Place of Evidence in Apologetics."

[57] Vern S. Poythress, "God's Lordship in Interpretation," *Westminster Theological Journal* 50, 1 (Spring 1988): 35.

[58] Frame, *Systematic Theology*, 726.

Because there are no facts without laws or vice versa, when one understands a fact, he also understands some law.[59] Facts are law-laden even as laws are fact-laden (in our experience). As a consequence, "The message about presuppositions is implicit . . . to accept the kind of argument that presupposes a Christian world view and epistemology is at the same time to accept that world view and epistemology."[60] Further, this means that "Evidentialist apologetics is not cogent and persuasive because it is based on unbelieving or 'neutral' presuppositions but because it is (insofar as it is sound) based on Christian presuppositions."[61] In other words, Frame is suggesting that evidential apologetics is often useful *in practice* even when wrong *in its theory*.

The shift from Van Til's belief that we must engage at the starting point of revelation to the belief that we may engage at any starting point came with an article by Francis Schaeffer:[62] "I came out agreeing with Schaeffer, and not with Van Til, that it is legitimate to use the unbeliever's inconsistencies as a positive point of contact. 'OK: you believe in logic, but if you really believed in logic, you'd be a theist.'"[63] In other words, because the fact of logic could only be explained by the presupposition of the God of Scripture, Frame believed an apologist could start with the facts and work towards the presuppositions.

Consideration of the point of contact leads us to the second major motivation for Frame's apologetic position. Namely, Frame

---

[59] Frame says, "Even when the immediate appeal is not to law but to empirical fact or to subjective awareness, the law is never absent." Frame, "Epistemological Perspectives and Evangelical Apologetics."

[60] Frame, *The Doctrine of the Knowledge of God*, 354.

[61] Ibid.

[62] Francis Schaeffer, "A Review of a Review," *PCA History*, last modified 1948, accessed January 9, 2014, http://www.pcahistory.org/documents/schaefferreview.html.

[63] John M. Frame, "Some Thoughts on Schaeffer's Apologetics," interview by Steve Scrivner, Internet, 2010, accessed September 6, 2013, http://www.frame-poythress.org/some-thoughts-on-schaeffers-apologetics/.

believes that the transcendental argument is not unique; rather, it is one window through which we may view all theistic argumentation. All good arguments are transcendental, but then all good arguments are also evidential (true to the situation) and existentially orientated.[64] Thus, a classically evidential argument can be transcendental if it is argued in a way that indicates that the existence of God is the only possible source from which causation, design, etc., could possibly derive.[65] For Frame all good arguments must be transcendental, and evidential arguments—even when fashioned on a method that denies a transcendental goal—can be used by God to accomplish a transcendental end.[66]

According to Frame, unless an apologist explicitly indicates that he is working without transcendental presuppositions, we should assume that he is working with them. Consider what Frame says of Bahnsen at the Bahnsen-Stein debate: "he argues, 'If logic, then God;' 'If scientific laws, then God;' and 'If moral standards, then God.' Reading him in the most favorable way, I believe that Bahnsen regarded logic, scientific laws, and moral standards as meaningless without God; so his argument is really transcendental." Frame continues, "But if we give Bahnsen's own argument such a favorable reading, then I think we should give a similarly favorable reading to other apologists who use this procedure, such as Clark, Carnell,

---

[64] "That is to say that a complete argument for Christian theism, however many sub-arguments it contains, will be transcendental in character." John M. Frame, "Transcendental Argument," ed. W. C. Campbell-Jack, Gavin J. McGrath, and C. Stephen Evans, *New Dictionary of Christian Apologetics* (Leicester, England: InterVarsity Press, April 18, 2006), 716–17.

[65] Frame uses transcendental to indicate that without God there can be no meaning, intelligibility, rationality, etc. "I agree with Van Til that theistic argument should have a transcendental goal. Certainly our purpose is to prove nothing less than the full biblical teaching about God: that he is absolute personality, transcendent and immanent, sovereign, Trinitarian. And indeed, part of that teaching is that God is the source of all meaning. Certainly we must not argue in a way that misleads the inquirer to think that God is anything less than this." Frame, *Apologetics to the Glory of God*, 71.

[66] Ibid., 87.

and Schaeffer."[67] Thus, "It may no longer be possible to distinguish 'presuppositional' in distinction from 'traditional' apologetics merely by externals."[68]

Frame further argues that the classical arguments are appropriate because no one argument can prove all of Christian theism. The transcendental argument is in need of supplementation.[69] Consequently, we are forced to use various arguments to make the larger case. On this interpretation, the classical arguments can be viewed as individual elements of a larger, multifaceted transcendental argument. If so, one cannot critique evidential arguments on the basis that they do not prove the entire Christian worldview.

In sum of his position, Frame indicates that the major positions on apologetics are perspectival and complementary:

> Thus, all three methods are biblically legitimate, as long as neither seeks to claim ultimate priority or to exclude another as a complementary 'perspective.' In the current debate over apologetics, we must recognize the claim of the presuppositionalists that knowledge is impossible without law and that the ultimate law is the Scripture. We must also grant the claim of the evidentialists that the truth is found through the publicly observable events of nature and history. And we must grant the point made by many that no one will think rightly unless he is psychologically qualified to do so (there is much to be said here about the noetic effects of

---

[67] John M. Frame, "Review of Bahnsen's Presuppositional Apologetics," in *John Frame's Selected Shorter Writings*, vol. 1 (Phillipsburg, NJ: P&R Publishing, 2014), 184.

[68] Frame, *Apologetics to the Glory of God*, 87.

[69] Frame argues that the transcendental argument requires other arguments, because the premise, *without God there is no meaning*, must be substantiated. Frame asks, "How, then, is that premise to be proved? Is it that the meaning-laden character of creation requires a sort of designer? But that is the traditional teleological argument. Is it that the meaning-structure of reality requires an efficient cause? That is the traditional cosmological argument." Ibid., 71.

sin and the illumination of the Holy Spirit). Any of these approaches may be prominent in any particular apologetic encounter; but none will be successful unless the other approaches are also present implicitly. If we seek, to present God's requirements without relating them in any way to the individual's experience and consciousness, our apologetic is unintelligible. If we seek to examine the events of nature and history without organizing and interpreting these facts in a divinely acceptable way, and without addressing the unbeliever's capacity for doing such, we achieve nothing. And if we seek to address an individual's subjectivity without giving him a legal and historical basis for inner change, then we are being manipulative and are not presenting the gospel at all.[70]

A Critique of Frame's Position

The three key elements of Frame's apologetic method concern perspectivalism. First, he believes the three major methods (presuppositional, evidential, and subjectivist) are each perspectives on the one apologetic task. Second, he believes that presuppositions and evidences are perspectivally related. Third, he believes the major forms of argument (transcendental, evidential, and existential) are perspectival. We have noted how these insights have led him to argue continuity between presuppositional and evidential apologetics. Here, however, we will argue that a processional triperspectivalism will maintain the distinctiveness of presuppositionalism in both the overall method and in its chief mode of argumentation.

Methods of Apologetics and Perspectivalism

Are the three major apologetic methods the same method viewed from different perspectives? For presuppositionalists, the revelation of God is the explicit and ultimate starting point from

---

[70] Frame, "Epistemological Perspectives and Evangelical Apologetics."

which all other knowledge is viewed.[71] Alternatively, for evidential apologists, the existence of God (and thus the transcendental conclusion) is assumed to be off limits until some preliminary matters are autonomously decided.[72] Therefore, the three major positions Frame indicates in the above paragraph are certainly perspectival, but *they are all presuppositional*. Van Til would have agreed that "truth is found through the publicly observable events of nature and history."[73] He would have also agreed that "no one will think rightly unless he is psychologically qualified to do so."[74] Van Til did not deny the use of evidences or the need for bringing the transcendental argument to the needs of the people. What distinguished his method from others concerned the issue of autonomy—an autonomy that evidentialist apologists explicitly endorse.[75] In other words, non-presuppositionalists are unwilling to accept *all the implications* of the following: "that knowledge is impossible without law and that

---

[71] Van Til made a distinction between one's proximate starting point (reason) and the ultimate starting point (one's ultimate authority). Cornelius Van Til, *The Defense of the Faith*, ed. K. Scott Oliphint, 4th ed. (Phillipsburg, NJ: P&R Publishing, 2008), 100.

[72] A book written as a popular critique of presuppositional apologetics provides an example: "Reason first decides whom to believe then reason leads to a deeper knowledge and understanding of the authority that is believed." R. C Sproul, John Gerstner, and Arthur Lindsley, *Classical Apologetics* (Grand Rapids, MI: Zondervan, 1984), 192.

[73] "Every bit of historical investigation, whether it be in the directly Biblical field, archaeology, or in general history, is bound to confirm the truth of the claims of the Christian position." Van Til continues, "But I would not talk endlessly about facts and more facts without ever challenging the non-believer's philosophy of fact." Van Til, *The Defense of the Faith*, 257.

[74] Van Til considered everyone in either a regenerate consciousness or an unregenerate consciousness, and noted that only the former have the capacity to understand creation correctly. Ibid., 72–73.

[75] Frame recognizes this as a feature of evidential apologetics when he says that such apologists "tell the unbeliever to think neutrally during an apologetic encounter, and they do seek to develop a neutral argument, one that has no distinctively biblical presuppositions." Frame, *Apologetics to the Glory of God*, 6.

the ultimate law is the Scripture."[76] As such, Frame is not showing the perspectival harmony of all the views—as though they are the same position from three vantage points; rather, he is showing the inherent perspectival harmony of a robust presuppositionalism.

Presuppositions, Evidences, and Perspectivalism

It is true that one cannot view evidences without presuppositions or vice versa, but to claim that one can derive proper presuppositions from the evidences alone is problematic on several grounds. First, Frame defines a presupposition as "A belief that takes precedence over another and therefore serves as a criterion for determining the truth of another. An ultimate presupposition takes precedence over all other beliefs. The ultimate presupposition is the basic commitment of the heart."[77] Inherent within Frame's definition of presupposition is hierarchy. Thus, when evidences are faced with presuppositions, the presuppositions have a priority in determining the way the evidences are viewed. As Bahnsen says, "it is just because the sum of our beliefs do have priority that we call them presuppositions."[78]

Frame says the ultimate presupposition of a Christian is the content of Scripture. But if so, facts and evidences must be submitted to this ultimate presupposition. Again Frame says,

> To recognize a Lord is to believe and obey that Lord's words, above the words of anyone else. And to obey the Lord's words in that sort of way is to accept them as one's ultimate presupposition. An ultimate presupposition is a basic heart-commitment, an ultimate trust. We trust Jesus Christ as a matter of eternal life or death. We trust his wisdom beyond all other wisdom. We trust his promises above all others. He

---

[76] Ibid., 74.
[77] Frame, *Systematic Theology*, 1134.
[78] Bahnsen, "The Place of Evidence in Apologetics."

calls us to give him *all* our loyalty, not allowing any other loyalty to compete with him, Deut. 6:4ff.; Matt. 6:24; 12:30; John 14:6; Acts 4:12. We obey his law, even when it conflicts with lesser laws (Acts 5:29). Since we believe him more certainly than we believe anything else, he (hence his word) is the very *criterion*, the ultimate *standard* of truth.[79]

Frame's language indicates that people have basic heart commitments (presuppositions) that play a governing role in the way that evidences and facts are handled. For the Christian, it is natural for Scripture to play such a governing role, but as we will see that is not natural for the unbeliever.

Second, while it is true that facts and evidences are only possible in light of the Christian God, Frame realizes that unbelievers have their own presuppositions:

It is certainly reasonable to maintain that such data as causality, purposiveness and morality indicate the reality of God. But an unbeliever may seek to avoid the force of such arguments by postulating an essentially irrational universe in which such 'indications' are not to be trusted, or by insisting that for him the universe itself is a sufficient explanation of these data. At this point, the apologist must again talk about criteria of truth and rationality. And in that discussion, his Christian colors should inevitably be exposed.[80]

Indeed, a proper understanding of Romans 1 indicates that mankind's problem is *not evidences*; rather, the problem is their autonomous *presuppositions* that guide the way they understand those

---

[79] Frame, *Apologetics to the Glory of God*, 6–7.

[80] John M. Frame, "Presuppositional Apologetics: An Introduction," *IIIM Magazine Online*, April 1999, accessed September 11, 2013, http://www.thirdmill.org/files/english/html/pt/PT.h.Frame.Presupp.Apol.1.html.

evidences.[81] Part of the genius of Van Til's approach was to recognize the primacy of presuppositions in one's epistemological system.

Third, while facts and evidences may be law-laden, unbelieving systems of thought express both rationalism and irrationalism, providing an escape avenue from the true presuppositions implied by such facts and evidence. In order to illustrate this point, Van Til spoke of how an unbeliever might accept that Jesus rose from the dead but not accept the biblical implications of such a belief.[82] The fact is not the issue, but rather the interpretation of the fact, which is ultimately based on one's presuppositions. As we have argued, such presuppositions play a guiding role in the interpretation of the facts. The inherent flexibility of unbelievers' presuppositions indicates that what needs to be challenged is not the evidences themselves, but the very system being used to understand the evidences (i.e., presuppositions).

Processional perspectivalism is helpful here in that it maintains the integrative nature of presuppositions and evidences, but it allows a structure and order to them. Because presuppositions align with the normative perspective, they image the role of the Father. The evidences, aligning with the situational perspective, image the Son. And just as the Son proceeds from the Father, so a proper understanding of the evidences and facts of creation flows from a proper understanding of biblical presuppositions. Consequently, one's accepted epistemological norms (presuppositions) take a leading role over how the situation (evidence) is to be understood. Thus, while presuppositions and evidences are united, presuppositions maintain a relative priority over evidences.

Nevertheless, it is also true that the situation is revelational of the norms. The Father is revealed through the Son, and norms are

---

[81] For a helpful exegetical study of Romans 1 see, K. Scott Oliphint, "The Irrationality of Unbelief: An Exegetical Study," in *Revelation and Reason: New Essays in Reformed Apologetics*, ed. K. Scott Oliphint and Lane G. Tipton (Phillipsburg, NJ: P&R Publishing, 2007), 59–73.

[82] Van Til, *The Defense of the Faith*, 28.

recognized through the various situations the norms are expressed within. So it would seem that we could discover right presuppositions from evidences or derive the norms from the situation. For example, in science the accumulation of evidences can cause an overthrowing of the dominant normative assumptions. Frame frequently cites the pioneering work of Thomas Kuhn in his influential work, *The Structure of Scientific Revolutions*, wherein Kuhn argues that paradigm changes are strongly resisted and evidence against a dominant paradigm is often suppressed. When evidence against a position (anomalies)[83] mounts to a point where a crisis occurs, scientists part ways. Some may leave the field altogether.[84] Others will maintain the old paradigm, attempting to bring the new evidence within the grasp of that paradigm. Finally, some will propose new paradigms that make sense of the new evidence.

But even when evidence forces paradigms to change, the change does not come easily. The flexibility of older paradigms and the hope that the older paradigm will provide an answer in the future allow paradigms to live far beyond their explanatory power.[85] The problem is exacerbated by the fact that one must accept some explanatory paradigm in order to make sense of any data, meaning that one must embrace a set of norms in order to evaluate the evidence presented. According to Kuhn, this results in two important points. First, paradigms have logical circularity, because they cannot be evaluated from the outside. As a result, "paradigm choice can never be unequivocally settled by logic and experiment alone."[86] Second, when a new

---

[83] He defines an anomaly as when "a piece of equipment designed and constructed for the purpose of normal research fails to perform in the anticipated manner . . . that cannot, despite repeated effort, be aligned with professional expectation." Thomas S. Kuhn, *The Structure of Scientific Revolutions*, 4th ed. (Chicago, IL: University Of Chicago Press, 2012), 5–6.

[84] Ibid., 78.

[85] "Scientists may conclude that no solution will be forthcoming in the present state of their field. The problem is labelled and set aside for a future generation with more developed tools." Ibid., 84.

[86] Ibid., 94.

paradigm is accepted, the scientific convert evaluates a whole new world.[87] In other words, the norms he now accepts substantially changes the way he evaluates the world (situation) he experiences.

What can Kuhn's research indicate about presuppositional apologetics and processional triperspectivalism? Initially, we can see that even in science, norms have a functional priority over the situation. Kuhn does suggest that norms can be changed by the accumulation of evidence, and we would agree. However, we would note two points. First, the resistance shown in science to the modification of paradigms is magnified in the confrontation with unbelief, which seeks to actively suppress the knowledge of God (Rom. 1:18–32). Thus, the mere accumulation of evidence is not alone sufficient for normative alteration. Second, scientific enquiry and the knowledge of God are not parallel concepts. God has placed mankind in a position to seek out knowledge of the creation (Gen. 1:28), but he has not revealed all of the norms of science. On the other hand, God has provided the ultimate theological norms by which we should live. Further, he has made sure that every man knows such norms (Rom. 1:18–20). Thus, in science it is appropriate to hold loosely to paradigms in order to evaluate evidence, but this is not the case in theology. It is imperative that we maintain biblical presuppositions throughout the evaluation of evidence. Those autonomous and rebellious subjects who refuse to do so must be reminded of the presuppositions they are suppressing.

A second lesson we can learn from Kuhn is that the key to paradigm shifts is often the introduction to a new set of norms (paradigm) by which one may view the evidence in a new light.[88] Presuppositional apologetics seeks to do precisely this by means of

---

[87] "Paradigm changes do cause scientists to see the world of their research-engagement differently. In so far as their only recourse to that world is through what they see and do, we may want to say that after a revolution scientists are responding to a different world." Ibid., 111.

[88] Ibid., 88–89.

Van Til's two-step approach.[89] Thus, Frame's approach, while recognizing the ability of God to work through the evidence to lead to proper presuppositions, does not always take the tactical advantage of explicitly reminding the unbeliever of his suppressed presuppositions—a tactic offered in presuppositional apologetics and suggested by processional perspectivalism.

Third, Kuhn shows that norms/presuppositions/paradigms offer alternative interpretations of reality. For example, the very idea of causality on one paradigm may significantly differ on another paradigm. When norms differ, one cannot assume shared understanding at the level of the situation. It is necessary, therefore, to make mention of the norms that are being used to understand the world of experience.

In sum, Frame is correct to note that evidences and presuppositions are one. However, the unique status of biblical presuppositions, as having been revealed to all men, places theology in a different position than other fields of inquiry. While the scientist may not be strongly committed to any paradigm (though he must choose one in order to evaluate evidence), it is imperative that men embrace certain presuppositions in theology. The result is that evidences are often quite helpful in making paradigm shifts in scientific realms, but in the theological realm, evidences are designed to bolster the awareness of clearly revealed theological norms (Rom. 1:18–20).[90] And

---

[89] Van Til says, "The Christian apologist must place himself upon the position of his opponent, assuming the correctness of his method merely for argument's sake, in order to show him that on such a position the 'facts' are not facts and the 'laws' are not laws. He must also ask the non-Christian to place himself upon the Christian position for argument's sake in order that he may be shown that only upon such a basis do 'facts' and 'laws' appear intelligible." Van Til, *The Defense of the Faith*, 122–23.

[90] It is clear from Scripture that the knowledge of God (norms of revelation) comes through that which is made (Rom. 1:20), so there is a very close connection between evidence and presupposition. However, Frame's apologetics advocates times where the believer may "hide his presupposition in his heart" in order to engage the unbeliever. Frame is certainly not advocating

while it is true that God works through evidences to bring about biblical presuppositions (because evidences do truly entail biblical norms), those who do not explicitly express the inherent knowledge of God in mankind (i.e., man's suppressed biblical norms) do not take the revelation of biblical presuppositions to all men as seriously as they should.[91] Consequently, they lose the tactical advantage of presenting the presuppositions that will lead to a proper evaluation of the evidence, and they tacitly accept the unbeliever's right to view the evidence through twisted, fallen norms.

Transcendental, Evidential, and Existential Arguments and Perspectivalism

Finally, we will consider Frame's position on transcendental argumentation. Frame has taken much criticism for his belief that the transcendental argument is not unique. Don Collett published a critique of Frame's position, which he called the *reductionist*

---

autonomy on the part of the apologist, but he is concerned for persuasiveness. We would contend that on the basis of Kuhn's work, persuasion comes when one is confronted with an alternative set of norms that makes sense of the evidence presented. As such, hiding one's presuppositions becomes ultimately unpersuasive. To be fair, Frame clearly does not have in mind *always* hiding presuppositions. Nevertheless, if one takes seriously the relative priority of norm over situation, it would appear that it is best to present the proper paradigm to understand evidence whenever evidence is presented. Steve R. Scrivener, "Frame's and Van Til's Apologetic," in *Speaking the Truth in Love: The Theology of John M. Frame*, ed. John J. Hughes (Phillipsburg, NJ: P&R Publishing, 2009), 551.

[91] It is because evidences do reflect true presuppositions that evidential apologetics sometimes works. Our issue is not with the connection between true presuppositions and evidences; rather, we are suggesting that (1) a person who ignores the presuppositional elements of the discussion is not taking the tactical advantage offered him by the ineradicable knowledge of God instilled in every man, and the advantage offered by proposing an alternative system of interpreting the evidence. (2) And a person who ignores the presuppositional elements of the discussion is inviting the unbeliever to assume an interpretation of the evidence in light of his own fallen, twisted presuppositions.

objection.⁹² Such an objection rests on the idea that the transcendental argument is not substantially different from traditional forms of argumentation.⁹³ More specifically, "The reductionist objection to the unique character of transcendental argument rests upon the assertion that 'p implies q' and 'p presupposes q' are deductively equivalent propositions."⁹⁴

Collett, Bahnsen, and Anderson all critique Frame's understanding on the transcendental argument at the same point. Namely, they show that the conclusion of a transcendental argument obtains regardless of the truth-value of the antecedent premise.⁹⁵ In other

---

⁹² The article has been published three times, and has been edited for each consecutive publication: Collett, "Van Til and Transcendental Argument"; Donald Collett, "Van Til and the Transcendental Argument," in *Revelation and Reason: New Essays in Reformed Apologetics*, ed. K. Scott Oliphint and Lane G. Tipton (Phillipsburg, NJ: P&R Publishing, 2007), 258–78; Donald Collett, "Van Til and Transcendental Argument Revisited," in *Speaking the Truth in Love: The Theology of John M. Frame*, ed. John J. Hughes (Phillipsburg, NJ: P&R Publishing, 2009), 460–88.

⁹³ After noting that presuppositional apologists often align the transcendental argument with indirect arguments, Frame says, "any indirect argument can be made into a direct argument with some creative rephrasing." Frame, *Apologetics to the Glory of God*, 76.

⁹⁴ Collett, "Van Til and Transcendental Argument," 304.

⁹⁵ Anderson says, "I believe Frame is mistaken in his suggestion . . . that transcendental arguments are not substantially different from other forms of theistic argument. The former can be distinguished from the latter with respect to the scope, subject matter, and modality of their premises. For now, an analogy will have to substitute for an argument: traditional theistic arguments proceed from what we see, whereas transcendental arguments proceed from the possibility of sight." James N. Anderson, "Presuppositionalism and Frame's Epistemology," in *Speaking the Truth in Love: The Theology of John M. Frame*, ed. John J. Hughes (Phillipsburg, NJ: P&R Publishing, 2009), 451n48. Bahnsen adds, "To put it simply, in the case of 'direct' arguments (whether rational or empirical), the negation of one of their premises changes the truth or reliability of their conclusion. But this is not true of transcendental arguments, and that sets them off from the other kinds of proof or analysis." Greg Bahnsen, *Van Til's Apologetic: Readings and Analysis* (Phillipsburg, NJ: P&R Publishing, 1998), 501. Finally, Collett states, "To qualify as a transcendental conclusion, the truth of the conclusion in a direct argument would have to be in some

words, the transcendental conclusion is necessary for either the truth or falsity of whatever is being considered. This is not a function of *modus ponens* or *modus tollens* and, therefore, is unique to the transcendental argument.

In response, Frame said that he would "no longer claim that presuppositional argument is the same thing as traditional implication." Nevertheless, he continued, "I will, however . . . claim that one may reach presuppositional conclusions by traditional argument forms."[96] His chief example comes from the Bahnsen-Stein debate, where Frame claims Bahnsen used many of the traditional arguments in order to make his ultimate transcendental conclusion: "[Bahnsen] argued 'logic, natural law, and morality, therefore God.' . . . This is a straight modus ponens argument, not essentially different in this respect from arguments used by Thomas Aquinas and other traditional apologists."[97]

How could Bahnsen, who argued for the distinctiveness of the transcendental argument use the same arguments as Aquinas? Collett gives the answer: "In those argumentative contexts where *modus ponens* is operative, or where the operative semantic relation is that of implication proper, methodological differences between presuppositional and traditional approaches do not register themselves on a formal level."[98] Or in the words of Fraassen, "Presupposition and implication are not the same, but they have something in common. What they have in common is that, if A either presupposes or implies B, the argument from A to B is valid."[99] In other words, there is overlap between transcendental and traditional arguments such

---

sense independent of the truth value of its antecedent premise. However, both *modus ponens* and *modus tollens*, two classic forms of direct argument, fail to meet this criterion." Collett, "Van Til and Transcendental Argument," 302.

[96] Frame, "Reply to Don Collett," 307.

[97] Ibid., 308.

[98] Collett, "Van Til and Transcendental Argument," 305.

[99] Bas C. Van Fraassen, "Presupposition, Implication, and Self-Reference," *Journal of Philosophy* 65, 5 (March 1968): 138.

that when an argument is examined *without context* one may not be able to distinguish the transcendental and traditional argument.

The integral relationship between facts and presuppositions must be remembered. One cannot examine facts without bringing his presuppositions to bear on those facts. In the same way, one cannot look at the logical conclusion of a series of facts (i.e., an argument) without bringing his presuppositions to bear on the argument. What Frame desires is that people accept the arguments and derive a biblical presupposition from them. But what presuppositions will be brought to bear on the arguments? Again Romans 1 is explicit. Without challenging the presuppositions directly, we are encouraging the unbeliever to use his ungodly presuppositions to bear on the evidences or logical arguments. As even Frame says, "Non-Christians do not share the presuppositions we have discussed. Indeed, they presuppose the contrary, as they suppress the truth."[100] Further, "Our ultimate commitment plays an important role in our knowledge: it determines our ultimate criteria of truth and falsity, right and wrong. While we maintain our ultimate commitment, we cannot accept anything as true or right that conflicts with that commitment."[101]

But if we explicitly challenge presuppositions, or the normative foundations, then we are addressing the core issue. Norms concern necessity and the range of possibility, and so when we offer a proper norm, which is the triune God of Scripture, as the ultimate presupposition, we define the range of possibility. In this light, the transcendental argument flourishes, for it defines both what is necessary and provides the range of possibility for which argumentation can be made. Once the proper presupposition has been stated, arguments that include implication are appropriate to use. Now, however,

---

[100] John M. Frame, "Presuppositionalism," ed. Jack Campbell, *IVP Dictionary of Apologetics* (Leicester, England: InterVarsity Press, 2006), 375–76, accessed September 5, 2013, http://www.frame-poythress.org/presuppositionalism/.

[101] John M. Frame, *Cornelius Van Til: An Analysis of His Thought* (Phillipsburg, NJ: P&R Publishing, 1995), 136.

such arguments are framed *within the context* of the ultimate biblical transcendental.

Greg Bahnsen at the Bahnsen-Stein debate offers a great example. Frame notes that Bahnsen uses implication-based arguments to prove his transcendental conclusion. However, it is important to note the *broader context* of the debate. Bahnsen prefaced his debate with these words:

> It is necessary at the outset of our debate to define our terms; that is always the case. And in particular here, I should make it clear what I mean when I use the term 'God.' I want to specify that I'm arguing particularly in favor of Christian theism, and for it as a unit or system of thought and not for anything like theism in general. . . . My commitment is to the Triune God and the Christian world view based on God's revelation in the Old and New Testaments. So, first I am defending Christian theism.[102]

Having established his presuppositions, Bahnsen could build implication-like arguments that developed from his overall presuppositions. His arguments were used in a broader context in which his interlocutor was aware of the presuppositions that he brought to bear on the evidence. As such, Bahnsen was explicitly (not merely implicitly) challenging the unbeliever's view of presuppositions, showing that only with the right foundations are knowledge, logic, etc., possible. However, if Bahnsen had not started with his introductory statements, what would have been the normative assumptions? The answer is clear: Stein assumed autonomous presuppositions whereby he was capable of determining whether God exists.[103]

---

[102] Greg Bahnsen and Gordon Stein, "The Great Debate: Greg Bahnsen and Gordon Stein," *The Domain for Truth*, last modified 2006, accessed April 26, 2011, http://veritasdomain.wordpress.com/2006/12/05/greg-bahnsen-vs-gordon-stein-the-great-debate/.

[103] Stein was prepared to refute the classical arguments for God's existence,

On this basis, there are at least two distinct types of argumentation. The *transcendental* type expressly states the presuppositions of Scripture and places the opponent in direct exposure to his denial of biblical presuppositions. In the following example of a transcendental argument, *A* references any number of evidential facts (logic, morality, causality, etc.) while *G* references the triune God.

[A presupposes G ∴ A ⊃ G]	(Pre-stated Presupposition)
A ⊃ G	(Stated Premise 1)
A	(Stated Premise 2)
∴ G	(Logical Conclusion)

Notice that in this argument, we do not begin with an argument from implication; rather, the argument from implication flows out from our biblical presupposition already stated. For this reason, our interlocutor does not have a right to believe that the existence of God rests on the conclusion of the argument.

The second type of argumentation, i.e., the *traditional* type, also includes presuppositions. However, because the unbeliever is not challenged with biblical presuppositions, he assumes presuppositions for himself and his interlocutor.[104] In the following, *U* stands for any unbelieving presuppositions:

---

but he did not prepare to answer a presuppositional argument. In this way, Stein showed that he believed the existence of God should be open to discussion, while Bahnsen showed that it was presupposed even at the beginning of the argument. Stein was showing faithfulness to the presuppositions Paul says unbelievers will express (Rom 1:18–32).

[104] The interlocutor may not assume that the Christian has the *exact same* presuppositions as himself. However, unless he is told otherwise, it is likely that modern man will assume that man is the ultimate arbiter of truth. For even as Frame recognizes, "The autonomy of thought has been routinely assumed in secular thought since the days of Greek philosophy." Frame, *Apologetics to the Glory of God*, 74.

[A presupposes U ∴ A ⊃ U]	(Unstated Presupposition)
A ⊃ G	(Stated Premise 1)
A	(Stated Premise 2)
∴ G	(Logical Conclusion)

The problem with this second form of argumentation is manifold. First, as noted above, presuppositions have a guiding role concerning how one views evidences and argumentation. In this case, if we are speaking to a naturalistic unbeliever concerning the implication of causation, his presupposition that causation implies other *natural* causation will limit the rest of the argument. Why is the existence of God required in light of the explanatory power of nature?

Second, the argument allows the unbeliever to consider that the existence of God is dependent on the conclusion of the argument. If the argument stands, then God exists. If it fails, then God does not exist. However, as Van Til has perceptively noted, God's existence is not dependent on the conclusion to an argument, for he is the very foundation for argumentation itself.[105] When arguing transcendentally, the believer is capable of indicating that whatever the unbeliever decides concerning the argument, the existence of God is already settled.[106] The implication argument is merely one way of expressing the *broader* transcendental point, which has been previously made explicit.

Third, if we substitute causality for A in the second argument,

---

[105] Collett summarizes Van Til's position, when he says that unbelievers "unwittingly assign to the concept of God's existence a logically derivative rather than logically primitive status." Collett, "Van Til and Transcendental Argument," 291.

[106] So Collett says, "In Van Til's Christian-theistic construction of the transcendental argument the truth of God's existence is not a deductive consequence of the premises of the argument, but rather the metaphysical and logical ground for the very possibility of the premises themselves." Ibid.

we are allowing the unbeliever to think of causality without reference to the absolute God of Scripture. That is, when we present the argument in the context of a larger transcendental argument, we are establishing the nature of causality and how we are using it in the argument. For the broader transcendental argument, causality includes in its very definition the necessary existence of God. However, in the more traditional argument, we are arguing from the unbeliever's conception of causality. Frame himself notes this limitation when, after expressing that traditional argumentation can lead towards a transcendental conclusion, he notes,

> If the argument is to be sound, however, we must of course, interpret causality in a way that is itself consistent with the God of the Bible, risking the charge of circularity . . . We should not suggest that the unbeliever can assume some secular philosophical concept of causality (like those of Aristotle, Hume or Kant) and reason from that. Causality itself is not a religiously neutral notion, providing a common ground between believing and unbelieving worldviews, from which Christian conclusions can be reached. No, without God there would be no causal order, nor any possibility of causal argument.[107]

We wholeheartedly agree with Frame here, but we wonder how a traditional argument can argue for a biblical concept of causality without first indicating that causality presupposes God's existence. If we do not make such an indication, we are arguing from the unbeliever's "secular philosophical concept of causality."[108] In this

---

[107] Cowan et al., *Five Views on Apologetics*, 221.

[108] Frame does respond to an argument like the one being made here. He notes, "The causal argument assumes that everything in creation has a cause. That premise is true according to a Christian worldview, but it is not true (at least in the traditional sense) in a worldview like that of Hume or Kant. . . . once one defines 'cause' as Hume or Kant does, the argument goes nowhere.

light, Frame's last statement is absolutely true and is the foundation from which any type of causal argument might be made. Granting this, it is also where the formulation of such an argument should be founded as well.

Fourth, only the broader transcendental type of argument is capable of communicating the *necessary* existence of God. Because ultimate presuppositions concern necessity, because God is a necessary being, and because God has made man to know him as a necessary being (Rom. 1:18–20), it is both disingenuous and ultimately unhelpful to present God in any other light. If we present an argument in the traditional mode above without reference to the necessary existence of God, we allow the unbeliever to continue in autonomy, ignoring the truth he suppresses and assuming the constructed reality he wishes to exist. It is for this reason that the transcendental argument is uniquely fitted to communicate God's aseity, for it is the type of argument that indicates that God's existence is necessary for any other reality.

Frame's alternative suggestion—that we might want to keep our presuppositions hidden—is based upon an appeal for persuasion.[109]

Now many people can be led to accept the existence of God through the traditional argument because *they agree to a Christian concept of cause*. This is part of God's revelation that they have not repressed, what Van Til calls 'borrowed capital.' But once they become more sophisticated and philosophical (i.e., more self-conscious about suppressing the truth) they are likely to raise objections to such proofs on the basis of a more consistently non-Christian frame of reference. At that point, the apologist must be more explicit about differences of presupposition, differences of worldview, differences in concepts like that of causality. Then the argument becomes more explicitly 'transcendental.' But not every inquirer requires this, and for many it actually hinders communication." Frame, *Apologetics to the Glory of God*, 71–72. In response, we would say that if they have not repressed the fact that causality presupposes God, it should not be problematic to bring it up in conversation. If they have done so, to assume that they have not, leads to using an unbiblical definition of causality to argue for God's existence.

[109] Frame notes in published personal correspondence with Scrivener: "The apologist may, for part of the discussion at least, want to hide his presupposition

According to Frame, a good argument can be described according to three perspectives: "It needs to be valid (i.e., it follows the laws of logic), sound (its premises are true and therefore its conclusion is true), and persuasive (it is effective in bringing people to believe the conclusion)."[110]

For Frame there are two problems with transcendental arguments as it concerns persuasion. First, some of the implications are clearly not persuasive. Frame gives the following example:

> If causality exists, God exists (in the sense that God is the presupposition or transcendental ground of causality).
>
> There is no causality.
>
> Therefore God exists.[111]

Second, the first premise needs to be explained and not just stated. As stated, Frame asks, "*Why* should anyone grant that the God of the Bible is the presupposition of causality?"[112] We will address these questions in reverse order. As for the second question, the reason people should grant that God is the presupposition of causality is because of the revelation already given to them. According to Romans 1:20, all of mankind knows God's eternal power and Godhead, and while the unbeliever suppresses such knowledge, it is not illegitimate to confront him with the truth he refuses to acknowledge. Indeed, this appears to be the most powerful tool of the apologist.

---

in his heart." Scrivener, "Frame's and Van Til's Apologetic," 551.

[110] In a footnote Frame says, "validity is normative (following laws); soundness is situational (stating true facts about the world); and persuasiveness is existential (appealing to the hearts and minds of its audience)." John M. Frame, "Responses to Some Articles," in *Speaking the Truth in Love: The Theology of John M. Frame*, ed. John J. Hughes (Phillipsburg, NJ: P&R Publishing, 2009), 964.

[111] Ibid., 965.

[112] Ibid.

The prior question is admittedly more difficult. Clearly an argument denying causality in order to prove God's existence is not initially persuasive. However, processional perspectivalism offers a helpful way forward. Norms refer to the range of possibility under which the situation may be fashioned. It is possible that God would create causality, or he could refrain from creating causality.[113] Nevertheless, having fashioned causality, it appears existentially unpersuasive to argue from non-causality. This is because that which is existentially experienced flows out of *both* the norm and situation. That is, existential persuasion occurs most naturally when observing events that occur within the realm of both possibility (normative) and actuality (situational).

Nevertheless, Frame's argument for non-causality can still be persuasive. Philosophers of modal logic often imagine different worlds, which are potential worlds limited by the norms that are said to obtain in *all worlds*. Is it possible that God could have made a world without causality? Yes. So while the common man may not find an argument from non-causality to be persuasive (because of the existential experience he has in this world), it is hardly on that basis that we can say an argument is unhelpful. The field of possible world cosmology is rich in philosophy today,[114] and is a result of the existential ability to imagine the norms of creation being fashioned according to a different situation. Christians have argued for God's necessary existence in all possible worlds,[115] and so the argument for non-causality could be successfully and persuasively used as a part of the larger transcendental and modal argument.

---

[113] Here we are referencing only that type of causality that is a product of God's free choice to create.

[114] For a summary of possible world cosmology and an extensive bibliography see, Christopher Menzel, "Possible Worlds," ed. Edward N. Zalta, *The Stanford Encyclopedia of Philosophy*, 2014, accessed September 25, 2014, http://plato.stanford.edu/archives/fall2014/entries/possible-worlds/.

[115] For instance, see Plantinga's modal ontological argument for God's existence on the basis of possible worlds. Alvin Plantinga, *The Analytic Theist: An*

To conclude our criticism of Frame's apologetics we would say that Frame appears to misunderstand the nature of the Christian's ultimate presupposition. He claims that Van Til's system is insufficient because it only seeks to prove that God is the author of meaning or purpose.[116] However, Van Til was using meaning and purpose as elements of his larger presuppositional argument. For Van Til, the ultimate presupposition concerns the metaphysical —i.e., God's existence.[117] For Frame, presuppositions are foundationally epistemological, and one's ultimate presupposition is not God's ontological existence but Scripture: "For a Christian, the content of Scripture must serve as his ultimate presupposition."[118] God's metaphysical reality has significant epistemological results, and Van Til's transcendental argument addresses the epistemological *because of the metaphysical*.[119] Thus, the epistemological point is a product of the metaphysical reality, which must be presupposed.

This misunderstanding of presupposition leads Frame to say, "Must we bring [the transcendental] point up explicitly in every apologetic encounter? I would say not. . . . If someone has a

---

Alvin Plantinga Reader, ed. James Sennett (Grand Rapids, MI: Eerdmans, 1998), 65–71.

[116] "If we grant Van Til's point that a complete theistic argument should prove the *whole* biblical doctrine of God, then we must prove *more* than that God is the author of meaning and rationality. Ironically, at this point, Van Til is not sufficiently holistic . . . the 'transcendental' argument requires supplementation by other arguments." Frame, *Apologetics to the Glory of God*, 73.

[117] Indeed, Metaphysics, Epistemology, and Axiology show processional triperspectivalism in that what is (metaphysics) determines what can be known (epistemology). Finally, what is (metaphysics) and what can be known (epistemology) together establish what should be valued (axiology).

[118] Frame, *Systematic Theology*, 707–8.

[119] Oliphint's definition of presupposition is more reflective of Van Til in that includes not only propositions but states of affairs: "Any religious, foundational proposition, principle or state of affairs assumed to be necessary for another given proposition, principle or state of affairs." K. Scott Oliphint, "Presuppositionalism," *Simple Apologetics (blog)*, 2014, accessed August 28, 2014, http://simpleapologetics.com/presuppositionalism.html.

particular problem recognizing Christ's intellectual lordship, then we should make an issue of it; otherwise, no."[120] Here we would agree with Frame, for the transcendental argument is chiefly concerned with how *metaphysics leads to epistemological and axiological results*.[121] Necessarily, if one truly recognizes the intellectual lordship of Christ, then he believes the ontological necessity of God's existence and the authority his absolute nature requires of creatures. But those who accept the intellectual authority of Christ are believers, and those who do not are unbelievers. For those outside Christ the issue at hand is the Lord's intellectual authority, ultimately founded on God's necessary existence and aseity.

Summary of Processional Perspectivalism and Presuppositional Apologetics

Frame has helpfully noted the perspectival relationship that exists between presuppositions and evidences. However, his failure to appropriate a processional triperspectivalism caused him to argue that presuppositions and evidences lacked priority. We have sought to show that as much as Frame has aligned presuppositions with the normative and evidences with the situational, and as much as he has noted that the normative is representative of the Father, and the situational is representative of the Son, there should be a function of

---

[120] Frame, *Apologetics to the Glory of God*, 74.

[121] In his response to Collett, Frame claims to have "imploded" the transcendental argument and shown its fault through a *reductio*. He does so by positing the following argument:
If anything is intelligible, God exists.
Nothing is intelligible.
Therefore, God exists.
The problem with such an argument is that it does not truly presuppose the God of Scripture. It ignores the ultimate metaphysical norm (God himself) when forming the argument. If we truly presuppose God's existence, then some arguments cannot be properly fashioned. Because it is the very nature of God to be intelligible in the intra-Trinitarian context, it is impossible, while presupposing God, to argue for *nothing* being intelligible. Frame, "Responses to Some Articles," 966–67.

priority and order between presuppositions and evidences. The situation (evidence) is what it is because of the norm (presupposition), and consequently, man determines the range of possible interpretation within the realm of his accepted presuppositions. While it is possible to derive proper presuppositions from evidences, Kuhn shows that it is tactically expedient to express the presuppositions which make sense of the data. Further, such presuppositions are already known by the unbeliever, indicating that such knowledge should be made explicit in an encounter with an unbeliever.

We also noted that while Frame has accurately described transcendental, evidential, and existential arguments as individual perspectives on a good argument, a failure to embrace processional triperspectivalism caused Frame to believe the transcendental argument was not unique. However, aligning the transcendental with the normative, evidential with situational, and existential with the existential perspective indicates that just as the Father, Son, and Spirit (which Frame aligns with the normative, situational, and existential) proceed in order and priority, so do the three types of arguments. Evidential arguments are existentially persuasive as much as they are built upon properly stated presuppositions. These presuppositions cannot simply be assumed in the argument, since the presuppositions of sinful men mar the truth (Rom. 1:18–20). Rather, we should situate the evidences within proper presuppositions in order to provide the most existentially persuasive account of Christian theism.

In sum, Frame's divergence from Van Til's apologetics is partly reflective of his perspectival methodology. But if processional triperspectivalism is correct, Van Til's apologetics should be retained, for, on that account, there is no conflict between a properly understood perspectivalism and a properly understood presuppositionalism.

Summary of Processional Triperspectivalism

Because triperspectivalism is a reflected image of the Trinitarian God in creation, it is necessary to discern whether that image also includes priority and order. And as much as Frame has developed patterns based on the individual Trinitarian persons who proceed in a particular order and priority, it should not be surprising to find that the reflected images display similar priority and order. We have suggested how embracing processional triperspectivalism could enhance Frame's perspectivalism. More specifically, we have shown how processional triperspectivalism helps explain the priority of Scripture and how it also provides the resources for maintaining the unique elements of Van Til's apologetic.

Processional triperspectivalism should be pursued to a fuller extent than this dissertation is capable. We have sought to show two areas where it might help, but there are others. Namely, Frame has been reticent to include the elements of the *ordo salutis* in his perspectival methodology. Even when he has included justification, sanctification, and adoption within a triad, he noted, "I am not claiming they are ultimately identical."[122] In light of Frame's lack of perspectival methodology in the *ordo* Sailer notes, "one might raise a question about the viability of a method that seems to stumble when applied to the heart of the gospel."[123] Could the major elements of the *ordo salutis* be described in light of perspectivalism? It does not appear that they can on Frame's model, but if we embrace a processional triperspectivalism, it appears that they can. Justification is the normative, adoption is the situational, and regeneration, conversion, and sanctification are all aspects of the existential. While space prevents us from fleshing such a program out, it would seem that perspectivalism provides the needed resources to provide a systematic exposition of the distinct-yet-inseparable elements of salvation that come with union with Christ.[124]

---

[122] Frame, *Systematic Theology*, 938.

[123] William S. Sailer, "Review of Doctrine of the Knowledge of God by John Frame," *Evangelical Journal* 6, 1 (Spring 1988): 51.

[124] For an excellent development of the biblical-theological development of the doctrine of union in Reformed Theology see, Lane G. Tipton, "Union With Christ and Justification," in *Justified In Christ: God's Plan for Us in Justification*, ed. Oliphint K. Scott (Great Britain: Mentor, 2007).

9

Conclusion

Nearly thirty years ago, Meredith Kline challenged his colleagues; "If we are to be responsible guardians of Reformed orthodoxy we must add to our agenda of study and discussion a scrutiny of multiperspectivalism."[1] This study has been an effort in providing a partial answer to this call. Much more labor needs to be done in order to provide a full answer to Kline, but this dissertation has sought to show the foundations of perspectivalism in the Trinitarian nature of God. If the dissertation has been effective, then the three foundational claims of perspectivalism are strengthened. Normatively, perspectivalism is an outworking of the one and many relationship originally present in the persons and attributes of the triune God. Situationally, we have sought to show that some of the major themes of perspectivalism derive from Reformed soil, and, because Trinitarian, perspectivalism should be accepted by any who believe Reformed theology is *semper reformanda*. Existentially, perspectivalism is useful as an aid to understanding creation, because creation is reflective of the one and many nature of its Creator.

While we have attempted to show the foundational role Herman Bavinck and Cornelius Van Til have had in the development of perspectivalism, more work needs to be done on the origins of

---

[1] Meredith G. Kline, *A Paper Pursuant to the Faculty Forum* (Escondido, CA: Westminster Seminary in California, 1986).

perspectivalism. Normatively, what are the fundamental ideas that have shaped perspectivalism? How does Calvin's work on covenant and epistemology affect Frame and Poythress's development of the method?[2] Does Frame's background in language philosophy play a dominant role or merely a secondary role to the development?[3] Poythress first learned the method from the works of Kenneth Pike, who was a pioneering linguist.[4] Does this shared concern for language philosophy explain the continuity of thought between Frame and Poythress on perspectivalism? Situationally, how do Frame's semi-liberal youthful inclinations,[5] his time at Princeton with the fundamentalist Evangelical Fellowship,[6] his time at Westminster

---

[2] Frame begins his first major book detailing perspectivalism by citing Calvin's first few pages of the Institutes where Calvin expresses the intimate connection between man's knowledge of God and self. Frame takes this to later suggest that his own perspectivalism is "generic Calvinism." John M. Frame, *The Doctrine of the Knowledge of God* (Phillipsburg, NJ: Presbyterian and Reformed, 1987), 1–5, 90.

[3] Wittgenstein's influence on Frame's theology is important. Frame calls him, "perhaps the most important philosopher" of the twentieth century, a "thinker I often turn back to." John M. Frame, "Backgrounds to My Thought," in *Speaking the Truth in Love: The Theology of John M. Frame*, ed. John J. Hughes (Phillipsburg, NJ: P&R Publishing, 2009), 22; John M. Frame, "Review of High's New Essays on Religious Language," *Westminster Theological Journal* 33, 1 (Fall 1970): 126–31. William Dennison believes Frame's departures from Van Til towards perspectival methodology can be traced to Wittgenstein and other language philosophers, ultimately leading to an abandonment of the philosophy of history evident in Van Til. William Dennison, "Analytic Philosophy and Van Til's Epistemology," *Westminster Theological Journal* 57, 1 (Spring 1995): 43–44.

[4] Poythress notes that Kenneth Pike was the first to introduce him to perspectivalism. Vern S. Poythress, *Redeeming Philosophy: A God-Centered Approach to the Big Questions* (Wheaton, IL: Crossway, 2014), 75.

[5] Frame mentions that when he was in high school he was "somewhat liberal theologically." John M. Frame, *John Frame's Selected Shorter Writings* (Phillipsburg, NJ: P&R Publishing, 2014), 291.

[6] For Frame's own understanding of the Evangelical Fellowship's influence in his life, see the following: John M. Frame, "Remembering Donald B. Fullerton," *The Works of John Frame and Vern Poythress*, last modified 2005, accessed

CONCLUSION

under Murray and Van Til,[7] and his time with the Yale School of Postliberal Theology factor into the development of perspectivalism?[8] Existentially, how have his deeply held ecumenical beliefs and his relationship with conservative Reformed brothers and institutions influenced the development of perspectivalism?[9] Each of these questions is important and should be further pursued.

Because Kline was most concerned with the theological results of perspectivalism, more work needs to be done to ascertain the

---

September 5, 2013, http://www.frame-poythress.org/remembering-donald-b-fullerton/. Frame, "Backgrounds to My Thought."

[7] Tim Trumper has argued that John Murray, who had a significant impact on Frame, began the sympathetic-critical approach to theology and the Reformed confessions. Frame appears to follow in his footsteps. Further, the development of doctrine during Frame's years as a student in the fields of apologetics (Van Til) and biblical theology (Kline) undoubtedly influenced the way Frame considered his own role as a professor. Tim J. R Trumper, "John Frame's Methodology: A Case Study in Constructive Calvinism," in *Speaking the Truth in Love: The Theology of John M. Frame*, ed. John J. Hughes (Phillipsburg, NJ: P&R Publishing, 2009), 149; Tim J. R. Trumper, "Covenant Theology and Constructive Calvinism," *Westminster Theological Journal* 64, 2 (Fall 2002): 388–405.

[8] Three of his professors at Yale appeared to make a significant impact. First, Frame says that it was under George Lindbeck and at Yale that "My ecumenicism and my perspectivalism were drawing together." Frame, "Backgrounds to My Thought," 21; John M. Frame, "Review of Lindbeck's The Nature of Doctrine," *The Presbyterian Journal* 43 (February 1985): 11–12. A second Yale professor, David Kelsey, wrote what Frame called "possibly the most significant writing on the subject [of Scripture] since Warfield." John M. Frame, "Review of Kelsey's The Uses of Scripture in Recent Theology," *Westminster Theological Journal* 39, 2 (Spring 1977): 328–53. Paul Holmer, the third Yale professor, was a disciple of Wittgenstein's thought, who sought to wed Wittgenstein's language philosophy to Christian theology. John M. Frame, "Review of Holmer's The Grammar of Faith," *Westminster Theological Journal* 42, 1 (Fall 1979): 219–31. Each of these professors impacted Frame in different ways, and it would be helpful to develop those ways more fully.

[9] Bahnsen indicates that Frame's aligning the transcendental argument with others forms of argument in a perspectival way was ultimately based on his deeply held ecumenical beliefs. Greg Bahnsen, "Answer to Frame's Critique of Van Til," Covenant Media Foundation Transcript (Escondido, CA,

developmental role perspectivalism has played in the theology of Frame and Poythress. For example, Frame has been criticized for his theological positions, and he often establishes those positions with a defense based on a perspectival grouping.[10] While the triad may not be directly responsible for Frame's overall position, it is important to determine what role perspectivalism has in the overall development of his theology. Further, it appears that most of Frame's distinct theological positions are in some way related to his view of unity and diversity. A study of Frame's outworking of unity and diversity in his theology would complement this study well, for it would show how Frame recognizes vestiges of the Trinity throughout all of God's theological revelation.

So while this dissertation has sought to strengthen the claim that perspectivalism is a vestige of the Trinity, it has only provided a glimpse of God's reflection in creation. It is hoped that through this dissertation, and the work that might follow it, more glory and praise might be given to our Trinitarian God, who through creation has revealed his eternal power and Godhead (Rom 1:20).

April 1994), 36, accessed January 25, 2014, http://www.cmfnow.com/answer toframescritiqueofvantil.aspx. And R. Scott Clark has argued that perspectivalism has been embraced by Frame because it provides Frame the resources to broaden the gates of Reformed theology, allowing more evangelical brothers into the fold. R. Scott Clark, "Peace (with Evangelicalism) in Our Time," *The Heidelblog*, last modified October 7, 2009, accessed October 2, 2013, http://heidelblog.net/2009/10/subjectivism-and-peace-with-evangelicalism-tim-keller/.

[10] The following are some of the distinctive theological positions Frame defends through perspectival analysis: his disregard for encyclopedia in theology; his lack of a fine distinction between law and grace; his unifying meaning and application; his lack of a distinction between life and worship as evidenced in the debate over the regulative principle of worship; his view of the definition and role of biblical theology and systematic theology; and his criticism of the primacy of the intellect.

Bibliography

Adams, Jay. "Reflections on Westminster Theology and Homiletics." In *The Pattern of Sound Doctrine*, edited by David Van Drunen, 261–68. Phillipsburg, NJ: P&R Publishing, 2004.

Alston, William P. "Does God Have Beliefs." *Religious Studies* 22, 3/4 (October 1986): 287–306.

———. *Illocutionary Acts and Sentence Meaning*. Ithaca, NY: Cornell University Press, 2000.

———. "Meaning and Use." *The Philosophical Quarterly* 13, 51 (November 2013): 107–24.

———. *Philosophy of Language*. Upper Saddle River, NJ: Prentice Hall, 1964.

Anderson, James N. *Paradox in Christian Theology: An Analysis of Its Presence, Character, and Epistemic Status*. Milton Keynes, UK: Paternoster, 2007.

———. "Presuppositionalism and Frame's Epistemology." In *Speaking the Truth in Love: The Theology of John M. Frame*, edited by John J. Hughes, 431–59. Phillipsburg, NJ: P&R Publishing, 2009.

———. "Review of God Without Parts by James Dolezal." *Themelios* 37, 2 (July 2012): 362–67.

Annis, David. "A Contextual Theory of Epistemic Justification." In *The Theory of Knowledge*, edited by Louis P. Pojman, 248–54. 3rd ed. Belmont, CA: Wadsworth, 2002.

Aquinas, Thomas. *On The Power of God*. Translated by by the English Dominican Fathers. Westminster, MD: Newman Press, 1952. Accessed July 29, 2014. http://dhspriory.org/thomas/QDde Potentia.htm.

———. *Summa Contra Gentiles*. Edited by Joseph Kenny. Translated by Anton Pegis, James F. Anderson, Vernon J. Bourke, and Charles J. O'Niel. New York, NY: Hanover House, 1957. Accessed July 30, 2014. http://dhspriory.org/thomas/Contra Gentiles1.htm.

———. *Summa Theologica*. New York, NY: Cosimo, 2013.

Armstrong, John. "John Frame's Missional-Ecumenical View of the Church: Unity in Christ Alone." In *Speaking the Truth in Love: The Theology of John M. Frame*, edited by John J. Hughes, 669–86. Phillipsburg, NJ: P&R Publishing, 2009.

Ashford, Bruce R. "Wittgenstein's Theologians? A Survey of Ludwig Wittgenstein's Impact on Theology." *Journal of the Evangelical Theological Society* 50, 2 (June 2007): 357–75.

Augustine. "On the Trinity." Translated by Arthur West Haddan. *New Advent*. Last modified December 1, 2009. Accessed December 1, 2009. http://www.newadvent.org/fathers/1301.htm.

Awad, Najeeb. *God Without a Face?: On the Personal Individuation of the Holy Spirit*. Mohr Siebeck, 2011.

Bahnsen, Greg. *Always Ready: Directions for Defending the Faith*. Edited by Robert Booth. Texarkana, AR: Covenant Media, 1996.

———. "Answer to Frame's Critique of Van Til." Covenant Media Foundation Transcript. Escondido, CA, April 1994. Accessed January 25, 2014. http://www.cmfnow.com/answertoframes critiqueofvantil.aspx.

———. "The Encounter of Jerusalem With Athens." *Ashland Theological Bulletin* 13 (Spring 1980): 4–40.

———. *Theonomy in Christian Ethics*. 3rd ed. Nacogdoches, TX: Covenant Media, 2002.

———. "The Place of Evidence in Apologetics." Audio Lecture,

January 17, 1986. Accessed June 27, 2014. http://www.cmfnow.com/theplaceofevidenceinapologetics.aspx.

———. *Van Til's Apologetic: Readings and Analysis.* Phillipsburg, NJ: P&R Publishing, 1998.

Bahnsen, Greg L., and Gordon Stein. "The Great Debate: Greg Bahnsen and Gordon Stein." *The Domain for Truth.* Last modified 2006. Accessed April 26, 2011. http://veritasdomain.wordpress.com/2006/12/05/greg-bahnsen-vs-gordon-stein-the-great-debate/.

Barber, John. "John Frame's Theology in the Present Cultural Context." In *Speaking the Truth in Love: The Theology of John M. Frame,* edited by John J. Hughes, 884–907. Phillipsburg, NJ: P&R Publishing, 2009.

Barker, William, and W. Robert Godfrey. *Theonomy: A Reformed Critique.* Grand Rapids, MI: Zondervan, 1991.

Bavinck, Herman. *Reformed Dogmatics.* Edited by John Bolt. Translated by John Vriend. Grand Rapids, MI: Baker, 2003.

Behe, Michael J. *Darwin's Black Box: The Biochemical Challenge to Evolution.* New York, NY: Simon and Schuster, 1996.

Betzold, John, Eugene Bradford, R. B. Kuiper, LeRoy Oliver, N. B. Stonehouse, Murray Thompson, William Welmers, et al. "The Text of a Complaint: Against Actions of the Presbytery of Philadelphia in the Matter of the Licensure and Ordination of Dr. Gordon H. Clark," 1944. Accessed July 23, 2014. http://godshammer.wordpress.com/2010/07/the-complaint.pdf.

Biggs, Charles R. "Epistemology According to Michael Polanyi, Cornelius Van Til, and John Calvin." *A Place for Truth.* Last modified 2005. Accessed September 16, 2013. http://www.aplacefortruth.org/essay.htm.

Blosser, Phillip. "Review of The Doctrine of the Knowledge of God by John Frame." *Eternity,* May 1988.

Boa, Kenneth, and Robert Bowman. *Faith Has Its Reasons: Integrative Approaches to Defending the Christian Faith.* Milton Keynes, UK: Paternoster, 2006.

Bosserman, Brant. "The Trinity and the Vindication of Christian Paradox: An Interpretation and Refinement of the Theological Apologetic of Cornelius Van Til." PhD Diss., Bangor, Wales: University of Bangor, 2011.

Bozzo, Greg. "Are Propositions Divine Thoughts?" Philosophia Christi, 2011. http://www.epsociety.org/userfiles/art-Anderson-Welty%20 (In%20Defense%20of%20the%20Argument%20for%20God%20from%20Logic).pdf.

Brown, Stephen W. "John Frame: The Closet Radical." In *Speaking the Truth in Love: The Theology of John M. Frame*, edited by John J. Hughes, 137–42. Phillipsburg, NJ: P&R Publishing, 2009.

Bultmann, Rudolf. "New Testament & Mythology." In *New Testament & Mythology*, 1–44. Minneapolis, MN: Fortress Press, 1984.

Butler, Michael R. "Frame on Van Til and Transcendental Arguments." *PenPoint Newsletter*, June 1997.

Calvin, John. *Institutes of the Christian Religion: 1536 Edition*. Translated by Ford Battles. Grand Rapids, MI: Eerdmans, 1995.

Carson, D. A. "Personal Words: D. A. Carson." In *Speaking the Truth in Love: The Theology of John M. Frame*, edited by John J. Hughes, xxxix. Phillipsburg, NJ: P&R Publishing, 2009.

Cathey, Robert Andrew. *God in Postliberal Perspective: Between Realism and Non-Realism*. Transcending Boundaries in Philosophy and Theology. Burlington, VT: Ashgate, 2009.

Claiborne, Nathaniel. "Hollywood, Geneva, and Athens: A Reformed Philosophy of Film." Th.M. thesis, Dallas, TX: Dallas Theological Seminary, 2011.

———. "Perspectives on Triperspectivalism." *Nate Claiborne (blog)*. Last modified September 25, 2011. Accessed February 19, 2014. http:// nathanielclaiborne.com/perspectives-on-triperspectivalis/.

———. "Triperspectivalism: More Than Church Leadership Analysis." *Nate Claiborne (blog)*. Last modified July 26, 2011. Accessed February 19, 2014. http://nathanielclaiborne.com/triperspectivalism-more-than-church-leadership-analysis/.

Clark, Gordon. "The Defense of the Truth: John Frame and Cornelius Van Til." MP3, presented at the Gordon-Conwell Lecture on Apologetics, Hamilton, MA, 1980. Accessed June 26, 2014. http://thegordonhclarkfoundation.com /defending-the-faith/.

Clark, R. Scott. *Recovering the Reformed Confession: Our Theology, Piety, and Practice*. Phillipsburg, NJ: P&R Publishing, 2008.

Clowney, David. *Earthcare: An Anthology in Environmental Ethics*. Edited by Patricia Mosto. Lanham, MA: Rowman & Littlefield, 2009.

Clowney, Edmund. "Professor John Murray at Westminster Theological Seminary." In *The Pattern of Sound Doctrine*, edited by David Van Drunen, 27–40. Phillipsburg, NJ: P&R Publishing, 2004.

Collett, Donald. "Van Til and the Transcendental Argument." In *Revelation and Reason: New Essays in Reformed Apologetics*, edited by K. Scott Oliphint and Lane G. Tipton, 258–78. Phillipsburg, NJ: P&R Publishing, 2007.

———. "Van Til and Transcendental Argument." *Westminster Theological Journal* 65, 2 (Fall 2003): 289–306.

———. "Van Til and Transcendental Argument Revisited." In *Speaking the Truth in Love: The Theology of John M. Frame*, edited by John J. Hughes, 460–88. Phillipsburg, NJ: P&R Publishing, 2009.

Conn, Harvie. *Eternal Word and Changing Worlds: Theology, Anthropology, and Mission in Trialogue*. Phillipsburg, NJ: P&R Publishing, 1992.

Cooper, John. *Panentheism: The Other God of the Philosophers-From Plato to the Present*. Grand Rapids, MI: Baker, 2006.

Cowan, Steven, Stanley N. Gundry, Gary Habermas, William Lane Craig, Paul D. Feinberg, Kelly James Clark, and John M. Frame. *Five Views on Apologetics*. Grand Rapids, MI: Zondervan, 2000.

Cross, Richard. *Duns Scotus*. New York, NY: Oxford University Press, 1999.

———. *Duns Scotus on God*. Burlington, VT: Ashgate, 2005.

———. "Duns Scotus: Ordinatio." In *Central Works of Philosophy: Ancient and Medieval*, edited by John Shand, 217–41. Quebec: McGill-Queen's Press, 2005.

Cunningham, Ralph. "A Critical Examination of Jonathan Edwards's Doctrine of the Trinity." *Themelios* 39, 2 (2014): 224–40.

Dahms, John. "The Subordination of the Son." *Journal of the Evangelical Theological Society* 37, 3 (September 1994): 351–64.

Dennison, William. "Analytic Philosophy and Van Til's Epistemology." *Westminster Theological Journal* 57, 1 (Spring 1995): 33–56.

DeYoung, Kevin. "Review of Systematic Theology by John Frame." *The Gospel Coalition*. Last modified November 14, 2013. Accessed November 21, 2013. http://thegospelcoalition.org/blogs/kevin deyoung/2013/11/14/book-review-systematic-theology-by -john-frame/.

Dolezal, James E. *God Without Parts: Divine Simplicity and the Metaphysics of God's Absoluteness*. Eugene, OR: Pickwick Publications, 2011.

———. "God Without Parts: Simplicity and the Metaphysics of Divine Absoluteness." PhD Diss., Philadelphia, PA: Westminster Theological Seminary, 2011.

———. *God Without Parts: The Doctrine of Divine Simplicity*. MP3. Vol. 185. Reformed Forum. Philadelphia, PA, 2011. Accessed March 13, 2014. http://reformedforum.org/podcasts/ctc185/.

———. "Trinity, Simplicity and the Status of God's Personal Relations." *International Journal of Systematic Theology* 16, 1 (January 2014): 79–98.

Driscoll, Mark. "Fighting the Air War and Ground War." MP3 presented at the CCEF National Conference, 2008. http://www .ccef.org/fighting-air-war-and-ground-war-1.

Edgar, William. "Frame the Apologist." In *Speaking the Truth in Love: The Theology of John M. Frame*, edited by John J. Hughes, 399–430. Phillipsburg, NJ: P&R Publishing, 2009.

Edwards, Bruce L. "Tagmemic Discourse Theory." Faculty Webpage.

Bowling Green State University. Last modified 2013. Accessed March 3, 2014. http://personal.bgsu.edu/~edwards/tags.html.

———. "Tagmemic Theory and Its Contribution to Composition Teaching." Master's thesis, Kansas State University, 1979. Accessed March 3, 2014. http://krex.ksu.edu/dspace/handle/2097/9293.

Elliott, Paul M. "What Is Perspectivalism, and Why Is It Dangerous?" In *Christianity and Neo-Liberalism*. Unicoi, TN: The Trinity Foundation, 2005. Accessed January 25, 2014. http://www.teachingtheword.org/apps/articles/?articleid=74632&columnid=5772.

Ellis, Brannon. *Calvin, Classical Trinitarianism, and the Aseity of the Son*. New York, NY: Oxford University Press, 2012.

Ellis Jr, Carl F. "Doing Theology Today." In *Speaking the Truth in Love: The Theology of John M. Frame*, edited by John J. Hughes, 908–29. Phillipsburg, NJ: P&R Publishing, 2009.

Enns, Peter. *Inspiration and Incarnation: Evangelicals and the Problem of the Old Testament*. Grand Rapids, MI: Baker, 2005.

Feinberg, John S. *No One Like Him: The Doctrine of God*. Wheaton, IL: Crossway, 2006.

———. "Personal Words: John Feinberg." In *Speaking the Truth in Love: The Theology of John M. Frame*, edited by John J. Hughes, xliii. Phillipsburg, NJ: P&R Publishing, 2009.

Fesko, John V. "Salvation Belongs to the Lord: A Review." *Ordained Servant Online*. Last modified November 2008. Accessed September 10, 2013. http://www.opc.org/os.html?article_id=123.

Field, Hartry. "Epistemology Without Metaphysics." *Philosophical Studies* 143, 2 (Macrh 2009): 249–90.

Fourth, Michael. "Christian Reflections on the Phenomenological Epistemology of Maurice Merleau-Ponty." *IIIM Magazine Online* 5, 22 (June 2003). Accessed October 18, 2014. http://thirdmill.org/files/reformedperspectives/hall_of_frame/HOF.Fourth.Merleau.Pointy.epistemology.pdf.

Frame, John M. *A History of Western Philosophy and Theology*. Phillipsburg, NJ: P&R Publishing, 2015.

———. "Abortion and the Christian." *The Presbyterian Guardian*, November 1970.

———. "Above the Battle?" *The Works of John Frame and Vern Poythress*. Last modified 2003. Accessed September 5, 2013. http://www.frame-poythress.org/above-the-battle/.

———. "A Fresh Look at the Regulative Principle: A Broader View." *The Works of John Frame and Vern Poythress*. Last modified 2008. Accessed September 6, 2013. http://www.frame-poythress.org/a-fresh-look-at-the-regulative-principle-a-broader-view/.

———. "Antithesis and the Doctrine of Scripture" presented at the Inagural Lecture on assuming the J. D. Trimble Chair of Systematic Theology, Reformed Theological Seminary, Orlando, FL, 2006. Accessed September 5, 2013. http://www.frame-poythress.org/antithesis-and-the-doctrine-of-scripture/.

———. "Apologetics." Edited by Kevin Vanhoozer. *Dictionary for the Theological Interpretation of the Bible*. Grand Rapids, MI: Baker, 2005. Accessed September 5, 2013. http://www.frame-poythress.org/logic/.

———. "Apologetics at Westminster Seminary." *The Works of John Frame and Vern Poythress*. Last modified 1990. Accessed September 3, 2013. http://www.frame-poythress.org/apologetics-at-westminster-seminary/.

———. *Apologetics to the Glory of God: An Introduction*. Phillipsburg, NJ: P&R Publishing, 1994.

———. "A Primer on Perspectivalism." In *John Frame's Selected Shorter Writings*, 3–18. Phillipsburg, NJ: P&R Publishing, 2014.

———. "A Reply to Mark Karlberg." *Mid-America Journal of Theology* 9, 2 (Fall 1993): 297–308.

———. "A Response to 'Redeeming the Arts.'" *Creative Spirit* 4, 2 (November 2005): 19–21.

———. "A Testimony." In *John Frame's Selected Shorter Writings*, 275–77. Phillipsburg, NJ: P&R Publishing, 2014.

Bibliography

———. "A Van Til Glossary." *The Works of John Frame and Vern Poythress*. Last modified 2000. Accessed September 4, 2013. http://www.frame-poythress.org/a-van-til-glossary/.

———. "Backgrounds to My Thought." In *Speaking the Truth in Love: The Theology of John M. Frame*, edited by John J. Hughes, 9–30. Phillipsburg, NJ: P&R Publishing, 2009.

———. "Bahnsen at the Stein Debate." *The Works of John Frame and Vern Poythress*. Last modified 2006. Accessed September 5, 2013. http://www.frame-poythress.org/bahnsen-at-the-stein-debate/.

———. "Between the Apostles and the Parousia: Bearing the Burdens of Change and of Knowledge." *The Works of John Frame and Vern Poythress*. Last modified 1993. Accessed September 3, 2013. http://www.frame-poythress.org/between-the-apostles-and-the-parousia-bearing-the-burdens-of-change-and-of-knowledge/.

———. "But God Made Me This Way!" *Tabletalk*, March 1997.

———. "Calvin Center Research Book Mirrors Secular Thinking." *Christian Renewal*, June 2013.

———. "Certainty." Edited by Jack Campbell. *IVP Dictionary of Apologetics*. Leicester, England: InterVarsity Press, 2006. Accessed September 5, 2013. http://www.frame-poythress.org/certainty/.

———. "Christianity and Contemporary Epistemology." *Westminster Theological Journal* 52, 1 (Spring 1990): 131–41.

———. "Christianity and Culture," Pensacola Theological Institute, July 2001. Accessed September 11, 2013. http://thirdmill.org/magazine/article.asp/link/http:%5E%5Ethirdmill.org%5Earticles%5Ejoh_frame%5EFrame.Apologetics2004.ChristandCulture.html/at/Christ%20and%20Culture.

———. "Contexts." In *John Frame's Selected Shorter Writings*, 52–58. Phillipsburg, NJ: P&R Publishing, 2014.

———. "Cornelius Van Til." Edited by Walter A. Elwell. *Handbook of Evangelical Theologians*. Grand Rapids, MI: Baker, 1993.

Accessed September 3, 2013. http://www.frame-poythress.org/cornelius-van-til/.

———. "Cornelius Van Til." Edited by Jack Campbell. *IVP Dictionary of Apologetics*. Leicester, England: InterVarsity Press, 2006. Accessed September 5, 2013. http://www.frame-poythress.org/certainty/.

———. *Cornelius Van Til: An Analysis of His Thought*. Phillipsburg, NJ: P&R Publishing, 1995.

———. "Covering Ourselves: A Charge to Graduating Seminary Students." *The Journal of Pastoral Practice* 7, 4 (1985): 2–6.

———. "D. Clair Davis: A Grateful Appreciation." In *The Practical Calvinist: An Introduction to the Presbyterian and Reformed Heritage*, edited by Peter A. Lillback. Scotland, UK: Mentor, 2003. Accessed September 5, 2013. http://www.frame-poythress.org/d-clair-davis-a-grateful-appreciation/.

———. "Determinism, Chance, and Freedom." Edited by Jack Campbell. *IVP Dictionary of Apologetics*. Leicester, England: InterVarsity Press, 2006. Accessed September 5, 2013. http://www.frame-poythress.org /certainty/.

———. "Developing a Frame Work for the Doctrine of Scripture: John Frame Speaks About the God Who Speaks." *Towers*, January 2011.

———. "Directory of Frame's Major Ideas." In *Speaking the Truth in Love: The Theology of John M. Frame*, edited by John J. Hughes, 977–93. Phillipsburg, NJ: P&R Publishing, 2009.

———. "Directory of Frame's Major Triads." In *Speaking the Truth in Love: The Theology of John M. Frame*, edited by John J. Hughes, 994–1001. Phillipsburg, NJ: P&R Publishing, 2009.

———. "Divine Aseity and Apologetics." In *Revelation and Reason*, edited by K. Scott Oliphint and Lane G. Tipton, 115–30. Phillipsburg, NJ: P&R Publishing, 2007.

———. "Epistemological Perspectives and Evangelical Apologetics." Biola University, CA, 1982. Accessed September 3, 2013.

http://www.frame-poythress.org/epistemological-perspectives-and-evangelical-apologetics/.

———. "Ethics and Biblical Events." *The Works of John Frame and Vern Poythress*. Last modified 2006. Accessed September 5, 2013. http://www.frame-poythress.org/ethics-and-biblical-events/.

———. "Ethics, Preaching, and Biblical Theology." *The Works of John Frame and Vern Poythress*. Last modified 1999. Accessed September 4, 2013. http://www.frame-poythress.org/ethics-preaching-and-biblical-theology/.

———. "Euthyphro, Hume, and the Biblical God." *The Works of John Frame and Vern Poythress*. Last modified 1993. Accessed September 3, 2013. http://www.frame-poythress.org/euthyphro-hume-and-the-biblical-god/.

———. *Evangelical Reunion: Denominations and the One Body of Christ*. Grand Rapids, MI: Baker, 1991.

———. "Frame to Dennison." *Journey*, October 1988.

———. "God." *Zondervan Pictorial Bible Encyclopedia*, 1975.

———. "God and Biblical Language: Transcendence and Immanence." In *God's Inerrant Word*, edited by John W. Montgomery, 159–77. Grand Rapids, MI: Baker, 1974. Accessed October 10, 2014. http://www.ccel.us/godsinerrantword.ch7.html.

———. "History of Epistemology." Course Notes, Reformed Theological Seminary, Orlando, FL, 2009. Accessed March 27, 2014. http://reformedperspectives.org/hof2009.asp#epist2009.

———. "How to Be Confident Amid Millennial Frenzy." *Reformed Perspectives Magazine*, May 3, 1999. Accessed June 30, 2014. http://thirdmill.org/magazine/article.asp/link/http:%5E%5Ethirdmill.org%5Earticles%5Ejoh_frame%5EPT.Frame.Millennial_Confidence.html/at/How%20to%20be%20Confident%20amid%20Millennial%20Frenzy.

———. "In Defense of Christian Activism vs. Michael Horton and Meredith Kline." *The Works of John Frame and Vern Poythress*. Last modified 2006. Accessed September 5, 2013. http://www

.frame-poythress.org/in-defense-of-christian-activism-vs-michael-horton-and-meredith-kline/.

———. "In Defense of Something Close to Biblicism: Reflections on Sola Scriptura and History in Theological Method." *Westminster Theological Journal* 59, 2 (Fall 1997): 269–91.

———. "Infralapsarianism." Edited by Donald McKin. *Encyclopedia of the Reformed Faith*. Louisville, KY: Westminster John Knox Press, 1992. Accessed September 3, 2013. http://www.frame-poythress.org/infralapsarianism/.

———. "Is Intelligent Design Science?" *The Works of John Frame and Vern Poythress*. Last modified 2008. Accessed September 6, 2013. http://www.frame-poythress.org/is-intelligent-design-science/.

———. "Is Natural Revelation Sufficient to Govern Culture?" *The Works of John Frame and Vern Poythress*. Last modified 2006. Accessed September 5, 2013. http://www.frame-poythress.org/is-natural-revelation-sufficient-to-govern-culture/.

———. "Is Realignment a Biblical Option?" *New Horizons*, July 1989.

———. "John Frame's Bibliography." *The Works of John Frame and Vern Poythress*. Last modified 2013. Accessed February 14, 2014. http://www.frame-poythress.org/bibliographies/john-frame-bibliography/.

———. *John Frame's Selected Shorter Writings*. Phillipsburg, NJ: P&R Publishing, 2014.

———. "Letter Concerning William White." *Journey*, February 1989.

———. "Logic." Edited by Kevin Vanhoozer. *Dictionary for the Theological Interpretation of the Bible*. Grand Rapids, MI: Baker, 2005. Accessed September 5, 2013. http://www.frame-poythress.org/logic/.

———. "Machen's Warrior Children." In *Alister E. McGrath and Evangelical Theology*, edited by Sung Wook Chung, 113–46. Grand Rapids, MI: Baker, 2003.

———. "Muller on Theology." *Westminster Theological Journal* 56, 1 (Spring 1994): 438–42.

———. "My Books: Their Genesis and Main Ideas." In *Speaking the Truth in Love: The Theology of John M. Frame*, edited by John J. Hughes, 3–8. Phillipsburg, NJ: P&R Publishing, 2009.

———. "My Use of the Reformed Confessions." *The Works of John Frame and Vern Poythress*. Last modified 2005. Accessed September 5, 2013. http://www.frame-poythress.org/my-use-of-the-reformed-confessions/.

———. "No Scripture, No Christ." *The Presbyterian Guardian*, January 1979.

———. "Ontological Argument." Edited by Jack Campbell. *IVP Dictionary of Apologetics*. Leicester, England: InterVarsity Press, 2006. Accessed September 5, 2013. http://www.frame-poythress.org/certainty/.

———. "Open Theism and Divine Foreknowledge." In *Bound Only Once*, 83–94. Moscow, ID: Canon Press, 2001. Accessed September 4, 2013. http://www.frame-poythress.org/open-theism-and-divine-foreknowledge/.

———. "Penultimate Thoughts on Theonomy." *Reformed Perspectives Magazine*, August 2001.

———. *Perspectives on the Word of God: An Introduction to Ethics*. Phillipsburg, NJ: Presbyterian and Reformed, 1990.

———. "Preface." In *Always Reforming: Explorations in Systematic Theology*, 9–12. Downers Grove, IL: InterVarsity Press, 2007.

———. "Presuppositional Apologetics: An Introduction." *IIIM Magazine Online*, April 1999. Accessed September 11, 2013. http://www.thirdmill.org/files/english/html/pt/PT.h.Frame.Presupp.Apol.1.html.

———. "Presuppositionalism." Edited by Jack Campbell. *IVP Dictionary of Apologetics*. Leicester, England: InterVarsity Press, 2006. Accessed September 5, 2013. http://www.frame-poythress.org/presuppositionalism/.

———. "Providence in All of Life." *The Works of John Frame and Vern*

Poythress. Last modified 2006. Accessed September 5, 2013. http://www.frame-poythress.org/providence-in-all-of-life/.

———. "Rationality and Scripture." In *Rationality and the Calvinian Tradition*, edited by Nicholas Wolterstorff, Hendrik Hart, and Johan Van Der Hoeven, 239–317. Lanham, MD: University Press of America, 1983. Accessed September 3, 2013. http://www.frame-poythress.org/rationality-and-scripture/.

———. "Recommended Resources." In *Speaking the Truth in Love: The Theology of John M. Frame*, edited by John J. Hughes, 1064–1070. Phillipsburg, NJ: P&R Publishing, 2009.

———. "Reformed and Evangelicals Together." In *John Frame's Selected Shorter Writings*, 100–114. Phillipsburg, NJ: P&R Publishing, 2014.

———. "Reformed Ethics." Edited by Carl F. Henry. *Baker's Dictionary of Christian Ethics*. Grand Rapids, MI: Baker, 1973. Accessed September 2, 2013. http://www.frame-poythress.org/reformed-ethics/.

———. "Reply to Don Collett on Transcendental Argument." *Westminster Theological Journal* 65, 2 (Fall 2003): 307–9.

———. "Responses to Some Articles." In *Speaking the Truth in Love: The Theology of John M. Frame*, edited by John J. Hughes, 971–73. Phillipsburg, NJ: P&R Publishing, 2009.

———. "Review of Bahnsen's Presuppositional Apologetics." In *John Frame's Selected Shorter Writings*, 1:174–86. Phillipsburg, NJ: P&R Publishing, 2014.

———. "Review of Bahnsen's Theonomy in Christian Ethics." *The Presbyterian Journal* 36 (August 1977): 18.

———. "Review of David Van Drunen's A Biblical Case for Natural Law." *The Works of John Frame and Vern Poythress*. Last modified 2012. Accessed September 6, 2013. http://www.frame-poythress.org/review-of-david-van-drunens-a-biblical-case-for-natural-law/.

———. "Review of Enns' Inspiration and Incarnation." *The Works of John Frame and Vern Poythress*. Last modified 2008. Accessed

September 5, 2013. http://www.frame-poythress.org/review-of-enns-inspiration-and-incarnation/.

———. "Review of Esther Meek's Longing to Know." *Presbyterion* 29, 2 (Fall 2003).

———. "Review of Holmer's The Grammar of Faith." *Westminster Theological Journal* 42, 1 (Fall 1979): 219–31.

———. "Review of Kaufman's Systematic Theology." *Westminster Theological Journal* 32, 1 (Fall 1969): 119–24.

———. "Review of Kelsey's The Uses of Scripture in Recent Theology." *Westminster Theological Journal* 39, 2 (Spring 1977): 328–53.

———. "Review of Michael Horton, Christless Christianity: The Alternative Gospel of the American Church-Part One." *Ecclesia Reformanda* 2, 1 (April 2010): 5–25.

———. "Review of Michael Horton, Christless Christianity: The Alternative Gospel of the American Church-Part Two." *Ecclesia Reformanda* 2, 2 (October 2010): 107–23.

———. "Review of Ogden's On Theology." *Westminster Theological Journal* 50, 1 (Spring 1988): 157–65.

———. "Review of Paul Helm's The Providence of God." *Westminster Theological Journal* 56, 2 (Fall 1994): 438–42.

———. "Review of The Nature and Extent of Biblical Authority (Christian Reformed Church, Report 44)." *IIIM Magazine Online*, September 2001. Accessed September 4, 2013. http://www.frame-poythress.org/review-of-the-nature-and-extent-of-biblical-authority-christian-reformed-church-report-44/.

———. "Review of White's Van Til–Defender of the Faith." *Westminster Theological Journal* 42, 1 (Fall 1979): 198–203.

———. "Revised Foreword." In *Backbone of the Bible*, edited by P. Andrew Sandlin. Nacogdoches, TX: Covenant Media, 2004. Accessed September 5, 2013. http://www.frame-poythress.org/foreword-to-sandlin-ed-backbone-of-the-bible/.

———. *Salvation Belongs to the Lord: An Introduction to Systematic Theology*. Phillipsburg, NJ: P&R Publishing, 2006.

———. "Scientia Media." Edited by Walter A. Elwell. *Evangelical Dictionary of Theology*. Grand Rapids, MI: Baker, 1984. Accessed September 3, 2013. http://www.frame-poythress.org/scientia-media/.

———. "Scripture Speaks for Itself." In *God's Inerrant Word*, edited by John W. Montgomery, 178–200. Grand Rapids, MI: Baker, 1974. Accessed October 10, 2014. http://www.ccel.us/gods inerrantword.ch8.html.

———. "Some Questions about the Regulative Principle." *Center for Reformed Theology and Apologetics*. Last modified 1992. Accessed September 3, 2013. http://www.reformed.org/misc/index.html?mainframe=/misc/frame_regulative_principle.html.

———. "Studying Theology as a Servant of Jesus." *Reformation & Revival* 11, 1 (Winter 2002): 45–69.

———. "Systematic Theology and Apologetics at the Westminster Seminaries." In *The Pattern of Sound Doctrine*, edited by David Van Drunen, 73–98. Phillipsburg, NJ: P&R Publishing, 2004.

———. *Systematic Theology: An Introduction to Christian Belief*. Phillipsburg, NJ: P&R Publishing, 2013.

———. *The Doctrine of God*. Phillipsburg, NJ: P&R Publishing, 2002.

———. *The Doctrine of the Christian Life*. Phillipsburg, NJ: P&R Publishing, 2008.

———. *The Doctrine of the Knowledge of God*. Phillipsburg, NJ: Presbyterian and Reformed, 1987.

———. *The Doctrine of the Word of God*. Phillipsburg, NJ: P&R Publishing, 2010.

———. "The Institutes of Biblical Law: A Review Article." *Westminster Theological Journal* 38, 2 (Winter 1976): 215–17.

———. "The Lord's Authority." *The Works of John Frame and Vern Poythress*, October 2000. Accessed March 25, 2014. http://www.frame-poythress.org/the-lords-authority/.

———. "The Spirit and the Scriptures." In *Hermeneutics, Authority, and Canon*, edited by D. A. Carson and John D. Woodbridge, 213–35. Grand Rapids, MI: Zondervan, 1986.

———. "Traditionalism." *The Works of John Frame and Vern Poythress*. Last modified 1999. Accessed September 4, 2013. http://www.frame-poythress.org/traditionalism/.

———. "Transcendental Argument." Edited by W. C. Campbell-Jack, Gavin J. McGrath, and C. Stephen Evans. *New Dictionary of Christian Apologetics*. Leicester, England: InterVarsity Press, April 18, 2006.

———. "Trinitarian Analogies." *The Works of John Frame and Vern Poythress*. Last modified 1999. Accessed September 4, 2013. http://www.frame-poythress.org/trinitarian-analogies/.

———. "Van Til: His Simplicity and Profundity." *The Works of John Frame and Vern Poythress*. Last modified 1985. Accessed September 3, 2013. http://www.frame-poythress.org/van-til-his-simplicity-and-profundity/.

———. "Van Til on Antithesis." *Westminster Theological Journal* 57, 1 (Spring 1995): 81–102.

———. "Van Til Reconsidered." *Reformed Perspectives*. Last modified 2005. Accessed September 5, 2013. http://reformedperspectives.org/article.asp/link/http:%5E%5Ereformedperspectives.org%5Earticles%5Ejoh_frame%5EFrame.Apologetics2004.VanTilReconsidered.doc/at/Van%20Til%20Reconsidered.

———. "Van Til: The Theologian." *The Works of John Frame and Vern Poythress*. Last modified 1976. Accessed November 20, 2009. http://www.frame-poythress.org/frame_articles/1976VanTil.htm.

Frame, John M., and Steve Hays. "Johnson on Van Til." *Evangelical Quarterly* 76, 3 (July 2004): 227–39.

Frame, John M., and Paul Kurtz. "Do We Need God to Be Moral?" *Free Inquiry*, 1996. Accessed September 4, 2013. http://www.frame-poythress.org/do-we-need-god-to-be-moral/.

Frame, John M., and P. Andrew Sandlin. "Reflections of a Lifetime Theologian: An Extended Interview with John M. Frame." In *Speaking the Truth in Love: The Theology of John M. Frame*, edited by John J. Hughes, 75–110. Phillipsburg, NJ: P&R Publishing, 2009.

Gaffin, Richard B. "Systematic Theology and Biblical Theology." *Westminster Theological Journal* 38, 3 (Spring 1976): 281–99.

Gamble, Richard C. "The Relationship Between Biblical Theology and Systematic Theology." In *Always Reforming: Explorations in Systematic Theology*, 211–39. Downers Grove, IL: InterVarsity Press, 2007.

Garcia, Mark A. "The Word Made Applicable." In *Speaking the Truth in Love: The Theology of John M. Frame*, edited by John J. Hughes, 233–47. Phillipsburg, NJ: P&R Publishing, 2009.

Gettier, Edmund L. "Is Justified True Belief Knowledge?" In *The Theory of Knowledge*, edited by Louis P. Pojman, 125–27. 3rd ed. Belmont, CA: Wadsworth, 2002.

Godfrey, Robert. "Westminster Seminary, the Doctrine of Justification, and the Reformed Confessions." In *The Pattern of Sound Doctrine*, edited by David Van Drunen, 127–48. Phillipsburg, NJ: P&R Publishing, 2004.

Good, Charles. "The Doctrine of the Knowledge of God: A Theology of Lordship." *Master's Seminary Journal* 1, 1 (Spring 1990): 79–82.

Goodmanson, Drew. "Triperspectivalism." *Goodmanson: Leadership, Church Web & Tech, Mission Alignment (blog)*. Last modified 2014. Accessed February 17, 2014. http://www.goodmanson.com/category/church/triperspectivalism/.

Grant, Jr., James H., and Justin Taylor. "John Frame and Evangelicalism." In *Speaking the Truth in Love: The Theology of John M. Frame*, edited by John J. Hughes, 262–83. Phillipsburg, NJ: P&R Publishing, 2009.

Griffith, Howard. "Frame as a Reformed Theologian." In *Speaking the Truth in Love: The Theology of John M. Frame*, edited by John J. Hughes, 305–29. Phillipsburg, NJ: P&R Publishing, 2009.

Grudem, Wayne. "Biblical Evidence for the Eternal Submission of the Son to the Father." In *The New Evangelical Subordinationism*, edited by Dennis Jowers and Wayne House, 223–61. Eugene, OR: Pickwick, 2012.

———. *Systematic Theology: An Introduction to Biblical Doctrine*. Grand Rapids, MI: Zondervan, 2000.

Gunton, Colin E. *The One, the Three and the Many: God, Creation and the Culture of Modernity*. New York, NY: Cambridge University Press, 1993.

Halsey, Jim. *For a Time Such as This: An Introduction to the Reformed Apologetic of Cornelius Van Til*. Nutley, NJ: Presbyterian and Reformed, 1976.

———. "Preliminary Critique of Van Til, the Theologian." *Westminster Theological Journal* 39, 1 (Fall 1976): 120–36.

Hart, D. G. "Systematic Theology at Old Princeton Seminary: Unoriginal Calvinism." In *The Pattern of Sound Doctrine*, edited by David Van Drunen, 3–26. Phillipsburg, NJ: P&R Publishing, 2004.

Hasker, William. "Yes, God Has Beliefs!" *Religious Studies* 24, 3 (September 1988): 385–94.

Hause, Jeffrey. "John Duns Scotus." *Internet Encyclopedia of Philosophy*, 2007. Accessed June 20, 2014. http://www.iep.utm.edu/scotus/.

Hays, Steve. "Westminster's Westering Star." *Triablogue*. Last modified February 11, 2006. Accessed September 6, 2013. http://triablogue.blogspot.com/2006/02/westminsters-westering-star.html#comment-form.

Helm, Paul. "Charles Hodge & The Method of Systematic Theology." *Paul Helm's Deep (blog)*, September 1, 2007. Accessed April 21, 2014. http:// paulhelmsdeep.blogspot.com/2007/09/charles-hodge-method-of-systematic.html.

———. "Frame's Doctrine of God." In *Speaking the Truth in Love: The Theology of John M. Frame*, edited by John J. Hughes, 284–304. Phillipsburg, NJ: P&R Publishing, 2009.

———. "Salvation Belongs to the Lord: An Introduction to Systematic Theology." *Reformation21 (blog)*. Last modified July 2007. Accessed January 25, 2014. http://www.reformation21.org/shelf-life/salvation-belongs-to-the-lord-an-introduction-to-systematic-theology.php.

Hodge, Archibald Alexander. *A Commentary on the Confession of Faith*. Philadelphia, PA: Presbyterian Board of Publication, 1869.

Hodge, Charles. *A Commentary on Romans*. Edinburgh, Scotland: Banner of Truth, 1972.

———. *Systematic Theology*. Vol. 1. New York, NY: Scribner, 1873.

Horton, Michael S. "A Response to John Frame's The Escondido Theology." *White Horse Inn (blog)*. Last modified February 2012. Accessed September 10, 2013. http://www.whitehorseinn.org/blog/2012/02/10/a-response-to-john-frames-the-escondido-theology/.

———. *The Christian Faith: A Systematic Theology for Pilgrims on the Way*. Grand Rapids, MI: Zondervan, 2011.

Horton, Michael S., and William Willimon. *Christless Christianity: The Alternative Gospel of the American Church*. Grand Rapids, MI: Baker, 2008.

Howie, John. *Ethical Issues for a New Millennium*. Carbondale, IL: SIU Press, 2002.

Hughes, Christopher. *On a Complex Theory of a Simple God: An Investigation in Aquinas' Philosophical Theology*. Ithaca, NY: Cornell University Press, 1989.

Hughes, John J., ed. *Speaking the Truth in Love: The Theology of John M. Frame*. Phillipsburg, NJ: P&R Publishing, 2009.

———. "The Heart of John Frame's Theology." In *Speaking the Truth in Love: The Theology of John M. Frame*, edited by John J. Hughes, 31–74. Phillipsburg, NJ: P&R Publishing, 2009.

Immink, Frederik Gerrit. *Divine Simplicity*. Kampen, Netherlands: J. H. Kok, 1987.

Jeancake, Paxson. "Rethinking, Reforming: Frame's Contributions to Contemporary Worship." In *Speaking the Truth in Love: The Theology of John M. Frame*, edited by John J. Hughes, 724–55. Phillipsburg, NJ: P&R Publishing, 2009.

Johnson, Dennis E. "A Triperspectival Model of Ministry." In *Speaking the Truth in Love: The Theology of John M. Frame*, edited by

John J. Hughes, 631–58. Phillipsburg, NJ: P&R Publishing, 2009.

Johnson, John J. "How a Muslim Could Employ Van Til's Apologetic System: A Response to Frame and Hays." *Patrick Henry College*. Last modified 2003. Accessed January 25, 2014. http://www.phc.edu/gj_john%20johnson%20frame%20hayes%20rebuttal1.php.

———. "Is Cornelius Van Til's Apologetic Method Christian, or Merely Theistic." *Evangelical Quarterly* 75, 3 (2003): 257–68.

Karlberg, Mark W. "John Frame and the Recasting of Van Tilian Apologetics: A Review Article." *Mid-America Journal of Theology* 9, 2 (Fall 1993): 279–96.

———. "On the Theological Correlation of Divine and Human Language." *Journal of the Evangelical Theological Society* 32, 1 (March 1989): 99–105.

Keller, Timothy. "A Model for Preaching: Part One: Three Perspectives on Preaching & the Biblical Aspect,." *Journal of Biblical Counseling* 12, 3 (1994): 36–42.

———. "A Model for Preaching: Part Three: The Personal Aspect." *Journal of Biblical Counseling* 14, 1 (1995): 54–62.

———. "A Model for Preaching: Part Two: The Situational Aspect." *Journal of Biblical Counseling* 13, 1 (1994): 39–48.

———. "The 'Kingly' Willow Creek Conference." *Redeemer City to City (blog)*, September 13, 2009. Accessed February 17, 2014. https://redeemercitytocity.com/blog/2009/the-kingly-willow-creek-conference/.

Kemp, Robert. "Aesthetic Perspectivalism and the Nature of Art: Two Proposals." *IIIM Magazine Online* 5, 22 (June 2003). Accessed October 18, 2014. http://www.thirdmill.org/files/english/practical_theology/6280~6_12_2003_2-36-48_PM~PT.Kemp.epistemology.hall.frame.pdf.

Kim, Ezra Hyun. "Biblical Preaching Is Apologia: An Analysis of the Apologetic Nature of Preaching in Light of Perspectivalism." DMin, Escondido, CA: Westminster Theological Seminary, 2000.

Kline, Meredith G. *A Paper Pursuant to the Faculty Forum*. Escondido, CA: Westminster Seminary in California, 1986.

———. "Comments on an Old-New Error." *Westminster Theological Journal* 41, 1 (Fall 1978): 172–89.

———. *Images of the Spirit*. Eugene, OR: Wipf and Stock, 1999.

———. "Kline on Multiperspectivalism." *Meredith G. Kline*. Last modified February 28, 1986. Accessed October 4, 2013. http://www.meredithkline.com/klines-works/articles-and-essays/kline-on-multiperspectivalism/.

———. "The Intrusion and the Decalogue." *Westminster Theological Journal* 16, 1 (Fall 1953): 1–22.

———. *The Structure of Biblical Authority*. Eugene, OR: Wipf and Stock, 1997.

———. *Treaty of the Great King: The Covenant Structure of Deuteronomy: Studies and Commentary*. Eugene, OR: Wipf and Stock, 2012.

Krieglstein, Werner. "Perspectivist Manifesto." *Perspectivism*. Last modified 2010. Accessed March 8, 2014. http://perspectivism.com/perspectivist-mephesto/.

Kuhn, Thomas S. *The Structure of Scientific Revolutions*. 4th ed. Chicago, IL: University Of Chicago Press, 2012.

Lacewig, Michael. "Nietzsche's Perspectivism." In *Philosophy for A2: Philosophical Problems*, 200–201. New York, NY: Routledge, 2014.

Landry, Eric. "A Response to Professor John Frame." *White Horse Inn (blog)*. Last modified October 2009. Accessed September 11, 2013. http://www.whitehorseinn.org/blog/2009/10/22/a-response-to-professor-john-frame/.

Lane, A. N. S. "B. B. Warfield On the Humanity of Scripture." *Vox Evangelical* 16, 16 (1986): 77–94.

Leftow, Brian. *God and Necessity*. New York, NY: Oxford University Press, 2012.

———. *Time and Eternity*. Ithaca, NY: Cornell University Press, 2009.

Letham, Robert. *The Holy Trinity: In Scripture, History, Theology, and Worship*. Phillipsburg, NJ: P&R Publishing, 2004.

Lister, Rob. *God Is Impassible and Impassioned: Toward a Theology of Divine Emotion*. Wheaton, IL: Crossway, 2012.

Lloyd, Tony. "A Equivocation in Anderson and Welty's Argument for God from Logic." Philosophia Christi, 2011. http://www.epsociety.org/userfiles/art-Anderson-Welty%20(In%20Defense%20of%20the%20Argument%20for%20God%20from%20Logic).pdf.

Locke, John. "A Representational Theory of Perception." In *The Theory of Knowledge*, edited by Louis P. Pojman, 75–88. 3rd ed. Belmont, CA: Wadsworth, 2002.

Manastireanu, Danut. "Perichoresis and the Early Christian Doctrine of God." *Archaevs* 11/12 (October 2008): 61–93.

Mattei, Tobias Alecio. "The 'Corrupted-Will' Model: A Reformed Theological Appraisal of Neuroscience and Cognitive Psychology of Human Will and Responsibility: A Mutliperspectival Endeavour Against Free-Will." *Reformed Perspectives* 13, 12 (March 2011).

Maxwell, Paul. "The Formulation of Thomistic Simplicity: Mapping Aquinas's Method for Configuring God's Essence." *Journal of the Evangelical Theological Society* 57, 2 (June 2014): 371–404.

McCormack, Bruce. *Engaging the Doctrine of God: Contemporary Protestant Perspectives*. Grand Rapids, MI: Baker, 2008.

McDermott, Gerald. "Jonathan Edwards and God's Inner Life: A Response to Kyle Strobel." *Themelios* 39, 2 (2014): 241–50.

McGowan, A. T. B. "The Doctrine of God." *Reformation & Revival* 12, 3 (2003): 178–87.

McGrath, Matthew. "Propositions." Edited by Edward N. Zalta. *The Stanford Encyclopedia of Philosophy*, 2014. Accessed July 10, 2014. http://plato.stanford.edu/archives/spr2014/entries/propositions/.

McKim, Donald. "Review of The Doctrine of the Knowledge of God by John Frame." *Reformed Review*, Spring 1988.

McKinley, Michael. "Triperspectival Leadership." *9 Marks (blog)*. Last modified July 3, 2009. Accessed September 5, 2013. http://www.9marks.org/blog /triperspectival-leadership.

Meek, Esther. *Longing to Know*. Grand Rapids, MI: Brazos Press, 2003.

———. *Loving to Know: Introducing Covenant Epistemology*. Eugene, OR: Cascade Books, 2011.

———. "Servant Thinking: The Polyanyian Workings of the Framean Triad." In *Speaking the Truth in Love: The Theology of John M. Frame*, edited by John J. Hughes, 611–30. Phillipsburg, NJ: P&R Publishing, 2009.

Menzel, Christopher. "Possible Worlds." Edited by Edward N. Zalta. *The Stanford Encyclopedia of Philosophy*, 2014. Accessed September 25, 2014. http://plato.stanford.edu/archives/fall2014 /entries/possible-worlds/.

Molnar, Paul. *Thomas F. Torrance: Theologian of the Trinity*. Burlington, VT: Ashgate, 2013.

Monaghan, Tony. "Review of Doctrine of the Christian Life by John Frame." *Orthodox Presbyterian Church*. Last modified August 30, 2013. Accessed September 11, 2013. http://www.opc.org /review.html?review_id=238.

Moo, Douglas J. "A Review of John M. Frame, The Doctrine of the Christian Life" presented at the Evangelical Theological Society National Conference, New Orleans, November 2009.

Moreland, James Porter, and William Lane Craig. *Philosophical Foundations for a Christian Worldview*. Grand Rapids, MI: InterVarsity Press, 2003.

Morris, Leon. *The Epistle to the Romans*. The Pillar New Testament Commentary. Grand Rapids, MI: Eerdmans, 1988.

Morris, Thomas V. "On God and Mann: A View of Divine Simplicity." *Religious Studies* 21, 3 (September 1985): 299–318.

———. *Our Idea of God: An Introduction to Philosophical Theology*. Vancouver, BC: Regent College, 2002.

Muller, Richard A. *Post-Reformation Reformed Dogmatics: The Rise* and Development of Reformed Orthodoxy, Ca. 1520 to Ca. 1725 (Divine Essence and Attributes). 2nd ed. Vol. 3. Grand Rapids, MI: Baker, 2003.

———. *Post-Reformation Reformed Dogmatics: The Rise and Development of Reformed Orthodoxy, Ca. 1520 to Ca. 1725 (Divine Essence and Attributes)*. 2nd ed. Vol. 4. Grand Rapids, MI: Baker, 2003.

———. "The Study of Theology Revisited: A Response to John Frame." *Westminster Theological Journal* 56, 2 (Fall 1994): 409–17.

Munson, Jamie. "Prophet, Priest, King | The Resurgence." *The Resurgance*. Last modified 2010. Accessed February 17, 2014. http://theresurgence.com /2010/12/13/prophet-priest-king.

Murray, John. "Corporate Responsibility." In *Collected Writings of John Murray*, 1:273–79. Edinburgh, Scotland: Banner of Truth, 1976. Accessed April 21, 2014. http://banneroftruth.org/us/store/collected-workssets/collected-writings-of-john-murray/.

———. "Systematic Theology (Part One)." *Westminster Theological Journal* 25, 2 (May 1963): 133–42.

———. "Systematic Theology (Part Two)." *Westminster Theological Journal* 26, 1 (Fall 1963): 33–46.

Nanzianzen, Gregory. "Orations." In *Nicene and Post Nicene Fathers*, edited by Kevin Knight, Philip Schaff, and Henry Wace, translated by Charles Gordon Brown and James Edward Swallow. Vol. 7. Buffalo, NY: Christian Literature Publishing, 1894. http://www.newadvent.org/fathers/3102.htm.

Netland, Harold A. "Apologetics, Worldviews, and the Problem of Neutral Criteria." *Trinity Journal* 12, 1 (Spring 1991): 40–59.

Notaro, Thom. *Van Til & the Use of Evidence*. Phillipsburg, NJ: Presbyterian and Reformed, 1980.

Obitts, Stanley. "The Doctrine of the Knowledge of God: A Review Article." *Trinity Journal* 9, 1 (Spring 1988): 112–15.

Oliphint, K. Scott. *Covenantal Apologetics: Principles and Practice in Defense of Our Faith*. Wheaton, IL: Crossway, 2013.

———. *God with Us: Divine Condescension and the Attributes of God*. Wheaton, IL: Crossway, 2011.

———. "Presuppositionalism." *Simple Apologetics (blog)*, 2014. Accessed August 28, 2014. http://simpleapologetics.com/presuppositionalism.html.

———. *Reasons for Faith: Philosophy in the Service of Theology*. Phillipsburg, NJ: P&R Publishing, 2006.

———. *The Battle Belongs to the Lord: The Power of Scripture for Defending Our Faith*. Phillipsburg, NJ: P&R Publishing, 2003.

———. "The Irrationality of Unbelief: An Exegetical Study." In *Revelation and Reason: New Essays in Reformed Apologetics*, edited by K. Scott Oliphint and Lane G. Tipton, 59–73. Phillipsburg, NJ: P&R Publishing, 2007.

Packer, J. I. Foreword to *Speaking the Truth in Love: The Theology of John M. Frame*, edited by John J. Hughes, XV–XVII. Phillipsburg, NJ: P&R Publishing, 2009.

Pecknold, C. C. *Transforming Postliberal Theology: George Lindbeck, Pragmatism and Scripture*. London: T&T Clark, 2005.

Perez, Joshua. "Frame's Apologetics and the Challenges of Our Time." In *Speaking the Truth in Love: The Theology of John M. Frame*, edited by John J. Hughes, 559–74. Phillipsburg, NJ: P&R Publishing, 2009.

Phillips, Rick. "Tim Keller's Review of Willow Creek: What About Gospel Clarity?" *Reformation21 (blog)*. Last modified October 2009. Accessed January 25, 2014. http://www.reformation21.org/blog/2009/10/tim-kellers-review-of-willow-c.php.

Plantinga, Alvin. *Does God Have a Nature?*. Milwaukee, WI: Marquette University Press, 1980.

———. *God, Freedom, and Evil*. Grand Rapids, MI: Eerdmans, 1974.

———. *The Analytic Theist: An Alvin Plantinga Reader*. Edited by James Sennett. Grand Rapids, MI: Eerdmans, 1998.

Plantinga, Cornelius. "Social Trinity and Tritheism." In *Trinity, Incarnation, and Atonement*, edited by Ronald J. Feenstra, 21–47. Notre Dame, IN: Notre Dame Press, 1989.

———. "The Threeness/Oneness Problem of the Trinity." *Calvin Theological Journal* 23, 1 (April 1988): 37–53.

Poitiers, Saint Hilary of. *The Trinity*. Translated by Stephen McKenna. Vol. 25. The Fathers of the Church. Washington, DC: Catholic University of America Press, 1954.

Powlison, David. "Frame's Ethics: Working the Implications for Pastoral Care." In *Speaking the Truth in Love: The Theology of John M. Frame*, edited by John J. Hughes, 759–77. Phillipsburg, NJ: P&R Publishing, 2009.

Poythress, Vern S. "A Biblical View of Mathematics." In *Foundations of Christian Scholarship: Essays in the Van Til Perspective*, edited by Gary North, 158–88. Sandy, UT: Ross House, 1976.

———. "Adequacy of Language and Accommodation." In *Hermeneutics, Inerrancy, and the Bible*, edited by Earl D. Radmacher and Robert D. Preus, 349–76. Grand Rapids, MI: Zondervan, 1984.

———. "A Framework for Discourse Analysis: The Components of a Discourse, from a Tagmemic Viewpoint." *Semiotica* 38, 3–4 (2009): 277–98.

———. "Canon and Speech Act: Limitations in Speech-Act Theory, with Implications for a Putative Theory of Canonical Speech Acts." *Westminster Theological Journal* 70, 2 (Fall 2008): 337–54.

———. *Chance and the Sovereignty of God: A God-Centered Approach to Probability and Random Events*. Phillipsburg, NJ: P&R Publishing, 2014.

———. "Christ the Only Savior of Interpretation." *Westminster Theological Journal* 50, 2 (Fall 1988): 305–21.

———. "Divine Meaning of Scripture." *Westminster Theological Journal* 48, 2 (Fall 1986): 241–79.

———. *God-Centered Biblical Interpretation*. Phillipsburg, NJ: P&R Publishing, 1999.

———. "God's Lordship in Interpretation." *Westminster Theological Journal* 50, 1 (Spring 1988): 27–64.

———. *Inerrancy and the Gospels: A God-Centered Approach to the Challenges of Harmonization*. Wheaton, IL: Crossway, 2012.

———. *Inerrancy and Worldview*. Wheaton, IL: Crossway, 2012.

———. *In the Beginning Was the Word: Language: A God-Centered Approach*. Wheaton, IL: Crossway, 2009.

———. *Logic: A God-Centered Approach to the Foundation of Western Thought*. Wheaton, IL: Crossway, 2013.

———. "Multiperspectivalism and the Reformed Faith." In *Speaking the Truth in Love: The Theology of John M. Frame*, edited by John J. Hughes, 173–200. Phillipsburg, NJ: P&R Publishing, 2009.

———. *Philosophy, Science, and the Sovereignty of God*. Phillipsburg, NJ: P&R Publishing, 2004.

———. *Redeeming Philosophy: A God-Centered Approach to the Big Questions*. Wheaton, IL: Crossway, 2014.

———. *Redeeming Science: A God-Centered Approach*. Wheaton, IL: Crossway, 2006.

———. *Redeeming Sociology: A God-Centered Approach*. Wheaton, IL: Crossway, 2011.

———. "Reforming Ontology and Logic in the Light of the Trinity: An Application of Van Til's Idea of Analogy." *Westminster Theological Journal* 57, 1 (Spring 1995): 187–219.

———. *Symphonic Theology*. Grand Rapids, MI: Zondervan, 1987.

———. "The Presence of God Qualifying Our Notions of Grammatical-Historical Interpretation: Genesis 3:15 as a Test Case." *Journal of the Evangelical Theological Society* 50, 1 (March 2007): 87–103.

———. *The Shadow of Christ in the Law of Moses*. Phillipsburg, NJ: P&R Publishing, 1995.

———. *Understanding Dispensationalists*. 2nd ed. Phillipsburg, NJ: P&R Publishing, 1994.

———. "Vern Poythress's Bibliography." *The Works of John Frame and Vern Poythress*. Last modified 2014. Accessed February 17, 2014. http://www.frame-poythress.org/bibliographies/vern-poythress-bibliography/.

———. "Why Lying Is Always Wrong: The Uniqueness of Verbal

Deceit." *Westminster Theological Journal* 75, 1 (Spring 2013): 83–95.

———. "Why Must Our Hermeneutics Be Trinitarian?" *The Southern Baptist Theological Journal* 10, 1 (Spring 2006): 96–98.

———. "Why Scientists Must Believe in God." *Journal of the Evangelical Theological Society* 46, 1 (March 2003): 111–23.

Pratt, Richard L. "John Frame and the Future of the Church." In *Speaking the Truth in Love: The Theology of John M. Frame*, edited by John J. Hughes, 933–60. Phillipsburg, NJ: P&R Publishing, 2009.

Pruss, Alexander. *Actuality, Possibility and Worlds*. London: Bloomsbury, 2011.

Reed, Baron. "Certainty." Edited by Edward N. Zalta. *The Stanford Encyclopedia of Philosophy*, 2011. Accessed July 15, 2014. http://plato.stanford.edu /archives/win2011/entries/certainty/.

Richard of Saint Victor. *On the Trinity*. Translated by Ruben Angelici. Cambridge, UK: James Clarke & Co, 2012.

Richards, Jay W. *The Untamed God: A Philosophical Exploration of Divine Perfection, Simplicity and Immutability*. Downers Grove, IL: InterVarsity Press, 2009.

Ridderbos, Herman N. *Paul: An Outline of His Theology*. Grand Rapids, MI: Eerdmans, 1997.

Robertson, O. Palmer. *The Christ of the Covenants*. Grand Rapids, MI: Baker, 1980.

Ronen, Shoshana. "Nietzsche and Wittgenstein: On Truth, Perspectivism, and Certainty." *Dialogue & Universalism* 11, 5/6 (August 2001): 97.

Rosen, Gideon. "Abstract Objects." Edited by Edward N. Zalta. *The Stanford Encyclopedia of Philosophy*, 2014. Accessed July 14, 2014. http://plato.stanford.edu/archives/fall2014/entries/abstract-objects/.

Rysiew, Patrick. "Epistemic Contextualism." Edited by Edward N. Zalta. *The Stanford Encyclopedia of Philosophy*, 2011. Accessed

March 27, 2014. http://plato.stanford.edu/archives/win2011/entries/contextualism-epistemology/.

Sailer, William S. "Review of Doctrine of the Knowledge of God by John Frame." *Evangelical Journal* 6, 1 (Spring 1988): 48–51.

Sandlin, P. Andrew. "Frame's Unique Contributions to the Christ-and-Culture Debate." In *Speaking the Truth in Love: The Theology of John M. Frame*, edited by John J. Hughes, 833–54. Phillipsburg, NJ: P&R Publishing, 2009.

Schaeffer, Francis. "A Review of a Review." *PCA History*. Last modified 1948. Accessed January 9, 2014. http://www.pcahistory.org/documents/schaefferreview.html.

Schnabel, Eckhard J. *Acts*. Exegetical Commentary on the New Testament. Grand Rapids, MI: Zondervan, 2012.

Schreiner, Thomas R. "Response to Gerald Bray." *Themelios* 39, 1 (April 2014): 26–29.

Scoti, Ioannis Duns. *Opera Omnia*. Edited by C. Balić, M. Bodewig, S. Bušelić, P. Čapkun-Delić, B. Hechic, I. Jurić, B. Korošak, et al. Vol. 4. Città del Vaticano: Typis Polyglottis Vaticanis, 1956.

Scott, James. "Review of Doctrine of the Word of God by John Frame." *Orthodox Presbyterian Church*. Last modified February 2012. Accessed September 10, 2013. http://www.opc.org/review.html?review_id=368.

Scrivener, Glen. "How Frame's Doctrine of the Knowledge of God Might Shape and Inform the Christian Study of Ethics." Bth Paper, London: Oak Hill Theological College, 2006. http://www.christthetruth.org.uk/Frame.htm.

Scrivener, Steve R. "Frame's and Van Til's Apologetic." In *Speaking the Truth in Love: The Theology of John M. Frame*, edited by John J. Hughes, 525–58. Phillipsburg, NJ: P&R Publishing, 2009.

Shannon, Nathan. "Necessity, Univocism, and the Trinity God: A Response to Anderson and Welty." Philosophia Christi, 2011. http://www.epsociety.org/userfiles/art-Anderson-Welty%20(In%20Defense%20of%20the%20Argument%20for%20God%20from%20Logic).pdf.

Smith, Barry D. *The Oneness and Simplicity of God*. Eugene, OR: Wipf and Stock, 2013.

Smith, Ralph. *Paradox and Truth: Rethinking Van Til on the Trinity*. Moscow, ID: Canon Press, 2003.

———. "Van Til's Insights on the Trinity." *Global Missiology English* 2, 2 (2005): 1–19.

Smith, Scotty. "I've Been 'Framed'! The Influence of John Frame and His Teaching on This Pastor and Pastoral Ministry." In *Speaking the Truth in Love: The Theology of John M. Frame*, edited by John J. Hughes, 659–68. Phillipsburg, NJ: P&R Publishing, 2009.

Sproul, R. C, John Gerstner, and Arthur Lindsley. *Classical Apologetics*. Grand Rapids, MI: Zondervan, 1984.

Staniloae, Dumitru. *Orthodox Dogmatic Theology*. New York, NY: A & C Black, 2000.

Strobel, Kyle. *Jonathan Edwards's Theology: A Reinterpretation*. New York, NY: A & C Black, 2012.

Studebaker, Steven, and Robert Caldwell III. *The Trinitarian Theology of Jonathan Edwards*. Burlington, VT: Ashgate, 2012.

Taylor, Justin. "Doctrine of God: A Review Article." *Journal of the Evangelical Theological Society* 47, 2 (June 2004): 356–59.

Thomas, Derek. "Frame on the Attributes of God." In *Speaking the Truth in Love: The Theology of John M. Frame*, edited by John J. Hughes, 351–69. Phillipsburg, NJ: P&R Publishing, 2009.

Tichenor, Alan, Robert Strong, Floyd Hamilton, Edwin Rian, and Gordon Clark. "The Answer to a Complaint Against Several Actions and Decisions of the Presbytery of Philadelphia Take in a Special Meeting Held on July 7, 1944," 1944. Accessed July 23, 2014. http://godshammer.files.wordpress.com/2010/07/the-answer.pdf.

Tipton, Lane G. "The Triune Personal God: Trinitarian Theology in the Thought of Cornelius Van Til." PhD Diss., Philadelphia, PA: Westminster Theological Seminary, 2004.

Torrance, Thomas F. *Trinitarian Perspectives: Toward Doctrinal Agreement*. New York, NY: A & C Black, 2000.

Torres, Joseph Emmanuel. "John Frame's Approach to Knowledge and Apologetics." *KingdomView*. Last modified March 21, 2012. Accessed September 11, 2013. http://apolojet.wordpress.com/2012/08/21/john-frames-approach-to-knowledge-and-apologetics/.

———. "Perspectivalism 101." *KingdomView*. Last modified September 17, 2007. Accessed September 11, 2013. http://apolojet.wordpress.com/2007/09/17/perspectivalism-101/.

———. "Perspectives on Perspectivalism." In *Speaking the Truth in Love: The Theology of John M. Frame*, edited by John J. Hughes, 111–36. Phillipsburg, NJ: P&R Publishing, 2009.

———. "Van Til's Presuppositionalism & Frame's Perspectivalism." *KingdomView*. Last modified November 13, 2012. Accessed September 11, 2013. http://apolojet.wordpress.com/2012/11/13/van-tils-presuppositionalism-frames-perspectivalism/.

Trumper, Tim J. R. "Covenant Theology and Constructive Calvinism." *Westminster Theological Journal* 64, 2 (Fall 2002): 388–405.

———. "John Frame's Methodology: A Case Study in Constructive Calvinism." In *Speaking the Truth in Love: The Theology of John M. Frame*, edited by John J. Hughes, 145–72. Phillipsburg, NJ: P&R Publishing, 2009.

Van Drunen, David. "A System of Theology? The Centrality of Covenant for Westminster Systematics." In *The Pattern of Sound Doctrine*, edited by David Van Drunen, 195–220. Phillipsburg, NJ: P&R Publishing, 2004.

Van Fraassen, Bas C. "Presupposition, Implication, and Self-Reference." *Journal of Philosophy* 65, 5 (March 1968): 136–52.

Vanhoozer, Kevin. "On the Very Idea of a Theological System: An Essay in Aid of Triangulating Scripture, Church and World." In *Always Reforming: Explorations in Systematic Theology*, 125–82. Downers Grove, IL: InterVarsity Press, 2007.

———. "Personal Words: Kevin Vanhoozer." In *Speaking the Truth in Love: The Theology of John M. Frame*, edited by John J. Hughes, lxxix–lxxx. Phillipsburg, NJ: P&R Publishing, 2009.

———. *Remythologizing Theology: Divine Action, Passion, and Authorship*. Cambridge, UK: Cambridge University Press, 2010.

———. *The Drama of Doctrine: A Canonical-Linguistic Approach to Christian Theology*. Louisville, KY: Westminster John Knox Press, 2005.

Van Til, Cornelius. *A Christian Theory of Knowledge*. Nutley, NJ: Presbyterian and Reformed, 1969.

———. *An Introduction to Systematic Theology*. Nutley, NJ: Presbyterian and Reformed, 1974.

———. "A Sacramental Universe." *Westminster Theological Journal* 2, 2 (Spring 1940): 175–84.

———. *A Survey of Christian Epistemology*. Logos Digital Collection. Nutley, NJ: Presbyterian and Reformed, 1977.

———. *Christianity and Idealism*. Philadelphia: Presbyterian and Reformed, 1955.

———. *Common Grace and the Gospel*. Nutley, NJ: Presbyterian and Reformed, 1972.

———. "Confessing Jesus Christ." In *Scripture and Confession*, edited by John H. Skilton, 217–46. Nutley, NJ: Presbyterian and Reformed, 1973.

———. "Nature and Scripture." In *The Articles of Cornelius Van Til*, edited by Eric H. Sigward. Logos Digital Collection. New York, NY: Labels Army Company, 1997.

———. *Psychology of Religion*. Logos Digital Collection. Nutley, NJ: Presbyterian and Reformed, 1971.

———. "Review of Worship of God by James Vance." In *Reviews by Cornelius Van Til*, edited by Eric H. Sigward. Logos Digital Collection. New York, NY: Labels Army Company, 1997.

———. *The Defense of the Faith*. Edited by K. Scott Oliphint. 4th ed. Phillipsburg, NJ: P&R Publishing, 2008.

———. *The New Hermeneutic*. Nutley, NJ: Presbyterian and Reformed, 1974.

———. "The Will in Its Theological Relations." In *Unpublished Manuscripts of Cornelius Van Til*, edited by Eric H. Sigward.

Logos Digital Collection. New York, NY: Labels Army Company, 1997.

———. *Unpublished Manuscripts of Cornelius Van Til*. Edited by Eric H. Sigward. Logos Digital Collection. New York, NY: Labels Army Company, 1997.

Venema, Cornelis P. "The Doctrine of God: A Theology of Lordship." *Mid-America Journal of Theology* 14 (January 2003): 153–66.

Ventrella, Jeffrey J. "Passionately Demonstrating Truth: Triangulating Cultural Restoration." In *Speaking the Truth in Love: The Theology of John M. Frame*, edited by John J. Hughes, 855–83. Phillipsburg, NJ: P&R Publishing, 2009.

Volf, Miroslav. *Free of Charge: Giving and Forgiving in a Culture Stripped of Grace*. Grand Rapids, MI: Zondervan, 2009.

Wagner, Robert. "A Living and Active Word: Some Notes on Frame's View of Holy Scripture." In *Speaking the Truth in Love: The Theology of John M. Frame*, edited by John J. Hughes, 330–50. Phillipsburg, NJ: P&R Publishing, 2009.

Wallace, Daniel B. *Greek Grammar Beyond the Basics: An Exegetical Syntax of the New Testament*. Grand Rapids, MI: Zondervan, 1996.

Warfield, Benjamin Breckinridge. "The Example of the Incarnation." Sermon, Princeton Theological Seminary, January 8, 1893. Accessed July 16, 2014. The gospelcoalition.org/blogs/justin taylor/files/2010/09/Warfield-Imitating-the-Incarnation2.pdf.

Warren Jr., Michael H. "The Scope and Limits of Van Til's Transcendental Argument: A Response to John Frame." *Christian Civilization*. Last modified March 2013. Accessed September 11, 2013. http://christianciv.com/.

Weaver, Gilbert. "Man: Analogue of God." In *Jerusalem and Athens: Critical Discussions on the Theology and Apologetics of Cornelius Van Til*, edited by E. R. Geehan, 321–27. Nutley, NJ: Presbyterian and Reformed, 1971.

Welty, Greg. "An Examination of Theistic Concpetual Realism as an Alternative to Theistic Activism." M. Phil in Philosopical Theology, Oxford, UK: Oriel College, 2000. Accessed July 14, 2014. http://www.proginosko.com/welty /mphil.pdf.

———. "Persuasion or Proof?" Last modified 1994. Accessed September 13, 2013. http://www.proginosko.com/welty/langame .htm.

———. "Shall We Argue Transcendentally?" *Proginosko.* Last modified 1995. Accessed September 11, 2013. http://www .proginosko.com/welty /cvtframe.htm.

Welty, Greg, and James N. Anderson. "In Defense of the Argument for God from Logic." Philosophia Christi, 2011. http:// www.epsociety.org/userfiles/art-Anderson-Welty%20(In%20 Defense%20of%20the%20Argument%20for%20God%20 from%20Logic).pdf.

———. "The Lord of Noncontradiction." *Philosophia Christi* 13, 2 (2011): 321–38.

White, William. "Bill White Contra John Frame." *Journey*, June 1988.

———. "The Shroud of Textualism: The Problem Epitomized and the 'Way Out.'" *Journey*, December 1987.

Whitlock Jr, Luder G. "John Frame: Orthodoxy and Creativity." In *Speaking the Truth in Love: The Theology of John M. Frame*, edited by John J. Hughes, 248–61. Phillipsburg, NJ: P&R Publishing, 2009.

Wierenga, Edward R. *The Nature of God: An Inquiry Into Divine Attributes*. Ithaca, NY: Cornell University Press, 2003.

Williams, Michael D. *Far as the Curse Is Found: The Covenant Story of Redemption*. Phillipsburg, NJ: P&R Publishing, 2005.

Williamson, G. I. "Review of The Doctrine of the Knowledge of God by John Frame." *Journey*, October 1988.

Wippel, John. *Metaphysical Themes in Thomas Aquinas II*. Washington, DC: Catholic University of America Press, 2007.

Wittgenstein, Ludwig. *Philosophical Investigations*. Upper Saddle River, NJ: Prentice Hall, 1973.

Wood, Nathan. *The Secret of the Universe*. 6th ed. Boston, MA: Warwick Press, 1936.

Zachman, Randall C. *Image and Word in the Theology of John Calvin*. Notre Dame, IN: University of Notre Dame Press, 2009.

"Perspective." *Oxford Dictionaries*. Oxford, UK: Oxford University Press, 2014. Accessed July 3, 2014. http://www.oxforddictionaries.com/us/definition /american_english/perspective.

"Westminster Confession of Faith," 1646. Accessed December 9, 2009. http://reformed.org/documents/wcf_with_proofs/.

Index of Scripture

Genesis
1:1—211, 250
1:2—193
1:3—196
1:6—196
1:9—196
1:11—196
1:14—196
1:20—196
1:24—196
1:26–28—191
1:28—86, 297
2:7—109
3:8—252
3:15—346
3:23—252
5:3—192
45:5–8—250

Exodus
3:14—142, 242
14:4—242
20:2—246
20:3—249
21:13—250

Leviticus
14:1–20—224

Deuteronomy
4:35—242
29:6—242

1 Kings
8:43—242
8:60—242
18:37—242
20:13—242
20:28—242

2 Kings
19:19—242

Psalms
16:11—168
83:18—242
92:5—66
104:1–4—193
104:30—147
139:7–12—257
139:17—66

Job
40:1–5—249

Isaiah
37:20—242
55:8–9—66
66:1—193, 244

Jeremiah
16:21—242
23:24—257
24:7—242
32:27—250

Ezekiel
6:7–14—242
7:4—242
7:9—242
7:27—242
11:10—242

Matthew
6:24—294
11:27—56, 210
12:30—294

Index of Scripture

19:26—250
27:46—160–61

Luke
1:37—250
14:26—249

John
1:1—160, 196, 226, 229
1:3—147
1:14—160
1:18—160, 226
2:16—223
3:35—227
4:24—121, 160
5:18—160
10:27–29—60
10:28–30—115
10:30—140, 147
10:38—147, 160–61
14:6—210, 294
14:9–11—147
14:10—226
14:10–11—115, 160–61
14:18—147
14:20—147, 160–61
14:23–27—227
17:1–2—140

17:21—115, 140, 147, 160–61
17:21–23—227

Acts
2:23—250
4:12—294
5:29—294
17:22–34—252
17:28—97

Romans
1—277, 294–95, 302
1:18–20—57, 86, 96, 194, 223, 251, 272, 282, 297–98, 307, 312
1:18–32—297, 304
1:19–20—193–94
1:20—195, 239, 251, 298, 308, 317
1:32—252
2—277
8—255
8:34—60
9:20—249
11:33—168
11:33–36—92
14:23—249

1 Corinthians
2:6–16—88
2:10–11—56
2:14—210
10:31—249

2 Corinthians
1:22—60

Colossians
1:15—191
1:16—147
1:17—249
1:23—227
2:3—57

Titus
1:2—153

Hebrews
1:3—191, 227, 249
11:3—196

1 John
1:5—121
3:1—160
3:16—167
4:8—153, 121
4:16—121

Index of Subjects and Names

absolute personality, 24, 44–45, 49, 89, 124–25, 173, 176, 184, 194, 206, 289

analogical, 51–52, 67, 69, 136–37, 150, 154, 181, 206, 237, 239, 266

Anderson, James, 11, 21, 39, 66, 138, 214

apologetics, viii, ix, 2, 6, 10, 20–21, 26, 33, 43, 84, 155, 185, 194, 214, 253, 257, 260, 274, 283–95, 297–300, 302, 304, 306–7, 310–12, 316

Aquinas, Thomas, 24, 62, 64, 69, 71, 120, 125–43, 145–47, 150, 153–56, 158–59, 161–62, 169, 171–72, 176–78, 286, 301

archetypal, 23, 25, 46, 51, 53, 75, 189, 191–93, 197, 205, 229, 237, 239

aseity, 24, 44, 53, 54, 62, 92, 119–20, 138, 144, 169–70, 173–74, 184–85, 257, 265, 307, 311

attributes, 4, 17, 24–25, 42, 46, 63, 67–71, 73, 92, 105, 119–28, 130, 135–36, 138, 145, 149–53, 155–57, 159, 162–77, 179–83, 185–87, 190, 192, 194–95, 203–4, 206, 208–10, 213, 222–23, 230–34, 239, 241, 244–52, 254–60, 262, 265, 278, 314

Bavinck, Herman, 18, 21, 25, 46–47, 51, 53, 163, 176, 192, 198–208, 221–23, 268, 314

Calvinism, 13, 19–20, 31, 315–16

Clark, R. Scott, 5, 20, 27, 122, 165, 218, 273, 317

covenant, 4, 11, 26, 38, 47, 49–52, 54–55, 79, 88, 97–99, 165, 174–75, 222, 243–46, 248, 252, 254, 256–57, 261–62, 276, 280, 315–16

ectypal, 25, 75, 172, 189, 191–92, 197, 205, 207, 226, 229, 236–37

epistemology, 9–11, 16, 20–21, 29–30, 39, 45, 50, 75, 81,

Index of Subjects and Names

88–89, 95, 101, 103–4, 107, 118, 139, 155, 178, 205, 215–16, 223, 243, 259–60, 263, 282, 288, 300, 310, 315
equal ultimacy, 23, 46, 49, 54, 67–68, 148, 151, 158–59, 163, 269
essence, 23, 42–43, 45–46, 48–49, 51–52, 56, 62–63, 66, 68, 70–71, 113, 116, 119, 121, 126, 129, 132–35, 137, 139, 141–43, 145–46, 148–49, 152–55, 157–59, 162–63, 171, 176, 182, 203, 207, 212–13, 216–17, 249

general perspectivalism, 23, 30–33, 38–40, 60, 65, 74, 77, 83–84, 95–97, 99, 102–4, 106, 108, 189, 239, 265

Karlberg, Mark, 2, 20, 272–73
Kline, Meredith, 1–2, 38, 79, 193, 314
Kuhn, Thomas S., 296–99, 312

lordship, viii, 5, 7–8, 25, 30, 37, 58, 108–10, 165, 175, 186, 198, 208, 212, 217–18, 220–23, 225, 230–34, 237–39, 241–49, 251–62, 270–71, 286–87, 311
lordship triad, 25, 37, 109, 212, 218, 220, 222, 225, 233, 239, 255, 258, 260, 262, 270–71

Nietzsche, Friedrich, 23, 81, 83

Oliphint, K. Scott, iv, xiii, 33–34, 36, 44, 47, 63–64, 72, 79, 92, 97, 102, 123, 126, 144, 146, 149, 151, 185, 194–95, 257, 283, 292, 295, 300, 310, 313
one and many, 18, 23, 38, 42, 46, 48, 54, 57, 59, 67–68, 71, 124–25, 128, 151, 159–60, 162–63, 165, 186, 196, 215, 221, 229, 232, 237, 256, 259, 269, 314

perichoresis, vii, 18, 24–25, 48, 52, 54, 56–57, 59, 105–6, 108, 111, 115, 117–19, 121–25, 127, 145, 147–49, 157–59, 165, 167, 169, 173, 182, 187–88, 190, 209, 213, 216, 224, 226–28, 233, 255–57, 262, 264–65
perichoretic-simplicity, 24–25, 105, 126–27, 151, 155, 170, 182, 184–88, 195, 209, 216, 224, 255
perspecival dynamics, 25, 108, 187–88, 209–10
predication, 24, 120, 135–37, 150–51, 153, 155, 158, 160, 180
priority, viii, 26, 80, 89, 138, 145, 187, 213, 264–66, 270, 272–75, 279, 281–83, 290, 293, 295, 297, 299, 311, 313

relativism, vii, 23, 77–87, 94, 100, 103, 218, 220, 273, 275
revelation, 20, 24, 29, 36, 44, 54, 58,

Index of Subjects and Names

60, 68, 79, 81, 86–87, 95, 100, 137–40, 144–47, 150–52, 155–56, 158, 161, 171, 177, 180–82, 185, 194, 199–201, 203, 206–8, 210, 213, 219–20, 222–23, 228, 239, 257, 260, 267–68, 271, 273–74, 277–78, 280–81, 283, 288, 291, 295, 298–300, 303, 307–8, 317

Sabellianism, 24, 47, 114, 116, 128, 148
Scotus, Duns, 24, 166, 177–83
simplicity, vii, 24–25, 42, 61, 64–71, 73–74, 105–6, 108, 115, 118–39, 141–46, 150–52, 155, 157–59, 161–65, 167–70, 172–73, 175–77, 180–82, 184, 187–88, 203, 209, 214, 255–56, 262, 265
structure, 1, 7, 38, 49–50, 54–55, 59–60, 79, 105, 110, 154, 171, 177, 189, 195, 197–98, 212, 222, 243, 245, 247, 255, 263, 265, 270, 281–82, 295, 296

theonomy, 1–2, 79–80, 112–13
Tipton, Lane, xiii, 5, 46, 185, 194, 257, 295, 300, 313
transcendental argument, 18, 26, 83, 199–200, 208, 285–86, 289–92, 299–312, 316
triad, vii–viii, 3, 7, 10–12, 24–26, 106–9, 114, 197, 201–2, 208–9, 213, 217–20, 223, 225–31, 233–38, 241, 246, 248, 254–55, 264, 271–72, 274, 285, 313, 317
Trinity, a, iii–iv, vii–viii, xi, xiii, 2–3, 17–19, 21–26, 28–29, 38, 42–59, 62, 65, 67–68, 71, 74–75, 77, 81–82, 84, 97, 104–5, 108–19, 121–30, 132–36, 138, 140–42, 145, 147, 152, 156–57, 159–60, 163–66, 168–70, 174–75, 177, 183, 187–91, 194–213, 215–24, 226–33, 235–37, 239, 241, 247, 256, 259–60, 262–64, 266–70, 279, 281, 283, 289, 312, 314, 317
and economic, 57, 166, 206–7, 267–70
and ontological, 54, 57, 67–68, 82, 97, 111, 118, 123, 132, 173, 196, 201, 206–7, 215, 228–30, 235, 237, 239, 266–68, 270, 309–11
and *vestigia trinitatis*, 19, 21, 25, 198, 200, 204, 208, 224, 232, 317
order and priority, 26, 213, 264–67, 269–70, 281, 283, 312–13
triperspectivalism, a, vii–viii, xi, xiii, 6, 12–14, 16, 19, 23–25, 31–32, 77, 81, 102, 104–11, 113–14, 188, 190, 209, 235, 239, 241, 247, 254–55, 262, 264–66, 270–72, 281, 283, 291, 297, 310–13
Triune, i, iii–iv, viii, xiii–xiv, 23, 25, 32, 38, 46, 49–50, 52–55,

59, 74, 83, 85, 102, 115, 120, 123–24, 128, 133, 162–63, 165, 168, 184, 190, 192–93, 195, 199–201, 204, 209–10, 224, 226, 231, 239, 246–47, 255, 258, 265, 268, 270, 281, 286, 302–4, 314

unity and diversity, 24, 42, 46, 48–49, 54, 59, 61, 68, 71–72, 74, 105–6, 115, 119, 121, 123, 125, 127–28, 147–50, 161–63, 165, 167–68, 171, 182, 195, 203–4, 208, 217, 221, 229, 259–60, 262, 279, 317

Van Til, Cornelius, xiii, 2, 4, 10, 18–21, 23, 26, 28, 34, 37, 43, 44–59, 61, 67–68, 75, 78–79, 81, 85, 89, 100–101, 107, 111, 115–16, 123–25, 127–28, 146, 148–49, 154–56, 158, 163, 165–66, 168, 182, 184, 190, 198–99, 206, 217, 229, 251, 259, 261, 267–68, 283–89, 292, 295, 298–302, 305, 307–8, 310, 312–16

Westminster Theological Seminary, iv, xi, xiii, 1, 4, 7, 9, 14, 16, 30, 46, 71, 119, 164

Timothy E. Miller is Assistant Professor of Systematic Theology and Apologetics at Detroit Baptist Theological Seminary. He received his M.A. from Maranatha Baptist University, his M.Div. from Calvary Baptist Theological Seminary, and his Ph.D. in historical theology from Westminster Theological Seminary. Before teaching at DBTS, Tim taught for four years at Maranatha Baptist University. With previous experience as an assistant pastor in Philadelphia, he is also actively involved in pulpit supply with churches in the Detroit area.

Available in the Reformed
Academic Dissertation Series

◆

*How Should We Treat Detainees? An Examination of
"Enhanced Interrogation Techniques" under the Light of Scripture
and the Just War Tradition*,
by J. Porter Harlow

*From Inscrutability to Concursus: Benjamin B. Warfield's Theological
Construction of Revelation's Mode from 1880 to 1915*,
by Jeffrey A. Stivason

*Marks of Saving Grace: Theological Method and the
Doctrine of Assurance in Jonathan Edwards's* A Treatise
Concerning Religious Affections,
by Eric J. Lehner

*The Triune God of Unity in Diversity: An Analysis of Perspectivalism,
the Trinitarian Theological Method of John Frame and Vern Poythress*,
by Timothy E. Miller

Forthcoming

It Has Not Yet Appeared What We Shall Be: A Reconsideration of the
Imago Dei *in Light of Those with Severe Cognitive Disabilities*,
by George C. Hammond

Preaching with Biblical Motivation: How to Incorporate the Motivation Found in the Inspired Preaching of the Apostles into Your Sermons,
by Ray E. Heiple Jr.

*The Doctrine of the Spirituality of the Church in the Ecclesiology of
Charles Hodge*,
by Alan D. Strange

www.ingramcontent.com/pod-product-compliance
Lightning Source LLC
LaVergne TN
LVHW040748250326
834688LV00034B/503